A People's War on Poverty

A PEOPLE'S WAR ON POVERTY

Urban Politics and Grassroots Activists in Houston

WESLEY G. PHELPS

The University of Georgia Press   *Athens and London*

Parts of chapters 2 and 3 appeared as "Ideological Diversity and the Implementation of the War on Poverty in Houston," in Annelise Orleck and Lisa Gayle Hazirjian, eds., *The War on Poverty: A New Grassroots History, 1964–1980* (Athens: University of Georgia Press, 2011). Copyright 2011 by the University of Georgia Press. Part of chapter 3 appeared as "National Ideal Meets Local Reality: The Grassroots War on Poverty in Houston," in Richard B. McCaslin, Donald E. Chipman, and Andrew J. Torget, eds., *This Corner of Canaan: Essays on Texas in Honor of Randolph B. Campbell* (Denton: University of North Texas Press, 2013). Copyright © 2013 University of North Texas Press.

© 2014 by the University of Georgia Press
Athens, Georgia 30602
www.ugapress.org
All rights reserved
Set in Minion Pro by Graphic Composition, Inc., Bogart, Georgia
Manufactured by Thomson-Shore

The paper in this book meets the guidelines for permanence and durability
of the Committee on Production Guidelines for
Book Longevity of the Council on Library Resources.
Most University of Georgia Press titles are available from popular e-book vendors.

Printed in the United States of America
18 17 16 15 14 P 5 4 3 2 1

Library of Congress Cataloging-in-Publication Data

Phelps, Wesley G.
A people's war on poverty : urban politics and grassroots activists
in Houston / Wesley G. Phelps.
     pages cm
Includes bibliographical references and index.
ISBN 978-0-8203-4670-0 (hardcover : alk. paper) —
ISBN 0-8203-4670-5 (hardcover : alk. paper) —
ISBN 978-0-8203-4671-7 (pbk. : alk. paper) —
ISBN 0-8203-4671-3 (pbk. : alk. paper)
  1. Community Action Program (U.S.)—History.
  2. Community development—Texas—Houston—History—20th century.
  3. Poor—Services for—Texas—Houston—History—20th century.
  4. Poor—Political activity—Texas—Houston—History—20th century.
  5. Poverty—Government policy—Texas—Houston—History—20th century.
  6. Social action—Texas—Houston—History—20th century. I. Title.
  HN80.H8P44 2014
  305.5'69097641411—dc23   2013029149

British Library Cataloging-in-Publication Data available

FOR DEVON AND JORDAN

Perhaps the story of Community Action must be told by a poet or mystic rather than a politician or historian.

—Donald Rumsfeld, director, Office of Economic Opportunity

CONTENTS

ACKNOWLEDGMENTS

This book is the result of several years of research on the implementation of the War on Poverty in Houston. It began as a research paper in John Boles's graduate seminar on the history of the United States South at Rice University, grew into a doctoral dissertation, and finally matured into a book manuscript. It gives me great pleasure to acknowledge those who have provided the encouragement, resources, and academic stimulation I needed along the way.

Each member of my dissertation committee made unique contributions to my work. Allen Matusow initially sparked my interest in the 1960s even before I arrived at Rice in 2005, and he continually challenged me to think more critically about my subject. John Boles provided much-needed encouragement when times got rough, and he is as good as it gets when it comes to academic professionalism and compassion. Caleb McDaniel brought a fresh perspective to my project, and our many conversations have helped me immensely in thinking about my work more broadly. Chandler Davidson offered an interesting sociological perspective that will continue to benefit my work as a historian, and as a scholar-activist his work has helped me see the link between rigorous academic inquiry and progressive social change.

I could not have completed this book without the generous financial support of several institutions. An Albert J. Beveridge Grant for Research in the History of the Western Hemisphere from the American Historical Association and a Moody Research Grant from the Lyndon Baines Johnson Foundation funded the necessary research trips as I began this project. Additionally, the Rice University History Department generously funded research travel and provided significant institutional support. During each of their tenures as director of graduate studies, Ed Cox and Carl Caldwell unfailingly advocated for the graduate students and ensured we would be provided with the resources we needed to complete our work. Paula Platt, Rachel Zepeda, Anita Smith, and Lisa Tate guided me through the bureaucratic requirements for finishing my degree and made my time at Rice thoroughly enjoyable. I would also like to thank Dean Paula Sanders and the Office of Graduate and Postdoctoral Studies at Rice University for providing a generous dissertation completion fellowship. Finally, the Sam Houston State University History Department provided generous financial support to complete the manuscript.

Many archivists and librarians helped me locate the materials I needed to complete this book: Tab Lewis and Barbara Rust at the National Archives in College Park, Maryland, and Fort Worth, Texas; Tamara Jordan, Erin Norris, Tim Ronk, and Joel Draut at the Houston Metropolitan Research Center; Allen Fisher and Claudia Anderson at the LBJ Library; Ellen Brown at the Baylor University Library; and Lauren Meyers at the Woodson Research Center at Rice University. I would also like to thank Earl Allen, Iris Ballew, Lee Grant, and John Wildenthal for sharing with me their memories of Houston in the 1960s.

I had many opportunities to present portions of my research at several academic conferences during the past several years, including the University of Virginia's Conference on the War on Poverty and Grassroots Struggles for Racial and Economic Justice, the Texas State Historical Association, the Urban History Association, Houston Area Southern Historians, the American Historical Association, the Organization of American Historians, the University of South Carolina's Conference on Southern Student Activism in the 1960s and 1970s, and Rice University's Conference on the Past and Present of Race and Place in Houston. My work has benefited from the many intriguing conversations I have had with individuals at these conferences, particularly Susan Ashmore, Bob Bauman, Brian Behnken, Edwin Breeden, Bill Clayson, Laurie Green, Lisa Hazirjian, Tom Kiffmeyer, Max Krochmal, Guian McKee, Zachary Montz, Anna Roberts, Marc Rodriguez, Kyle Shelton, Jenna Steward, and Rhonda Williams.

Several individuals have read portions of my manuscript and have provided valuable comments and criticisms that I was able to incorporate into the finished product. Tom Jackson read an early version of a draft that eventually grew into several chapters and helped me conceptualize the project more coherently. Cary Wintz and Rick McCaslin provided excellent comments on chapter 3. Jeff Crane, Greg Eow, and Marty Wauck gave me some valuable feedback on the introduction. Bill Bush, Kent Germany, Randal Hall, Annelise Orleck, and Mel Piehl suggested improvements to chapter 2, by far the most difficult section for me to write. Everyone at the University of Georgia Press has been wonderful to work with during the publishing process, particularly Jon Davies, Kay Kodner, Derek Krissoff, and Beth Snead. I would also like to thank the anonymous readers for their thoughtful and incisive comments and suggestions.

Many friends and colleagues have had a profound influence on my work. My daily lunch conversations with Luke Harlow and Rusty Hawkins during our time together in Houston allowed me to test out new ideas on a sympathetic audience and forced me to temper some of my more tenuous claims. Blake Ellis, Gale Kenny, Andy Lang, Joe Locke, Allison Madar, Jim Wainwright, and

Ben Wright helped me think more critically about my project. I would also like to express my gratitude to the students who took my course titled "American Biography: The 1960s" at Rice University during the fall 2009 semester. It was a sincere pleasure to teach such bright, inquisitive, and ambitious students, and they helped me see how my project fits more broadly into the history of the 1960s in America.

When I was a student at the University of North Texas, Mike Campbell took me under his wing and shaped the kind of historian I would eventually become. Dr. Campbell encouraged me to explore more deeply the periods of history that had always fascinated me, even when they did not match up neatly with his own academic interests. Although I am certain to fall short, I strive to emulate him in so many ways ranging from his engaging teaching style to his genuine concern for the well-being of his students.

Members of my family have been a constant source of support during the writing of this book. My parents, Lee and Carol Phelps, instilled in me at an early age the value of an education and were patient with me when I lost sight of that for a few teenage years. My in-laws, Kip and Dana Inman, and my brother-in-law, Dustin Dodson, were there for me when I needed them most and often expressed genuine interest in my work as a historian and a teacher. I only wish my dad and Dustin were still with us to see the book's final publication. My siblings, Randy, Paul, Sherry, and Leigha, as well as my brother-in-law Brian Garrett and my best friend Jeff Hardin, have provided much encouragement over the years. Uncle Steve and Uncle Dale shared with me their memories of the 1960s and played a significant role in kindling my interest in the history of that turbulent decade. In a similar way, Claude Doane and Trisha Brown sparked my fascination with urban history and the plight of America's cities through our many tours of downtown Dallas in the mid-1990s.

There are two people in my life who have lived with this book project on a daily basis for just as long as I have. My partner, Devon, and our daughter, Jordan, have been my rock, my source of inspiration, and my unconditional cheering section. They have experienced with me the full range of emotions—from insecurity and exhaustion to joy and elation—that go along with writing a book. While I have spent most of my time writing, Devon has dedicated the last six years of her life to making the ideals of educational democracy and equality a reality in the lives of low-income Houston-area public school students. She is a powerful source of inspiration in my life and is a constant reminder that we all can make a unique contribution to the quest for social justice. I count myself lucky to share my life with these two wonderful individuals whom I admire and love so deeply. It is to them that I dedicate this book.

A People's War on Poverty

The War on Poverty and the Expansion of Democracy

On May 22, 1964, President Lyndon Johnson delivered the keynote address to the graduating class of the University of Michigan in Ann Arbor. In a speech designed to announce the launching of his Great Society, Johnson pledged "an end to poverty and racial injustice, to which we are totally committed in our time." In response to the African American civil rights movement, Johnson had made remarkable progress in using the power of the federal government to help movement activists tear down the walls of racial segregation in the American South. And indeed, the passage of the Civil Rights Act of 1964 was less than a month away. What the federal government could accomplish in the pursuit to end poverty, however, was a much more complicated and unprecedented matter. The president had made statements about fighting poverty before, most notably in his State of the Union address to Congress the previous January, in which he declared an "unconditional war on poverty in America." In the University of Michigan speech, however, Johnson's liberal optimism and his faith that Americans could solve any problem with enough will and determination bubbled to the surface; he spoke of an almost utopian vision of a perfect America, free from the problems plaguing it since the founding of the nation.[1]

In his quest to make the Great Society a reality, Johnson launched the federal War on Poverty, which Congress authorized with the passage of the Economic Opportunity Act in August 1964. Like the president's statements during the previous few months, the act called for a bold, ambitious series of initiatives fueled by the spirit of 1960s American liberalism. It created the Job Corps to provide unemployed and underemployed young men and women with marketable skills; Volunteers in Service to America (VISTA) to tap the great resource of idealistic youth eager to take an active role in fighting poverty; and the Community Action Program (CAP) to coordinate the delivery of new and existing local social services and to initiate the reform of institutions that affected the lives of the poor. Soon the War on Poverty would also include a number of additional programs, such as Legal Services and Head Start, designed to provide services for the poor to which they otherwise would not have access. This massive federal antipoverty program would be administered by the newly created Office of Economic Opportunity (OEO).[2]

Several policy analysts began writing about the War on Poverty while it was still being fought in the 1960s and early 1970s. But it was not until the 1980s—a decade that saw the systematic dismantling of much of the Great Society—that a significant number of historians and social scientists grew interested in Johnson's poverty war. The first generation of scholars writing about the antipoverty initiative were particularly concerned with the impact of its programs on the fate of American liberalism in the 1960s. As a result, they tended to focus on a broad national narrative, making assessments based on the president's ambitious pledge to eradicate poverty from American society. The most prominent scholars in this group—historian Allen J. Matusow and political scientist Charles Murray—approached the study of the War on Poverty from very different perspectives yet reached strikingly similar conclusions. The War on Poverty, argued Matusow and Murray, was a failure because it fell short of eradicating poverty in America. As Matusow stated, "[T]he War on Poverty was destined to be one of the great failures of twentieth-century liberalism." Arguing that antipoverty programs of the 1960s never attempted to redistribute the nation's wealth in a more equitable way, Matusow suggested that the epitaph for the War on Poverty should have read, "Declared but Never Fought." Murray argued that the government's social policy during the 1960s, particularly the War on Poverty, actually resulted in more poverty because it made more American citizens dependent on the welfare system for survival. "We tried to provide more for the poor," proclaimed Murray, "and produced more poor instead. We tried to remove the barriers to escape from poverty, and inadvertently built a trap." Like Matusow and Murray, recent accounts also approach the War on Poverty from a macrolevel, with many historians seemingly fixated on judging the success of this series of massive and complex federal programs through statistical national aggregates.[3]

Although national studies are necessary for understanding the ideas and politics that shaped federal policy, they tend to obscure the multitude of ways that poverty warriors actually implemented these policies in local communities. Two brief episodes from the War on Poverty in Houston illustrate this point. On the morning of September 6, 1966, two years after the president's declaration of a War on Poverty, Houston resident C. E. Moore led a group—consisting of about twenty low-income residents and a handful of community organizers employed by the city's local War on Poverty agency—into a Houston city council meeting. Moore, along with the residents and organizers, demanded that city officials begin paying attention to the plight of their neighborhood. These residents came from an area of northeast Houston known as Settegast, a low-income neighborhood where housing conditions were among the worst in the city. Community organizers affiliated with the federal War on Poverty began working in Settegast early in 1966 and had discovered a number of problems resulting from long-term neglect by city officials and a general lack of municipal services in the area.

By the summer of 1966, community organizers and Settegast residents had decided to confront the mayor and other city council members and force them to take notice of their neighborhood. On that particular day in September, they had come to demand sanitary drinking water and a working sewage system. Through their own extensive research, War on Poverty workers had discovered open sewage ditches prevalent throughout Settegast, which contributed to an estimated rat population that was roughly three times as large as the human population in the neighborhood. The quality of the drinking water supply in Settegast was even more appalling. Nearly 70 percent of residents received their water from shallow wells often contaminated from septic tanks and sewage backups from outhouses. War on Poverty officials believed that the extraordinarily high rate of kidney and bladder diseases among Settegast residents was directly connected to the contaminated water they drank on a daily basis.

Armed with this information, Settegast residents and community organizers affiliated with the War on Poverty demanded that Mayor Louie Welch and other city officials take immediate action to extend municipal water and sanitation services to their neighborhood. The strategy worked. Faced with this delicate political issue and clearly not wanting to appear to deny Houston residents sanitary drinking water, Mayor Welch and the council members immediately ordered city workers to place emergency water spigots on the city's fire hydrants in Settegast to provide clean water to the residents. The mayor also quickly drew up a plan to extend city water services to the area, and municipal workers arrived in Settegast the very next day to begin the project. The event produced such a surprising victory that a local newspaper reporter covering the story declared that the "dawn of a quiet revolution may have broken over Houston" when the Settegast group arrived at City Hall to begin receiving a redress of grievances that had been a long time coming.[4]

A few months after the confrontation at City Hall, another incident occurred in Settegast that illuminated how local residents fought the poverty war. Local civil rights activist and community organizer Earl Allen had just recently begun his new position as director of community organization for Houston's official War on Poverty agency when county authorities forcibly evicted Betty Gentry from her Settegast home. According to Gentry, who was eight months pregnant at the time, a deputy constable had brutalized her during the eviction, handcuffed her, thrown her across a bed, and arrested her for aggravated assault. Soon after Gentry was arrested, several hundred neighborhood residents began planning a confrontation with city and county authorities to force them to address the problem of police brutality.[5]

According to Earl Allen, the treatment of Gentry revealed the problems not only of poverty but of political powerlessness. Through extensive research, Allen and his staff had discovered the prevalence of unscrupulous mortgage-lending profiteers taking advantage of Settegast homeowners, a plethora of substandard housing, and countless stories of unfair treatment of residents by police. As Allen explained, Gentry's "eviction wasn't the real issue. The real issues are lack of adequate housing which permits profiteers to insist on unfair terms, and the intimidation of the poor by police." With the help of Allen and his staff, Settegast residents vowed to protest at city and county offices in downtown Houston until authorities addressed their problems. Protesting Gentry's treatment turned out to be a catalyst for neighborhood residents to confront such structural and institutional problems as inadequate housing, unfair business practices, and police brutality.[6]

These confrontations over municipal services, exploitative business practices, and police brutality in Settegast are just a few examples of how local activists and poor residents implemented the War on Poverty in Houston. As Matusow conceded nearly thirty years ago, and as the Houston case illustrates, the real story of the War on Poverty rests with organizations "in one thousand communities across the country" guided by their own antipoverty philosophies and implementing their own visions of how to combat poverty. Since historians know little about how the War on Poverty programs operated at the local level, Matusow said, no final judgment of them was possible "until an army of local historians recovers the program's lost fragments."[7]

Fortunately, over the last ten years a significant number of historians have begun to recover the fragments. By building upon and clarifying the important national studies while focusing on particular locations, these historians are forcing a reevaluation of the federal antipoverty programs of the 1960s and are broadening our understanding of twentieth-century American politics.[8] For example, in her study of the War on Poverty in Alabama, Susan Youngblood Ashmore has shown that the implementation of the federal poverty program helped African Americans become political actors by providing avenues to local power. In this way, according to Ashmore, the War on Poverty was a significant extension of the civil rights movement. In his investigation of New Orleans, Kent B. Germany argued that the War on Poverty rejuvenated liberalism in the Crescent City by helping southern liberals retain relevance in the midst of a conservative counterrevolution. Political organizations arising from the War on Poverty and other Great Society programs provided Louisiana's Democratic Party with a firm base of support for the next several decades. As Germany stated, "In the late 1960s and early 1970s, the South developed its first long-term, clearly legitimate political liberalism in which cultural tolerance, intellectual openness, and racial inclusiveness were guiding themes." Robert Bauman has discovered that the War on Poverty intersected with a wide variety of social movements in Los Angeles and helped activists redefine their own racial, ethnic, and gender identities. The implementation of the federal poverty program, according to Bauman, also provided a structure for activists to create Black Power, Chicano, and feminist political organizations.[9]

Perhaps most directly relevant to the present study of Houston is William S. Clayson's recent book, *Freedom Is Not Enough: The War on Poverty and the Civil Rights Movement in Texas*, published in 2010. Like Ashmore's study of Alabama, Clayson reveals the important links between the War on Poverty and the African American and Latino civil rights movements and argues that race, despite Lyndon Johnson's effort to pursue a colorblind poverty program, was always at the heart of the War on Poverty. As a result, while the War on Poverty uplifted economically and racially marginalized groups in Texas, it also engendered tensions between the state's African American and Latino populations as they struggled over who would control federal dollars.[10] As these few examples illustrate, the vast majority of recent scholarship on the War on Poverty attempts to explain the concrete effects of the federal poverty program on the ground and to move beyond questions of success or failure. By reevaluating the War on Poverty from the local level, historians have been able to pose new questions about the array of complex consequences—both intended and unintended—that resulted from the federal poverty war of the 1960s and 1970s.

This grassroots study of the War on Poverty in Houston is my own contribution to the growing scholarship on how the federal antipoverty program worked on the ground and the ways in which it affected the lives of those it targeted. The city of Houston offers a valuable location for a case study of the implementation of the poverty program. Houston was and continues to be the largest city in the American South, yet it is also one of the most understudied cities in the nation. The lack of scholarly attention paid to Houston is surprising since the city has a strikingly rich multicultural history and was near the center of so much of the country's development in the twentieth century, particularly in the post–World War II period. It was during the 1960s and 1970s that Houston underwent sudden and profound demographic changes that would soon be experienced nationally. As Houston transitioned into a modern urban metropolis during the 1960s, its boundaries expanded, its economy grew, its population diversified, and its municipal government became more powerful. The implementation of the War on Poverty was an important part of this story. Finally, because of Houston's status as the fifth-largest city in the United States, it had a well-funded and active community action agency to administer the War on Poverty.

The implementation of the War on Poverty in Houston reveals that the federal program did not operate in a vacuum. Rather, a diverse group of local actors, including public officials, local elites, grassroots antipoverty activists, program administrators, federal volunteers, civil rights activists, and poor people themselves, profoundly shaped the War on Poverty in the city. Similar to the findings in Ashmore's study of Alabama and Clayson's study of Texas, there were significant connections between the civil rights movement and the War on Poverty in Houston. Yet the Houston case also reveals how ideology determined the types of activism in which Houston's poverty warriors engaged. In Houston, the federal War on Poverty briefly opened a window of opportunity for grassroots activists to turn their ideology into action by empowering the poor and organizing them to confront certain pillars of the local power structure.

Although the War on Poverty contributed to the evolution of liberal ideology, as Matusow, Germany, and Clayson have demonstrated, grassroots activists in Houston created a local context for the poverty war that was much more diverse in its intellectual and political influences than the rather narrow confines of New Deal/Great Society liberalism. This moderate brand of liberalism, according to Matusow, sought to extend the blessings of American life to previously excluded citizens. "Liberals came to identify the main problems confronting the country as unemployment, racism, and poverty," Matusow said. "The solutions they sponsored were Keynesian management of the economy, civil rights laws, and special measures to bring the poor into the economic mainstream— measures that came to be called the War on Poverty." Eschewing any hint of redistributive radicalism or political conflict, liberals in the 1960s believed that a rising tide lifted all boats. The way to combat poverty, then, was to maintain continued economic growth, remove legal barriers to self-improvement, and recycle New Deal–style work and education programs.[11]

The moderate liberalism that motivated architects of the federal War on Poverty met a harsh reality on the ground in Houston. As in other cities, local activists had identified structural and institutional barriers facing the poor that stemmed from their political powerlessness. An assortment of local Houston activists had already formulated an antipoverty philosophy to combat this powerlessness that turned out to be quite different from what the liberals offered. Lyndon Johnson's brand of liberalism certainly helped galvanize local antipoverty activists in Houston. Even more prominent in their antipoverty philosophy, however, was a brand of Christianity focused on the teachings of the Hebrew prophets advanced by theologians such as Reinhold Niebuhr combined with visions of participatory democracy and community organizing espoused by members of the New Left and iconoclastic figures like Saul Alinsky.

Yet the history of the implementation of the War on Poverty in Houston reveals more than simply a national story with a local twist. As conflicts over municipal services, housing conditions, predatory lending practices, and police brutality in the neighborhood of Settegast show, the federal antipoverty program often ignited open confrontations among activists, the poor, and political and social elites. The implementation of the War on Poverty in Houston reveals that the fluid interaction between federal policies and grassroots activists created a significant site of conflict over the meaning of American democracy and the rights of citizenship that historians have largely overlooked. Grassroots activists in Houston were able to use the War on Poverty to advance an agenda of social change that included empowering the city's poor and helping them engage in confrontations with local elites. In so doing, they contested mainstream definitions of democracy. These confrontations revealed a fundamental disagreement over what democracy meant, how far it should extend, and who should benefit from it. Many of the program's implementers embraced the federal mandate to empower the poor, pushing for a participatory form of democracy that would include more citizens in the political, cultural, and economic life of the city. The small victories that activists were able to achieve in their quest to expand democracy provoked a strong backlash from local public officials and other elites interested in maintaining the status quo. In Houston, therefore, the War on Poverty simultaneously created opportunities for grassroots activists to bring about social change and set limits on what those activists could ultimately achieve. Seen in this new light, the War on Poverty appears as an integral part of the democratic experiment in America, and its implementation in Houston reveals both the possibilities and the limits of American democracy.

The dynamics of the War on Poverty in Houston, particularly local activists' efforts to use the federal program to expand democracy, can best be understood within the conceptual framework provided by urban sociologist Manuel Castells in *The City and the Grassroots: A Cross-Cultural Theory of Urban Social Movements*. Castells theorized that cities are shaped by a series of continually conflictive processes through which competing interests attempt to define the meaning of urban space and to chart the future of the city. "Any theory of the city," Castells argued, "must be, as its starting point, a theory of social conflict." In his model for understanding the nature of urban movements and their potential to use conflict to bring about social change, Castells argued that social movements in cities tend to be remarkably diverse in their makeup. Stating that these urban movements cannot simply be reduced to another form of class struggle, gender struggle, or ethnic struggle, Castells wrote that urban activists "come from a variety of social, gender, and ethnic situations."[12]

My use of the term *grassroots* to describe antipoverty activists in Houston is informed by Castells's theory of urban social movements. The diverse group of local activists, administrators, and poor residents who implemented the War on Poverty in Houston had very few racial, ethnic, or class characteristics in common. Yet all of them in some way were engaged in a conflict with local public officials and other elites to determine the future of the city and to redefine the meaning of democracy. In this way, grassroots antipoverty activists in Houston created an urban social movement that transcended narrow class, racial, ethnic, or gender categories. It was a desire to expand the meaning of democracy in Houston, rather than an engagement in class or race conflict, that united these activists and opened a window of opportunity to effect real and meaningful social change.

The diversity of this urban movement to expand democracy in Houston also highlights the complexity of historical actors, particularly when it comes to political ideology. Most grassroots activists in Houston did not fit neatly into the liberal–conservative binary that permeates much of the history of the War on Poverty. The growing importance of political participation to many activists in the 1960s and 1970s, for example, illustrates the limitations of the liberal–conservative binary in explaining human behavior and beliefs. Beginning in the 1950s, a handful of political theorists and social critics, such as Paul Goodman and C. Wright Mills, began to voice their concerns about American democracy. Specifically, these intellectuals were troubled by what they saw as widespread political apathy and a disengagement from civic life. The remedy for apathy and the preventative for political disillusionment, they argued, would be to transform the United States into a participatory democracy. As historian Kevin Mattson has argued, "Politics was to be about more than just electoral activity; instead, it would relate directly to people's everyday lives." These and subsequent intellectuals looked to Jean-Jacques Rousseau, Thomas Jefferson, and John Dewey for a political philosophy that would empower ordinary citizens beyond mere voting and office holding. New Left thinkers in the 1960s, such as Arnold Kaufman and Tom Hayden, built upon these ideas. Most fully articulated in 1962 in the Port Huron Statement of the Students for a Democratic Society (SDS), participatory democracy called for all citizens to play significant roles in the decision-making processes that affected their lives.[13]

Rather than attempting to place complex human beings into narrow categories of political ideology, this study will illustrate the value of widening the lens to show the remarkable array of disagreement about the meaning of democracy in the 1960s and 1970s. Focusing on the implementation of the War on Poverty in a single location presents a valuable way of highlighting this disagreement. Historians have not yet paid sufficient attention to the relationship between the New Left philosophy of participatory democracy and the War on Poverty. The renewed emphasis on citizen participation during the 1960s found its way into federal guidelines for the Community Action Program (CAP), the most significant as well as the most combustible component of the War on Poverty. The concept of community action was ill defined, open to a multitude of interpretations, and it remains the most poorly understood element of the War on Poverty.

As historian John A. Andrew argued in his national study of the Great Society, CAP sought to "produce social change through participatory democracy." At its core, community action presented a new way of thinking about both the causes of and solutions for poverty. According to historian Allen J. Matusow, CAP called for local communities to create community action agencies that would be capable of "mobilizing local resources for a comprehensive attack on poverty." The goals of this direct attack on poverty would be threefold: (1) to create and provide new social services for the poor; (2) to provide centralized coordination of all social services available to the poor; and (3) to bring about institutional change that would benefit those living in poverty. This final CAP objective of reforming local institutions proved to be political dynamite in many communities because it implied a direct challenge to the balance of power, especially in the larger cities. A significant number of the architects of the federal War on Poverty, Matusow argued, had learned "to despise local schools, police, welfare departments, and private charity institutions for dispensing demeaning, fragmented services to the poor." While more and better services were certainly needed, many federal planners believed that a meaningful attack on poverty should include helping the poor engage in the political process in order to produce real social change. It was this original conception of community action that opened a space to contest the very meaning of democracy.[14]

This attempt to bring about meaningful social change was bound to be rife with tension and conflict. As Matusow pointed out, there were a few "closet radicals" among the War on Poverty planners who recognized that local institutions would be openly defiant of efforts to change them. Their solution to this problem was to declare that all community action agencies must be administered with the "maximum feasible participation" of a community's poor residents. "Community action," concluded Matusow, "would seek to reform institutions by empowering the poor." The edict of maximum feasible participation could operate in three ways: (1) poor residents could serve on the governing boards of local community action agencies; (2) the poor could be hired to work in the various programs; or (3) local community action agencies could employ community organizers to help empower the poor to make demands on local institutions and elected officials. Predictably, this final application of maximum feasible participation, which called for nothing short of the politicization and empowerment of the poor to demand a greater share of a community's resources, provoked the strongest response from local public officials and institutions. Therein lay the possibility of a broader critique of how democracy operated in the city.[15]

Historians have shown that President Lyndon Johnson and most OEO administrators poorly understood the ramifications of community action and maximum feasible participation of the poor. As Clayson argued, "The president probably envisioned noble unemployed men rolling up their sleeves and swinging pick axes like something out of the New Deal. He certainly did not anticipate that men and women from poor neighborhoods, people whom Johnson considered friendly constituents, would march into planning meetings demanding federal money from city governments controlled by the Democratic Party." Following a close analysis of Johnson's 296 recorded telephone conversations on the subject of the War on Poverty, historian Guian McKee concluded: "There is no evidence that President Johnson recognized, much less considered, the implications of maximum feasible participation and what it might mean either for community action itself or for the War on Poverty as a whole."[16]

Many OEO officials understood the implications of community action and maximum feasible participation little better and simply assumed the poor would be invited to help administer new social service programs in roles akin to junior partners and low-level employees. Yet the amorphousness of the community action concept and the maximum feasible participation edict left the goals of CAP wide open to interpretation. In Houston, a significant number of local activists and poor residents interpreted these ideals as an opportunity to organize communities; politicize the poor; and, if unable to redistribute wealth, at least to attempt to redistribute power by using conflict and confrontation. The seeds of social change, therefore, were embedded in the language of the federal War on Poverty guidelines regardless of the intentions of federal officials or the president himself. Local activists and poor residents in Houston, as in other cities, recognized this potential to bring about meaningful change and sought to capitalize on this significant opportunity to expand the meaning of democracy.

By pushing beyond the boundaries of liberalism and conservatism, the present study will reveal a complicated and meaningful conflict over the meaning of democracy centered on the important issue of citizen participation. Rather than continuing to highlight the debate between liberals committed to a New Deal–style welfare state and conservatives who advocated lower taxes and a more limited government, the implementation of the War on Poverty in Houston reveals a more important conflict in American society during the 1960s and 1970s over democracy and power. At stake was nothing less than the power to define the scope of democracy, the power individual citizens had over their own lives, the power to expand or limit access to finite resources, and the power to determine the future of the city.

These attempts to use the War on Poverty to expand the meaning of democracy and redistribute power—and especially the fierce political battles resulting from these attempts—were, of course, not confined to the city of Houston. As the recent outpouring of grassroots studies is showing, many local activists tried to renegotiate the boundaries of democracy in nearly every location where the War on Poverty was implemented. Although historians of the War on Poverty sometimes treat these attempts as peripheral to their narratives, in reality they are central to understanding how the War on Poverty operated on the ground in local communities. In other words, examining the role of the War on Poverty in expanding democracy in the 1960s and 1970s reveals a uniting thread that connects much of the recent outpouring of grassroots studies. Such analysis can also help reconceptualize the War on Poverty by restoring it to its rightful place in post-1945 American political history.

Viewing the War on Poverty through the conceptual lens of democracy also provides a historiographical advantage. The War on Poverty and the political battles its implementation sparked in Houston occurred during a time that has become known as "the sixties," a vague conceptual category and periodization that has tended to obscure more than it has revealed. Many scholars have correctly pointed out that historians of the 1960s have largely failed to bring any coherence to our understanding of the decade. As M. J. Heale has argued in his recent review of the field, historians of the 1960s in America have found it difficult to write synthetic histories of an era that itself seemed to reject the very idea of synthesis. As Heale stated, it was during the 1960s that "powerful currents of race, gender, class, and culture undermined the older notion of a consensual society." For periods of history before the 1960s, the result was a fragmentation of the writing of American history in its entirety—and that fragmentation came at the expense of synthetic history that already existed. "This could not be said of the Sixties," Heale concluded, "whose fate it was to be dissolved by the currents it spawned before a stable historiography could be written."[17]

Because it created such a significant site of conflict over American democracy in the 1960s, the War on Poverty can help integrate many of the decade's disparate historiographical threads that surprisingly remain unconnected by historians. The federal antipoverty program, particularly its implementation on local levels, intersected with several narratives of the 1960s in America. Most important among these are African American and Latino civil rights movements, postwar urban decline and the struggle for scarce resources, class conflict, debates over federalism and the persistence of localism, the rise and fall of the New Left, and the political polarization of American society. By connecting important trends in social history and political history, a close look at the implementation of the War on Poverty in a single location can help historians of the 1960s bridge these various strands of historical interpretation.

Most important, the implementation of the War on Poverty in Houston during the 1960s reveals the complex nature of how democracy works on the ground and how its very definition has been unstable and changing throughout history. As historian James T. Kloppenberg has recently reminded us, "Democracy in America has been a contest among diverse groups of people sharing neither common convictions nor common aspirations. . . . Democracy provides an attractive analytical framework precisely because it highlights the ceaseless wrangling—the deep disagreements over procedures as well as principles—that has marked American history." The 1960s marks a period in American history when the concept of democracy was especially in flux. Amid African American and Latino civil rights movements, the postwar decline of the American city, and increasingly volatile political and cultural conflict, Houstonians and Americans were engaged in intense debates about the nature and future of democracy during the 1960s.[18]

As this study shows, the most illuminating way to explore these debates about democracy during the 1960s and early 1970s is to view them, as historians such as Jesse Lemisch have long argued, "from the bottom up." By using the War on Poverty as a lens through which to investigate how ideas about democracy were rapidly changing, it also becomes possible to interrogate precisely how these ideas affected the lives of ordinary people—some poor, some not, but all affected by changing conceptions of how democracy was supposed to work. "If history is to be creative," Howard Zinn once wrote, "to anticipate a possible future without denying the past, it should, I believe, emphasize new possibilities by disclosing those hidden episodes of the past when, even if in brief flashes, people showed their ability to resist, to join together, occasionally to win." There were some brief flashes in Houston during the implementation of the War on Poverty when residents organized to resist oppression, democracy seemed to expand, and the poor even tasted victory. The fact that grassroots activists and poor Houston residents were able to transform a federal poverty program into a vehicle for social change, even for a short period of time, highlights the ingenuity and creativity of local people struggling to expand the meaning of democracy in America. When another window of opportunity to broaden the definition of democracy presents itself, perhaps today's democratic activists can draw on these lessons from the War on Poverty.[19]

Declaring a War on Poverty in the Midst of "Pervasive Conservatism"

The Tumultuous Road to Establishing a Community Action Agency, 1964–1965

"Through Houston's modern civic and social history seeps a pervasive conservatism," stated Houston historian David G. McComb in his landmark study of the city, "reflected in varying degrees in politics, public schools, and reactions to urban problems. It is the conservatism of a nineteenth-century robber baron — exploitative, laissez-faire, and at times generous in philanthropy. Its roots lie in the Southern heritage of the town, the expansive, opportunistic nature of the area, and the strong business orientation of the economy. It gives to the people a certain bold, reckless, stubborn, independent, and sometimes lawless attitude, which means that the conservatism both helps and hinders the development of the city."[1] The conservatism that McComb described certainly defined the city's politics in the mid-1960s, and it had a profound effect on the implementation of the War on Poverty in Houston.

The War on Poverty was not simply a top-down phenomenon imposed on local communities from Washington; rather, a multitude of local complications defined the program in significant ways, including its implementation in Houston. Between August 1964 and December 1965, federal program administrators, local public officials, politicians, grassroots antipoverty activists, and members of the city's traditional welfare bureaucracy wrangled over how the War on Poverty would be fought in the city. Much of the disagreement stemmed from divergent interpretations of the meaning of "community action," a concept developed by architects of the War on Poverty who had roots in the federal juvenile delinquency programs of the early 1960s. According to federal program developers, community action would offer a novel and aggressive method for attacking the root causes of poverty in American society. Despite pressure from War on Poverty administrators and some local advocates of this new antipoverty philosophy, Houston's public officials and members of the city's traditional welfare establishment viewed the concept of community action in a very cautious manner. The city's public officials, particularly Houston mayor Louie Welch, interpreted the federal mandate in a way that would increase their own political power.

During the first year of the War on Poverty, Welch attempted to use federal antipoverty funds to pay for services the city government had yet to provide, such as infrastructure improvements and increases in sanitation and other municipal services. The mayor could take credit for these improvements and reap the political rewards. Members of the city's traditional welfare bureaucracy similarly tried to use the community action concept to strengthen their control over the purse strings of private charitable giving in the city. Meanwhile, several federal program administrators and a few grassroots antipoverty activists in Houston began calling for nothing short of a revolution in the way the city addressed the needs of the poor. The contentious process of creating a community action agency to administer the War on Poverty in Houston was therefore shaped more by local power struggles and the contours of city politics than by debates in Washington on how to fight poverty.

The debates provoked by these differing interpretations of how to administer the War on Poverty in Houston resulted in two significant developments that altered political events in the city over the next several years. First, launching the War on Poverty suddenly made Houston's poor population visible, especially to governing elites. Dwight Macdonald's widely read 1963 *New Yorker* article, "Our Invisible Poor," aptly described the plight of low-income residents of Houston. Until then, they simply had not been noticed by anyone other than those involved in the city's relatively small, privatized charitable sector. Because Houston's poor were isolated in low-income neighborhoods, they were not part of the city's political and civic landscape. The War on Poverty, at the very least, directed attention toward these poor communities. With the promise of federal funding to help alleviate poverty, Houston's political and civic leaders took notice.[2]

Second, disagreements over how to implement the War on Poverty in Houston opened a space to debate the very meaning of democracy, which was made possible by divergent interpretations of community action. While many local activists viewed community action as an opportunity to organize and empower the poor, big-city mayors, as historian Allen J. Matusow has argued in his study of the War on Poverty, tended to be "guided by their own convenient conceptions of what community action should be." This was certainly the case in Houston, where Mayor Louie Welch and members of the traditional welfare establishment interpreted community action in a way that did not challenge the city's "pervasive conservatism" that McComb described so poignantly. Meanwhile, the persistent mandate of empowerment coming from Washington electrified many activists in Houston. It was this debate over how the War on Poverty should be implemented that brought the definition of democracy into question.[3]

Like other Sunbelt politicians, Louie Welch was a moderate who had an overtly favorable attitude toward business enterprise in Houston. Welch actually gained political clout and ultimately won the mayor's seat in 1963 by appearing as an outsider to the established political culture in the city. Most important, many people saw Welch as a commonsense moderate on racial issues. Although a sizable number of Houstonians resisted calls to desegregate the city in the late 1950s and early 1960s, the most powerful business interests recognized that ugly racial conflicts, such as those occurring in Birmingham, would only serve to hurt Houston's reputation as a business-friendly city. In response to an increasing number of calls from the city's civil rights leaders to desegregate businesses in Houston, the city's business and political elites gathered behind closed doors and decided to desegregate much of the city quietly and without fanfare.[4]

During his tenure on Houston's city council between 1950 and 1962, Louie Welch built a reputation both as a racial moderate sympathetic to the business community's efforts to avoid showdowns over desegregation and as a friend of and advocate for the city's African American community. In 1959, as an increasing number of black Houstonians lodged complaints of police brutality and harassment against the Houston Police Department, Welch demanded that the city attorney's office perform a complete investigation and take disciplinary action against any guilty officer. Coming on the heels of this political victory, one particular event in 1960 solidified Welch's reputation as a moderate whose commonsense approach would save the city from the bad publicity of tense racial confrontations. In March 1960, about thirty-five black and white students from nearby universities staged a sit-in at the segregated cafeteria located in the basement of City Hall, whose owner was one of the few holdouts resisting desegregation. As the students sat in the cafeteria waiting to be served, a crowd of angry whites began to gather inside the building and on the sidewalk outside the main window. Welch was upstairs in the council chambers, and when he got news of what was happening in the cafeteria, he rushed to the scene. The cafeteria manager sought out Welch and asked him what she should do. "Serve them," Welch responded, "because if you don't you are going to get into trouble. They are citizens of the city and this is a city building, so serve them." Welch then fought his way through the crowd and walked over to the table where the students were sitting. Someone from the crowd of onlookers yelled, "Get those niggers out of here!" Welch looked at the students, looked back at the crowd, and said, "Well, we don't all have to be damn fools, do we?" Welch then sat down beside the students and started up a conversation. In just a few minutes the cafeteria manager had served all the students, and Welch became an important part of this civil rights triumph in the city.[5]

Three years later, after two failed attempts, Welch finally won the mayor's race with the help of a substantial majority of black Houstonians. His opponent, the incumbent Lewis Cutrer, once had the overwhelming support of the city's black voters. As sit-ins began in the early 1960s, however, Cutrer found himself recast as a stubborn opponent of civil rights because he was not willing to support desegregation efforts publicly or help create more job opportunities for African Americans in city agencies. Most concerning to Houston's black citizens was Cutrer's hiring of the overtly racist and brutal Carl Shuptrine as police chief. Welch promised that as mayor he would fire Chief Shuptrine and clean up the police department to make it more professional and just in its treatment of all citizens. He also promised to address the problems of poverty in Houston.[6]

Welch's antipoverty philosophy was essentially traditional and cautious in nature, and his interpretation of the community action concept reflected his moderate approach. With the passage of the Economic Opportunity Act in August 1964, Welch declared that his office and the city council would work together to apply for some of the $5 million to which the city was entitled under the new antipoverty act. Welch envisioned using these funds to make infrastructural improvements to the city, such as extending water and sewage services to the outskirts of town and perhaps paving roads in some neighborhoods. What the mayor did not have in mind, however, was a community action program in Houston like national planners had advocated. As for the maximum feasible participation edict, Welch stressed that he and the city council alone were responsible for deciding when and how the city of Houston would participate in the federal War on Poverty. If the city did indeed apply for and receive federal antipoverty funds, Welch promised to appoint an antipoverty committee himself to oversee the use of these funds. So while Welch in some ways conformed to the new breed of Southern politician, moderate on racial issues and open to accepting federal funds to improve the city, his message was clear: he would be in control of the War on Poverty in the city of Houston.[7]

The 1964 national elections indicated to Welch that even his moderate and cautious positions would meet with resistance in Houston's more dogmatically conservative political environment. Houston's mayoral politics were ostensibly nonpartisan, and many of the city's past mayors had steered clear of national politics to focus instead on local issues. The War on Poverty, however, presented Welch with a new challenge because it intertwined national and local politics so closely. When the Democrats met in Atlantic City in late August 1964 for their national convention, they overwhelmingly endorsed the idea of making the War on Poverty a major campaign issue. Party leaders noted that Barry Goldwater, Johnson's challenger for the presidency, had voted against the Economic Opportunity Act. New York City mayor Robert F. Wagner Jr. implored convention delegates to highlight this important difference between the two candidates in the general election. Wagner stated, "The issue between the parties is clear. The platform must reflect this clearcut issue and give it the dramatic prominence it deserves." Platform writers agreed and made the War on Poverty a major theme of the party's campaign document. The final draft pledged that the Democratic Party would carry "the War on Poverty forward as a total war against the causes of human want" and relished that the party had been instrumental in getting the Economic Opportunity Act passed through Congress. In fact, the Democratic Party platform mentioned the War on Poverty seven times throughout the document, making it clear that the poverty program and civil rights for minorities would be the centerpieces of the campaign that year.[8]

A few weeks after the Democratic national convention, Mayor Welch, who was not part of the liberal wing of the Democratic Party in Texas, announced his approval of the party platform and his endorsement of the Johnson-Humphrey ticket. This proclamation prompted a flood of angry letters from Goldwater supporters and other conservatives in Houston, and many of these letters attacked Welch's implied support for Johnson's War on Poverty. Exemplifying the reaction of many conservatives in Houston, Virginia Eastham wrote to berate Welch for his support of Johnson and the Democratic Party's alleged left-wing agenda. "In my opinion, you favor socialism, destruction of free enterprise, [and] federal control (this is borne out by your request for federal anti-poverty funds)," she said. A letter from Mrs. John T. Carter accused Welch of playing politics with the federal antipoverty program. Carter stated, "I also note that you have been quick to seek Washington aid for local affairs, and these efforts, if fruitful, may enhance you in the eyes of some of the recipients of this government dole, but certainly I do not believe it will prove politically advantageous to you." Although Welch was open to the idea of obtaining federal funds through the War on Poverty, these kinds of letters reminded him that strong conservative forces would oppose him and undoubtedly served to temper the mayor's interpretation of the federal antipoverty mandate.[9]

The War on Poverty and the prospect of its implementation in Houston also opened serious political rifts that had been brewing for some time among the city's elected officials. Harris County judge Bill Elliott, whose position was akin to serving as chief financial officer for the county, was known as a staunch liberal and vocal critic of many of Welch's moderate probusiness policies. Elliott attacked the mayor's plan to control all the city's War on Poverty funding and said it "smelled to high heaven of being an election year gimmick." Elliott objected to the fact that Welch would have the power to appoint the board and director for any central antipoverty committee in the city of Houston. In September, in an attack on the War on Poverty from the right, the millionaire oilman George H. W. Bush launched his campaign as a Republican against liberal Democrat Ralph Yarborough for the U.S. Senate. During the first month of campaigning, Bush made the War on Poverty a central issue by accusing Yarborough and his liberal colleagues of being paternalistic in their antipoverty efforts. War on Poverty proponents, argued Bush, "assign the needy a number and tell them to get into a federal handout line." Bush said he would offer his own brand of "compassionate conservatism" as an alternative to Yarborough's "cold liberalism."[10]

The results of the 1964 election seemed quite favorable to the liberal War on Poverty both nationally and locally in Houston. In Harris County, the Johnson-Humphrey ticket won 63.1 percent of the popular vote and outpolled Goldwater by about seventy-five thousand votes. Since the Democratic Party had made the War on Poverty one of the campaign's major issues, it seemed there were many War on Poverty supporters in Houston. A further indication of this support was Senator Yarborough's defeat of Bush, who lost Harris County even though he lived there. Harris County voted overwhelmingly Democratic for the first time since 1948, and voters made Lyndon Johnson the first Democratic president to win Harris County since Harry Truman. President Johnson interpreted the 1964 election as a mandate to continue building the Great Society, and Houston civic leaders drew similar conclusions about Harris County returns. Mayor Welch and County Judge Elliott, in particular, began moving closer to direct participation in the War on Poverty.[11]

Welch and Elliott were not alone in supporting the War on Poverty in Houston. The Houston Community Council, the established bureaucratic agency responsible for coordinating activities of all the major public welfare agencies in the city, also supported the federal antipoverty initiative. The council was responsible for studying the needs of the poor in Houston, publishing its findings in an annual report, and ensuring that the city's various welfare agencies addressed these needs. Like similar welfare coordinating boards in other major cities across the United States, Houston Community Council members came mostly from the ranks of the city's white upper-middle class and worked closely with the city's public officials. In May 1964, as President Lyndon B. Johnson's Economic Opportunity bill made its way through Congress, the executive committee of the Community Council launched a study of how the new federal antipoverty initiative might be implemented in Houston once it became law. Members of the council's executive committee immediately recognized that the Economic Opportunity bill could have profound implications for poverty work in Houston. Like Welch, members of the council had a guarded view of the concept of community action, but they also recognized the need for an increased level of social services that would benefit the poor. Although Welch had tried to make it clear that he would control any War on Poverty funds that might come to the city, Houston's Community Council members remained confident that their organization would become the community action agency for Houston and the primary recipient of federal funds to fight poverty in the city.[12]

This confidence was reinforced in August 1964 when Joseph Zarefsky, executive secretary of the Community Council, traveled to Austin to attend a meeting of the State Mental Health Planning Committee. At that time he had a lengthy conversation with Fred Baldwin, who was a member of President Johnson's Task Force on Poverty. Baldwin stressed to Zarefsky (1) that the federal government would approve only one official community action agency per city and (2) that it would be very wise for that agency to work closely with public authorities and local politicians in order to ensure any proposed antipoverty programs would not meet resistance from those in power. The Houston Community Council, Baldwin argued, was in a great position to assume this leadership role for the War on Poverty in Houston, and it seemed to be on good terms with the mayor and the city council.[13]

As Welch began making statements asserting his authority over the implementation of the War on Poverty in Houston, Zarefsky responded by inviting the mayor and his staff to a Community Council board of directors meeting in late August to discuss the possibility of forming a coordinating committee to administer the War on Poverty in Houston. As Zarefsky stated during the meeting, the Community Council already possessed the tools and staff to administer the War on Poverty based on its previous welfare work in the community. Despite Welch's need to retain control, he seemed receptive to the idea of the Community Council being involved in the War on Poverty in the city, most likely because both he and the council shared similar interpretations of the concept of community action. Zarefsky and other board members made it clear that a traditional service-delivery philosophy would continue to guide the Community Council and that there would only be minimal participation of the poor in planning and implementing these antipoverty services. Community Council chairman J. Robert Reynaud noted that the War on Poverty, once implemented in Houston, would require the involvement of "lay people and professionals, official agencies and voluntary agencies, [and] school districts," and would need the same kind of participation from the "city, county, the Employment Commission, the Community Council, and many other agencies." The concept of "maximum feasible participation" of the poor seemed to have been lost on Community Council members in Houston.[14]

With Welch's informal approval, by late September 1964 the Houston Community Council was actively positioning itself as the logical board to administer the War on Poverty in the city. The executive committee met that month and decided to begin forming a community committee made up of the Community Council and several of its delegate agencies. The board of directors of the council then issued a public statement asking Mayor Welch to approve this committee as the central antipoverty agency for the city of Houston. In an effort to obtain that approval from Houston's public officials, council leaders also requested that Mayor Welch and County Judge Elliott each appoint some of the members of the committee. Welch and Elliott both responded favorably, and it seemed the War on Poverty might actually begin implementation in Houston during its first year.[15]

Despite giving tacit approval for the Community Council to become the central coordinating board for the War on Poverty in Houston, Welch still wanted to retain control of its implementation. He continued to favor obtaining federal grants to fund improvements to the city's infrastructure rather than using them to expand and improve social welfare services for the poor. Welch continued developing his own personal plan for using federal antipoverty funds in the city. Part of this plan included asking the Office of Economic Opportunity to award a grant to the city of Houston to improve water and sanitation services in Acres Homes, a poor, mostly African American neighborhood in the northwest part of Harris County. Welch announced that he would request $8 million from the federal government to install sanitary sewers, drainage equipment, and water lines and to provide training in construction industry skills for poor residents of the area. Meanwhile, Houston Community Council members continued their efforts to persuade Welch and Elliott to appoint a central committee to oversee the War on Poverty in the city. To make their case stronger, the council's board of directors began developing ideas for antipoverty programs that could be funded through the War on Poverty, particularly for the city's traditional welfare agencies such as the Harris County Welfare Department, the Opportunity Center for Retarded Children, the Texas Employment Commission, and the Houston Neighborhood Centers Association.[16]

While adequate sanitation services and the delivery of traditional welfare services are important in any city, Houston's city leaders and welfare bureaucracy refused to accept fully the implications of the Economic Opportunity Act. Architects of the federal War on Poverty, especially when they developed the community action component of the act, envisioned a different kind of poverty program than what traditional welfare agencies offered. New and expanded social services and centralized coordination of those services were certainly components of the Community Action Program. But equally significant was the idea of reforming local institutions by promoting the participation of poor residents in the planning, development, and implementation of poverty programs designed not simply to alleviate the symptoms of poverty but also to attack the root causes of poverty. The War on Poverty was neither intended to subsidize the building of infrastructure, which was the responsibility of cities and municipalities, nor designed simply to increase funding to traditional welfare agencies.

It is possible that Mayor Welch and members of the Houston Community Council simply failed to understand the new antipoverty philosophy that motivated the designers of the War on Poverty. A more likely explanation for their actions, however, is that both the mayor and the Community Council board wanted to retain control over the traditional welfare bureaucracy in Houston. In order to accomplish this, they intentionally worked to limit and control the poverty program in order to prevent poor residents from participating. The Reverend John F. Stevens, director of Christian Social Relations for the Episcopal Diocese of Texas and the head of the Episcopal Society for Cultural and Racial Unity in Houston, recognized this power play and advocated a more aggressive interpretation of the concept of community action. Stevens offered a powerful critique of the philosophy of the service-oriented welfare agencies in Houston. He stated that Houston's traditional welfare agencies had become "just another outside service to a poverty-ridden area" and had "lost touch with local leadership." Stevens said this happened because members of these organizations had a faulty understanding of the remedy for poverty, "which sees the dominant (affluent Anglo-Saxon) community providing a solution for the depressed area on its own terms, while being distrustful of any exercise of power on the part of residents in the depressed area." As a result, "no real solution is possible until the status quo in society is changed to give residents of depressed areas equal educational and job opportunities, competitive pay and equal access to good housing." As Welch, Elliott, and the Community Council moved forward with their plans for a piecemeal antipoverty effort in Houston that they could control, critical voices like that of Rev. Stevens grew louder and more forceful and began to gain an increasing amount of legitimacy in the poor neighborhoods of the city.[17]

In addition to a few vocal critics, who called attention to the way Houston's public officials and traditional welfare bureaucracy were handling the declaration of the War on Poverty in the city, several additional antipoverty agencies actually began to compete for a share of this new pool of federal money. The Neighborhood Centers Association, an organization created in the early twentieth century as part of the Progressive-era settlement house movement, teamed up with the Houston Independent School District (HISD) in January and submitted a proposal for using War on Poverty funds to create a program to keep at-risk high-school students in school by providing them with remedial education and job training. In April the federal government also approved a Neighborhood Centers Association application to administer a Neighborhood Youth Corps program in Houston.[18]

The antipoverty organization that eventually forced public officials and members of the Houston Community Council into action was Houston Action for Youth (HAY). Professional social workers in Houston created HAY in the summer of 1964 as part of the Kennedy-Johnson effort to curb juvenile delinquency in the nation's cities. The organization was already funded by the Department of Health, Education, and Welfare through May 1965. HAY administered traditional programs such as homeless shelters and job-training centers for impoverished young people in Houston. In April 1965 HAY partnered with the HISD school board to draw up a proposal to administer a summer Head Start preschool program in Houston funded by OEO, intended to reach approximately 2,500 children living in poverty.[19]

Members of the Community Council board wanted to avoid losing any control or influence over the development of the War on Poverty in Houston, and they were threatened by an organization like HAY that was conceivably large enough to administer the federal antipoverty program in the city and already receiving federal funds. The board members began to put additional pressure on Mayor Welch to give formal approval for the appointment of a central antipoverty committee for the city made up of Community Council members. Board chairman Reynaud met with Welch in January and reiterated the need for a committee in Houston, yet Welch continued to be coy about his intentions. At a board meeting near the end of February, Community Council board member William Ballew expressed alarm about the fact that some antipoverty agencies in Houston were already submitting funding applications to the Office of Economic Opportunity. Ballew argued that despite the difficulties the Community Council had been experiencing with Mayor Welch, it was time to move forward with creating a committee to oversee War on Poverty funding in Houston regardless of whether or not the mayor gave his approval. There were simply too many organizations calling for the Community Council to take an active leadership role in the War on Poverty, according to Ballew, and those voices could no longer be ignored.

Ballew, who would later become the head of Houston's community action agency and move the organization in a more confrontational direction, was a very politically astute individual. As a successful attorney with one of the city's oldest and largest law firms, Ballew understood the intricacies of Houston's local politics. In an effort to push Welch more forcefully, Ballew began making overtures toward County Judge Bill Elliott, Welch's political rival, and asked him to help convene an antipoverty committee. He then persuaded the Community Council board to appoint a task force, to be chaired by Ballew, whose sole responsibility was to perform a study of how War on Poverty programs could be implemented in Houston and convince the mayor to name a committee.[20]

Federal War on Poverty administrators also ramped up their efforts to persuade Welch to help establish a community action agency for Houston. Sargent Shriver, director of OEO, helped smooth the process of appointing an antipoverty committee by sending a letter to Mayor Welch expressing his desire to work closely with local leaders in the implementation of the War on Poverty across the country. Shriver stated, "I have always felt and OEO policy has always supported the position that local public officials have a major role to play in community action—a role which they have in fact carried out with great dedication and intelligence. Successful programs in over 600 American communities attest to the effectiveness of this participation." In March 1965 Vice President Hubert Humphrey invited thirteen mayors from the nation's largest cities to Washington to discuss the possibilities for implementing the War on Poverty at the local level. During this meeting Welch told Humphrey that he wanted to apply for OEO grants, but he was unsure how to get the process started. In response, Humphrey and federal OEO officials promised to send representatives from their office to Houston in the coming weeks to help work out a plan for implementation of the new federal antipoverty program. On March 22 and 23, 1965, two OEO officials visited Houston, and after their visit neither was optimistic about the War on Poverty's future in the city. The officials noted the presence of multiple power struggles occurring simultaneously, and all seemed to revolve around the question of who would control the War on Poverty in the city.[21]

Although federal War on Poverty planners wanted each city to have a community action agency to provide centralized administration of the implementation of federal antipoverty programs, Welch told the visiting OEO representatives that he was only interested in obtaining no-strings-attached federal grants to make improvements to the city; he also said that he in no way wanted a community action agency in Houston. In fact, the more Welch learned about the Community Action Program in the national media, the more he became opposed to its implementation in his city. The only logical avenue for federal funding in Houston, Welch told the OEO officials, was to help build the city's infrastructure as reflected in his proposal for an $8 million grant to improve the water quality and sanitation system in Acres Homes. Welch said that if certain groups in Houston forced him to create a community action board, then he would follow the example of Chicago mayor Richard Daley and create a "blue ribbon group." By this tactic, Welch would appoint all of the members himself from the elite business community, and the board would have no authority except to investigate poverty conditions in Houston and report back to the mayor. Under no circumstances, however, would Welch share the responsibility for appointing the members of such a board with anyone, especially not County Judge Bill Elliott, whom OEO officials called "a liberal political rival." It became clear to OEO officials that the mayor was reinterpreting the concept of community action in order to turn the War on Poverty into a vehicle for increasing his own political power in the city.[22]

While in Houston, OEO officials also scheduled meetings with other individuals and groups in the community who were interested in the War on Poverty.

In a meeting with Bill Elliott, the county judge indicated that he would accept any number of compromise positions on the appointment of an antipoverty committee for Houston but strongly oppose a board whose members were all appointed by Welch. During a meeting with the board of directors of the Houston Community Council, OEO officials learned that the council had developed a proposal for the creation of an antipoverty committee whereby the mayor, county judge, and the Community Council would each appoint an equal number of members. OEO officials noted that this proposal would be acceptable in Washington but would be entirely irrelevant if Welch stuck to his guns and refused to share appointment power. Members of Houston Action for Youth told OEO officials that they planned on moving forward with their own antipoverty plans for Houston and that they wanted to expand their services into more areas of the city. Finally, a small group of Mexican Americans who had attended a War on Poverty conference in Tucson, Arizona, that month had begun meeting weekly in an attempt to form their own antipoverty committee for Houston.[23]

Upon returning to Washington, OEO officials who had visited Houston made several recommendations to the OEO office. First, they advised senior OEO staffers that if Welch insisted on appointing all the members of a central antipoverty committee, then they should press the mayor as hard as possible to make the committee community-wide and "representative of more than the conservative wing of the Democratic party." While OEO officials were resigned to the fact that the committee would indeed probably be a "blue ribbon group," they nevertheless stressed the need to encourage some decentralization of decision-making power in Houston in an attempt to get some policymaking authority into the hands of neighborhood organizations, if not the poor residents themselves. The OEO representatives recognized, however, that Welch would strongly and vocally oppose this because he had already made it known that he was against "a Philadelphia situation," a reference to the rumored corruption said to have already occurred with the War on Poverty there. Finally, the OEO officials recommended that while Welch organized his blue ribbon group, OEO should go ahead and fund the programs being carried out by Houston Action for Youth in some of Houston's poor neighborhoods. OEO should not, however, fund HAY at a level that would allow the organization to expand its services into additional areas of the city, as this would "give HAY an invitation to empire-building, to which its chairman, Mrs. Helen Lewis, seems prone." Rather, OEO should partially fund HAY as a way to put pressure on Welch to appoint a community action agency that would meet federal CAP requirements.[24]

Between March and May 1965 several factors came together to force the mayor to accept a compromise position on the appointment of a committee. Immediately after OEO officials left Houston at the end of March, the Mexican American group that had been meeting weekly to discuss the implementation of the War on Poverty in Houston officially formed the Anti-Poverty Council of Houston. The Reverend James Novarro, pastor of a local Baptist church in a predominantly Mexican American neighborhood and chairman of the new antipoverty council, urged the Latino community in Houston to unify its political and social agencies into one force in order to claim a policymaking voice in the War on Poverty. During a rally at the end of March organized by the city's chapter of the Political Association of Spanish-Speaking Organizations (PASSO) in support of bringing the War on Poverty to Houston, Novarro told his audience that rivalry among the various antipoverty agencies could threaten the whole program. "There are many power structures in Houston," Novarro warned, and "we must encompass all these organizations or the anti-poverty program will have passed us by." Novarro said his new council "hopes to serve as a bridge of communication between the agencies that are going to help and the people who need it."[25]

Rev. Novarro and other members of the Anti-Poverty Council of Houston grew tired of waiting for Mayor Welch to act. During the first Houston city council meeting in April 1965, Novarro and several other members spoke in an effort to put added pressure on the mayor to appoint a central committee to administer the War on Poverty in the city. Novarro stressed to the city council that minority groups in Houston, many of whom were disproportionately affected by poverty, desperately needed help through the federal War on Poverty. Members of the city council responded by giving Mayor Welch a two-week deadline to come up with a plan for the implementation of the War on Poverty in Houston.[26]

Later in April 1965, the Houston Community Council's Task Force on the Economic Opportunity Act, chaired by William Ballew, finally completed its report titled "Tentative Proposal for Community Action Program for Metropolitan Houston." The report revealed a level of poverty in Houston that many thought had been eradicated by the general prosperity the Sunbelt city enjoyed following the end of World War II. Using the currently accepted yardstick for defining poverty, which included all families earning less than $3,000 annually and all individuals earning less than $2,000 annually, the study showed that there were 227,000 people—about one-fifth of the population of Harris County—whose total household incomes were below the poverty line, and 78 percent of these individuals lived inside Houston's city limits. This number included 57,000 poor families and more than 76,000 children. The study found that the twenty-five poorest census tracts in Houston housed 21 percent of Houston's population, yet they also accounted for 29 percent of the city's deaths, 36 percent of the city's infant deaths, 58 percent of deaths from tuberculosis, and 54 percent of the city's homicides. The report also indicated that 41 percent of Houston's poor families lived in deteriorated or dilapidated housing. Not surprisingly, authors of the study argued that nonwhite families were most vulnerable to poverty. The report stated that a "caste system" existed in the city for nonwhites and that African American and Mexican American families were disproportionately represented among poor families. Though nonwhites in Houston accounted for only 23 percent of the total population, half of the families living in poverty were nonwhite.[27]

As the task force's report suggested, a closer look at the median income of Houston's thirty-five poorest census tracts revealed the extent of poverty in the city. There were significant sections of Houston that suffered from unemployment rates two to three times the average rate in the city and that had average incomes less than half of the citywide average. In many of these poor sections of Houston, there was a very low rate of home ownership and a significant amount of housing was considered substandard. The statistics also showed that while much of the poverty was concentrated around the inner city, there were also many impoverished neighborhoods interspersed throughout the rest of the city and county. In other words, there was no single, concentrated poverty "ghetto" in Houston.[28]

Welch was up for reelection in November and apparently realized there was substantial popular support for at least some parts of the War on Poverty program in Houston. Word had also gotten back to Welch that OEO officials were considering funding Houston Action for Youth as the major War on Poverty agency for the city, a development that both Welch and members of the Community Council greeted with trepidation. Additionally, the Community Council's report confronted Welch with concrete statistics about poverty in Houston that he simply could not ignore. In response, Welch began meeting with representatives of the Community Council and with County Judge Bill Elliott in an effort to find a way to appoint a central committee that would satisfy everyone and still allow public officials to retain control of the poverty program. The compromise they reached was that each party—the mayor, the county judge, and the Community Council—would appoint five members to a fifteen-member executive committee that would serve as the central antipoverty board for the city of Houston. As the Community Council's report recommended, the members of the executive committee would then select a sixty-person advisory council to assist in developing an antipoverty program for Houston.[29]

When Welch, Elliott, and members of the Community Council board got around to naming the executive committee in May 1965, the fears that federal OEO administrators had of a blue ribbon group came to fruition. Many of the appointed members came from the ranks of wealthy businessmen in the city. George H. W. Bush, an oil industry executive, Republican politician, and recent critic of the War on Poverty, found his name on the committee roster, as did *Houston Post* vice president William P. Hobby Jr. and Texas National Bank vice president Charles W. Hamilton. The mayor, county judge, and Community Council also appointed a few middle-class African American business leaders to the executive committee, including Sid Hillard, a real estate agent, and Francis Williams, a prominent African American attorney in Houston. Welch appointed Houston attorney Leon Jaworski, who several years later would become known for his role as a special prosecutor in the Watergate scandal, to chair the committee.[30]

The newly appointed executive committee charged with overseeing the creation of a community action agency for Houston used the Community Council's report as a framework for how the poverty program would operate in the city. Since the Community Council had been the coordinating agency for the traditional welfare establishment in Houston for some time, the task force's report predictably highlighted the role of social service delivery in efforts to eradicate poverty. Community Council members were willing to accept the call to increase social services and coordinate programs of the traditional welfare agencies in Houston. What Community Council members would not accept, and what Welch would never have approved, was the idea that the poor could be empowered to reform the institutions that affected their lives. The majority of the programs suggested by the task force's report therefore were simply extensions of social services already offered by welfare agencies in Houston. The only difference was the additional funding provided by OEO that these agencies would have at their disposal. Considering the circumspect way in which members of the Community Council interpreted the concept of community action and the fact that Welch was very much in control, it is not surprising that the report envisioned no role whatsoever for poor people themselves in the planning, development, or implementation of antipoverty programs in Houston's poor neighborhoods. Authors of the report indicated that the board of directors of the new agency would be made up of an equal number of representative directors and directors-at-large. The representative directors would come from the ranks of elected and public officials in Houston, such as the mayor, the president of the school board, and the president of the chamber of commerce. These representative directors would, in turn, appoint the directors-at-large during the first meeting of the board. This board of directors would serve as a repository for information on War on Poverty programs and policies, and the traditional welfare organizations would act as delegate agencies to administer the antipoverty programs. The report never even mentioned the possibility of including the poor on the board of the community action agency. In fact, some of the hypothetical programs presented in the report were quite paternalistic and condescending.[31]

By the beginning of May 1965, OEO administrators were pleased that local officials in Houston were following at least the minimal procedures for establishing a community action agency for the city. This optimism was quickly dashed, however, when the OEO office in Washington dispatched a representative to travel to Houston and report on progress there. Vince Ximenes, an OEO consultant stationed in Lubbock, Texas, arrived in Houston in mid-May and began sending highly critical reports back to Washington as soon as he arrived. His first complaint was that the appointment of the city's poverty committee was motivated entirely by local politics: Mayor Welch was running for reelection, and County Judge Elliott was most likely going to run for the U.S. representative office in 1966 from the newly created congressional district in Houston. According to Ximenes, Welch and Elliott agreed to split evenly the number of members each would appoint to the committee to satisfy the political aspirations of both politicians.[32]

Ximenes was most troubled by the complete absence of poor people on the executive committee. For this reason he believed the Houston antipoverty board would fail to meet the minimum community action specifications for poverty resident participation. When Fred Baldwin, an OEO official working out of the Washington community action office, read this report, he immediately contacted the Houston Community Council to urge members of the new antipoverty committee to include the poor in the planning and implementation of War on Poverty programs in Houston. A representative from the Community Council assured Baldwin that although neither the politicians nor the council had appointed any poor people to the executive committee, it was the understanding of the council board that the executive committee would appoint a sixty-person advisory council that would indeed include poor residents.[33]

When the executive committee members appointed the advisory council a few days later, they did include a few representatives from the poor neighborhoods in Houston. Of the sixty total members of the advisory council, fifteen were considered "poor," including eight African Americans and four Mexican Americans. The announcement issued to the public by Welch, Elliott, and the members of the Community Council stated that the members of the advisory council "were jointly chosen to represent the viewpoints of the broadest number of people in the community, and each person accepted the nomination enthusiastically." While on the surface it appeared that Houston's poor residents in some small way might begin to have a voice in the planning, development, and implementation of antipoverty programs in the city, Ximenes quickly discovered that this advisory council would in fact have no influence over the executive committee and very little voice in making policy or developing antipoverty programs. According to Ximenes, this advisory council would "serve no purpose except window dressing."[34]

Ximenes attended a meeting of the new antipoverty organization's executive committee while he was in Houston and was unimpressed with what he saw. Several individuals, including Ximenes, urged the executive committee to include the sixty-member advisory council in making major decisions and in developing programs, and each time executive committee chairman Leon Jaworski and other committee members turned down the suggestions. Jaworski announced that the executive committee would agree to meet with the advisory council only four times per year, and during these meetings the executive committee, rather than seeking the advice of the advisory council, would simply keep the advisory council abreast of the committee's activities in the community. Ximenes pointed out to Jaworski and the rest of the executive committee that the Economic Opportunity Act, as well as OEO guidelines, required community participation in the War on Poverty, but the committee members quickly dismissed Ximenes's argument and told him to come back and talk to them at a later date. As the meeting drew to a close, Ximenes reported that he "was given to understand that the community development concept has no place in Houston."[35]

"If Houston is an example of what is being done in other towns," Ximenes wrote in his report, "then I suppose the self-help ideal will once again be defeated. . . . There is an obvious fear of including minorities or poor people in any kind of function, administrative or operative." Even the middle-class African American representatives on the executive committee, according to Ximenes, would not be allowed to have any voice, "except as it may have been pre-determined." Ximenes urged OEO officials to take note of the "predominance of millionaires" on the executive committee and argued that there was "every reason to believe that the board as it is constituted now has no intention of allowing communities to formulate their own programs much less decide policy." Ximenes warned that if Houston's antipoverty committee continued to insist on its present course of action, the residents of the poverty areas in the city would continue to insist on true representation on the policymaking committee, possibly using mass demonstrations to get their point across. It was just in the previous week that two thousand African American students and supporters had marched through the streets of Houston to demand that public school desegregation proceed more quickly. If a mass demonstration in support of poor and minority representation on the antipoverty committee occurred, OEO would be forced to side with the poor residents against Houston's public officials, a situation most OEO officials would have rather avoided.[36]

Federal OEO administrators were concerned enough about the events in Houston that they passed on Ximenes's reports to OEO director Sargent Shriver. Ximenes recommended that OEO go ahead and fund other antipoverty agencies in Houston, such as Houston Action for Youth, and argued that this might put more pressure on the executive committee to comply with OEO guidelines on representation of the poor. His report, however, ended rather pessimistically.

Ximenes warned that he was not at all convinced that Houston's antipoverty committee was "a sincere effort to utilize OEO funds on any basis. It could be a typical Houston delaying tactic. The kind that finally caused the Negroes to march in support of school integration." Shriver agreed with Ximenes's assessment of the gravity of the situation in Houston and immediately issued a memo instructing OEO officials to "please watch Houston closely." After reading Ximenes's report, Fred Baldwin recommended that OEO fund Houston Action for Youth at the highest amount possible, even though OEO had serious doubts about the competence of HAY's staff. There were simply no other options available. As Baldwin stated, "HAY is the only vehicle for getting substantial services into its target areas."[37]

By the time that Welch, Elliott, and members of the Community Council got around to establishing a committee to oversee the implementation of the War on Poverty in Houston, Houston Action for Youth had become a major contender for federal antipoverty funding. Its members positioned themselves as a viable alternative for a community action agency for the city. During the summer and fall of 1965, as federal OEO inspectors expressed serious reservations about the officially appointed antipoverty board in Houston, it appeared that federal administrators might designate HAY as the official recipient and coordinator of War on Poverty funds in the city. OEO officials did not want to see the city of Houston left out of the national War on Poverty during the first year of funding. Even though HAY was a traditional welfare organization, it seemed to be the most desirable outlet for OEO funding given the dearth of alternatives in Houston.

This relationship between OEO and local HAY administrators eventually provoked the newly appointed antipoverty board into action and forced them to come up with a plan for the War on Poverty in Houston acceptable to federal program officials. HAY's application for OEO funding submitted in late May 1965 revealed the traditional nature of this welfare agency, which focused on social service delivery to poor residents in Houston. HAY requested $2.8 million to continue delivering services like foster care for homeless youth, family education projects, family planning, counseling services for troubled youth, nursery school services, and Boy Scout and Girl Scout projects. HAY also had a very limited reach in the city. According to its application, HAY proposed to carry out these services in just a few neighborhoods north of downtown Houston. HAY delivered most of their social services out of neighborhood service centers, and despite the agency's claim to include poor residents in the implementation of these services, there was no indication that there were any neighborhood residents in leadership positions at these centers. Although CAP guidelines required the maximum feasible participation of poor residents in the planning, development, and implementation of War on Poverty programs, HAY's application remained quite vague about how poor residents would be involved at all other than informally telling HAY staffers what services they desired.[38]

OEO decided to approve HAY's request in spite of the organization's limitations and the improbability it would carry out the community action program that War on Poverty architects had envisioned. It was even more unlikely that the newly created antipoverty board that the mayor, county judge, and Community Council appointed would be prepared to implement a program that year, so it seemed that HAY offered the only possibility for any substantial OEO funding to be used in Houston. Every OEO official who visited Houston during the spring of 1965 agreed with the sentiment expressed in an internal OEO memo in early May, which stated that HAY "is the only vehicle for getting substantial services into its target area" and therefore should be funded by OEO "in large amounts." OEO officials announced on July 2 they would immediately grant HAY $2 million to carry out the programs outlined in its application. In addition to the general antipoverty grant, OEO also approved HAY's application to administer Head Start preschool centers in its target neighborhoods in conjunction with the Houston Independent School District.[39]

When it became clear that OEO would fund HAY as the primary community action agency for the city of Houston, the central antipoverty committee appointed by the mayor, county judge, and Community Council—now called the Houston–Harris County Economic Opportunity Organization (H-HCEOO)— moved into action. Fearful that their organization would be rendered irrelevant if they were unable to secure funding and determined to retain control of the War on Poverty in the city, members of the H-HCEOO executive committee quickly wrote up an application for a community action grant. Submitted during the second week in June, H-HCEOO's CAP application requested the relatively small amount of $40,000 to carry out an in-depth survey of poverty in Houston and to develop a plan for action in conjunction with existing antipoverty agencies and residents of the target neighborhoods. This initial survey and development grant, according to the application, would allow H-HCEOO to ascertain the necessary information to submit a full community action grant application at some time in the following months.[40]

OEO officials, who were fed up with the delaying tactics and inadequate makeup of H-HCEOO's executive committee and advisory board, denied the CAP grant application because H-HCEOO made no top staff positions available to any of the residents of the poor neighborhoods in Houston, despite the fact that many of these residents were well qualified for the jobs. While executive committee members promised to employ poor people in lower-level jobs like clerks and interviewers, OEO officials objected because none of the poverty residents would have a voice in the policymaking decisions of H-HCEOO. To make matters worse, a Houston minister affiliated with Protestant Charities wrote an anonymous letter to OEO protesting the makeup of H-HCEOO's executive committee and advisory board. He pointed out that of the seventy-six members of the executive committee and board, only six were African American and only three were Mexican American. In addition to inadequate minority representation, only three of the sixty-one advisory board members actually lived in any of the poverty areas in Houston. The most blatant failure to live up to OEO guidelines, according to the minister, was the fact that none of the fifteen executive committee members, who held the policymaking power of the organization, represented the poor. The unnamed minister's letter only reinforced the OEO officials' original decision to fund HAY as the sole community action agency for Houston. They recommended that H-HCEOO adjust the makeup of its governing body and resubmit an application at a later date. OEO officials held out hope that H-HCEOO's executive committee and advisory board would comply with OEO guidelines and eventually serve as Houston's community action agency, but they realized that this restructuring would probably not occur until the next year.[41]

When OEO announced that they were going to fund HAY as the community action agency for the city in July 1965, however, some H-HCEOO members panicked. H-HCEOO executive committee member George H. W. Bush sent a letter to chairman Leon Jaworski that same month and declared that he was "disturbed to see yesterday's newspaper article" announcing OEO funding of HAY and several other smaller antipoverty projects in the city of Houston. "I think it would be a mistake," Bush continued, "if the Office of Economic Opportunity started approving all sorts of miscellaneous requests from Houston. I hope that our Board of Directors can make a strong plea to OEO to funnel its grants through our Committee. It seems to me that if all types of groups are able to go directly to OEO, the effectiveness of your committee will be minimized and all kinds of confusion could result." This "confusion," of course, meant that the business elites on H-HCEOO's executive committee might lose control of the War on Poverty in Houston.[42]

A majority of H-HCEOO's executive committee and advisory board agreed with Bush's assessment of the situation, and in late August they hastily prepared and submitted to OEO a full grant application requesting $1.2 million for a ten-month antipoverty program in Houston. In a letter included in the application, H-HCEOO board chairman Leon Jaworski informed OEO officials that since HAY only targeted a small section of the city north of downtown Houston, H-HCEOO would direct its antipoverty programs toward the rest of the city. Conveying a sense of urgency, Jaworski urged OEO officials in Washington to approve the request quickly, especially since H-HCEOO was "far behind in its previous schedule for developing a complete Community Action Program."[43]

H-HCEOO's application outlined several antipoverty projects that members of the organization intended to initiate in Houston, including research and survey projects that were part of the previous initial program development grant application submitted to OEO. Beyond ascertaining the nature and prevalence of poverty in Houston, H-HCEOO members proposed several antipoverty programs for the city. Much like the HAY grant application, the program proposals included in this application were social services such as vocational training and child care for working mothers. In order to meet OEO requirements for including poor residents in policymaking and program development decisions, H-HCEOO's new grant application stated that the organization would appoint counselors for each poor neighborhood. Their job would consist of seeking out opinions from neighborhood residents concerning the programs and services they wanted for their communities.[44]

In September OEO once again rejected H-HCEOO's application and its bid to become Houston's community action agency. Despite the new proactive attitude evidenced by H-HCEOO's application, OEO officials continued to be critical of the organization's provisions for including poor residents in policymaking and program development. Donald Mathis, regional OEO director based in Austin, Texas, pointed out to H-HCEOO members that the poor were insufficiently represented on the staff and in leadership positions within the organization. In addition, there were no provisions or procedures to establish cooperation among the social service agencies in Houston necessary to carry out H-HCEOO's programs. "The law is quite specific," argued Mathis, "in requiring representation from these groups to the maximum extent feasible. . . . There are only one or two on the board of directors representing the poor." Mathis continued his criticism of H-HCEOO's application by stating, "Most of the projects require the cooperation of several organizations and we see no evidence of how they would achieve this cooperation." Though he offered several ways to remedy these problems, Mathis reminded H-HCEOO members that the solutions should come from the people of Houston.[45]

This most recent rejection of H-HCEOO's application for a community action grant set off a firestorm of criticism directed at OEO from high-ranking officials in Houston. Mayor Welch blasted OEO's decision in the newspapers the next day and proclaimed that he had no intention whatsoever of naming a new antipoverty committee for Houston to meet OEO guidelines. Referring to Mathis's statement about H-HCEOO's shortcomings, Welch replied, "Apparently a bureaucrat is setting up new rules. I have full confidence in the committee and in Leon Jaworski, the chairman. I have no intention of naming a new committee because I think the present committee is doing a good job."[46]

H-HCEOO executive committee chairman Leon Jaworski echoed Welch's remarks and argued that it was "illogical, to put it mildly," to think that simply appointing additional poor members to the advisory board would improve the function of H-HCEOO as a community action agency. Jaworski continued, "The mayor and the county judge with the advice of civic leaders carefully selected this committee and it is to be regretted that an individual who knows so little about the qualifications of those selected should undertake arbitrarily to say that a number of other persons should be added to this group whose sole quali-fication needs to be that of being poor." In a statement that clearly indicated his complete rejection of the new antipoverty philosophy of the War on Pov-erty, Jaworski argued that the boards of the "great charitable organizations in our community consist of men and women dedicated to aiding those in need, and one's financial standing has never been a test for serving." These men and women, according to Jaworski, were "dedicated and determined in the pursuit of endeavors for the benefit of *others*."[47]

Jaworski's statements once again revealed an unwillingness to accept the phi-losophy that drove the architects of the federal War on Poverty, namely that poor people themselves should be involved in the planning, development, and imple-mentation of antipoverty programs in their own communities. While it seemed "illogical" to Jaworski to include members on the committee simply because they were poor, the logic behind this OEO guideline was based on the notion that poor residents themselves were most familiar with the nature of poverty in their communities and therefore were in the best position to plan and develop antipoverty programs for their own neighborhoods. Further, War on Poverty architects believed that rather than developing programs and services from afar and then implementing them in poor neighborhoods—how traditional welfare organizations typically operated—the new antipoverty initiatives of the 1960s would ask poor residents to take active leadership roles in carrying out what-ever programs they planned and developed. H-HCEOO remained steadfast in its refusal to adhere to these OEO guidelines because the city's elected officials and members of the traditional welfare bureaucracy were fearful of losing control of federal funding and the administration of antipoverty services in the city.

The furor over this latest OEO rejection, however, died down rather quickly as H-HCEOO members, under threat from HAY, quickly searched for ways to com-ply as best they could with OEO guidelines. During a closed-door meeting of the executive committee a few days after OEO officials turned down their grant request, H-HCEOO members agreed to create a seventy-five-member board of directors with fifteen members coming directly from the poverty neighbor-hoods. Though both Jaworski and Welch claimed that there had simply been a misunderstanding between H-HCEOO and OEO—and that the plan had al-ways been to add poor residents to the board once H-HCEOO was funded—it seems unlikely that this explains why the H-HCEOO executive committee had such a quick change of heart. If Jaworski and other members of the executive committee had planned on adding more poor people to the board of directors eventually, it seems unlikely he and Welch would have made such harsh statements about OEO's recent rejection of their grant application. It is more likely that some members of H-HCEOO's executive committee were in favor of doing whatever it took to get funding approval before the organization was excluded completely from the implementation of the War on Poverty in Houston. A clear indication of this was Jaworski's statement to the press after the organization made the decision to comply with OEO guidelines. He said, "Some of these requirements in my view are unsound but we will work it out with them." Clearly the H-HCEOO executive committee was not happy about sharing any power with poor residents, but it seems many were willing to work toward a compromise if it meant retaining control over the War on Poverty in Houston.[48]

In October 1965 H-HCEOO submitted its revised grant application to OEO, and War on Poverty officials in Washington expressed relief that the showdown ended peacefully. OEO staffer Bill Crook, who would soon be appointed southwest regional director of OEO and who had recently admitted that the situation in Houston "could have been a bad one," sent a memorandum to Sargent Shriver lauding the resolution as "an excellent example of what the courteous but unrelenting pressures of 'maximum feasible participation' can bring about in a city. . . . I consider the favorable turn of events to be an important breakthrough that will make easier the work that we have to do state-wide." Shriver passed this memo on to the White House and stated, "The President can see in this specific case exactly how 90% of the 'fighting' develops, and how solutions have been reached in more than 1,100 cities, towns, and counties." Although they still wanted further indications that H-HCEOO members shared their commitment to community action and maximum feasible participation of the poor, OEO officials had a renewed sense of confidence after their apparent victory. For the time being, OEO decided to fund a portion of H-HCEOO's grant request to get the organization off the ground and to begin planning some antipoverty programs for the city of Houston. Rather than fund the entire $1.1 million that H-HCEOO asked for, OEO officials decided on a lesser amount of $130,000 to fund exploratory projects designed to ascertain the needs of Houston's poor communities. OEO informed H-HCEOO that once it was able to plan a few antipoverty programs, the Washington office would grant funding for those projects.[49]

By the end of 1965, Houston Action for Youth and the Houston–Harris County Economic Opportunity Organization had been funded for a combined total of $3 million, had planned programs for various poor neighborhoods in the city, and were ready to begin implementing the War on Poverty in Houston. In October Harlem congressman Adam Clayton Powell brought his House Committee on Education and Labor to Houston as one of thirty-three major cities to receive an investigation of the progress of the War on Poverty around the country. Following two days of meetings with antipoverty organization staff and touring the target neighborhoods, Powell's committee concluded that after a shaky beginning, the War on Poverty was progressing smoothly in Houston. A Powell aide told the local newspapers, "We have received no flack or letters or anything else from Houston so you must have a very model program down there." Sam Price, HAY's director of neighborhood organization, reported, "From all indications, we got a perfectly clean bill of health."[50]

Yet more trouble lay ahead for the implementation of the War on Poverty in Houston. At the end of October, OEO in Washington sent Ivan Scott, an inspector hired by War on Poverty administrators to investigate community action boards and report on compliance with federal guidelines, to Houston to spend a day at H-HCEOO headquarters. Though he recommended that OEO approve the grant application, Scott had serious concerns about H-HCEOO's outright refusal to include poor residents in any decision-making processes. Scott discovered that of the fifteen additional members of the board of directors that the H-HCEOO executive committee appointed to comply with OEO guidelines, only two were actually poor. H-HCEOO administrators assured Scott, however, that they would reorganize the board once OEO funded the organization and promised that more poor people would be included. Scott also uncovered a problem of a different sort that would continue to hamper antipoverty activities in Houston for the next two years. A rivalry had emerged between H-HCEOO and HAY over which organization could operate in particular areas of the city and what types of programs each group could offer. While Scott concluded that most of the problems could be solved in a satisfactory way for each antipoverty organization, important questions remained about whether H-HCEOO and HAY would be able to work together to administer the War on Poverty in Houston. It would take the next two years to answer these remaining questions in any satisfactory way.[51]

Even though the War on Poverty was a national program, local circumstances profoundly shaped its implementation in Houston. The cautious way in which local elected officials and members of the city's traditional welfare bureaucracy interpreted the concept of community action had significant consequences for the early years of the federal antipoverty initiative. Yet Houston's "pervasive conservatism" that McComb described left open a small window of opportunity for those who had a different understanding of what the Community Action Program should be. These disagreements provided a space to debate not only how to implement the War on Poverty but also, of more importance, how democracy should work in the city. The federal Community Action Program emphasized the role of citizen participation and called into question the neglect of the poor in the city's political decision-making processes. The battle lines had been drawn; the ideas of citizen empowerment embedded in the federal guidelines could not easily be quashed once they were unleashed. Although in their first year of operation members of the city's official community action agency interpreted the community action concept in a limited way, the possibility remained that at any time the H-HCEOO board could decide to reinterpret their federal mandate and change the direction of the entire poverty program. Beginning in 1966, this is precisely what happened. Before this shift could transpire in Houston, however, grassroots antipoverty activists operating outside of H-HCEOO would have to present an alternative interpretation of the concept of community action and maximum feasible participation of the poor.

Creating an Alternative Antipoverty Philosophy for Houston

Grassroots Religious Activists and VISTA Workers Outside the City's Community Action Agency, 1964–1966

In May 1966 Winifred Pollack, a volunteer with the federal War on Poverty's Volunteers in Service to America (VISTA) program, was assigned to work in an impoverished African American neighborhood in Houston's old Fifth Ward. Pollack helped organize a group of forty area residents to protest several recent actions by the Houston Independent School District board. Pollack was first made aware of problems in the neighborhood when a resident approached her for assistance shortly after she arrived in early spring 1966. He told Pollack he had received an offer from school board members to buy his Fifth Ward home in order to build a new elementary school. According to this resident, the school board offered the meager sum of $7,000 for his home even though it was valued at more than $20,000. The school board's offer to buy the home was also accompanied by a threat: if the homeowner failed to sign the necessary paperwork to sell the house within seven days, school board members, as they had done in other neighborhoods, would petition the city to condemn the property and turn it over to the school district. Pollack immediately recognized the unfairness of the situation and promised to arrange a meeting of all neighborhood residents who had received similar threats from the school board.

In response, forty neighborhood residents met with Pollack a few days later to discuss the school board's efforts to purchase their homes. While Pollack came into the meeting convinced that the real issues that needed to be addressed were the unfair prices being offered by the school board and the threatening tone of their communications with residents, she quickly discovered that area residents had a larger critique of the school board's actions. Despite pressure from the federal government and civil rights activists in the city, many Houston school board members continued to resist public school desegregation in the mid- and late 1960s by using subtle and devious tactics to prevent African American and Mexican American students from attending white schools. One way they accomplished this was to build new schools in African American neighborhoods that bordered white areas of the city where the existing white schools were in close proximity to nonwhite residents. Fifth Ward residents explained to Pollack that the school board's effort to build a new school in their neighborhood was simply another part of their plan to transform the crumbling system of de jure segregation into a more permanent system of de facto segregation. As Pollack stated in an interview shortly after the meeting, she "was very impressed that these elderly and not particularly literate people were so aware of the situation."[1]

As a VISTA volunteer, Pollack had received some training in the tactic of community organizing. The response of Fifth Ward residents to the school board's exploitative actions provided her with an opportunity to try the strategy on the ground. After holding a series of neighborhood meetings to discuss the issue and develop a plan of action, Pollack mobilized this group of forty residents to appear at several school board meetings to voice their disapproval. Much to the surprise of Pollack and the residents, school board members, undoubtedly caught off-guard by this politically mobilized group, agreed to back off from their coercive actions. This small victory emboldened Pollack and the residents to continue their efforts to organize the Fifth Ward in order to empower the poor to make demands on the institutions that affected their lives. As Pollack stated in an interview shortly after the protest, the only way for VISTA volunteers to leave a lasting impact on the area was to help residents learn how to organize in order to gain power. "This power," continued Pollack, "can help them acquire many of their smaller, mutual needs such as streetlights and better facilities. . . . If the fight against the School Board works, [community] organization may lead in the long run to the possibility of a quality education." Pollack's antipoverty philosophy and her efforts to attack poverty in one of Houston's poor neighborhoods were in stark contrast to the vision laid out by the members of the Houston–Harris County Economic Opportunity Organization (H-HCEOO), the city's official community action agency. The preceding narrative documents only one example of the many ways in which grassroots antipoverty activists operating outside the official community action agency in Houston used the War on Poverty to empower the poor by organizing them to confront powerful city institutions and bring about meaningful social change.[2]

Experiences like Pollack's show how grassroots antipoverty activists constructed the intellectual ground upon which the War on Poverty was implemented in Houston. Between 1964 and 1966, grassroots antipoverty activists unaffiliated with H-HCEOO created a local context in which to implement the War on Poverty. This approach was much more diverse in its intellectual and political influences than the rather narrow confines of New Deal/Great Society liberalism, with its inherent commitment to social harmony and reluctance to offend the middle class. The moderate liberalism that motivated the architects of the federal War on Poverty certainly helped galvanize local antipoverty activists in Houston. Even more prominent in the antipoverty philosophy of many grassroots activists in Houston, however, was an activist-oriented brand of Prophetic Christianity combined with the ideal of participatory democracy. These local Houston activists promoted an aggressive interpretation of the community action concept. Thus they created an environment in which it became possible to imagine using the War on Poverty to advance an agenda of social change by empowering the poor, helping them engage in confrontations with the city's public officials and other elites, and challenging mainstream definitions of democracy. Most important, local activists helped open a small window of opportunity for members of Houston's official community action agency to reinterpret the concept of community action and begin to implement a more vigorous and confrontational program in the city. In Houston, therefore, the local political and intellectual environment, even more than federal politics, determined how the War on Poverty was fought and ultimately made an expansion of democracy possible.

Perhaps no one did more to create the local context for the implementation of the War on Poverty in Houston than the Reverend Wallace B. Poteat, a local minister of the Ecumenical Fellowship United Church of Christ (UCC), whose grassroots antipoverty organization became one of the official sponsors of the VISTA program in 1966. The young minister articulated his model of community organization and empowerment of the poor through his work with VISTA volunteers in the city. His influence on the manner in which local activists implemented the War on Poverty in Houston, however, extended far beyond the VISTA program. By 1967, nearly all of the community organizers affiliated with the War on Poverty in Houston had begun implementing Rev. Poteat's model of community organization and empowerment.

When the War on Poverty was launched in 1964, the recent history of the Ecumenical Fellowship helped shape the way its members would interpret their role in the fight against poverty. The Ecumenical Fellowship emerged out of a bitter split between two factions within the Garden Villas United Church of Christ, an all-white congregation in southeast Houston, that occurred during the summer of 1964. Garden Villas was located in an area of the city that was gradually transitioning from an all-white neighborhood to a majority African American and Latino neighborhood. Many Garden Villas members, including Rev. Poteat, the young pastor of the congregation, wanted to reach out to welcome their new neighbors to the area. In order to begin this outreach program, Rev. Poteat and several members teamed up with a nearby African American congregation to sponsor a racially integrated vacation church school for children during the summer of 1964. A significant majority of Garden Villas's members, however, remained steadfastly opposed to challenging entrenched patterns of segregation in that part of the city. After several months of factional battles within the walls of Garden Villas, the congregation voted to dismiss Rev. Poteat as pastor in October. This decision prompted several dozen members of the church to withdraw their membership from Garden Villas and to commit themselves to establishing a new church under Rev. Poteat's leadership.[3]

Rev. Poteat maintained that he and the younger Garden Villas members who left the congregation were simply trying to carry out the mission of the United Church of Christ, which had a strong commitment to supporting multiracial and multicultural congregations. When the prospect of racial integration appeared, however, Rev. Poteat exclaimed that "the traditional patterns of Houston's characteristic church life of serving the interest of constituents only and the interests of the immediate vicinity reasserted themselves." The group of Garden Villas members who opposed his actions, according to Rev. Poteat, "have made the decision to participate in the mission of the church only in those areas of life which would not violate the 'time honored' taboos, patterns, and prejudices of the ringed in and defensive community of Garden Villas." Above all, Rev. Poteat and his followers believed that the "race issue" was the most important problem confronting the modern church. This racial prejudice had to be overcome in order for the church to be a positive force in Houston.[4]

The desire to be actively involved in the communities of Houston beyond the church walls propelled Rev. Poteat and his supporters to create the Ecumenical Fellowship United Church of Christ immediately upon leaving Garden Villas. Rev. Poteat argued that the city of Houston desperately needed a new congregation whose members engaged with the outside world, because most churches in the city had become "spiritual retreats from the rapidly changing patterns of urbanization." Rather than cutting itself off from the social problems in Houston, like Garden Villas had done, this new church congregation would seek solutions for societal ills and attempt to be a transformative force in the city.[5]

Rev. Poteat and his followers had been profoundly influenced by several recent trends advanced by prominent Protestant theologians in the early and mid-1960s, particularly the renewed emphasis on original sin and the Old Testament prophets spearheaded by Reinhold Niebuhr, the call for people of faith to engage with the world more directly by Harvey Cox, and the ecumenical push coming from the National Council of Churches. In creating the Ecumenical Fellowship United Church of Christ, Rev. Poteat and his supporters hoped to combine these three elements into a theology that called church members into the slums of Houston to be a prophetic voice exposing the evil of poverty in an ecumenical way. These trends had significant implications for the way Rev. Poteat and his congregation viewed the opportunities created by the federal War on Poverty.[6]

In January 1965 Rev. Poteat urged members of his new congregation to read carefully *Moral Man and Immoral Society*, Reinhold Niebuhr's most widely known book. Often labeled a neo-orthodox theologian by contemporary observers, Niebuhr called for a renewed emphasis on man's original sin and the depravity of humankind. He also criticized liberal theology (and postwar liberalism in general) for purporting that man could be ultimately perfected. American liberals, going back to John Dewey and other political theorists during the first few decades of the twentieth century, had an unshakeable faith in the inevitable progress of human civilization that would be brought about by education and democracy. As society improved, conflict between groups and individuals would accordingly decline. Niebuhr, on the other hand, disagreed with this faith in progress and argued that social conflict was inevitable because of man's depraved and fallen nature. Liberals, Niebuhr said in the book, "completely disregard the political necessities in the struggle for justice in human society by failing to recognize those elements in man's collective behavior which belong to the order of nature and can never be brought completely under the dominion of reason or conscience. They do not recognize that when collective power, whether in the form of imperialism or class domination, exploits weakness, it can never be dislodged unless power is raised against it. If conscience and reason can be insinuated into the resulting struggle they can only qualify but not abolish it." In other words, the liberal's belief in inevitable human progress and the perfectibility of man failed to take into account that man's very nature was imperfect because of original sin. Once this basic fact about human nature was accepted, Niebuhr argued that the only way justice could be achieved on earth was through conflict and coercion. "Conflict is inevitable," Niebuhr stated, "and in this conflict power must be challenged by power."[7]

Niebuhr also tried to restore the prophetic voice to Christianity. According to historian David L. Chappell, this was his most significant intellectual contribution to mid-twentieth-century struggles for justice in the United States. In his provocative book *A Stone of Hope: Prophetic Religion and the Death of Jim Crow*, Chappell argued that the core beliefs of civil rights intellectuals, particularly Martin Luther King Jr., consisted not of liberalism, with its faith in the ability of education and inevitable moral progress to bring about racial justice and an end to segregation, but rather of a prophetic brand of Christianity advanced by Niebuhr. Contrary to the views of most American liberals, Niebuhr argued that real evil existed in the world. For many African Americans, living with segregation and racism meant that they too had firsthand experience with human depravity and societal evil. The Jim Crow system in the American South and the white racism that propped up this racial caste system were evils that had to be confronted. According to Chappell, King and other movement leaders believed that whites would relent and the Jim Crow system would crumble only when those in power were coerced into allowing it to occur. By bringing the prophetic voice to the American South, civil rights activists hoped to expose this grave societal evil and deliver blacks in the South from its clutches. It was also this brand of Prophetic Christianity that sustained the civil rights movement and brought about some measure of success while many liberals abandoned the goals of the movement.[8]

Rev. Poteat and his followers were similarly influenced by Niebuhr and Prophetic Christianity. In response to a question about whether the new church congregation would be "liberal" or "conservative," Rev. Poteat responded by arguing that "the words Liberal and Conservative which we sometimes use with abandon really confuse the issue because of the varied connotation of these terms." Rather than being concerned with where the new church would fall on the American political or theological spectrum, Rev. Poteat insisted that he and his supporters were concerned to maintain a "creative dialectic between the priestly and prophetic aspects" of their faith. "If we sound weighted to prophecy," Rev. Poteat concluded, "it is perhaps because we believe that the prophetic voice in the local church needs to be strengthened in Houston."[9]

In addition to being greatly influenced by Niebuhr, Rev. Poteat and his followers saw themselves as part of a religious movement whose participants were dedicated to establishing Christian missions in the country's urban centers. Foremost among the influential theologians in this movement was Harvey Cox, whose 1965 publication *The Secular City* synthesized the increasing calls to reengage with the outside world. In January 1966 Rev. Poteat asked his congregation to read this book, in which Cox lambasted Christians who were fearful of secularization. Rather than something to fear, Cox argued, the process of secularization was "the liberation of man from religious and metaphysical tutelage, the turning of his attention away from other worlds and toward this one.... The task of Christians should be to support it and nourish it." In the secular city, which, as Cox argued, every part of the country was quickly becoming, traditional religion, with its preoccupation with otherworldliness, had no place. Modern Christians, he said, should reject that kind of traditional religion and enter freely into the secular world as full participants. Most attractive to Rev. Poteat and his congregation, however, was Cox's attempt to develop a theology of social change. "We are trying to live in a period of revolution without a theology of revolution," exclaimed Cox. "Our task is that of developing a theology of politics, and in particular a theology of revolutionary social change.... The secular city provides the starting point for such a theology." For antipoverty activists like Rev. Poteat and his congregation, Cox provided a theological basis for a thorough democratization of the economy to produce a world without the evils of poverty.[10]

Rev. Poteat looked to theologians like Cox for guidance in his attempt to establish an urban church in Houston. As Rev. Poteat explained to his congregation, the trend of contemporary church congregations to leave the inner city and retreat to the suburbs meant that the city of Houston needed a new church that would actively and ambitiously reach out to the urban poor. "It is our conviction," proclaimed Rev. Poteat, "that those who stand outside the doors of the churches in an exploding metropolis with its problems and promise deserve to be served by faithfully witnessing churches rather than pious professions of concern."[11] In a brochure advertising the founding of the Ecumenical Fellowship, Rev. Poteat asked, "Will Sunday morning begin your eager week of involvement or will it hear your prayer of relief that toil is done? Will you attend a sanctuary where an inordinate claim on your time drags you out of the world and makes life one big retreat? . . . where the emphasis is on ceremony, ritual, narrow-minded minutiae, pious platitudes? . . . where exalted ideals are proclaimed but no attempt is made to implement them or live up to them? . . . where charity is only a food basket from Lady Bountiful?" Or, Rev. Poteat asked, will you attend a "church . . . where the whole church means the whole world? . . . where the emphasis is on our common needs, racial and social justice, the brotherhood of man? . . . where concern is courageous and the church will take a stand on issues? . . . where charity recognizes human dignity and helps others raise themselves?" The Ecumenical Fellowship, according to Rev. Poteat, would be this new brand of urban church "committed to seeking a faith adequate to the challenge of today and the promise of tomorrow."[12]

In addition to Prophetic Christianity and a commitment to establishing an urban mission in Houston, a significant national trend that had a profound effect not only on Rev. Poteat and his supporters but on the entire body of the United Church of Christ was the ecumenical movement that began at the turn of the twentieth century. In 1950 the National Council of Churches was formed, capping off a half-century of efforts to create an interdenominational organization capable of encouraging dialogue between believers of different faiths. Members of the National Council of Churches wanted to shift the focus away from the relatively small doctrinal differences that served to divide people of faith and toward the many commonalities among the denominations. As they stated in their message "To the People of the Nation" during their founding meeting in 1950: "[W]e have forged an implement for cooperation such as America has never seen before. . . . The Council itself is a demonstration of [Jesus's] power to unite his followers in joyous cooperation. Let nation and nation, race and race, class and class unite their aims in his broad purposes for man, and out of that unitedness there will arise new strength like that of which we ourselves already feel the first sure intimations."[13]

As Rev. Poteat explained to his congregation in March 1966, "Denominational parochialism, static concepts, and competition [were] and [are] the worst enem[ies]" of the modern urban church, and they represented "a curse on the seamless robe of Christ." Whereas suburban church congregations could cling to their denominational differences and remain financially viable, Rev. Poteat argued that "competition and isolation spells doom to the inner city church," as evidenced by the fact that "in the cruel heart of the city, traditional middle class neighborhood churches are closing their doors and are objects of indifference and hostility." To cling to outdated denominational differences and peculiarities while holding up one's own as the only true way to worship, according to Rev. Poteat, is "to take the historical position that the Christian Church in 2000 years has only produced a limited few models for the development of churches and missions that can be both Christian and successful. . . . To claim that there is only one structure, one way of development, one valid way of becoming a self sustaining church, one restricted mission of the church is ultimately to castrate the future of the church and its mission." There was, however, reason for hope. The growth of the National Council of Churches and the increasing strength of the ecumenical movement, according to Rev. Poteat, were encouraging developments showing that "the walls of hostility between diverse religious groups, ethnic groups, economic groups, between suburb and inner city are being broken" in order to serve "the poor, the blind, the deaf, the oppressed, the captives."[14]

These diverse theological trends played a determining role in the creation of the Ecumenical Fellowship in Houston. As members of the congregation set out to engage with the secular world, they quickly discovered that the problem of urban poverty would also require a political solution. Rev. Poteat believed that Niebuhr provided a coherent philosophy for exposing and attacking the evils of poverty, but he also attempted to combine Niebuhrian Prophetic Christianity with the confrontational political vision of Saul Alinsky. Over time, Rev. Poteat became a firm believer in what was known as the "Saul Alinsky method."

Alinsky was an aggressive community organizer who helped create the Back of the Yards Neighborhood Council in Chicago in 1939. He received national attention by traveling around the country and training organizers in his methods. Alinsky argued that individuals, especially those trapped in poverty, had little hope of successfully dealing with any city's public officials, government agencies, or welfare organizations because of the overwhelming amount of power an urban bureaucracy possessed over its poor citizens. According to Alinsky, it was only through organization, such as what labor accomplished through the creation of industrial unions, that the poor could attempt to match the power of a city's government and bring about needed changes in their communities. Alinsky's method of organizing and mobilizing poor communities was attractive to some antipoverty workers across the country because Alinsky seemed to understand that the problems of poverty boiled down to one core issue—power relations. Alinsky's followers believed that only through upsetting the traditional balance of power between a city's power structure and its poor residents, thereby implementing a vision of participatory democracy, could the evils of poverty be resolved.[15]

Alinsky's most coherent articulation of his ideas was his 1946 book *Reveille for Radicals*. In the first half of the book, Alinsky defined what it meant to be an American radical and differentiated radicals from American liberals. He explained, "The Radical is not fooled by shibboleths and facades. He faces issues squarely and does not hide his cowardice behind the convenient cloak of rationalization. The Radical refuses to be diverted by superficial problems. He is completely concerned with fundamental causes rather than current manifestations. He concentrates his attack on the heart of the issue. . . . The Radical recognizes that constant dissension and conflict has been the fire under the boiler of democracy." Alinsky warned that radicals should not be confused with liberals, who "are hesitant to act" and whose "opinions are studded with 'but on the other hand.'" Alinsky continued, "Caught on the horns of this dilemma, [liberals] are paralyzed into immobility. They become utterly incapable of action. They discuss and discuss and end in disgust." The true American radical, however, "does not sit frozen by cold objectivity. He sees injustice and strikes at it with hot passion." Because of the American radical's propensity for action, according to Alinsky, "[s]ociety has good reason to fear the Radical. Every shaking advance of mankind toward equality and justice has come from the Radical. He hits, he hurts, he is dangerous. Conservative interests know that while Liberals are most adept at breaking their own necks with their tongues, Radicals are most adept at breaking the necks of Conservatives."[16]

The most important difference between liberals and radicals with regard to bringing about meaningful social change, according to Alinsky, was in their disparate understandings of power. "Liberals fear power or its application," he argued. "They labor in confusion over the significance of power and fail to recognize that only through the achievement and constructive use of power can people better themselves. They talk glibly of a people lifting themselves by their own bootstraps but fail to realize that nothing can be lifted or moved except through power." Radicals, on the other hand, "precipitate the social crisis by action—by using power." Alinsky concluded that the only sure way for common people to attain and use power effectively was through organization. He argued, "If we strip away all the chromium trimmings of high-sounding metaphor and idealism which conceal the motor and gears of a democratic society, one basic element is revealed—the people are the motor, the organizations of the people are the gears. The power of the people is transmitted through the gears of their own organizations, and democracy moves forward."[17]

In the second half of *Reveille for Radicals*, Alinsky offered a blueprint for establishing "People's Organizations" capable of organizing communities and empowering them to challenge any structure or institution that oppressed them. A People's Organization, according to Alinsky, was not simply a community council, designed by liberals, merely to remedy the symptoms of the problems of a community; rather, it was a radically inspired group of citizens empowered to attack the root causes of society's ills. Alinsky explained, "You don't, you dare not, come to a people who are unemployed, who don't know where their next meal is coming from, whose children and themselves are in the gutter of despair—and offer them not food, not jobs, not security, but supervised recreation, handicraft classes and character building! Yet *that is what is done!* Instead of a little bread and butter we come to them with plenty of bats and balls!" Alinsky highlighted the futility of job-training programs, arguing, "To train men for a job when there is no job is like dressing up a cadaver in a full-dress suit; in the end you still have a cadaver." Alinsky readily admitted that most charity and social workers would surely disagree with his assessment, primarily because traditional charity and social workers "pride themselves upon their techniques and talents for adjusting people to difficult situations. They come to the people of the slums under the aegis of benevolence and goodness, not to organize the people, not to help them rebel and fight their way out of the muck—NO! They come to get these people 'adjusted'; adjusted so they will live in hell and like it too. A higher form of social treason would be difficult to conceive—yet this infamy is perpetrated in the name of charity." Alinsky designed the People's Organizations to be a radical alternative to the largely ineffective liberal programs of the various community councils around the country.[18]

In order to build an effective People's Organization, Alinsky argued that native leadership must be identified through which the organization could be created. Only the people themselves could form an organization that would be respected by the majority of a community's members. The role of the community organizer was to come to a thorough understanding of the life of the community, including specific customs and traditions. Though many members of the community would initially view the organizer with suspicion and distrust, the organizer must remain honest and selfless as he or she reached a level of personal identification with the community as a whole. By respecting the dignity of the people, Alinsky argued, the organizer would eventually earn the trust of the community and would be able to begin organizing its members and start solving the problems of the community. According to Alinsky, once a community was organized it would become imperative for the People's Organization to engage in conflicts that would upset the status quo. He stated, "A People's Organization is dedicated to an eternal war. It is a war against poverty, misery, delinquency, disease, injustice, hopelessness, despair, and unhappiness." Alinsky argued that only by empowering People's Organizations to disrupt the status quo could its members begin to solve the problems of their community.[19]

Alinsky concluded his book by arguing that the continuation of democracy itself was dependent upon the successful organization of the American people. "The fundamental issue that will resolve the fate of democracy is whether or not we really believe in democracy," he concluded. "The only hope for democracy is that more people and more groups will become articulate and exert pressure upon their government." Alinsky also issued a dire warning to those who opposed the organization and empowerment of relatively powerless communities. "Those who fear the building of People's Organizations as a revolution also forget that it is an orderly development of participation, interest, and action on the part of the masses of people. It may be true that it is revolution, but it is *orderly revolution*. To reject orderly revolution is to be hemmed in by two hellish alternatives: disorderly, sudden, stormy, bloody revolution, or a further deterioration of the mass foundation of democracy to the point of inevitable dictatorship. The building of People's Organizations is orderly revolution, it is the process of the people gradually but irrevocably taking their places as citizens of a democracy."[20]

Rev. Poteat recognized the value of combining his religious beliefs with Alinsky's powerful message about community empowerment in order to attack poverty in the city of Houston. In February 1965 he urged members of the Ecumenical Fellowship to read a recent article in the United Church of Christ's *Social Action* newsletter titled "Strategies for Community Change," which outlined the Alinsky method. In a church newsletter that same month, Rev. Poteat also criticized an editorial in the *Christian Century*, which "unwarrantedly leveled its guns at the Saul Alinsky approach" that had been advocated by officials at the UCC Department of Urban Churches. A few months later Rev. Poteat sent a representative from his congregation to a UCC denominational executive meeting to hear a church official speak about the cooperation between several inner-city churches and Alinsky's antipoverty organization in northern cities. The speaker said UCC churches were involved in community programs organized by Alinsky's group in Syracuse, Rochester, and Buffalo, New York, and he implored members present to follow the same trend in their own cities or risk becoming irrelevant.[21]

Rev. Poteat and his supporters envisioned the Ecumenical Fellowship carrying out this prophetic Christian mission in Houston's inner-city neighborhoods through the use of Alinsky-style community organization. He and the members of the congregation immediately went about implementing this vision in their community in the fall of 1964. The most important role of a prophet, of course, is to expose evil, and Ecumenical Fellowship members explicitly set out to expose and confront a racial caste system that kept certain Houston residents mired in poverty. As a beginning, Rev. Poteat and his congregation founded the Ecumenical Fellowship Latin American Channel (EF-LAC) project, a program designed in conjunction with Protestant Charities of Greater Houston that focused on the predominantly Mexican American population living near the ship channel in southeast Houston. As Rev. Poteat told a reporter with the *Houston Chronicle*, "Building a church must be based on mission, not just going out to some suburb and building." The stated goals of the project included a commitment to support "the development of indigenous 'grassroots' community organizations through which they can together prevent further deterioration of the area, effect community redevelopment, and attack the root causes of economic, political, social, cultural, and spiritual deprivation, alienation, and discrimination," as well as to "provide a means whereby the barriers which prevent the exercise and enjoyment of the rights and responsibilities [of] full and equal citizenship by all the residents of the area may be overcome."[22]

Rev. Poteat and EF-LAC activists attempted to enhance their commitment to New Left ideas about participatory democracy by welcoming members of Houston's chapter of Students for a Democratic Society (SDS) into the ranks of their antipoverty crusade. SDS was a New Left organization formed in 1962 whose members set out to transform the United States into a participatory democracy. In their "Port Huron Statement," issued the year of their founding, SDS activists stated, "As a social system we seek the establishment of a democracy of individual participation, governed by two central aims: that the individual share in those social decisions determining the quality and direction of his life; [and] that society be organized to encourage independence in men and provide the media for their common participation." In 1965 Houston SDS members decided to try implementing their vision of turning America into a participatory democracy by working with the EF-LAC project. As the Houston SDS newsletter stated in November 1965, by working closely with EF-LAC volunteers on "programs ranging from literacy work to recreation to tenants' organization work, we will get to know the community, and then perhaps branch out into more specifically political programs—whatever issue, be it garbage, schools, housing or jobs, that the community feels is of importance . . . and at the same time work to involve the people in political action." Rev. Poteat even arranged a training session with Houston's SDS to teach the students how to go into communities and organize the poor, and he named a Houston SDS member, Gil Campos, as the EF-LAC project's youth director. The attitude of many SDS members about the possibilities of transforming the War on Poverty into a vehicle for aggressive political action was revealed in their announcement of this training session: "Do come! The possibilities for a dedicated, militant and sensitive organization are fantastic. The dedication, the militancy, and the sensitivity to people's needs depends on YOU." Although the EF-LAC project would receive ample criticism for welcoming these student activists into their ranks, EF-LAC organizers remained steadfast in their support for Houston SDS and saw it as a major accomplishment that theirs was the only antipoverty organization in Houston that welcomed the involvement of this increasingly high-profile New Left organization.[23]

Before applying for OEO funding or requesting VISTA volunteers from Washington, EF-LAC project activists initiated several programs in poor neighborhoods on the east side of Houston near the ship channel. Early in 1965 EF-LAC volunteers established a teen recreation center to provide activities for youth, especially in the summer months when school was out and nearly all of the parents worked full-time. They also created a "Swap Shop" where neighborhood residents could swap items no longer needed for ones they did need.

In addition to these service-oriented programs, EF-LAC volunteers also began organizing the poor into action groups such as the East End Teen Club, the Manchester Broadway Mothers Club, and the Golden Age Sewing Club. In the spring of 1965 the teen club staged a peaceful protest against the Houston school district's policy of busing African American students past white schools to majority black schools, and the mother's club spearheaded the creation of a credit union to serve the needs of neighborhood residents. EF-LAC volunteers also organized a citizenship education and voter registration drive in the area. As the projected program for the EF-LAC project stated, "Political indifference of Latin Americans and Ghetto Negros [sic] has enabled [Houston's] political establishments to persuade the few who vote to often vote against their interests." The authors of EF-LAC's projected program also recognized the need to develop community organizations to put pressure on the city's elected officials. These types of activities would continue to grow with OEO funding. EF-LAC activists established a few service-delivery programs in their neighborhoods, but it was clear early on that they recognized the value of empowering the poor through community organization. Although these early efforts were small in scale and lacked clear direction, they nevertheless represented the beginning of significant community-organizing initiatives in the city of Houston.[24]

Rev. Poteat and his followers designed their antipoverty program to be the first of its kind in Houston and recruited volunteers to make an ambitious effort not only to provide services to the poor but, more important, to empower the city's poor residents through community organization. As Rev. Poteat explained to a potential EF-LAC project volunteer, Houston had the ability to escape the fate of the northern ghettos "not by lady bountiful with a charity basket at Christmas, not by professional 'do-gooders,' not by expecting the government to do it all—but by voluntary, person-to-person involvement in projects in which the people, the churches, the businessmen, the clubs, and the schools are motivated and given an instrument and the necessary outside support by which they can unite in a concerted common effort to break the bonds of poverty— themselves!" Neighborhood residents would be organized with the goal of effecting widespread social change in Houston, according to Rev. Poteat, such as pressuring local businesses and institutions to comply with federal desegregation laws; registering voters and mobilizing them politically to prevent them from voting "against their own interests"; and organizing residents to demand more public housing options from the city of Houston and from the federal government, more rapid desegregation of local schools, adequate funding for schools in poor neighborhoods, the creation of more job opportunities, the upgrading of medical and welfare services, and an end to police harassment of poor and minority residents. As Rev. Poteat and other EF-LAC members stated in a recruitment brochure, "We believe in grassroots democracy. . . . We believe in Racial Justice now. . . . We believe in community organization and action. . . . We work with religious and secular organizations for justice now, for a new day in Houston." The time had come, according to Rev. Poteat, to force the churches in the city "to practice what [they] preach—i.e., Peace, instead of killing. Brotherhood instead of Segregation. Release of the Captives and Oppressed of our cities instead of Subjugation and Oppression of the weak." Rev. Poteat and the members of the EF-LAC project stood poised to use the federal War on Poverty to organize and empower the poor in Houston. But first, they had to contend with a city bureaucracy vying to control the implementation of the federal antipoverty program in the city.[25]

Soon after Rev. Poteat and other members of the Ecumenical Fellowship initiated the EF-LAC project, Houston mayor Louie Welch, Harris County judge Bill Elliott, and members of the city's welfare bureaucracy created H-HCEOO to administer the War on Poverty in the city. Rev. Poteat and other members of the EF-LAC project had little hope for the recently created community action agency to make much of an impact in Houston. In response, Rev. Poteat and EF-LAC members began to look for ways to become actively involved in implementing the federal antipoverty program. While it was unlikely federal War on Poverty officials would fund more than one community action agency for the city, Rev. Poteat and EF-LAC project activists turned their attention toward the VISTA program and proposed using these young volunteers to organize and empower the poor in Houston.

Scholars have paid a surprising lack of attention to the significant role of the VISTA program in the War on Poverty, presumably because it has been difficult to discover exactly what these volunteers were doing in the country's poor neighborhoods. As a result, historians know very little about VISTA experiences on the ground or the ideologies of local VISTA-sponsoring organizations. Contrary to the view of many historians of the War on Poverty, the VISTA program was often crucial for the implementation of the War on Poverty at the local level and greatly contributed to the proliferation of community organizing and confrontational tactics. By placing young and idealistic volunteers in poor communities under the supervision of local activist organizations, the VISTA program produced several unintended consequences that caught many federal policymakers by surprise. Broadening the original intent of the War on Poverty, many VISTA volunteers employed community organization, mobilization, and confrontational tactics in order to empower the poor to demand increased participation in the local democratic process. And in Houston, the VISTA program had a direct impact on the activities of the official community action agency as well.[26]

To most national and local government officials in the 1960s, most of whom were committed to the ideals of social harmony and preservation of the status quo, the VISTA program seemed benign enough. Attorney General Robert Kennedy and his task force on juvenile delinquency first came up with the idea for a "domestic Peace Corps" in 1962 to give young people a way to serve their country at home. Though a bill to establish the National Service Corps stalled in Congress, architects of the War on Poverty picked up the idea, renamed it VISTA, and included the volunteer program in the Economic Opportunity Act of 1964. The federal government would train and fund volunteers to serve one-year tours of duty in the War on Poverty, most often in conjunction with local antipoverty organizations. What Peace Corps volunteers had done in remote villages in distant lands would be translated domestically. These young volunteers could assist families who lived in poverty in meeting everyday challenges associated with being poor.[27]

Most historians of the War on Poverty agree with this contemporary assessment, and this seems to be the main reason why the VISTA program remains one of the most understudied parts of the poverty war. There were some individuals, however, including a few early architects of the federal War on Poverty, who recognized the potential of the VISTA program to become a transformative force in American society. According to War on Poverty planner Stephen J. Pollak, the most progressive members of the War on Poverty Task Force—people like Robert Kennedy, Richard Boone, and David Hackett—were the strongest proponents of including the VISTA program in the federal antipoverty effort.[28]

Edgar May, another War on Poverty Task Force member, argued more than a decade after the War on Poverty ended that the VISTA volunteers had undoubtedly been "agents of change." During an interview in 1981 May described how a VISTA volunteer could have inevitably become a force for social change in his or her community:

> It didn't take the VISTA volunteer a hell of a long time, whether he was in Harlem or in the South Side of Chicago or in Appalachia or in a Navajo reservation . . . to figure [out] who the bad guys are in these dramas. . . . In the latter, for example, it didn't take him long to figure out that if the white people have got a municipal

water system, and the Indians have got to travel in the same county five miles to get enough water in a bunch of five-gallon cans, then there's something the matter with the public system, and if you're down there to do something about poverty, you begin showing up at the water authority meetings, and you say things that they really don't want to hear. That's when the genie's out of the bottle. Yes, they're agents of change. We didn't need social workers. We didn't need a lot of people to teach little kids how to read.[29]

As May points out, the local context in which the VISTA volunteers were placed played a significant role in determining the tactics they would use to attack poverty. These conditions applied to many VISTA volunteers who came to Houston in the 1960s. Although the national legislation had within it the seeds of possibilities for the VISTA program to become a vehicle for social change, it was in the local implementation of the program that these seeds were fertilized and allowed to grow. As these VISTA volunteers began to discover that the roots of many problems of the poor were tied to their relative powerlessness, and as they were exposed to a wide array of ideas about social change through their sponsoring agencies, many became more assertive and confrontational the longer they lived in Houston's impoverished neighborhoods.

The first VISTA volunteer arrived in Houston in late February 1966, and then a steady stream of volunteers trickled into the city over the next several months. By the end of April, the city had twenty VISTA volunteers who were actively working in the targeted areas. Faced with the extreme deprivation of many of Houston's poor neighborhoods, most of the VISTA volunteers upon arriving immediately set out to provide desperately needed social services. They established after-school tutoring sessions in their homes, set up information centers directing young people to employment centers and the Job Corps, and held informal meetings with neighborhood residents to come up with solutions to the most pressing problems in these impoverished areas. What is evident in the following narrative of the volunteers' activities in Houston's poor neighborhoods, however, is that the VISTA volunteers modified much of their antipoverty philosophy and tactics after spending just a few months in the target neighborhoods. Whereas initially many VISTA volunteers focused on the delivery of services, within a short period of time most of the volunteers shifted to an emphasis on community organizing and empowerment of the poor. Actual on-the-ground experiences and the influence of Rev. Poteat and the EF-LAC project activists, therefore, shaped the VISTA volunteers' philosophy and methods in significant ways.[30]

Michael Hayward, a twenty-one-year-old former navy seaman from Indiana, completed his VISTA training early in 1966 and was assigned to work in an African American neighborhood in northeast Houston in the old Fifth

Ward. Immediately Hayward recognized the stark reality in the neighborhood: crowded and inadequate schools with skyrocketing dropout rates, desperately poor housing, exploitative white business owners, absentee landlords, a general lack of any sense of community spirit, churches aloof from community issues, a prevalence of low-paying unskilled jobs, and persistent racism among business owners and hiring officials. Most distressing to Hayward was a pervasive sense of hopelessness among the area's residents.[31]

After finding a house to rent, in which he could live and also use as a central meeting place for community organizations, Hayward spent his first few days trying to make contacts with influential members of the community in churches, bars, and pool halls. After assessing some of the most significant needs of the community, Hayward began with a service-delivery approach. One of the most pressing issues, according to neighborhood residents, was not necessarily unemployment but a lack of jobs that paid well and offered opportunities for advancement. Hayward began expanding an existing training program to equip black workers with the necessary skills to become machine operators for various types of mechanized industry. In order to build some community spirit, Hayward also began to organize Little League baseball teams in the neighborhood both to keep the young people occupied and to create a sense of cohesiveness among the neighborhood's youth.[32]

After a few months in the neighborhood, however, Hayward learned from residents that the problems of poverty did not necessarily stem from inadequate services but from a lack of power among poor residents. In order to remedy this power imbalance between the city's poor people and local public officials and institutions, Hayward and several residents began using the tactic of community organizing to empower the neighborhood's poor people. A group of African American workers who belonged to several union locals under the AFL-CIO umbrella worked with Hayward to pressure union leaders to commit themselves to addressing problems like hiring discrimination and unequal access to union membership. Although this commitment produced few tangible results, Hayward and the union members recognized that the process of organizing and putting pressure on a large and powerful institution showed many poor residents that they could organize and use their collective power to effect change. Just a few months after arriving in the Fifth Ward, Hayward was convinced that the organization of the community was "essential if the work of the [VISTA] volunteers is to be of lasting value." Only through organized action, Hayward argued, could poor residents begin to challenge the urban structures that kept them mired in poverty.[33]

Hayward also began laying the groundwork for future use of the tactic of community organizing to empower the poor. He convened periodic neighborhood meetings during which residents could get to know each other and select leaders who would serve as advocates for the interests of the neighborhood at city hall and other bureaucratic institutions. Hayward believed that the organization of neighborhood residents into a self-conscious bloc was the only way reforms and improvements to the neighborhood would remain permanent. At these meetings Hayward encouraged neighborhood dwellers to voice their concerns about conditions and to come up with solutions to their problems.[34]

Winifred Pollack, the VISTA volunteer who helped organize neighborhood residents to protest the Houston school board's exploitation of poor homeowners in Houston, also arrived in the city in 1966. Like Hayward, Pollack gradually shifted from a focus on social service delivery to community organizing and empowerment tactics. Whereas Michael Hayward lived and worked in a predominantly African American neighborhood, Pollack worked in a majority Mexican American neighborhood in the industrial section of the Fifth Ward. Despite the different racial makeup of the two neighborhoods, Pollack identified many of the same problems when she arrived, such as poor public educational facilities, few community organizations, general idleness among neighborhood residents, alienation from local churches, and the horrible condition of rental properties. Pollack was struck by visible inequality in the neighborhoods, particularly with regard to the quality of schools and the level of services provided by the city. One of the junior high schools in the area was very old, overcrowded, and in obvious need of repair. Just across town, however, was a school in a white neighborhood that was brand new and often had empty classrooms because it was so large. City services were almost nonexistent; Pollack was appalled when she discovered that in the Fifth Ward few streets had proper lighting and the roads were almost impassable because of huge potholes. There was also a clear lack of drainage, as evidenced by puddles in many roads that had been there so long they were full of tadpoles. After quite a rough start due to her lack of transportation or any prearranged community contacts, Pollack slowly began building a network of concerned residents to combat the negative effects of the neighborhood's poverty.[35]

Like Hayward, Pollack initially set out to solve the immediate needs of neighborhood residents, which required social programs. One of the first issues Pollack and neighborhood residents attempted to tackle was the lack of material needs of those living in destitute poverty. She gathered a group of members from the two churches in the neighborhood and organized a collection and distribution system providing food and clothing to families in need. Clothing was a particular concern once Pollack realized that many families were not sending their children to school because they did not have adequate clothing for them. Pollack also set up a tutoring project in her home and began organizing recreational activities in which schoolchildren could take part after school and on weekends. To meet the needs of a group of unemployed women, she set up a training center in which neighborhood women taught each other secretarial and other office skills.[36]

After spending the first few months trying to provide much-needed services in the neighborhood, Pollack began modifying her philosophy and tactics to attack poverty in a more direct way. Like Hayward, Pollack came to believe that only through community organizing could any real positive changes occur in her neighborhood. Accordingly, she arranged meetings of neighborhood residents to discuss their common interests and make decisions about actions to take. One of these actions was an organized protest of the Houston school board. Through community organizing and the achievement of small victories, Pollack hoped to help empower poor residents to take control of their own lives. In addition to organizing protests to address specific neighborhood problems, Pollack also tried to unite residents in a concerted effort to gain power. While organizing residents to protest, Pollack discovered that there was mutual dislike and distrust between Mexican Americans in her neighborhood and African Americans living in surrounding areas. Pollack quickly realized that only a united community of poor residents could effectively challenge the institutions that had such a profound effect on their lives. To encourage a more united community in the Fifth Ward, Pollack focused much of her energy toward alleviating tensions between the Mexican American and African American neighborhoods. At the local community center on the edge of her neighborhood, which was frequented mostly by young African Americans, Pollack organized a fiesta event to bring members of the two groups together and open channels of communication. She also included black residents who lived close to the Mexican American neighborhood in organizational meetings in order to get a wide array of perspectives on what needed to be done. And she helped ease the tension created when an African American family bought a house in the Mexican American neighborhood by scheduling discussion groups where residents had an opportunity to air their particular concerns. This was a clear attempt by Pollack to bridge racial divides within the community and organize residents along class lines. As she told an interviewer, improving relations between the two groups would "show them that they will both gain if they work together."[37]

Whether the designers of the War on Poverty intended it or not, Pollack saw no way of addressing issues of poverty without taking race and racism into consideration simultaneously with economic factors, and this determination ultimately meant challenging the white power structure. While Pollack claimed that she had no preconceived intentions of becoming involved in local politics, increasingly she saw her role as one of an initiator of organized action on behalf of poor residents in order to show them how to attain "real power" to challenge the "white establishment." While she entered Houston's Fifth Ward determined to provide services to poor residents, her on-the-ground experiences convinced her that community organization and empowerment of the poor were the most effective avenues through which to attack the ills of poverty.[38]

Stuart Buman and Donald Szeszycki were two VISTA volunteers assigned to an area in northwest Houston known as South Heights, a rather oddly placed low-income and predominantly African American area surrounded by a white middle-class neighborhood on the north side and River Oaks on the south side—one of the wealthiest areas in the entire city. Buman was a graduate of the University of North Dakota with a degree in public administration who was especially interested in politics and social problems, and Szeszycki was a high-school graduate from Chicago who had spent the previous year in the U.S. Army stationed in Germany. Buman and Szeszycki, like other VISTA volunteers in Houston, attempted to establish service programs in their target neighborhoods such as tutoring and recreation centers. They quickly realized, however, that residents had no desire for those types of services. Neighborhood residents were suffering from chronic unemployment and underemployment, and they wanted Buman and Szeszycki to help with this most pressing problem.[39]

Unlike in the Fifth Ward, where the major employment problem was not a lack of jobs but a lack of skilled and well-paying jobs, in South Heights the biggest issue was persistent unemployment. Buman and Szeszycki began a recruiting effort for the Job Corps in their neighborhood as a way to channel unemployed workers into training programs that would prepare them for skilled jobs in Houston's factories and plants. The VISTA volunteers also created job-training facilities to provide typing, general office, and secretarial skills. Buman and Szeszycki also helped neighborhood residents open an employment club for teenagers to find work outside of school hours to supplement their family incomes. Their other efforts included initiating a neighborhood cleanup project, a voter registration and education drive, a campaign for the construction and funding of a public health facility, and a neighborhood center that would serve as a staffed day-care center for working parents. Only by living in the target neighborhood and ascertaining what types of programs residents wanted could these VISTA volunteers initiate service programs that residents would approve of.[40]

Like Hayward and Pollack, Buman and Szeszycki quickly concluded that the delivery of services alone was inadequate for solving the problems of poverty. Soon after they initiated these modest service programs they began receiving criticism from a wide array of established interests in the neighborhood. This criticism came from traditional charities that wanted to continue their discriminatory practices; middle-class organizations like the Heights Community Council, whose members felt their authority threatened; a city councilman who represented the area and was fearful of political organizing; middle-class business interests who were paranoid about possible demonstrations and boycotts;

and even Houston Action for Youth leaders who wanted their organization to be the sole poverty agency in the neighborhood. All of this resistance from established interests in South Heights convinced Buman and Szeszycki that poor residents must organize and use their power to attack the effects of poverty on their daily lives. And like Winifred Pollack, Buman and Szeszycki worked to ease racial tensions between the black children in their neighborhood and the white children in the adjacent areas by organizing mutual sports and recreational events and community meetings. By creating lines of communication between the groups of children, Buman and Szeszycki hoped to bridge the racial divisions between their parents and create biracial alliances based on class.[41]

By the end of 1966, Rev. Poteat and EF-LAC project activists were supervising more than twenty VISTA volunteers in the city. VISTA volunteers in other parts of Houston contributed to the operation of Head Start centers and other tutoring programs, taught classes to help Latin American immigrants on their way to obtaining American citizenship, and administered youth education programs. One volunteer, a registered nurse, opened a free health clinic funded by donations from area businesses, while another VISTA volunteer created a public information center and held voter-education classes that focused on local issues important to area residents. Finally, all of the VISTA volunteers working with the EF-LAC project began organizing neighborhood residents in order to empower them to claim a voice in the decisions that affected their lives.[42]

In Houston, a broad range of ideas and philosophies shaped the intellectual ground upon which the War on Poverty operated. This local ideological environment included Prophetic Christianity, religious ideas about Christian missions in the nation's urban centers, ecumenism, participatory democracy, and the Saul Alinsky method, all of which were outside the paradigm of New Deal/Great Society liberalism that shaped national policy. Yet these ideas were integral to the implementation of the federal antipoverty program in Houston and therefore defined the War on Poverty just as much as the moderate liberalism that drove national policymakers.

Although the EF-LAC project was small and meagerly funded, Rev. Poteat and grassroots antipoverty activists were able to create a local intellectual and political environment conducive to a confrontational interpretation of the community action concept. In so doing, they provided an important model for how the War on Poverty could be implemented in Houston that differed sharply from the vision offered by local public officials and more cautious members of the city's official community action agency. Rev. Poteat and his supporters showed that the federal antipoverty program could be used to broaden the definition of democracy in the city. Most important, this alternative interpretation of the concept of community action offered by Rev. Poteat and other grassroots antipoverty activists had an immediate effect on the official community action agency in Houston. Initially the majority of H-HCEOO board members had cautiously interpreted the meaning of community action. Once Rev. Poteat and grassroots activists affiliated with the EF-LAC project began implementing their own vision of what the War on Poverty could become in the city of Houston, however, several members of the H-HCEOO board took notice. And when William Ballew, himself a believer in the Saul Alinsky method and very much impressed with Rev. Poteat's use of VISTA volunteers in Houston, assumed the chairmanship of H-HCEOO, the War on Poverty in the city took a decidedly more aggressive turn.

THREE

An Aggressive Vision for the Community Action Program

Confrontational Politics and the Expansion of Democracy, 1966–1967

If the first twelve months of the War on Poverty in Houston had been little more than a minor skirmish, the year 1966 proved to be a much more eventful and conflict-ridden episode. Precipitating this dramatic shift was a change in the leadership of the Houston–Harris County Economic Opportunity Organization (H-HCEOO), the city's official community action agency. William Ballew, a prominent Houston attorney with a reputation for championing the rights of the city's underprivileged population, replaced Leon Jaworski as board chairman in January. This change in leadership ushered in a new direction for the organization because of Ballew's more confrontational interpretation of the concept of community action, which followed the example set by the Reverend Wallace B. Poteat and grassroots antipoverty activists affiliated with the Ecumenical Fellowship's Latin American Channel (EF-LAC) Project. Ballew placed heavy emphasis on community organization and empowerment of the poor in order to challenge local public officials and institutional bureaucracies and to upset the status quo that kept poor residents locked in a cycle of poverty. Ballew and his supporters in H-HCEOO began implementing an aggressive Community Action Program in Houston through a three-pronged attack on poverty. This included the creation of a robust Legal Services program in the city, the expansion of crucial social service programs in many of Houston's poor neighborhoods, and, most important, a clear focus on organizing poor residents to challenge local officials and institutions in an effort to bring about lasting social change in the city. Meanwhile, Houston Action for Youth (HAY) leaders continued to implement their limited interpretation of community action by focusing on the delivery of small-scale social services through the city's traditional welfare agencies and also by refusing to entertain any suggestion of organizing residents or challenging the status quo. By the spring of 1967, OEO officials were clearly favoring Ballew's approach to community action and encouraging H-HCEOO members to continue applying the program in Houston.

In 1966, as the War on Poverty took a confrontational direction in Houston, local circumstances not only continued to dictate the shape and contours of the federal antipoverty program but also created a window of opportunity for activists to expand the meaning of democracy. For a brief moment between the fall of 1966 and the spring of 1967, grassroots antipoverty activists in Houston were able to shape national War on Poverty policies by implementing their own confrontational interpretation of the community action concept and locating sympathetic allies in Washington. Ballew and other H-HCEOO members implemented an aggressive Community Action Program that called for the organization and empowerment of Houston's poor communities. This approach showed some encouraging signs of effectiveness in forcing the city's public officials and local institutions to begin responding to the demands of poor residents. While HAY leaders continued carrying out a cautious vision of community action, Ballew and his staff were proving that, if given the chance to succeed, a confrontational Community Action Program could be effective in winning some small victories in the fight against poverty. Armed with an aggressive ideology that called for the empowerment of the poor, Ballew and other H-HCEOO members challenged HAY's limited approach to community action and the local power structure's resistance to change. They also exposed the fallacies and naiveté of the liberal dream of a War on Poverty that would neither confront city governments and other pillars of local power nor upset the status quo. By illustrating very vividly that the problems of the poor were often structural and institutional in nature, H-HCEOO leaders showed that confrontational tactics could be effective in addressing the needs of the poor and in changing the meaning of democracy on the ground in Houston.

The first step in the transition of H-HCEOO into an aggressive community action agency was the change in leadership that occurred in January 1966. When Houston mayor Louie Welch and Harris County judge Bill Elliott approached Leon Jaworski to head up the city's new antipoverty organization in 1965, Jaworski made it clear to the two men that, due to his rather busy schedule, he would only be able to assist in getting the new agency started. Jaworski told the mayor and the county judge that once the H-HCEOO executive committee named the members of the board of directors and the organization became operational, he would resign as chairman in order to pursue other activities. By early January 1966, Jaworski was satisfied that H-HCEOO was operating effectively, and as promised he tendered his resignation to Welch and Elliott. President Johnson had recently appointed Jaworski to the President's Commission on Law Enforcement and Administration of Justice, and Texas governor John Connally had appointed him to his committee on public education in the state. Because of these added responsibilities, in his resignation letter the sixty-one-year-old Jaworski asked to be immediately relieved of his duties as chairman of H-HCEOO.[1]

Jaworski's resignation brought Houston attorney William Ballew into the position of H-HCEOO chairman and signaled dramatic changes for the poverty program in the city. Ballew had been a member of the Houston Community Council's board of directors for several years and had chaired the organization's task force that studied the possibilities of implementing the Economic Opportunity Act in Houston in 1965. The Community Council had appointed Ballew as the first vice chairman of the antipoverty committee created for the city. So when Jaworski resigned in January 1966, Ballew was the logical choice as his successor. Not only did he have ample experience with welfare and antipoverty efforts in the city, but Ballew was also an early advocate among Community Council members for the implementation of the new federal War on Poverty in Houston and had remained a strong proponent of an active antipoverty program in the city. The composition of the H-HCEOO board and executive committee also changed at the beginning of 1966 as some of the wealthier and more cautious members resigned and Ballew replaced them with poor residents from the target neighborhoods. For example, George H. W. Bush resigned from the H-HCEOO board in mid-January in order to launch his campaign to capture the Republican Party's nomination for Congress representing the newly created Seventh Congressional District on the west side of Houston. As a federal inspector commented about the new leadership of the poverty program in Houston, "The course and pace of Houston's War on Poverty may have changed for the better." Over the next few years, the changes Ballew brought to the War on Poverty in the city were viewed with acclaim or hostility, depending on one's philosophy for attacking poverty. This proved to be a contentious issue in both Houston and Washington.[2]

Though observers of the War on Poverty in Houston would be divided over how the programs developed over the next several years, in early 1966 there was one issue that almost everyone involved agreed on—the election of William Ballew as the new head of H-HCEOO certainly meant a dramatic shift in the program's focus and direction. Most of the early H-HCEOO organizers appointed by city officials had a guarded interpretation of community action, and they were cautious about maximum feasible participation of the poor. But Ballew firmly believed that community organization and mobilization with the goal of empowerment of the poor to challenge the city's elected officials and institutions were the most important parts of the War on Poverty. This was fundamentally a different definition of community action from the one adopted by Jaworski and other H-HCEOO members when they created the organization the previous year. It is doubtful that very many of the H-HCEOO board members were aware of Ballew's political views because they unanimously elected Ballew to replace Jaworski. They would find out soon enough exactly what the new chairman had in mind for the War on Poverty in Houston.[3]

The story of Houston's official community action agency illustrates that terms such as "community action" and "maximum feasible participation of the poor" had no real meaning outside of the local context in which the War on Poverty was implemented. Federal legislators and War on Poverty policymakers ambiguously defined these terms. As a consequence, local implementers of the poverty program were responsible for interpreting the meanings of these concepts and for giving them clear definitions for the thousands of foot soldiers working in the program. It was possible, therefore, for activists to turn the War on Poverty into a vehicle for expanding democracy. When Mayor Welch and County Judge Elliott created Houston's first incarnation of the city's community action agency in 1965, it was clear that the two men interpreted these concepts very narrowly. They intended to keep the War on Poverty small, with a focus on improving the city's infrastructure and delivering a few social services. As H-HCEOO's first chairman, Jaworski agreed with Welch's and Elliott's assessment. So for the first few months of the poverty war, members of the city's community action agency simply gathered data and had no intention of expanding the War on Poverty beyond Welch's and Elliott's narrow vision. Ballew had a drastically different interpretation of the meaning of concepts like "community action" and "maximum feasible participation," and his tenure as H-HCEOO chairman provides further evidence that the local context in Houston, particularly the grassroots intellectual environment that existed in the city, profoundly determined the shape of the War on Poverty—and ultimately made it possible to challenge mainstream definitions of democracy.

As soon as Ballew took over as H-HCEOO chairman, it became apparent that not only did he have a different interpretation of community action but also, like Rev. Poteat and EF-LAC project activists, he believed in the Saul Alinsky method. To remove any doubt about his antipoverty philosophy and commitment to community organizing, Ballew required that all H-HCEOO board members carefully read Alinsky's *Reveille for Radicals*, a book published in 1946 that laid out Alinsky's blueprint for the organization of poor communities to challenge urban power structures.[4]

In February 1966, one month into Ballew's tenure as head of H-HCEOO, Alinsky brought his message directly to Houston's poverty workers when he spoke on the campus of the University of Houston about his experiences organizing several poor communities and how these organizational tactics could be used in the federal War on Poverty. The main shortcoming of the national antipoverty effort, according to Alinsky, was that it "looks at deprivation only in terms of money and not of power. . . . To expect to funnel federal funds through local administrations is like giving an employer money to funnel into the organization of labor unions that someday might strike against him." Alinsky argued that the only way to make the War on Poverty successful in eradicating poverty in Houston was to organize poor people into powerful blocs that could confront the city's public officials and force them to address the needs of impoverished neighborhoods. Apparently this suggestion that poor people should organize to claim power and control over their own lives was too much for some audience members to withstand. After just a few minutes of Alinsky's speech, one woman in the front row jumped out of her seat and shouted, "Well, that's enough for me!" and walked out of the auditorium. About twenty-five others followed her, including a dozen Ku Klux Klan members in full regalia. When asked about Alinsky's visit a few days later, Mayor Welch stated, "I don't think extreme philosophies of either side are needed in this community. Any philosophy which sets class against class is, in my opinion, un-American." Ballew undoubtedly faced an uphill battle in following the Alinsky model of community organizing in Houston.[5]

In the spring and summer of 1966, Ballew personally launched a public relations campaign in Houston to explain how the Alinsky method would be applied to the implementation of the War on Poverty in the city. During a speech delivered to a group of Houston businessmen, Ballew echoed Alinsky's sentiments and argued that the grassroots antipoverty activists were "fast replacing the Civil Rights movement as the number one domestic effort of our people." Ballew continued, "Its basic concept is radical, yes, even revolutionary; but so was the beginning and the development of our American democracy and economy. . . . Recall the labor movement in America. Most manufacturers did not improve wages and working conditions until workers in America organized and became a political and economic force in our country." Ballew argued that, just as with the labor movement, poor people in the United States had to be organized to pressure and, if necessary, force confrontations with the city's local elected officials to make sure their needs were addressed. For this reason, argued Ballew, "the war on poverty cannot be a mere extension of existing social and welfare programs. Existing agencies, for all their decent efforts and good intentions, were not getting through to the poor." Instead, Ballew pledged that H-HCEOO would encourage poor people themselves to plan, develop, and implement antipoverty programs in their own communities, even though this plan was "not necessarily welcomed by existing power structures." This goal would be reached through community organization, a tactic Ballew referred to as

our single most important program. This is more than an extension of social and welfare services; it is a new departure—it is grass roots involvement of the poor in their own programs and decisions in connection with meeting their needs in the community. . . . When these people meet in their civic organizations and clubs, get to know each other and articulate their needs, requests are bound to be made upon the county courthouse, the city hall for services, etc. As labor organizers in the 20s and 30s were labeled agitators, or worse, community organizers today in the war on poverty may be likewise reviled. If we are wise, we will exercise extreme patience and understanding while these people go about their work.[6]

Ballew was committed to the Saul Alinsky method and to a confrontational antipoverty philosophy, but he still needed a way to turn the War on Poverty into a vehicle for social change in the city. As he was searching for a way to implement his vision in Houston, Ballew increasingly turned to Rev. Poteat and the EF-LAC project activists who were using federal VISTA volunteers to organize the poor. Near the end of September 1966, Ballew arranged an informal meeting between himself, Rev. Poteat, EF-LAC project activists, and recently arrived VISTA volunteers. Ballew reported being struck by the effectiveness of the city's VISTA volunteers who, after being in the city for only a few months, were organizing residents around important issues and empowering them to make demands on local officials and institutions. While H-HCEOO's current community organizers were mostly social workers who traveled daily into Houston's poor neighborhoods and were under strict supervision from the H-HCEOO board, the VISTA volunteers lived in the neighborhoods where they worked and enjoyed the freedom to pursue courses of action they deemed necessary for the empowerment of the residents. The result was a suspicion of H-HCEOO community organizers, while residents seemed to trust the VISTA volunteers. Ballew concluded that "we are doing it precisely wrong" and that H-HCEOO administrators must reevaluate the purpose of the organization and the role of their community organizers.[7]

After witnessing how Rev. Poteat and EF-LAC project activists were using the VISTA program to bring about social change in Houston, Ballew decided to commit the majority of H-HCEOO's resources to the organization and empowerment of Houston's poor. In early November 1966, Ballew sent a confidential memorandum to H-HCEOO executive director Charles Kelly in which he stated, "Since money . . . is not only in short supply but is also restricted in many cases, our effective area of operation is in community organization, development and action. Our primary effort, I repeat, is in the neighborhoods and our primary responsibility is placing good people there as community organizers and neighborhood developers. This is essential." Just like the VISTA volunteers in the city, Ballew argued that H-HCEOO community organizers should live in Houston's poor neighborhoods with the residents they were attempting to empower through community organization. Community organizers, therefore, should be chosen based on whether or not they could commit to this new focus.

"This requires a special commitment," Ballew continued, "not normally found in some social worker types who want a good paying job and spend too much time protecting that job. In the war on poverty, we are all expendable." Like the VISTA program, Ballew also advised giving individual community organizers as much freedom as possible to carry out their efforts. "Once we have good people working in the neighborhoods," Ballew stated, "we should give them as much independence and responsibility as possible." The ultimate goal, according to Ballew, was to get community-organizing activities initiated quickly in order to begin empowering the poor to make demands on public officials and local institutions that affected their daily lives.[8]

As Ballew laid out his plans for the course of the War on Poverty in Houston, and particularly after he saw how Rev. Poteat and EF-LAC project activists were using VISTA volunteers, he remained steadfast in his commitment to Alinsky-style community organizing and maximum feasible participation of the poor—despite some opposition. Although conflict did arise with other board members, Ballew was able to lead H-HCEOO in a more activist direction focused on organizing poor communities to challenge the city's public officials, primarily because he located an important ally in the regional OEO office. William Crook, who was the regional director of the southwest division of OEO and would later become national director of the VISTA program in 1967, strongly supported the use of community organizing and favored more aggressive community action agencies like the one Ballew was trying to build in Houston.

Ballew arranged for Crook to speak at H-HCEOO's first annual dinner meeting in 1966. Crook used the occasion to stress that the Community Action Program should be used to expand democracy in cities like Houston. Though the program had come under fire from mayors of some of the nation's largest cities, and despite the fact that Mayor Welch had tried to avoid creating a community action agency in Houston, Crook argued that community action "contains whatever hope we have for a successful conclusion to the war on poverty." In response to those who opposed the idea of community organization, Crook pointed out that it was the only part of the federal antipoverty effort that attempted to restore the initiative to local citizens and for this reason should be welcomed rather than feared. According to Crook, the ideas fueling the Community Action Program, including the prospect of organizing and empowering the poor, "is as valid a form of democratic decision [making] as the Constitution of the United States. It is as much a part of the tradition of this land as the old New England town meetings. . . . It is the philosophy of a free people applied practically to a local situation." Rather than bowing to the irrational fears of local politicians, Crook implored those present at the H-HCEOO meeting to expand the Community Action Program and community organization in Houston and to use these tools to bring about lasting democratic change.[9]

Effecting lasting social change in Houston was, of course, Ballew's ultimate and abiding goal throughout his time as H-HCEOO chairman, and he attempted to realize this goal in three significant ways between the spring of 1966 and the spring of 1967. First, Ballew placed heavy emphasis on the establishment of a Legal Services program for the poor in Houston, because he firmly believed the legal system was one of the best vehicles for empowering poor residents. Second, he sought expansion of those social services that he believed were absolutely necessary for a decent standard of living in the city's poor neighborhoods and that were also capable of bringing about institutional reform. Finally, and most importantly, Ballew redirected H-HCEOO's board and staff toward a clear focus on community organizing in an effort to empower poor Houston citizens to confront local institutions and the city's public officials. Through this three-pronged attack on the root causes of poverty, Ballew hoped to broaden the definition of democracy in Houston by giving poor residents a voice in the decisions that affected their lives.

Upon taking control of the Community Action Program in Houston, Ballew made it a priority to assist in the creation of a massive and far-reaching Legal Services program in the city. H-HCEOO officials designated the Houston Legal Foundation as the delegate agency to administer the Legal Services program. After the Supreme Court began handing down a series of decisions in the early 1960s that upheld the rights of citizens accused of a crime and also their right to be provided an attorney if they were unable to afford one, a group of Houston attorneys began raising money to create an organization that would provide attorneys free of charge to needy Houstonians. After securing a sizable grant from the Ford Foundation, these attorneys formed the Houston Legal Foundation to operate a public defender program in the city, and they named retired district judge Sam Johnson as the organization's director. By the spring of 1966 Johnson was able to secure a service commitment from more than 3,000 attorneys in the city, enabling the Houston Legal Foundation to begin providing legal defense to Houston residents who were without the means of hiring a lawyer.[10]

It quickly became apparent to members of the Houston Legal Foundation, however, that a significant number of Houston's poor residents had not been charged with any crime but needed legal assistance of a civil nature. Director Sam Johnson began exploring the idea of creating a civil division that would supply attorneys to poor residents in civil cases involving divorce and child custody issues, property disputes, and consumer credit problems. More than doubling the number of clients the Houston Legal Foundation would serve required a substantial increase in the level of funding. Johnson decided to seek War on Poverty money through the newly created Legal Services division to accomplish his goal of expanding the foundation's services in Houston. In March 1966 Johnson submitted a request for $700,000 to OEO to initiate the Houston

Legal Foundation's civil law division and begin providing legal services to all of the city's poor residents who were in need.[11]

Ballew was very enthusiastic about bringing the Houston Legal Foundation into the city's War on Poverty during the spring of 1966. Over the next year he worked to make the foundation live up to his vision of using the War on Poverty to empower Houston's poor. First and foremost, however, the Houston Legal Foundation provided an important service to those living in poverty. The poor seldom had access to legal counsel, advice, or representation in cases involving divorce, child custody, and other domestic legal issues. Attorneys working through the foundation would help remedy this situation by providing free legal services in neighborhood law centers. Ballew certainly understood the value of providing these much-needed legal services in Houston's poor neighborhoods, but even more attractive was the potential of the Houston Legal Foundation to empower the city's poor residents. By providing legal educational programs and attorneys who could help the poor initiate lawsuits, the foundation could help level the playing field when it came to legal matters. For example, the foundation could make poor residents more aware of their legal rights and provide attorneys to represent the poor in their dealings with landlords, local welfare offices, police, local businesses, employers, and any other individual or institution affecting their lives. As Ballew recognized, in addition to providing an important service, the foundation could also contribute to empowering the poor to deal more equally with the city's public officials and institutions. As the program grew larger and as poor neighborhoods became more politically organized, the foundation could also pursue institutional reform through the legal system.

The Houston Legal Foundation's application for OEO funding laid out plans for one the most far-reaching Legal Services programs in the country. Clinton Bamberger, national director of OEO's Legal Services program, commented on the foundation's funding application during an address he delivered to the southwest regional OEO office in March 1966. Bamberger told his audience that attorneys working in conjunction with Legal Services programs around the country not only provided legal aid to poor citizens but also served as agents of change in their communities. He stated, "Some may think it curious to consider lawyers as leaders of what may be called a social revolution. Yet no role could be more true to the traditions of our profession. It is and has been for centuries the task of lawyers to change the status quo. It is fallacious to think of lawyers as guardians of tradition. Rather, we are the guardians and watchdogs of orderly change. . . . Lawyers have been the architects—as well as the artisans—of social reform; to redesign, reform and create not only legal institutions but social, economic and political institutions as well." Bamberger praised the Houston Legal Foundation for living up to these expectations and reminded his audience that in order for the Houston program to be successful, the attorneys "must be free to challenge even the local government and the community action agency if the cause warrants and the client's interest demands." Bamberger was confident that Houston's program would become "one of the most comprehensive and extensive programs in the country." These statements undoubtedly bolstered Ballew's confidence in the Houston Legal Foundation. Bamberger shared his vision of a strong Legal Services program in Houston that could potentially upset the city's traditional balance of power by providing a more equal footing for the poor in the legal arena.[12]

With Ballew's assistance and encouragement, the Houston Legal Foundation (HLF) quickly established an extensive Legal Services program in Houston. OEO approved the foundation's application in April 1966 and granted the organization more than $700,000 to create its proposed civil law division. According to the plan, the public defender program would continue to be funded by a grant from the Ford Foundation, but the two programs would work in conjunction with each other. Once the Houston Legal Foundation had received the funds, members began establishing neighborhood law centers in several target communities in the city. Although the foundation began with only three neighborhood centers, over the course of the next several months the HLF established a law center in each of H-HCEOO's target neighborhoods, with two attorneys assigned to each center. According to Judge Sam Johnson, the attorneys working for the foundation were allowed to accept any civil case whatsoever except for personal injury lawsuits, which were fee-generating cases that a private attorney would most likely accept. The only other limitation was that the person receiving legal aid from the HLF must be considered as living below the poverty level. Houston Legal Foundation attorneys envisioned themselves accepting cases involving disputes with landlords, unfair contracts for home repairs, adverse rulings on social security and welfare benefits, and an array of other cases where the relative powerlessness of poor residents would otherwise hamper their ability to resolve these legal issues in a satisfactory way.[13]

By the fall of 1966 the Houston Legal Foundation had accepted more than seven hundred of these types of cases. In September, however, the foundation reached a turning point in the development of the Legal Services program in the city when local circumstances forced attorneys to decide whether they would become a catalyst for social change in Houston. The question that prompted this development was whether HLF attorneys would be allowed to handle civil rights cases. As Houston's public schools reopened that fall, Mrs. Melvyn Davis and her school-aged son Darrell walked into a Houston Legal Foundation neighborhood office and complained that the Houston Independent School District had not allowed the black student to attend a predominantly white school in the city, despite recent court rulings ordering Houston's public schools to desegregate. Davis wanted to sue the school district to allow her son to attend the school that year, but attorneys at the neighborhood center soon discovered that she earned too much income to qualify for free legal services through the foundation. The attorneys subsequently turned down her case for that reason, but the matter was complicated a few days later when the HLF's director, Judge Johnson, reviewed the denial of services. Johnson stated to the press that even if Mrs. Davis had qualified for free legal services, attorneys at the neighborhood center would have refused this particular case because national Legal Services program requirements and federal War on Poverty policies forbade the Houston Legal Foundation from accepting cases involving alleged civil rights violations. Johnson reasoned that since the Civil Rights Act of 1964 gave the U.S. attorney general the authority to initiate lawsuits of this kind, and the Economic Opportunity Act of 1964 prevented any War on Poverty agency from duplicating the duties or services of other government agencies, the Houston Legal Foundation could not legally prosecute civil rights cases because that would indeed be a duplication of services and duties.[14]

Judge Johnson's pronouncement to the Houston press set off a flurry of activity among War on Poverty officials in the southwest regional office and in Washington. It was undoubtedly an unsettling development in Ballew's effort to use the Houston Legal Foundation to bring about social change in Houston. The issue finally reached the desk of Anthony Partridge, deputy general counsel for OEO in Washington, in October. Partridge disagreed with Judge Johnson and offered his legal opinion that the Economic Opportunity Act did not prevent local Legal Services programs from accepting civil rights cases because the clause of the act in question only prohibited the duplication of services offered by the federal government. The Houston Legal Foundation, however, was a private nonprofit organization, and despite the fact that it received funding from the federal government, it was not technically a federal agency. The national OEO office forwarded Partridge's opinion to the southwest OEO regional office's director William Crook, who notified Judge Johnson and other members of the Houston Legal Foundation that their organization should indeed accept cases involving civil rights laws. OEO officials in Washington stressed that the situation in Houston had received national media attention and that the outcome would have consequences for Legal Services programs all over the country. In response, Crook informed Ballew that the Houston Legal Foundation not only was allowed to accept civil rights cases but also that its attorneys were in fact required to accept these cases to fulfill their obligations under War on Poverty guidelines. Judge Johnson agreed to comply, but it was evident he was bristling under this latest criticism. "It's like being a bird dog," Johnson said of leading the Houston Legal Foundation in the wake of the civil rights controversy. "If you get too far ahead of the hunter, you get shot. If you stay too close, you get kicked." Despite Johnson's uneasiness and much to Ballew's satisfaction, Houston Legal Foundation attorneys were further encouraged to act as agents of democratic change rather than to restrict themselves to handling only cases of family law.[15]

By the beginning of 1967, the Houston Legal Foundation seemed to be off to a promising start toward fulfilling Ballew's hopes for a Legal Services program in Houston that not only could provide important services to the poor but also possessed the potential to bring about social change in Houston. In just a few months, the Houston Legal Foundation had opened eight neighborhood law offices in the city's poor neighborhoods, served hundreds of clients, initiated a legal education program, and opened the door to pursuing civil rights cases to speed the pace of school desegregation in the city. The fiasco over whether or not Houston Legal Foundation attorneys could accept these kinds of cases, however, should have indicated to Ballew that the H-HCEOO board would need to keep pressuring Houston's Legal Services administration to continue pursuing cases that had the potential to empower the poor. Without this pressure and support from Houston's community action agency, the Houston Legal Foundation might not be as willing to pursue such a confrontational strategy.[16]

After successfully initiating an active Legal Services program in Houston through the Houston Legal Foundation, Ballew turned his attention to the second component of his vision for the Community Action Program in the city—the expansion of services in poor neighborhoods that both were needed to ensure a decent standard of living and also had the potential to encourage institutional reform. Ballew first worked to expand the Head Start program in the city. During the previous year the small and relatively unorganized Head Start program administered by Houston Action for Youth and the Neighborhood Centers Association was able to show some positive results despite the uncoordinated nature of the operation. A team of researchers from the University of Texas in Austin published a study in February 1966 in which they compared low-income first-grade students in several Houston elementary schools who had participated in a Head Start program the previous summer with similar students who had not been enrolled in a Head Start center. The results showed that those first graders who had been participants in the Houston Head Start program exhibited great improvement in reasoning skills, social competence, and verbal knowledge. Dr. Alberta Baines, the Houston school official who administered part of the Head Start program the previous summer, commented on the report by stating, "The evidence is in classrooms in our district this year. We have noted great change in both the children and their parents when compared with those who did not choose to participate in Head Start last summer. I believe it is fact to say that the average IQs of our children in the program were raised several points and I am convinced that at least 40 percent—1200 of

3000 in Houston public school classes—moved toward the middle class level in classroom performance." Now that the city of Houston had a central community action agency in H-HCEOO, many Head Start proponents were hopeful for a more organized program for the summer of 1966 that would reach many more underprivileged preschoolers in Houston.[17]

Ballew undoubtedly recognized the potential for institutional reform that Head Start offered. The preschool program not only provided an important educational service to low-income families but also held possibilities for educational reform in Houston's schools, particularly with regard to desegregation efforts. Federal program guidelines prohibited racial segregation in Head Start centers, and since most of the centers were located in Houston public school buildings, many local reformers hoped to use Head Start to expose the irrationality of attempts to keep the city's schools segregated. Armed with the report showing the success of the Head Start program in Houston, Ballew and other supporters persuaded the city's school board to approve a plan that nearly doubled the enrollment capacity for students who would be eligible for Head Start during the summer of 1966. Members of the H-HCEOO board of directors and the Houston school board collaborated on a plan for an expanded program that would reach more than six thousand preschool-aged children in sixty schools all across the city and county. Though several OEO officials in Washington expressed some reservations about using the Head Start program to promote desegregation efforts in Houston, southwest regional OEO director William Crook convinced the national office to approve H-HCEOO's $1.4 million Head Start funding request by pointing to several key factors: Mayor Welch's recent display of goodwill toward the poverty program in Houston, the apparent restiveness of residents of the target areas anxious to see concrete programs implemented in their neighborhoods, and Sargent Shriver's pending visit to Houston. In early June OEO announced its approval of H-HCEOO's request, and the Head Start program was once again underway in Houston. As with the Legal Services program, the success of using Head Start to encourage reform in Houston's educational system and to promote desegregation efforts depended on reformers like Ballew keeping pressure on the local school board and local Head Start administrators.[18]

Contrary to the charge Ballew's critics later leveled at H-HCEOO—that the organization completely neglected social service programs in Houston—Ballew and the H-HCEOO board expanded some programs in several of Houston's poor neighborhoods that they deemed vital to the overall War on Poverty effort in the city. Ballew attempted to take seriously all elements of the community action concept, and a significant part of community action was the expansion and coordination of social services available to the poor. In March 1966 OEO approved funding for a parent education program, to be administered by H-HCEOO and

Houston's Family and Children's Service Center in the Fourth Ward, to deal with an array of family problems through family-counseling discussion groups. According to the program description, topics of discussion would include family budgeting, teenage problems, job seeking, and the availability of educational and welfare services in the area. H-HCEOO members also began administering a summer youth recreation program in 1966 that reached six thousand young people in Houston between the ages of six and eighteen. The stated goal of the program was "to channel their energies during school vacation into constructive rather than destructive channels." The recreation program operated out of twenty-six community centers spread out all over the city and provided activities such as organized sports competitions and trips to Houston's many cultural attractions. In July Houston's Alley Theatre, a small theater company started by a high-school drama teacher in the 1940s and funded by the Ford Foundation, treated six hundred of the program participants to a free production of *Winnie the Pooh*. A few weeks later all of the youths involved in the program got to see the Houston Astros play the New York Mets in an afternoon baseball game in the newly opened Houston Astrodome.[19]

Ballew's third component of his three-pronged attack on poverty in Houston placed much more emphasis on including poor residents living in the target neighborhoods in the development and implementation of antipoverty programs. Most important in this approach was the need to organize communities, politicize and empower poor residents, and force institutional change in the city. To increase the participation of poor residents, H-HCEOO obtained an OEO grant of $1.7 million in June 1966 to establish thirty fully staffed neighborhood centers all across the city. Through the neighborhood centers, H-HCEOO would be able to hire neighborhood residents to staff the centers; to offer meeting rooms for neighborhood organizations and periodic workshops, which would bring residents into the decision-making processes of the poverty program; and to allow them to play a role in determining program policy. As the OEO press release stated, these neighborhood centers in Houston "will greatly enhance the concept of community action, . . . increase the scope of services to be performed, and will provide direct participation of target area residents in the selection of programs designed to help them help themselves." H-HCEOO members estimated that 300,000 poor Houston residents would greatly benefit from the creation of these neighborhood centers in addition to the more than 250 staff employees that H-HCEOO promised to hire directly from the target neighborhoods.[20]

As an extension of his efforts to carry out the directive of maximum feasible participation of the poor, Ballew strove to begin organizing Houston's poor communities in order to reform local institutions and challenge the status quo. Rev. Poteat and EF-LAC project activists had had a profound impact on Ballew earlier in the year with their use of VISTA volunteers to organize poor neighborhoods in order to empower poor Houston residents to make demands on local public officials and institutions. By mid-1966 Ballew was itching to use the H-HCEOO staff to experiment with Alinsky-style community organization. During the summer of 1966 Ballew and H-HCEOO executive director Charles Kelly hired a community organizing specialist from Chicago to administer a four-week training program to prepare an army of H-HCEOO community organizers to go into Houston's poor neighborhoods and begin organizing residents.[21]

In order to give H-HCEOO's community-organizing effort clear direction, as well as to build some credibility in the poor neighborhoods, Ballew appointed the Reverend Earl Allen as director of community organization. Allen was a native Houstonian, a local Methodist minister, and director of the Wesley Foundation at Texas Southern University, Houston's all-black university located in one of H-HCEOO's target neighborhoods in the Third Ward. Allen certainly had plenty of experience with community organizing. He had been a regional representative of the Congress of Racial Equality (CORE) in Dallas while he attended seminary at Southern Methodist University. In that position, Allen had organized a month-long civil rights protest in 1964 to desegregate downtown restaurants and cafeterias. Like Ballew, Allen had read Saul Alinsky's work on community organizing and was committed to the idea of empowering the poor in Houston to confront the city's public officials and institutions. "I wanted to change the status quo," Allen said in a recent interview, "so I was abrasive and not afraid of confrontation." In hiring Allen to focus solely on community organizing, Ballew sent a clear message that neighborhood organization, community empowerment, and even protest activity would be a major thrust of H-HCEOO's effort to implement the War on Poverty in the city of Houston.[22]

Beginning in the fall of 1966, Ballew began shifting the majority of H-HCEOO's resources and energy into community organizing. In November Ballew asked Allen to head up an H-HCEOO project called "Operation Discovery," which Ballew had designed in order to begin applying some of Saul Alinsky's ideas about community organization in Houston's poor neighborhoods. Because Ballew was an Alinsky disciple, he understood perfectly well that power relations were at the heart of the problems of poor people. Ballew often could be heard during these months in the fall of 1966 repeating a phrase he had picked up from one of his aides: "Poverty isn't the absence of money; it's the absence of power." Operation Discovery was meant to rectify the imbalance of power between Houston's poor population and the city's institutions by organizing the poor into powerful groups of citizens with the ability to put pressure on city hall, local welfare agencies, and other representatives of the city's power structure. During the month leading up to its launch, Ballew decided to give

Operation Discovery top priority and reassigned several key staff members to Allen's special task force dedicated to community organizing.[23]

As soon as Allen took charge of the community organization task force and Operation Discovery, he immediately recognized that the staff would need to be retrained in Alinsky-style community organizing. For example, Allen discovered that many H-HCEOO staff members lacked even the basic skills needed to relate to poor Houston residents on a personal basis. In order to define clear goals and objectives for his staff, Allen issued a memorandum in early December in which he stated that the purpose of Operation Discovery was to determine an effective method for organizing Houston's poor residents so as to allow them to take control of their own lives. Rather than simply gathering more statistical information about the target neighborhoods, Operation Discovery was an attempt to find what was "both a relevant and a realistic approach to achieving the maximum feasible participation of the poor in the total decision-making process in Houston–Harris County. More specifically, Operation Discovery is the vehicle we have chosen to determine what are the quickest and best possible methods for perfecting indigenous organization[s] within the poverty areas of Houston–Harris County through which the poor can 'help themselves.'" What is evident from these kinds of statements is that Allen had an extremely broad interpretation of the meanings of community action and maximum feasible participation of the poor. Allen certainly agreed with both Ballew and federal War on Poverty planners that poor residents should be involved in the planning and implementation of antipoverty policies and programs in their own communities, but he carried this edict even further by arguing that poor Houston residents should also enjoy full participation in the social, political, and economic life of the city. In short, Allen advocated the New Left philosophy of participatory democracy and believed that the Community Action Program called for the use of community organizing in order to restore to Houston's poor population a degree of power over their own lives.[24]

Operation Discovery allowed Allen to design a comprehensive plan for organizing the poor communities of Houston. The plan itself was an excellent illustration of how differently Allen and his community organization team viewed both the causes of and the possible solutions for poverty compared to the traditional welfare agencies and many social workers. The traditional view of poverty posited that poor people themselves were the cause of their own poverty because they had failed to adapt to an advanced industrial economy with an increasing number of highly skilled jobs. In order to remedy this, welfare agencies and social workers sought to change the individual behavior of poor people. Other antipoverty activists, however, including Allen and a few national War on Poverty planners, believed there were structural limitations that severely reduced the power poor people had over their own lives. Institutional racism, discrimination, complex and aloof municipal bureaucracies, cumbersome local welfare service agencies, and a lack of educational and employment opportunities were just a few examples of the structural forces that oppressed poor people and that were completely out of their control. One of the solutions to poverty, therefore, which was included as a small but significant component of the Community Action Program within the federal War on Poverty, was community organizing with the ultimate goal of empowering the poor. According to Allen and other community organization proponents, Saul Alinsky had been correct: the only effective solution to the problem of poverty was to restore power to poor communities through organization.[25]

In his plan for community organization in Houston, Allen argued that there were myriad reasons why poverty existed, but four significant factors stood out above the rest: (1) inadequate housing; (2) inadequate educational opportunities and facilities; (3) inadequate health facilities; and (4) inadequate employment opportunities. To begin addressing these inadequacies, Allen, as a good Alinsky disciple, instructed his community organization staff first to enter a poor neighborhood and develop a profile of the community that would present a "realistic picture" of the particular area and uncover specific problems that needed to be resolved. Once the community organizer had identified the major problems of a particular neighborhood, Allen instructed them to draw the attention of neighborhood residents to a "gut issue," which was a specific situation that served to dramatize a particular problem. For example, specific gut issues stemming from the problem of inadequate housing in poor neighborhoods could be rat infestation, high rents, unresponsive landlords, a lack of trashcans, or a wide array of other issues that would serve to dramatize the larger problem of inadequate housing. Allen told his community organizers to rally residents around these gut issues and bring those citizens who were concerned about particular issues together in order to work on possible solutions and initiate any necessary action. Allen stated, "Your job is to dissect a poor community and find out what's buggin' it. You have to build a concern for participation— find a gut issue, but find one which can be solved quickly. We need victories. Victories build confidence." By bringing residents together to work on common problems in the community, according to Allen, organizers would be able to identify leaders within the community and could begin developing this leadership to tackle future problems and issues. This process could be repeated for a series of gut issues until the neighborhoods were organized into action groups capable of successfully confronting the city's public officials and dedicated to solving the problems of the community. Allen stated that these various action groups should eventually convene to form neighborhood councils that would try to deal with problems affecting the entire neighborhood. Similarly, these neighborhood councils would eventually form area councils that would be sufficiently large and diverse enough to address problems affecting an entire area of Houston. Allen argued that once these area councils had been formed, community organizers should work to strengthen each organizational group so they would be able to carry on without the leadership provided by the professional organizer.[26]

Ballew was so impressed with Allen's plan for community organization that he immediately assigned a 140-member staff to Allen's community-organizing department. Ballew and Allen decided to focus H-HCEOO's first community-organizing efforts on a large African American neighborhood northeast of downtown Houston known as Settegast. Allen himself had once been a resident of Settegast, so he knew firsthand the conditions there. For several years residents of the area had registered various complaints to the city government about poor and unsanitary living conditions in their neighborhoods, but they had very little success in getting any of their grievances addressed. In many ways the Settegast area was an attractive location to experiment with community organizing. As Allen stated, Settegast had clear geographic boundaries that would allow organizing efforts to be concentrated where they were needed most. There existed several indigenous community groups in the area that could be mobilized to put pressure on local institutions and on the city's public officials.[27]

H-HCEOO staff members already had broad knowledge about the Settegast area. The H-HCEOO board's interest in this section of Houston began in the summer of 1966 when staff members conducted an extensive survey of the neighborhood that resulted in the publication of "The Settegast Report," a study commissioned by H-HCEOO executive director Charles Kelly to gain a better understanding of the problems and issues in one of the city's poorest neighborhoods. At one time Settegast had been a haven for lower-middle-class African Americans who wanted to own their own homes, but by the mid-1960s the neighborhood had deteriorated primarily because it failed to keep pace with standard city improvements through the years, such as modern sewage systems and paved roads. By 1960 the median income in Settegast was little more than half the average income for Harris County. And despite the fact that home-ownership rates remained high, housing conditions were among the worst in the city. During the summer of 1966 Kelly sent a team of researchers and interviewers into the Settegast area in order to ascertain the root causes of poverty in that part of the city. What they discovered shocked many people who were completely unaware of the magnitude of deprivation in the area.[28]

Authors of the report identified four major areas of concern in Settegast. The first concern noted was the rampant profiteering and exploitation of area residents by unscrupulous businessmen, especially those in the homebuilding and home mortgage lending industries. H-HCEOO interviewers found that neighborhood residents were "too trustful" of representatives from these types of businesses who scoured the area selling substandard homes and offering loans that could never be paid off. Because homes were already being built before the Settegast area was officially incorporated into the city of Houston, homebuilders were not required to conform to Federal Housing Authority (FHA) standards, and as a result most of the homes did not qualify for FHA mortgage insurance. Surveyors found that more than 30 percent of the homes in Settegast were in a deteriorated or dilapidated condition, and they reported that as a result "the cost in human suffering is high."[29]

Surveyors found that even though 80 percent of respondents in Settegast owned their own home, "the term *ownership* must be used in the loosest possible sense" (emphasis in original). H-HCEOO staff discovered that mortgage lenders in Settegast had found a way to take advantage of residents who could not afford to make a large down payment to purchase a home in the area. Lenders had devised a "contract for deed" arrangement whereby a prospective homebuyer was allowed to make payments each month until an agreed-upon amount had been collected by the lender that would be used as the down payment. Once this amount was reached, the buyer would acquire the title to the property and the balance of the total purchase price would be financed through a mortgage loan. On the surface, this arrangement appeared to offer new homebuyers the means to make a down payment when they would otherwise be unable to afford it. But H-HCEOO surveyors found that in reality many of these contracts for deed were designed in such a way that borrowers found it impossible to reach the agreed-upon amount because of a multitude of hidden fees and exorbitant finance charges. For example, the surveyors interviewed one prospective homeowner whose contract price was $6,100 and called for monthly payments of $52. After paying this amount every month for almost nine years, the total payments equaled $5,608. According to the contract, however, the unpaid balance on the contract remained at $5,800. Mortgage lenders were clearly exploiting Settegast residents, who were often unable to decipher the contract terminology and unaware of their own legal rights.[30]

The second major area of concern that the H-HCEOO staff found in Settegast involved the closely related issues of poor health and sanitation services. The most shocking discovery was that there were absolutely no healthcare facilities in Settegast or in any of the surrounding communities. There was not a single doctor or dentist who practiced in the area, and if residents needed medical attention, they were forced to travel twenty miles to Ben Taub Hospital, which was the nearest public health facility to the Settegast community. Many residents lacked the means of transporting themselves or family members to the hospital, and since ambulance services were only available to those who could pay for them, most Settegast residents simply received no medical attention when they were sick or injured. With regard to sanitation in Settegast, surveyors also found open sewage ditches and a complete lack of drainage facilities, which provided extremely favorable environments for the breeding of rodents and other vermin. They estimated that the size of the rat population in Settegast was easily three times as large as the human population in the area. The water supply in Settegast was also a major problem because nearly 70 percent of residents received their water from shallow wells that were often contaminated from septic tanks and sewage backups from outhouses. Though no official study had been conducted, H-HCEOO staff believed that the extraordinarily high rate of kidney and bladder diseases among Settegast residents was directly connected to the contaminated water they drank on a daily basis.[31]

The third major area of concern was a general lack of educational and employment opportunities. H-HCEOO interviewers found that a majority of Settegast residents desperately wanted a Head Start program initiated in their neighborhood, and many more expressed a desire for some type of day care program so their children would not be left at home alone. Surveyors also found that there was no community library in the area. While more than two-thirds of residents lacked a high-school education, interviewers found that most were not content to remain uneducated; many expressed a strong desire for an adult education program in their community. The authors of the report concluded that an adult education program would be impossible without an adequate library. Surveyors also recognized the need for a consumer education program in Settegast to alert residents to the premium prices they were paying for consumer goods in neighborhood stores. There were no supermarkets in the area, so H-HCEOO staff conducted a shopping survey in Settegast and compared prices with those paid at supermarkets just outside the neighborhood. The results were surprising. The prices for nearly every item most families bought on a regular basis were considerably higher at the local neighborhood stores than at the nearby supermarkets. With minimal transportation options, Settegast residents were forced to use their limited income to buy overpriced goods from local grocers. Surveyors also found that there were no adult or youth vocational training programs in Settegast, even though nearly 70 percent of the residents stated they wanted these types of programs for their neighborhood.[32]

The final problem area in Settegast discovered by H-HCEOO surveyors was insufficient transportation options for residents. Interviewers found that poor residents constituted the largest group of Houstonians who needed access to public transportation, but they were also in the group who resided in parts of the city often neglected by urban transportation planners. Surveyors discovered that public transportation in Houston was inadequate, slow, and expensive, and in Settegast it was also incredibly inefficient, inconvenient, and time consuming. Three main bus lines served the city of Houston, all of which radiated out from downtown. For Settegast residents, this often meant they had to take a lengthy bus ride into downtown Houston just to transfer to another bus line that would take them to their destination, which was often closer to Settegast than it was to downtown. All riders on Houston's buses paid a one-dollar roundtrip fare, but for many Settegast residents this amounted to more than their hourly take-home pay.[33]

H-HCEOO's "Settegast Report" exposed a neglected area of Houston many people in the city were totally unaware of and revealed a degree of deprivation most thought had been eradicated during the post–World War II economic boom. Settegast residents suffered from a number of problems, not the least of which stemmed from the indifference of the city's public officials to their problems and exploitive actions by business and real estate developers directed at the relatively powerless and uneducated community. When the H-HCEOO board of directors reviewed the report, they were presented with two options for how to address the problems in Settegast. Since there was a clear lack of services being provided in the neighborhood, H-HCEOO staff could have implemented federally funded service projects in Settegast by coordinating local agencies to improve housing conditions, clean up the water supply, help people with their mortgage payments, assist residents who needed medical attention, recruit the unemployed into programs like the Job Corps, or otherwise deliver needed services. If the traditional welfare bureaucracy in Houston had targeted the Settegast area, residents could have reasonably expected those service-oriented organizations to begin providing these types of social welfare programs.

Earl Allen was able to convince the H-HCEOO board of directors, however, that the delivery of services to Settegast residents would only provide a temporary solution to their problems. What was needed in the area, argued Allen, was the other option for fighting poverty: community organization to bring about lasting social change capable of producing permanent improvements in the lives of Settegast residents. Only by organizing the residents of Settegast could they be mobilized and empowered, which would enable them to make demands on the city government, local businesses, and other institutions to remedy the problems associated with poverty in the neighborhood. Ballew agreed with Allen that Settegast could be used to experiment with an Alinsky-style community organization project, and he was able to convince enough H-HCEOO board members to agree to a ninety-day demonstration program. With H-HCEOO board approval, in the last two months of 1966 Allen placed eighty members of his community-organizing staff in Settegast with the hopes of proving that his philosophy of community organization would be effective in addressing the problems of the poor in Houston.[34]

The community organization tactics developed by Ballew and Allen produced almost immediate results. When Allen's community organization staff began searching for a gut issue in Settegast in November, it was clear that the grotesquely unsanitary water supply in the area would serve as a very effective issue to dramatize the problem of inadequate city services in this poor section of Houston. Organizers discovered that the majority of homes in Settegast were served by backyard water wells, which frequently became contaminated with bacteria and parasites because disease-carrying sewage was seeping into the wells from septic tanks and outhouses. Armed with this information, H-HCEOO community organizers and a group of Settegast residents walked into a city council meeting and demanded that Mayor Louie Welch extend city water services to their neighborhoods. Faced with this delicate political issue and clearly not wanting to appear to deny Houston residents sanitary drinking water, Welch immediately ordered city workers to place emergency water spigots on the city's fire hydrants in Settegast to provide clean water to the residents. Welch also quickly drew up a plan to extend city water services to the area and instructed one of Houston's city attorneys to investigate the possibility of filing a lawsuit against the company that knowingly sold water from contaminated wells to unsuspecting families in Settegast. Ballew immediately claimed victory for this exercise in Alinsky-style community organization and pointed out that at the urging of community organizers, residents "went to City Hall and demanded a city water supply to replace their contaminated one. They got it." The event produced such a surprising victory that a *Houston Post* reporter covering the story declared that the "dawn of a quiet revolution may have broken over Houston," referring to when the Settegast group arrived at City Hall to begin receiving a redress of grievances that were a long time coming. "In a modern city such as Houston," a *Houston Post* editorial asserted a few days later, "no person should be threatened by contaminated water, or be dependent upon a fire hydrant for pure water. Our consciences should not permit it."[35]

Ballew and Allen even encouraged the community organizers to help plan and participate in organized protest activities to bring attention to the plight of their communities. While some Settegast residents were putting pressure on Welch and the Houston City Council to address their water problems, others began staging demonstrations at local schools to protest the lack of sanitary conditions. Not only was there contaminated water coming into many of the schools, but there simply was not enough water pressure for using drinking fountains or even flushing toilets. Many students and teachers had to bring Thermoses to school filled with enough water for the entire day. After protesting for several weeks with no response from the all-white Northeast Houston School District Board, several Settegast neighborhood councils, which had been formed with assistance from Allen's staff, launched a write-in campaign to elect to the board two African American residents who promised to address the problems. These two candidates lost by a very narrow margin, but nevertheless the neighborhood councils were successful in encouraging more residents to assume an active role in the administration of their local schools. A *Houston Post* reporter commented, "With almost 1,000 Settegast votes to reckon with, it is doubtful that the school board out there will ever be quite the same again." The protests also had an effect on Welch—he ordered his staff to obtain water samples from Settegast schools to check for contamination.[36]

After achieving some success in getting city officials to address the problem of sanitation in Settegast, Allen's community organizers focused on the absence of medical treatment facilities. Rather than establishing a temporary federally funded health clinic or hospital in the area, members of Allen's staff began organizing neighborhood residents to put pressure on the Harris County Hospital District to build and maintain a permanent branch of the public hospital system in Settegast. One H-HCEOO organizer argued that the proposed Settegast healthcare facility would set an example for the rest of the city and become the first of several clinics established in poverty neighborhoods. One H-HCEOO staff member in the area stated, "These clinics would help decentralize charity medicine in Harris County and make services available to the poor in outlying areas, many of whom have no means of transportation to Ben Taub," the central general hospital in Houston. As Allen's staff began organizing residents into pressure groups, Harris County Hospital District officials responded slowly but mostly favorably to the idea of creating a branch of the city's charity hospital in Settegast. By early January the hospital district board had placed the issue on the agenda for their meeting that month.[37]

In order to make sure that members of the Harris County Hospital District would address the absence of healthcare facilities in Settegast, H-HCEOO community organizers and neighborhood residents held a rally in downtown Houston near where the meeting was taking place to demand the creation of a branch of the charity hospital in their neighborhood. The strategy worked—the hospital district voted to establish a branch of the charity hospital in Settegast immediately. Hospital district member Quentin Mease, a prominent African American civic leader in Houston and executive director of the downtown YMCA, was especially receptive to the idea of establishing branch hospitals in poor neighborhoods, and he worked tirelessly to obtain the approval of the Settegast Clinic. Located inside a building donated by the Houston City Council, the new Settegast Clinic opened during the last week in January and served 175 poor residents in its first week of operation. The staff consisted of hospital district employees and volunteers from the Houston Medical Forum, an organization made up of African American doctors in Houston. In the wake of the clinic's opening, Ballew expressed optimism about the course of the War on Poverty in the city. The opening of the Settegast Clinic was "a breakthrough event," Ballew told Texas senator Ralph Yarborough, and clear evidence that the "War on Poverty in Houston is beginning to go."[38]

After some early successes, Ballew encouraged the spirit of organized protest to carry beyond the neighborhood of Settegast. For example, H-HCEOO community organizers and a group of residents from Blossom Heights, a mostly African American neighborhood on the west side of town, organized a twenty-mile protest march to call attention to the fact that their children were bused that far to attend school when an all-white school was just two miles from their homes. In the Sunnyside neighborhood, a poor area south of downtown, H-HCEOO community organizers found that residents had recently formed the Sunnyside Housing Committee through which they were attempting to put pressure on the Houston city council to prevent slumlords from building inadequate and unsafe housing in that part of the city. Members began showing up at Houston city council meetings in October to demand a change in the city's building code and an end to land zoning practices that allowed unscrupulous residential builders to erect high-density, low-quality housing that had a tendency of turning older neighborhoods into "instant slums." When H-HCEOO community organizers arrived in Sunnyside, they did not have to search for very long to find a major gut issue. With the help of the organizers, Sunnyside Housing Committee members launched a protest campaign against the real estate developers who were beginning to build slum housing in the area. In November 1966 approximately fifty people marched in front of the proposed building sites carrying signs that read "Don't Move In" and "I Wouldn't Let My Dog Live in These Shacks." Clarence White, leader of the protest, told members of the press to spread their message all across the city of Houston. "This is pathetic," White exclaimed. "What kind of kids could you raise in those shacks? This is what breeds crime. People say, 'Why so much crime among the Negroes?' Then they come out here and help build crime." Addressing the other marchers, White pointed out that the slums were being built by two real estate developers—one white and one black, although the race of the guilty parties was of no real importance. White continued, "It doesn't matter what color your skin is. If you're moving shacks into Sunnyside, we're your enemy." Other marchers told the reporters that this protest was only the beginning of their effort to take control of their own neighborhood.[39]

The involvement of H-HCEOO employees in protest activities provoked many questions from city officials and Houston residents about the proper role of poverty workers and community organizers around the city. In response to these questions, Ballew defended both the organizers' actions and the use of protest demonstrations. "It seems to me our organizers are going to have to be with the people and work with them," argued Ballew to a *Houston Post* reporter.

"As long as the protests are peaceful, I see nothing wrong with our people taking part in them." Federal OEO officials helped bolster Ballew's confidence in Allen and the use of Alinsky-style community organization. During an official inspection of the War on Poverty in Houston conducted in February 1967, members of an OEO inspection team concluded in their report that Ballew had improved the antipoverty effort in Houston when he became H-HCEOO chairman through the hiring of Earl Allen and an increased focus on community organizing. One OEO inspector noted that the success of the community-organizing effort was apparent all over the city and that Allen's community organization staff was "reaching someone in Houston since they are creating a great deal of foment." Another inspector commented that Allen was "bright, imaginative, and knowledgeable about the process of community organization" and possessed the necessary competence to iron out any problems that naturally would arise from trying to organize the poor. This kind of encouragement from federal War on Poverty administrators undoubtedly made it easier for Ballew to answer local criticism of applying the Alinsky method in Houston.[40]

It was clear by the spring of 1967 that Earl Allen's community-organizing efforts, particularly in the Settegast area, were paying dividends to poor residents and were actually changing the meaning of democracy. Ballew could finally boast that the Community Action Program being carried out by H-HCEOO was waging a concerted attack on the root causes of poverty in Houston and was enjoying a degree of success and a series of small but important victories. The organization's neighborhood centers were bringing poor residents into the administration of the poverty program, and Allen's staff was organizing residents into powerful blocs capable of forcing the city's elected officials and institutions to respond to the needs of poor communities. The Saul Alinsky method seemed to be off to a great start during Ballew's first year as H-HCEOO chairman, primarily because he enjoyed a tremendous amount of support from his staff and OEO officials in Washington. Ballew's organization was not the only agency attempting to implement a Community Action Program in Houston, however, as HAY members continued to compete with H-HCEOO leaders to make their organization the sole community action agency in the city.

While H-HCEOO members focused on community organizing in an attempt to empower poor communities to challenge Houston's public officials and local institutions, HAY directors continued to use a service-delivery approach and employed professional social workers in their attempt to eradicate poverty in one small section of the city on the north side of town. In January 1966 HAY contracted with Houston's Day Care Association to administer a small Head Start program in their target neighborhood that would reach approximately ninety preschoolers. In April HAY members teamed up with the Texas Employment Commission to seek out neighborhood residents considered unemployable and begin training them for unskilled and low-skilled jobs in the city. The assumption driving the program, of course, was that Houston's unemployed citizens lacked jobs simply because they were unaware of how to locate them. A representative from the Texas Employment Commission (TEC) stated that "it's quite possible that we can tap a labor supply that heretofore we were not able to reach." There is no evidence that the HAY-TEC program developers ever considered the role of institutional racism and discrimination, or the lack of power poor citizens had over their own lives, in their unemployment status. Soon after HAY and TEC initiated the program, many neighborhood residents began complaining about the attitudes of the HAY canvassers who were seeking out the unemployed. It seems a paternalistic and condescending attitude had taken hold among the HAY staff. One antipoverty activist who worked in the target neighborhood but was not affiliated with HAY commented that several residents "say some of the canvassers act as though they are afraid of getting dirty when they enter the neighborhood."[41]

HAY members also administered traditional services that dated back to the organization's founding mission to address problems of juvenile delinquency in Houston. For example, HAY continued funding homeless shelters for runaway youths, family counseling services, home management programs, counseling services for troubled youths, day care and nursery services, and neighborhood activity centers. In addition to these services, HAY launched a new program in the spring of 1966 called "Operation Medicare Alert." When OEO officials realized late in 1965 that only a few eligible elderly persons across the country had registered for Medicare benefits, planners developed a program to increase the number of older Americans enrolled in the new federally funded hospital insurance program. OEO officials exported this new program to local community action agencies in January 1966, and HAY personnel decided to participate in its implementation in their target neighborhood. With a $7,500 grant from OEO, HAY staff members knocked on doors in their target neighborhood in search of elderly residents who had not yet signed up for Medicare benefits. By the end of March, they had assisted more than 1,000 residents in applying for Medicare.[42]

Ballew realized that although the services offered by HAY administrators were indeed helpful to poor residents, the fact remained that HAY leaders were doing virtually nothing in Houston's poor neighborhoods to address the problem of powerlessness. Indeed, there were fundamental philosophical differences between the way each antipoverty organization approached the War on Poverty and particularly the Community Action Program. The federal OEO inspection team that visited Houston in February 1967 recognized the clear dichotomy between HAY's nearly total focus on the delivery of social services, to the exclusion of community organizing, and H-HCEOO's devotion to community organization but reluctance to administer programs or services. OEO officials unanimously agreed that H-HCEOO was more successful than HAY in attacking the root causes of poverty and in making a real difference in their target neighborhoods. One OEO inspector stated in her report that H-HCEOO was clearly the stronger anti-poverty organization and that Earl Allen's efforts to provide a way for the poor to identify their own needs and exert pressure on the city's public officials were proving fruitful. Because H-HCEOO community organizers were successful in "creating ripples" in the power structure, they had been able to achieve some small victories and cause some changes to occur. The inspection team concluded that Ballew's pronouncement that the city's white power structure was "afraid of us" might indeed be true given the responsiveness of local institutions to the various protests and demonstrations that H-HCEOO had been involved in over the previous few months. Another OEO inspector stated that H-HCEOO more clearly resembled a legitimate and effective community action agency, noting that Allen's community organization effort was enjoying some success in mobilizing the poor communities of Houston and empowering poor residents to exert pressure on the city's institutions. While they expressed some concern about the lack of service programs offered by H-HCEOO, OEO officials concluded that Ballew's agency, and especially Earl Allen's community organization efforts, were showing clear signs of effecting needed change in Houston.[43]

The OEO inspection team's assessment of HAY's antipoverty activities in Houston, on the other hand, was in sharp contrast to their evaluation of H-HCEOO. Though OEO officials recognized that HAY's social service programs were well administered, they nevertheless reported that the majority of these programs were in the "low-priority category." One federal inspector was especially concerned that HAY only operated in one fairly isolated part of the city and that even in this small area, HAY directors had been unable to perform any comprehensive community planning. While a few of the programs provided social services that residents desperately needed, the inspection team reported that the programs were "geared toward alleviating the symptoms of poverty rather than effecting its causes." Though HAY enjoyed a good reputation among the traditional welfare and social service organizations in the city, unfortunately it had "minimal success in mobilizing those resources" to initiate a concerted and unified assault on poverty. Another federal inspector commented that HAY's board of directors was "primarily a rubber stamp" and had very little control over the actual operations of the agency. More alarming to the inspection team, however, was the assessment that although HAY had been operating in Houston for five years, it "has had almost no impact" on the plight of the poor in the city and had the reputation of being a "nice program" that did not "rock the boat." To make matters worse, federal OEO inspectors discovered that many African American and Mexican American residents of HAY's target neighborhood considered HAY director Helen Lewis to be quite prejudiced in her decisions concerning the poverty program.[44]

The relatively safe and nonconfrontational tactics of HAY sharply contrasted with the direct-action approach of H-HCEOO under Ballew's leadership. Federal OEO inspectors clearly favored Ballew's more confrontational interpretation of the community action concept because it seemed to offer an effective method for attacking poverty in Houston. While HAY's professional staff delivered a few social services in one isolated community in the city, H-HCEOO members organized poor residents into powerful blocs capable of making demands on the city's officials and institutions and offering a challenge to mainstream definitions of democracy. Ballew recognized the fact that when the federal War on Poverty funding inevitably dried up, most of HAY's service programs would disappear and the agency itself would return to being a small-scale traditional welfare organization with a severely limited impact on poverty in Houston. By bringing about lasting democratic change in the city, Ballew and other H-HCEOO leaders hoped to address the needs of the poor by empowering residents to take control of their own lives. As any good Saul Alinsky disciple would have argued, Ballew operated on the idea that community organization and empowerment of the poor held the keys to effecting significant and permanent change in Houston's poor neighborhoods and attacking the root causes of poverty in the city.

Although Ballew's interpretation of the community action concept delivered some significant victories in Houston's poor neighborhoods in the fall of 1966, it is clear in hindsight that there were several external factors that allowed H-HCEOO members to implement their aggressive vision in an uninhibited way, despite the city's "pervasive conservatism" that Houston historian David G. McComb described. First, the overwhelming support Ballew received from OEO officials in Washington was essential for H-HCEOO leaders to continue implementing an aggressive Community Action Program in Houston. In the days before a conservative mood took hold in Washington in 1967, which resulted in the decision to allow public officials to take control of the Community Action Program, OEO officials were often openly supportive of aggressive and confrontational community action agencies around the country. When OEO officials began retreating from this confrontational interpretation of the community action concept in 1967, however, it produced a negative effect on antipoverty organizations like H-HCEOO, whose leaders had depended on support from Washington. Second, for a few months during the fall of 1966, Ballew implemented his aggressive vision in a relatively friendly environment free of vocal opposition from Houston's elected officials, primarily because H-HCEOO staff members initiated their activities quickly and the city's public officials had little time to devise an attack on Ballew and Allen's methods. By the spring of 1967, however, the situation had changed as Houston's mayor and police chief began cracking down on Ballew's activities, particularly with regard to community organization. Finally, during the fall of 1966, Ballew enjoyed the support of the majority of the H-HCEOO board and staff, and this undoubtedly emboldened him to implement his ambitious program without restraint. During the following year, however, as local elected officials launched an attack on H-HCEOO and OEO officials backed away from their open support of Ballew's vision, the H-HCEOO board and staff members began defying Ballew's leadership. In other words, the window of opportunity for using the War on Poverty to expand democracy began to close by the beginning of 1967. While Ballew had all three of these things working in his favor as 1966 drew to a close, the spring of 1967 brought significant changes to the situation in Houston that threatened to undo Ballew's aggressive Community Action Program and completely destroy the reputation of the Saul Alinsky method in the city.

Louie Welch, mayor
of Houston from
1964 to 1973. Photo
reprinted with permission
from the Houston
Metropolitan Research
Center (HMRC), Houston
Public Library, Houston,
Tex., Mayor Book-Welch.

Louie Welch (left) and Leon Jaworski (right) speaking to two unidentified women, 1964. Photo reprinted with permission from the HMRC, *Houston Post* Negatives, RGD006-1964-6568 FR002.

Herman Short being sworn in as Houston's chief of police, 1964. Photo reprinted with permission from the HMRC, *Houston Post* Negatives, RGD006-1964-7698 FR020.

The Reverend Wallace "Bud" Poteat (left), pastor of the Ecumenical Fellowship United Church of Christ and creator of the Latin American Channel Project, raises a flag with an unidentified man. Photo reprinted with permission from the HMRC, VISTA Collection, RGF10-0040.

African American and white children participate in an integrated summer church school led by the Reverend Wallace "Bud" Poteat, 1964. Photo reprinted with permission from the HMRC, VISTA Collection, RGF10-0022.

A VISTA volunteer plays pool with neighborhood teenagers at the Ecumenical Fellowship's LAC Project Teen Center. Photo reprinted with permission from the HMRC, VISTA Collection, RGF10-0032.

A VISTA volunteer makes a sign for the Ecumenical Fellowship's LAC Project Teen Center. Photo reprinted with permission from the HMRC, VISTA Collection, RGF10-0017.

William V. Ballew Jr., chairman of the Houston–Harris County Economic Opportunity Organization (H-HCEOO) from 1966 to 1967. Photo reprinted with permission from the HMRC, *Houston Post* Negatives, RGD006 FR004.

REV. EARL ALLEN announcing his resignation as director of HOPE.

Earl Allen, Methodist minister and director of community organization for the Houston–Harris County Economic Opportunity Organization from 1966 to 1967. Photo reprinted with permission from the HMRC, *Voice of Hope* Collection, 10-6-64 p001.

Sunnyside residents march in protest of real estate developers building "instant slums" in November 1966. Photo reprinted with permission from the HMRC, *Houston Post* Negatives, RGD006-11-7-66 FR18A.

Francis Williams, prominent Houston attorney and NAACP chapter president, served as the board chairman and later as executive director of the merged Harris County Community Action Association (HCCAA) beginning in 1967. Photo reprinted with permission from the HMRC, *Houston Post* Negatives, RGD006-1969-0432 FR025.

Hartsell Gray, an Episcopal minister involved in Houston's poverty program since 1965, was put in charge of Earl Allen and his community organization staff in 1967. Photo reprinted with permission from the HMRC, *Houston Post* Negatives, RGD006-1976-1223 FR017.

Houston police officers arrest TSU student and activist Lee Otis Johnson,
April 1967. Photo reprinted with permission from the HMRC, *Houston Post*
Negatives, RGD006-2654.

Texas Southern University students (from left) Lee Otis Johnson, F. D. Kirkpatrick, and James Alexander in court after their arrest, May 1967. Photo reprinted with permission from the HMRC, *Houston Post* Negatives, RGD006-1420 FR19A.

FOUR

A Closing Window of Opportunity for Expanding Democracy

Houston's Public Officials and the Taming of the Community Action Program, 1967

For several months in the winter of 1966–1967, William Ballew encountered few obstacles in his quest to implement an aggressive vision for Houston's Community Action Program based on the Saul Alinsky method. Ballew helped launch a comprehensive Legal Services program, expanded social services in the city's poorest neighborhoods, and, of most importance, dedicated much of H-HCEOO's resources to community organizing. With the hiring of Earl Allen to supervise a 140-member community organization staff, Ballew made a clear statement that H-HCEOO would place a heavy emphasis on empowering poor communities to challenge Houston's public officials and expand the meaning of democracy. For a brief moment it appeared that the Saul Alinsky method would be efficacious in the city as Ballew, Allen, and the community organization staff achieved a series of small yet significant victories. These ranged from improved city sanitation services to the creation of a badly needed health clinic in one of Houston's most impoverished neighborhoods. Ballew was able to make Houston's Community Action Program a success mainly because he enjoyed a supportive environment for the implementation of his vision along with little organized opposition from local elected officials or other defenders of the status quo. Between September 1966 and February 1967, OEO officials in Washington and Austin provided almost unconditional support for Ballew's vision, while Houston's public officials had yet to devise their own plan for resisting the rapidly increasing number of demands being made upon city officials by poor residents.

During the spring of 1967, however, many of Houston's public officials, particularly Mayor Louie Welch, U.S. congressman George H. W. Bush, and Police Chief Herman Short, launched a concerted assault on H-HCEOO and its leaders in order to reassert some degree of control over the changes occurring in the city and specifically over the activities of Allen's community organization staff. Welch and Bush had been active participants in the creation of H-HCEOO in 1965, and they handpicked several members of the organization's board of directors and executive committee. When William Ballew became H-HCEOO chairman in January 1966, however, he distanced the organization from city officials and curtailed any influence Welch and Bush might have previously enjoyed over the poverty program in the city. Since he was a believer in the Saul Alinsky method, Ballew cut H-HCEOO's ties with the city's public officials because he planned to organize Houston's poor residents to challenge that very structure and make demands on city officials. Only by liberating H-HCEOO from the constraints of Welch and Bush could Ballew effectively implement his confrontational vision for the Community Action Program in Houston.

Police Chief Short, on the other hand, who had a reputation as a notorious racist, seems to have opposed the idea of a War on Poverty in the city from the very beginning and was prepared to attack H-HCEOO's activities as soon as he could gain Welch's approval. By the spring of 1967 Welch and Bush found themselves completely alienated from the poverty program in Houston and were growing increasingly alarmed at the speed with which Ballew, Allen, and the community organization staff had mobilized many of the city's poor neighborhoods to engage in collective political action. Beginning in February 1967, Welch, Bush, and Short worked together to attack the community organization strategy developed by Ballew and Allen, to limit the expansion of democracy sought by activists, and to discredit the organization that had shut out the three of them from the poverty program in Houston.

A series of events during the spring of 1967 provided Houston's public officials with the ammunition they needed to attack Ballew's vision for the city's Community Action Program. Welch, Bush, and Short, growing more impatient with the community organization strategies developed by Ballew and Allen, exploited these events in order to discredit the Saul Alinsky method and reassert their control over the War on Poverty. While Ballew, Allen, and the H-HCEOO community organization staff had won some small yet important victories— organizing poor residents all over the city and empowering them to make demands on the city's public officials and local institutions—their efforts in Settegast, where they had enjoyed their greatest achievements in the spring of 1967, backfired when several powerful figures in the neighborhood revolted against H-HCEOO's efforts. The turmoil this revolt caused in Settegast provided the city's public officials with ammunition to attack H-HCEOO's activities. On the heels of the Settegast revolt, several H-HCEOO staff members became involved in a disturbance on the campus of Texas Southern University (TSU) that became known as the "TSU Riot." Amid the accompanying media coverage, several of Houston's public officials launched a public attack on H-HCEOO by appealing to widespread fear and paranoia about the threat of urban rioting—the specter of another Watts, Newark, or Detroit—and associating H-HCEOO's activities with events at TSU. The fallout from the Settegast revolt and the TSU riot pushed the H-HCEOO board of directors into a defensive position and persuaded them to rein in some of their community organization efforts. As a result, an uprising erupted among the H-HCEOO staff that split the agency into two competing factions. To complicate matters even further, OEO officials in Washington and Austin decided in the spring of 1967 that they could no longer fund two separate community action agencies in Houston, meaning that H-HCEOO and HAY would have to merge to form a single organization. Meanwhile, a citywide backlash formed against the practices of H-HCEOO community organizers, who were now viewed by many as troublemakers. This backlash, coupled with sustained attacks from the city's public officials, forced the H-HCEOO board into an even more defensive posture as a more cautious philosophy began to take hold among the board members.

These four events during the spring of 1967—the Settegast revolt, the TSU Riot, the H-HCEOO staff uprising, and the forced merger of H-HCEOO and HAY—were the precipitating factors that forced the H-HCEOO board of directors to go on the defensive and provided an opening for Houston's public officials and defenders of the status quo to attack H-HCEOO's activities. This sequence of events ultimately resulted in the abandonment of Ballew's aggressive vision for community organization and empowerment of the poor, allowing Welch, Bush, and Short to reassert their control over the poverty program. In only four months the concerted attack waged by Welch, Bush, and Short tamed H-HCEOO's activities in Houston, and by the end of May 1967 the environment in which H-HCEOO operated in Houston had changed dramatically. Just a few months after Ballew, Allen, and the H-HCEOO community organization staff achieved some of their greatest accomplishments, the H-HCEOO board, in response to the attack from the city's public officials, quickly retreated from its confrontational interpretation of the community action concept. The board forced Ballew out of office, reined in the activities of Allen and his community organization staff, and committed themselves to a limited program of social service delivery. Ballew's experiment in applying the Saul Alinsky method in Houston thus ended just as activists were beginning to achieve some small but important victories in their quest to expand democracy.

In Settegast, where Allen's community organization staff had experienced the most success, H-HCEOO's activities produced a backlash from Houston's public officials that was aided by several local business and religious leaders. These indigenous forces managed to use the mounting criticism of Allen's community organization staff, as voiced by the city's public officials, to ignite a revolt among some poor Settegast residents against many of H-HCEOO's activities. Though the marches, rallies, and other protest activities had produced tangible results for Settegast residents, they also undoubtedly alerted Houston's public officials that area residents had organized and were prepared and equipped to make demands for city services. The quest to obtain a branch of the general hospital in Settegast resulted in the final victory for residents that did not also produce a counterattack from public officials or disapproving Houstonians.

About the same time as the new Settegast Clinic opened its doors to area residents, H-HCEOO community organizers faced a major setback in their efforts to empower poor residents to use their constitutional right to vote. When Earl Allen's community organization staff first arrived in Settegast, they immediately began registering area residents to vote. In order to register as many new voters as possible, H-HCEOO staff members went door-to-door with voter registration forms and assisted neighborhood residents with filling them out correctly. As soon as an entire section of Settegast had been canvassed, community organizers delivered the voter registration forms to the Harris County Tax Assessor-Collector, who would add the new voters to the rolls. From the very beginning of the voter registration drive, H-HCEOO community organizers faced the accusation that their actions were illegal because they were not official deputies authorized to register voters. Jim Mayor, the Republican Party chairman for Harris County who was instrumental in the effort to break the hold of the Democratic Party in Houston and across the South, issued a statement in January 1967 criticizing H-HCEOO's voter registration efforts and claimed that the community organizers in Settegast were violating the Texas Election Code. George H. W. Bush, the newly elected Republican congressman from Houston, also publicly questioned the legality of the voter registration drive in Settegast. For Bush, of course, the prospect of a large group of new voters who were poor and mostly nonwhite had political implications that struck close to home. As Bush stated in a letter to a Houston business acquaintance, "I have heard that in Houston they undertook a voter registration drive but restricted it to the Negro areas. This, of course, would not bode well for yours truly at the polls. But, more importantly, I don't believe this has anything to do with the alleviation of poverty." H-HCEOO executive director Charles Kelly and Earl Allen responded to Bush's public criticism of the voter registration drive by pointing out that community organizers were not actually registering voters but simply assisting neighborhood residents in filling out the forms correctly and delivering the completed forms to the appropriate office. Kelly pointed out that the forms that H-HCEOO community organizers had been taking door-to-door in Settegast were exactly the same as the forms that were printed daily in the Houston newspapers. Not only were the community organizers clearly following local election laws, but the voter registration drive also had the prior approval of the Harris County Tax Assessor-Collector's office.[1]

On the morning of January 17, 1967, Republican fears of the addition of thousands of new voters, many of whom were expected to vote Democratic, were allayed when an arsonist set fire to the H-HCEOO community center in Settegast and destroyed more than two thousand completed voter registration forms that had yet to be turned over to the tax assessor-collector. Also destroyed in the fire were records from an H-HCEOO investigation into home contract sales in Settegast, which had uncovered the unfair "contract for deed" arrangements that were prevalent in the area. Houston arson investigators determined that the fire had been set deliberately, and in a more shocking discovery they concluded that there had been no forced entry into the community center building. In other words, whoever set the fire had in his or her possession a key to the center. Though Houston police investigators questioned a few suspects, they were unable to find the person or persons responsible for the fire. Appalled by the inconclusiveness of the investigation, Charles Kelly issued a public statement, in which he declared there was considerable evidence that the motive for the fire was the destruction of the voter registration forms. Kelly also announced that he had requested a full investigation from the Federal Bureau of Investigation, citing a violation of the Settegast residents' civil rights and an attempt to deny citizens' right to vote.[2]

The controversy surrounding H-HCEOO's voter registration drive in Settegast, as well as the arson that it provoked, caused some neighborhood residents to begin criticizing the activities of Earl Allen's community organization staff. In the wake of the arson came an event that further divided the Settegast community and served to undermine Allen's community-organizing efforts. In January 1967 a deputy constable appeared at the doorstep of Settegast resident Betty Gentry, who was pregnant, to carry out an eviction order. The deputy constable ordered Gentry out of her home and began removing her belongings from inside the house. When Gentry's plea that she was being wrongly evicted went unheeded, she began making a telephone call to her landlord. At that point the confrontation turned physical. "When I was on the phone," Gentry recalled, "one of the men pushed me. . . . I hit him with the phone to defend myself; he threw me by the hair into the bedroom and handcuffed me and threw me across the bed." After removing all of Gentry's belongings from the house, the deputy constable arrested her and charged her with aggravated assault. A few hours later, as news of the altercation spread throughout the neighborhood, hundreds of angry Settegast residents showed up at Gentry's home and staged a spontaneous protest that lasted until the early morning hours the next day.[3]

Later that evening more than two thousand Settegast residents met at a local Baptist church and signed a petition calling for the immediate dismissal of the deputy constable who evicted Gentry. The residents vowed to protest at City Hall until their demand was answered. Earl Allen immediately recognized this as a "gut issue" that could be used to mobilize Settegast residents to confront the city's public officials about the problems of unfair housing contracts and police brutality. As Allen later explained, "Eviction wasn't the real issue. The real issues are lack of adequate housing which permits profiteers to insist on unfair terms, and the intimidation of the poor by police. But the people are concerned because a pregnant woman was roughed up. We had to help them to do something right then. Once mobilized they can get at other issues." The way Allen and his community organization staff chose to assist the residents in mobilizing to protest the treatment of Ms. Gentry was to help them secure transportation to downtown Houston to carry out a protest at City Hall. H-HCEOO representatives contracted with Pioneer Bus Company to provide three buses, but in anticipation of criticism the arrangement disallowed using federal money for the protest or the buses. Settegast residents would pay the bill themselves by raising money in the community in support of Betty Gentry.[4]

Approximately eighty Settegast residents boarded buses a few days later and headed toward City Hall in downtown Houston. Though the protest did not result in the dismissal of the deputy constable, it did force a response from city and county officials. Precinct 1 constable W. H. Rankin, the deputy constable's immediate supervisor, told the protesters that Gentry was "agitated during the eviction proceedings" and at some point during the scuffle she struck the deputy constable. "We can't allow our men to be beaten and abused," argued Rankin. "We only serve the papers after the court has decided on the eviction." Earl Allen himself could not have portrayed the situation more succinctly and accurately. Betty Gentry was not simply roughed up by one county constable; rather, she was the victim of an intricate web of oppression that included unscrupulous profiteers, local city ordinances, the courts, and law enforcement officials. Protesting the treatment of Gentry was simply an avenue through which to confront the structural and institutional problems facing Settegast residents. As Allen had hoped, the protest at City Hall and the response by local officials were excellent illustrations of how a "gut issue" could alert poor residents to major problems like inadequate housing, unfair business practices, and police brutality.[5]

Even though H-HCEOO staff members had been careful not to use any federal funds to provide buses for the protest at City Hall, controversy soon arose because the Pioneer Bus Company overcharged the Settegast group and sent the bill directly to H-HCEOO. Community organizers initially believed they would need eight buses for the protest but at the last minute decided they only needed three. An H-HCEOO official was supposed to cancel the five extra buses, but because of a miscommunication, the cancellation never happened. As a result, Settegast residents were charged for eight buses, and the amount was more than they could afford. Local public officials finally had some potent ammunition with which to attack the community action agency's protest activities.

When Mayor Welch and Congressman Bush erroneously charged H-HCEOO with using federal funds to stage the protest, the local newspapers repeated the charge and provoked a firestorm of criticism aimed at the organization. Though H-HCEOO executive director Charles Kelly repeatedly assured the public that no federal poverty funds were used for the protest, the damage had been done. The reputation of Earl Allen's community organization effort in Settegast suffered a major setback.[6]

The controversy surrounding the voter registration drive and the protests at City Hall prompted some Settegast residents to begin voicing more loudly their opposition to H-HCEOO and Earl Allen's community-organizing efforts in their neighborhood. Several ministers and older residents complained that H-HCEOO organizers were bypassing existing community leadership and attempting to create a new force for change that was both more confrontational and less effective than groups that had already been established in the neighborhood. Local precinct judges voiced their displeasure about Allen's voter registration campaign because they believed there were adequate block workers and deputies to register everyone in Settegast who wanted to vote and that H-HCEOO workers' efforts were a wasteful duplication of services. Other residents of the area showed up at an H-HCEOO board of directors meeting in February 1967 to complain about being disrespected and even threatened by H-HCEOO staff members in Settegast. One neighborhood resident told the H-HCEOO board that staff members in Settegast had accomplished some good things, "but I'm saying OEO is not doing the job it was designed to do. It is causing neighbor to look funny at neighbor. OEO people shouldn't have a superior attitude and look down on people."[7]

In the wake of the demonstration at City Hall against the treatment of Betty Gentry, members of the Settegast Civic Club, an organization that had existed longer than the poverty program and included several business and religious leaders, expressed fear that protest activity in Settegast was going too far and that Earl Allen and his staff were encouraging violence. The Reverend Rancier Worsham, a prominent Baptist minister in Settegast, publicly disagreed with the way Allen and H-HCEOO staff members handled the eviction situation. Worsham stated, "I would have preferred to talk things over with the offended person and the constable before making a commitment. Then we would know how important it was. Instead, teen-agers have been stirred up by [H-HCEOO] staff . . . and are going off half-cocked." Another Settegast resident, who had been involved in the campaign to get pure drinking water for the neighborhood from the city, commented that there was danger of "a year's hard work being lost, with people trying to start trouble." One neighborhood resident, who had been active in the effort to improve public schools in Settegast, objected to the request by H-HCEOO community organization staff members for parents to keep their children out of the schools so they could join the protest at City Hall, saying, "It seems to me this stirs people up, that it hinders the community instead of helping it." A rumor that the H-HCEOO board was going to bring Stokely Carmichael, the Black Power advocate and head of the Student Nonviolent Coordinating Committee, into Settegast to help organize poor people also contributed to a feeling among the established leaders that their authority was being threatened.[8]

Earl Allen responded to these complaints and criticisms with characteristic poise. "Poverty communities are highly organized," he argued, "and the leaders feel threatened when the organization starts to change." These changes, according to Allen, were absolutely necessary to address the problems of poverty in Settegast in any meaningful way. "The problem is that the present structure isn't adequate for changing the situation," he continued. "If it was, we wouldn't have a poverty community. Either the leaders don't represent enough people or their methods haven't proved effective. People in these communities are apathetic, not because they don't want to change their situation, but because they're hopeless, deprived of dignity and frustrated from years of methods which don't work." Allen reiterated that his goal was to organize the Settegast community and create an environment where new and vigorous leadership could arise to help solve the problems of poverty. As for the charge that his staff was fomenting violence in Settegast, Allen responded that there "is more danger of violence in a leaderless community than in one with effective leadership." Despite Allen's reassuring comments about his community-organizing activities in Settegast, in March a large group of Settegast residents picketed H-HCEOO's neighborhood office and accused Allen's staff of "destroying our community" and "organizing children against their parents."[9]

Under Ballew's leadership, H-HCEOO had provided unequivocal support for Earl Allen and his community organization staff since the fall of 1966. Faced with the prospect of public demonstrations against H-HCEOO that might threaten the entire poverty program, however, the board changed course and launched an investigation into the activities of the community organization staff in Settegast. Though the investigation panel found no specific violations of OEO policy in Settegast, in order to cool down the immediate tensions the board's executive director Charles Kelly nevertheless ordered the removal of the entire community organization staff from the area and reassigned them to other parts of Houston. Kelly issued a tepid statement with his decision that hardly justified removing the staff from the area. He explained, "Some people seem to be unhappy with the way the kids are acting. Perhaps our staff has been involved in encouraging kids to become involved in community problems. I don't know. Some people just don't want their kids doing what they're doing. That is, being concerned with . . . improving things in the community." Despite the vague explanation he provided, it was clear that one of the factors motivating Kelly to re-assign the community organization staff was to prevent further protests against H-HCEOO and its activities around the city. His decision had the opposite effect, however, as approximately thirty young people staged a sit-in at the H-HCEOO office the following day and demanded the return of Allen's staff to Settegast.[10]

By April 1967, residents of Settegast were deeply divided over the role of community organizing in the War on Poverty, and the H-HCEOO staff had been pulled out of the area. More important, Charles Kelly and members of the H-HCEOO board of directors had begun a slight retreat from their determination to focus on community organizing and the empowerment of poor residents to challenge Houston's public officials and begin reforming its institutions. This backing-off from Ballew's vision hindered the way Ballew and Allen continued to implement their interpretation of the community action concept in Houston. The ordeal in Settegast, however, was only the first in a series of events that ultimately led to a complete retreat from community organizing and a subduing of H-HCEOO as a force for change in Houston. The three other major events that occurred during the spring of 1967—the riot on the campus of Texas Southern University, the H-HCEOO staff revolt, and the forced merger of H-HCEOO and HAY—followed the conflict in Settegast and together drove Ballew, Kelly, and the H-HCEOO board into a defensive position from which they never recovered.

The troubled spring semester of 1967 on the campus of Texas Southern University had its roots in the change in university leadership that occurred the previous fall. The Texas legislature had created TSU in 1947 to serve as a supposed educational equivalent to the University of Texas. Located in the lower-middle-class African American neighborhood known as the Third Ward, TSU would serve African American students and thus allow higher education in the state to remain racially segregated. TSU had been presided over since 1955 by Samuel Nabrit, who during his eleven-year tenure as president attempted to expand the role of the university in the Houston community and supported efforts to desegregate the city. For example, during the late 1950s and early 1960s Nabrit commended TSU students who took the lead in efforts to desegregate public facilities in Houston, which included several demonstrations and sit-ins. When Nabrit resigned his position in 1966 to assume an appointment to the Atomic Energy Commission, his replacement as TSU president held a different view of the proper role of the university and its students. Joseph A. Pierce, Nabrit's successor who served as president of the university for only one year from the fall of 1966 to the spring of 1967, was described by Houston historian Dwight Watson as "deferential to whites" and intent on controlling the TSU student population. Many TSU students characterized Pierce as "reactionary, rigid, and inflexible." As Watson argued, Pierce's "heavy-handed leadership set the stage for confrontations between students and the administration."[11]

During the fall of 1966 a group of TSU students formed an organization they called "Friends of SNCC" and requested official university recognition as a campus organization. One of the requirements for securing official university recognition was that each organization obtain a faculty sponsor, and to meet this condition the Friends of SNCC chose Mack Jones, a seasoned civil rights worker who came to TSU as an instructor in the social sciences department during the fall of 1966. The TSU administration did allow the Friends of SNCC to hold meetings on campus, but despite the fact that the organization's members had found a faculty sponsor, administrators never officially recognized them as a campus organization. Above all, TSU administrators, especially Pierce, feared that the leaders of Friends of SNCC were trying to stir up trouble on campus and were especially susceptible to the influence of outside agitators. In early March 1967, members of the Friends of SNCC led a rambunctious crowd of approximately a hundred participants in a downtown march protesting police brutality against African Americans in Houston, increasing Pierce's skepticism of the organization. Friends of SNCC members held the protest in response to accusations by four African American gospel singers that Texas highway patrolmen had brutalized them during a traffic stop just outside the Houston city limits. During the march some of the participants shouted slogans like "Black Power" and "Burn Baby Burn" as others carried signs reading, "Whitey, the days for black nonviolence are over—are yours?" and "Welch, help stop police brutality or Houston will be a billion dollar graveyard." After the demonstration, TSU administrators met with Friends of SNCC and Mack Jones, their faculty sponsor, to inform them that their organization would no longer be allowed to meet on campus and that further discussions concerning university recognition were out of the question.[12]

One week later TSU administrators further infuriated members of the organization by declining to renew Mack Jones's teaching contract for the next year. The firing of Jones rallied formerly uninterested students to the Friends of SNCC, and several members of the faculty called for an investigation into the administration's firing of Jones. The tension-filled weeks that followed were marked by a series of class boycotts that spilled into the university's final exam schedule. On April 13, 1967, in the midst of the turmoil, Stokely Carmichael came to Houston to speak on the nearby campus of the University of Houston. Though Mayor Welch and Houston police chief Herman Short were both fearful that Carmichael would incite TSU and University of Houston students to riot, Carmichael gave a rather moderate speech about the importance of reclaiming black culture and opposing the war in Vietnam. When asked about the demonstrations and class boycotts at TSU, Carmichael stated, "It was a long time coming," but he opted not to lead a march to the TSU campus after his speech.[13]

Though Carmichael's speech did not live up to the fears of Welch and Short, after Carmichael's visit to Houston the demonstrations and boycotts on the TSU campus intensified. The Friends of SNCC began with only two demands—that their organization be recognized by the university administration and that Mack Jones be reinstated as an instructor. By mid-April 1967, however, a campus-wide student uprising had gained momentum as the students' demands now included extended curfew hours, increased salaries for all faculty and university employees, removal of armed security officers from the campus, creation of a student court with authority equal to the dean of students, addition of black literature to the university library shelves, improved cafeteria food, freedom of student organizations to bring to campus any speaker of their choice, and removal of the dean of students from the local draft board. While the student movement was intensifying at TSU, the Houston police department began a surveillance operation on the campus designed to keep tabs on the student activists. Police Chief Short began securing arrest warrants for leaders of the boycotts. Short also increased the number of undercover and uniformed officers in and around the TSU campus, a move that further enraged the student demonstrators.[14]

Through this increased police presence city officials learned about the involvement of Houston's poverty workers in the demonstrations at TSU. Carl Moore, a TSU student and part-time employee of Houston Action for Youth, had participated in the demonstrations on campus in early April. Police also discovered that the Reverend Bill Lawson, who was the director of the Upward Bound program at TSU and often served as an informal adviser to Ballew, had provided blankets and food to students staging a sit-in at the city courthouse to demand the release of several activists who had been arrested at TSU. Most damaging, however, was the revelation that Pluria Marshall, a full-time H-HCEOO community organizer, actually led one of the major demonstrations at TSU during the month of April and supplied a bullhorn for student protesters making speeches on campus. Though Marshall had been a frequent critic of the antipoverty efforts of H-HCEOO and once called for the immediate resignation of Charles Kelly, Ballew and Kelly had hired Marshall in December 1966 and placed him on Earl Allen's community organization staff. Police Chief Short eagerly turned over this information to Mayor Welch, who in turn demanded an investigation by the H-HCEOO board and OEO officials in Washington.[15]

After the events in Settegast over the previous few months, H-HCEOO board members were becoming more cautious in their approach to community-organizing efforts and in their response to mounting criticism. After Houston Action for Youth officials terminated Carl Moore's employment for his participation in the TSU demonstrations, Ballew and Kelly decided that Pluria Marshall's actions also required a response from the H-HCEOO board of directors lest public officials use the incident to discredit their organization even further.

Rather than firing him, Earl Allen convinced Ballew and Kelly that Marshall should be placed on an indefinite leave that would allow him to continue leading protest demonstrations at TSU without being affiliated with the poverty program in Houston. Marshall agreed that this arrangement provided the best solution to the problem. In his letter requesting a leave of absence from his community-organizing duties with H-HCEOO, Marshall stated that an indefinite leave was necessary "in order to maintain communication with the [TSU] students to help them keep going in a rational direction. I feel that the respect that they have for me forces me to honor it and do whatever I can to help them." To prevent the appearance of being too soft on Marshall, Ballew and Kelly, in addition to accepting his request for a leave of absence from the organization, also docked Marshall's pay for the six days he abandoned his community-organizing responsibilities to participate in demonstrations on the TSU campus.[16]

Kelly, Ballew, and Allen had underestimated the determination of certain local public officials to attack H-HCEOO. The disciplinary action against Marshall was not enough to satisfy Police Chief Short or Mayor Welch, and in response the two public officials launched an all-out assault on the organization. At one time Welch had been fairly indifferent to the city's antipoverty program. The protests in Settegast, however, had caught the mayor by surprise, and H-HCEOO's participation in the TSU demonstrations embarrassed him. Like officials in other cities, Welch was also fearful of race riots, which had been regularly convulsing the nation's large cities since 1965. As Welch saw it, although H-HCEOO would probably never intentionally incite a riot, their actions might inadvertently contribute to igniting a racial explosion in Houston. When Ballew and Kelly failed to fire Pluria Marshall, Welch initiated a public smear campaign against individuals associated with the organization in order to rein in their more questionable activities. In mid-April, just after Marshall had been granted his indefinite leave of absence, Welch began turning over information to local Houston radio station KTRH 740 AM concerning the involvement of H-HCEOO employees in the uprising at TSU. KTRH broadcasters ran a daily morning report for an entire week alleging that Moore, Lawson, and Marshall had violated OEO policy by being involved in the TSU protests and had used federal funds to help the demonstrators. As the week progressed the accusations got more intense. Citing two officers who worked for the Houston Police Department's Intelligence Division, the radio station reported that Pluria Marshall had admitted to a reporter that he used OEO funds to supply a bullhorn to the TSU protesters, and then Marshall threatened the reporter by saying he would be "whipped" if he mentioned anything about his confession on the air.[17]

By the end of the second week of April 1967, Welch was turning over the full police records of certain H-HCEOO employees to KTRH producers. Although the radio station's broadcasters stopped short of stating the actual names associated with each police file, in many cases they provided just enough information so that nearly anyone who wanted to put the pieces together could figure out the individuals they were referencing. The radio station reported that one particular employee had been arrested for vagrancy and suspicion of being an army dissenter in Galveston in 1948, robbery by firearm in Philadelphia in 1955, and possession of narcotics in Illinois in 1957. The reporter also pointed out that this individual was known to wear Black Panther and SNCC buttons on the TSU campus and had been a leader in the Friends of SNCC organization. The radio station also aired the police record of Earl Allen, pointing out that he had been arrested in Dallas in connection with civil rights protests in the early 1960s and had been instrumental in the Settegast demonstrations at City Hall.[18]

Seeing a battle between the community action agency and local elected officials developing quickly in Houston, OEO officials in Washington wasted no time sending a representative from the Office of Inspection to investigate the allegations being made by Mayor Welch and Police Chief Short. On April 7, 1967, OEO inspector James Simons arrived in Houston and immediately began a thorough inquiry into the accusations against War on Poverty workers in the city. Mayor Welch initially welcomed the investigation, but his attitude toward Simons and OEO changed when Simons turned up no evidence of wrongdoing on the part of H-HCEOO. Simons concluded that no federal funds had been used by any H-HCEOO employee to help the demonstrators at TSU and that the role played by Bill Lawson was entirely "constructive," meaning he helped prevent the situation from becoming any worse by keeping the protesters calm and level headed. He also noted that Lawson had been instrumental in negotiating a truce between the university administration and the student demonstrators to allow for the class boycott to end in early April. As for the role played by Pluria Marshall, Simons found that if Marshall had provided a bullhorn for the protesters, he had definitely not used OEO money to buy it. He also concluded that the disciplinary action that Ballew and Kelly took against Marshall was appropriate for the situation. Simons concluded that no one involved had acted in a way that violated OEO policy and that no one "seemed upset over the involvement of OEO-funded groups except Mayor Welch and the Houston Police Department, who are thought to be opposed to most of the efforts of OEO in Houston." Once Simons sent his report back to OEO in Washington, the situation seemed to settle down in Houston. Another federal OEO official commented in mid-April that the "situation in Houston is presently relatively calm" and that "all is quiet on the Texas Southern University campus."[19]

Though it seemed that Simons's report settled the issue for H-HCEOO, the actual TSU "riot" was still weeks away. Despite the appearance of "quiet" on the campus of TSU, in reality students were still fuming about the heavy-handed leadership of Pierce and the increased police presence on the campus. During the second week of May 1967 several TSU students were involved in a demonstration in the Sunnyside neighborhood protesting the way the city administered a garbage dump in the area. Protesters initiated the demonstration after a young African American boy in the neighborhood was able to get inside the dump and then drowned in a water-filled pit. Houston police officers attempted to disperse the crowd on May 16 and arrested the Reverend Bill Lawson, Earl Allen, and several other protesters on the charge of failure to move on at a police order. Lawson remembered that the police officers got quite rough with the protesters, further infuriating TSU students who had been demonstrating against police brutality for more than a month. When these students returned to the TSU campus later that night and reported on the actions of the Houston police at the Sunnyside dump, tensions that had been seething for several weeks exploded into anger and open hostility toward the increased police presence on campus. When police officers arrested a student who was addressing a crowd about police brutality at the Sunnyside dump protest, angry students began throwing bricks and rocks at passing police cars and white onlookers. Police Chief Short responded by assembling additional officers in full riot gear on the periphery of the campus, a move that further angered the already-indignant student population.[20]

With the situation becoming more volatile by the minute, H-HCEOO officials decided to try to mend their relationship with city officials, particularly with Mayor Welch. Perhaps alarmed at the ease with which Welch carried out a public attack on the organization and possibly encouraged by OEO officials in Washington to hedge their bets, the H-HCEOO board contacted the mayor's office and offered the services of their organization to help restore peace on the TSU campus. This was quite a turnabout for an organization that just a few months prior was totally committed to the organization and empowerment of poor communities to challenge the city's power structure. But the campaign conducted by the mayor and the police chief against H-HCEOO had a profound effect on the organization's leadership. The strategy seemed to work; Welch agreed to release Earl Allen and Bill Lawson from jail if H-HCEOO officials agreed to send them to the TSU campus to talk to the students. In the wake of this development, one OEO official in Houston remarked that H-HCEOO had begun to work actively and cooperatively with representatives of the mayor's office and with the police department, and that the mayor himself had "high praise for their efforts in this difficult situation." As the OEO official proclaimed, "This endorsement under these circumstances . . . represents a major turn around of opinion by the Mayor's office about OEO in Houston."[21]

By the time Lawson and Allen arrived on the TSU campus, many students had already begun destroying property and had barricaded themselves inside one of the student residence halls. A rumor had been circulating on campus that a white man had shot and killed a young African American boy in northeast Houston. Although this rumor proved to be false, the story's circulation at TSU simply added more fuel to the fire. Police officers allowed Lawson and Allen to enter the hall to speak with the students, but to no avail. Moments after Lawson and Allen left the building, gunfire erupted on the campus. It remains unclear whether it was a student or a police officer who fired the first shot, but when it ended, Houston police officers had fired more than five thousand rounds into the dormitory and one officer, Louis R. Kuba, lay dead in a pool of blood. Police Chief Short initially reported that Kuba had been killed by sniper fire coming from the dormitory, but a later investigation concluded that Kuba had been struck by a ricocheting bullet fired from another police officer's gun. Police responded to Kuba's death by storming the dormitory and, as historian Dwight Watson has written, "they went berserk, destroying everything in their path." By night's end Houston police officers had arrested more than five hundred students and turned the TSU campus into an occupied territory.[22]

Though the H-HCEOO leadership had attempted to improve their relationship with the city's public officials, tensions remained as some city officials, particularly Police Chief Short, continued to attack the poverty program in Houston and blamed some of its employees for causing the "riot." An additional OEO inspector dispatched to Houston in the wake of the TSU riot met with Short and reported that "it was very evident that the Chief was incensed that it cost the city of Houston a considerable sum of money to police demonstrations backed by OEO-Federal money." The inspector went on to state that Short "did not believe that the TSU demonstrations were anything but H-HCEOO inspired, citing Pluria Marshall's part in the incidents." Though Marshall was not on the campus during the riot in May and the H-HCEOO board attempted to restore peace on the campus the night of the riot, the police chief continued to believe H-HCEOO employees were behind the turmoil. After the riot, Short sent Welch a photograph of a message spray-painted on the wall of a TSU building: "Everybody Rejoice— We Killed a White, Racist, Punk-Ass, Blue-Eyed, Stringy-Haired, Pussy Eating COP!" Attached to the photograph was a personal note from the police chief that read, "Mayor, this is the 'great society' that deserves so much help." Clearly Short did not interpret H-HCEOO's overtures toward the city's public officials as altruistic, and he continued his assault on the poverty program in the city.[23]

Much like the events in Settegast, the TSU riot served to put H-HCEOO leaders on the defensive and forced them to put the brakes on their community organizers. Ballew and Kelly witnessed firsthand the power of the mayor and police chief and the weapons at their disposal if they chose to attack the poverty program. After the TSU riot, Kelly and the board forbade H-HCEOO staff members and community organizers from participating in protests or demonstrations in the city. In an even more shocking development, after the TSU riot the

H-HCEOO personnel committee agreed to submit the names of all current and prospective employees of the organization to Police Chief Short for prescreening. If any employee or future employee was found to have a questionable police record, that person could be denied employment with the poverty program in Houston. Though this only partially satisfied Short, Mayor Welch was pleased with the new arrangement. In fact, Welch told an OEO inspector in late May that "H-HCEOO could be an effective organization" in Houston now that its leaders were willing to coordinate their activities with city officials.

H-HCEOO had traveled a long distance from the idealistic days when Ballew first took the helm. Ballew had committed the organization to the Alinsky model of community organization and empowerment of the poor by hiring Earl Allen and devoting nearly all of the agency's resources to his community-organizing efforts. But Ballew and Allen were no match for Welch and Short. Alinsky had been right; power relations were at the very heart of the problems of the poor. When H-HCEOO leaders decided to forge a friendly relationship with Houston's public officials, they circumvented their own power in the fight against poverty.[24]

Satisfying local city officials largely ended the conflict with Welch and Short but it created an ever widening rift between the H-HCEOO board on the one hand and community organizers and the poor themselves on the other. While the situation was heating up on the TSU campus, Earl Allen and his community organization staff began voicing their opposition to the new cautious mood of the H-HCEOO board. OEO inspector James Simons met with Allen and a few other dissident community organizers during the second week in April 1967 to investigate this troubling conflict between the H-HCEOO board and its staff. Simons discovered that "mass disillusionment and bitterness" had overtaken many members of the community organization staff and poor residents of the target neighborhoods, because both groups believed that H-HCEOO leadership was attempting to block their efforts at organizing the poor in Houston. Allen and other community organizers warned Simons that the present course of H-HCEOO would invariably produce a "violent expression" of frustration in the poor neighborhoods where the War on Poverty had raised the expectations of poor residents but failed to deliver on its promises. One H-HCEOO community organizer in Settegast told Simons that he was losing both the respect of neighborhood residents and the credibility he once enjoyed as a representative of H-HCEOO. He exclaimed, "If I was hired to pacify angry folk with promises . . . I won't do it. . . . I'll starve first." With the firm belief that if H-HCEOO failed to change course soon there would be a violent uprising in Houston's poor neighborhoods, Allen and other community organizers met on April 8 and 9 to plan a demonstration and a public airing of their grievances at H-HCEOO headquarters.[25]

On the morning of April 10, 1967, as the H-HCEOO board of directors was busy considering disciplinary action against Pluria Marshall for his participation in the ongoing TSU demonstrations, Earl Allen and approximately fifty members of his community organization staff arrived at H-HCEOO headquarters in downtown Houston and began a protest vigil that lasted all day. Allen issued a statement explaining that he and his staff were demonstrating against the H-HCEOO board's waning support for community organization in Houston's poor neighborhoods and its lack of effective communication with the staff about the priorities and goals of the community action agency. Although Ballew was still chairman of H-HCEOO, he was rapidly losing support among members of the board due to the controversies in Settegast and on the TSU campus. To make matters worse, Ballew interpreted Allen's picketing of H-HCEOO headquarters as a personal insult that disregarded his support of community organizing over the past year. In response to Allen's demands, Ballew initially refused to negotiate with the demonstrators. H-HCEOO executive director Charles Kelly went a step further by suspending three community organizers involved in the protest indefinitely and docking the pay for all others present during the demonstration. When Allen promised continued protests outside H-HCEOO headquarters until the board addressed their demands, officials at the southwest regional OEO office in Austin pressured Ballew and other board members to call a special H-HCEOO executive committee meeting to hear the community organization staff's concerns.[26]

One week later Allen and other members of the community organization staff presented their list of grievances and demands to the H-HCEOO executive committee. After pointing out how several board members were attempting to defame the reputation of certain community organization staff members while, at the same time, criticizing their activities in Settegast and other areas where poor residents were being organized, the authors of the list arrived at the crux of their disillusionment with H-HCEOO as an organization. The report stated that the "Board is afraid of conflict, and as a result of that fear has allowed criticism of the program to be turned into condemnation of the Staff. . . . The fear of conflict results in our Board's reacting in a manner which is diametrically opposed to the concept of maximum feasible participation of the poor." The board was missing the point, the protesters said, because the "inevitability of internal and external conflict is inherent in the concept of Community Action itself; therefore, it is naïve to believe that one can conduct an effective Community Action Program without experiencing confrontation between the poor and the established power structures." H-HCEOO board members "oppose the actions of our group," the protesters argued, "because they know that we are fighting to bring about the realization of a program that will afford to the poor the opportunity to enter into direct confrontation with those forces which have kept them in a condition of deprivation."[27]

Several H-HCEOO board members in recent months had also accused Allen and his community organization staff of attempting to use the poverty program in Houston to advance a Black Power agenda. The authors of the list of grievances and demands answered this charge directly:

> If Black Power means an attempt at forming a power base in Negro communities in an effort to afford to those residents the opportunities to control their destinies, then we advocate Black Power. If Brown Power means an attempt at forming a power base in a Latin American community in an effort to afford to those residents the opportunity to control their own destinies, then we advocate Brown Power. If White Power means an attempt at forming a power base in White communities in an effort to afford to those residents the opportunities to control their own destinies, then we advocate White Power. If Human Power means an attempt to bring together all ethnic groups in an effort to create a harmonious and cooperative society which benefits from the participation of all its members, then we advocate Human Power.

The authors accused certain board members of using fears of Black Power and urban rioting in an attempt to discredit the community organization staff and diminish the effectiveness of its confrontational strategy.[28]

The authors concluded their statement of grievances and demands with a list of recommendations for the H-HCEOO board of directors. All the recommendations boiled down to the demand that the community organization staff be allowed to continue using the tactics developed by Earl Allen free from interference by the board. The authors argued that the board should confine its actions to policy decisions and leave the operation of the community action program to the staff. In order to restore the confidence of the community organization staff as well as the poor residents themselves, the authors of the report demanded that "a statement be issued by the board endorsing the use of direct confrontation as a strategy for social change" and that the board dedicate itself to giving "support to employees engaged in activities in keeping with effective community action even when those activities are contrary to interests represented on the Board." The dissident staff members recognized that they would not be able to continue organizing and empowering Houston's poor communities unless the H-HCEOO board of directors stood firmly behind their efforts. If Allen's staff continued to be hamstrung by the new cautious mood that had taken hold of the board, H-HCEOO community organizers realized they would continue to lose support and credibility in the target neighborhoods and a violent uprising would be a real possibility.[29]

Allen failed to persuade the board. He no doubt expected that, but what he could not have predicted was the resulting conflict within the community organization staff. A week later, an OEO inspector from Washington noted that after Allen and his staff made their demands on the H-HCEOO board the result was that, "due to a weak, ineffective executive director [Charles Kelly], two factions have evolved in H-HCEOO with diametrically opposed philosophies concerning community development." On one side of this philosophical rift was Earl Allen and his community organization staff, who the inspector described as displaying a "high degree of militancy" and being totally committed to "the use of direct confrontation as a strategy for social change." The opposing faction was led by Mrs. Keith Finlayson, an H-HCEOO community organizer who resigned in January 1967 and alleged that newly hired director of Community Organization, Earl Allen, was "accelerating the conversion of [community organization] staff personnel to the Black Muslim faith" and "turning the poverty program into a militant Black Power Organization." Though it must have seemed unlikely that a Methodist minister like Earl Allen would oversee the conversion of his operation into a black Muslim organization, a sufficient number of other H-HCEOO employees and board members believed Finlayson, even after the board investigated her allegations and found them to have no merit. Despite her patently false allegations, the H-HCEOO board refused to accept her resignation and simply reassigned her as a community organizer outside of the Settegast area and away from Allen's day-to-day operations. From that position Finlayson continued her assault on Allen's staff. According to H-HCEOO executive director Charles Kelly, she also began providing information to the Houston Police Department and the local news media about the inner conflicts within H-HCEOO. By April 1967, when Allen and his staff revolted against the H-HCEOO board, Finlayson had a solid group of supporters on both the H-HCEOO staff and the board of directors. This group rejected the idea that community organizing should be the centerpiece of H-HCEOO's activities in Houston's poor neighborhoods and instead advocated for the development and coordination of social services for the poor. Rather than provoking the city's public officials, Finlayson and her supporters argued that the status quo should be preserved and city leaders should be consulted and brought into the poverty program if possible. As the OEO inspector noted in his report, this dichotomy within the H-HCEOO staff seemed to be a harbinger of things to come in the future of the organization.[30]

While the H-HCEOO staff revolt was beginning to tear apart the organization from within, several of Houston's public officials continued their external assault on the poverty program in the city and exploited the staff divisions in order to shape the future of the organization. Despite Welch's gradually improving relationship with the H-HCEOO board, the mayor soon found himself in an ideal position from which to criticize the parts of the War on Poverty in Houston with which he disagreed. In March 1967 Lyndon Johnson had appointed Welch to the National Advisory Council of the Office of Economic Opportunity, and the mayor's first statement as a member of this council was to argue that some of the poverty programs needed to end, particularly the emphasis on community organizing. Welch told the *Houston Post* that protests were certainly not the intent of War on Poverty planners and that the "business of hiring buses to bus people to the wrong place in order to protest is certainly a waste of taxpayers' money." The protest at city hall, according to the mayor, was "misdirected and misguided and I hope will not recur."[31]

In May 1967 Mayor Welch, unable to control the H-HCEOO community organization staff completely and concerned that Earl Allen's faction might emerge victorious, submitted a formal complaint to the OEO office in Washington; he characterized the complaint as a "series of questions that this office feels it can no longer delay in raising." Welch continued, "As the OEO in both Washington and Austin knows, there has been deep concern about the poverty program in the Houston area for some time but it has only been in the last few weeks that the problem has reached a point where this office must bring the sort of information and questions contained in the attached to the attention of those in authority on a national level." The mayor's concerns were predictably centered on the question of the proper role of a community action agency in the fight against poverty. Welch expressed his outrage that H-HCEOO community organizers had promoted conflict between poor residents and the city's government when "remedies through mediation and negotiation have not been exhausted." After praising the service delivery approach of HAY, the mayor denounced H-HCEOO's criticism of that approach and asked if "revolution" was the goal of H-HCEOO. Welch also expressed his dissatisfaction with the involvement of H-HCEOO employees in protests in the city and in demonstrations on the TSU campus. The mayor stated, "Since it appears that the [H-HCEOO] program is based, at least in part, on that used by The Woodlawn Organization initiated by Saul Alinsky, is it the opinion of the OEO that confrontation and conflict are the only means by which the poor can be heard by 'the power structure' and mediation of problems is a method not open to the impoverished?" The mayor concluded his letter by reporting on the results of a survey conducted by his office that showed most poor residents in Houston were dissatisfied with H-HCEOO and the poverty program in general. OEO officials in Washington forwarded Welch's letter to the southwest regional OEO office, and director Walter Richter promptly responded to Welch's concerns and attempted to explain OEO policy regarding the activities of the H-HCEOO community organization staff. While Richter encouraged Welch to accept some degree of conflict in Houston as the natural outgrowth of poor people taking control of their own lives, he nonetheless wanted to prevent the situation from threatening the survival of the entire War on Poverty being conducted in Houston. Accordingly, Richter tried to assure the mayor that OEO policy would never allow a community action agency to promote "revolution" and promised that the poverty program in

Houston would strive to work closely with the city's elected officials to carry out a meaningful and effective attack on poverty.[32]

Republican congressman George Bush had a similar reaction to the activities of H-HCEOO's community organization staff, and there is evidence to suggest that he and Mayor Welch had begun working together as early as February 1967 to launch a public smear campaign against H-HCEOO in Houston and drive a wedge between community organizers and poor residents in Settegast.[33] It was during that month that the mayor's office began supplying Bush with confidential information about individual H-HCEOO community organizers. Bush especially took issue with H-HCEOO's voter registration campaign in Houston's poor neighborhoods; poor and black residents were not the type of voters Republicans wanted to add to the roles in their effort to make inroads into the Solid South. When the Texas attorney general ruled that H-HCEOO employees did not violate any voter registration laws with their actions, Bush called for a change in OEO policy that would forbid these kinds of voter registration activities. By March 1967 the freshman congressman was criticizing the poverty program in Houston so loudly that OEO officials in Washington sent an inspector to meet with Bush to discuss his concerns. During this meeting, Bush voiced his strong opposition to H-HCEOO chairman Ballew's confrontational philosophy and his emphasis on community organizing. Bush also charged that the H-HCEOO board of directors regularly hired community organizers who had police records, which was information he had received from Welch. As the OEO inspector wrote in his report, "It appears obvious that a number of Bush's concerns had been stimulated by the Mayor, particularly since he cited the Mayor as the source of information concerning employment of persons with police records and extremist backgrounds." The OEO inspector concluded that Bush was not antagonistic to the poverty program in Houston but that he preferred the service delivery approach of HAY and was incredibly fearful that H-HCEOO's community-organizing tactics would lead to a violent urban riot in Houston.[34]

An important matter that further complicated this volatile situation, and one that Welch, Bush, and Short also sought to exploit in order to gain more control over the poverty program in Houston, was the increasing pressure exerted by OEO officials in Washington and Austin for H-HCEOO and HAY to merge into a single community action agency. All of the OEO inspectors who visited Houston in February 1967 agreed that the most desirable solution would be a merger of H-HCEOO and HAY into one community action agency for the city of Houston. According to OEO officials, even though each community action agency operated in a different part of the city, just the mere presence of two separate organizations indicated a failure to coordinate the poverty program in Houston. More important, an effective community action agency needed to be able to perform both functions—community organization as well as the coordination of social services. By merging Houston's two community action agencies, OEO officials hoped to create a single agency that could carry out both objectives and at the same time improve the deficiencies of each organization by using the strengths of the other.[35]

Although the goal of a merged community action agency for Houston was clear, the method of achieving this goal proved to be more problematic. As one OEO inspector stated in her report, leaders of H-HCEOO and HAY shared a mutual distrust of each other. "HAY characterizes H-HCEOO as a rabble-rousing organization run by an ambitious Board Director and untrained staff, achieving little in the way of significant improvements for the poor and lacking the confidence of its constituency. H-HCEOO sees HAY as a paternalistic traditional social service agency, confining itself largely to providing some palliative services for the indigent with minimum interest in community organization and minimum impact on changing the lot of the poor." H-HCEOO seemed especially resistant to the idea of a merger between equals because its board of directors saw their organization as the legitimate community action agency for Houston and refused to enter into relationships with other antipoverty organizations unless the other agency agreed to give the H-HCEOO board of directors authority over their operations. For example, H-HCEOO refused to take part in the manpower and employment program administered in part by the Texas Employment Commission (TEC) because the TEC refused to place their operations under the authority of the H-HCEOO board. Additionally, under Ballew's leadership the H-HCEOO board had taken the focus off of the delivery and coordination of social services and had become devoted to the organization of the poor as a means of addressing the problems of poverty in Houston. This emphasis on community organizing was not simply a tactical decision but rather a deeply held philosophical belief, espoused most vocally by William Ballew and Earl Allen, that the only sure way to attack the root causes of poverty was to organize and empower the poor to make demands on local public officials and begin to reform the institutions that affected their lives. For Ballew and Allen, this meant discarding the notion that the delivery and coordination of social services was an effective way of permanently addressing the needs of the poor. Instead, antipoverty activists should be working in poor neighborhoods to identify "gut issues" and organizing poor residents to come up with their own solutions to these problems. According to Ballew and Allen, poverty workers must be prepared to work with and support neighborhood residents even to the point of participating in protests and demonstrations against the city's public officials. H-HCEOO activists simply had a vision of expanding democracy in Houston that was not shared by members of HAY. With these competing philosophies, it seemed unlikely indeed that H-HCEOO and HAY would ever be able to merge and carry out a united antipoverty effort in Houston.[36]

This philosophical difference between H-HCEOO and HAY, which had existed since the inception of the War on Poverty in Houston, played a major role during the spring of 1967 when southwest regional OEO officials finally insisted that the two organizations merge to form a single community action agency for the city of Houston. Although OEO officials had been politely suggesting that H-HCEOO and HAY merge to form one community action agency for the Houston area since the fall of 1966, H-HCEOO's emphasis on community organizing and confrontational tactics did not mesh well with HAY's almost total dedication to the delivery and coordination of social services for the poor. When asked about a possible merger in January 1967, H-HCEOO chairman Ballew pointed out that "each organization is approaching the poverty problem from vastly different viewpoints." Earl Allen stated that H-HCEOO's "community organizers are not community flunkies. Our staff is not out to run people back and forth to Ben Taub [General Hospital]. There are too many people looking for handouts already. Our idea is to get people to act for themselves, to involve people in the planning which affects their lives." HAY president Ed Bracher replied that HAY's approach "has shown itself to be effective" and argued that HAY had "a highly competent professional staff, which is not dominated by the opinions of lay people. . . . [H-HCEOO] seems to get groups together solely for the purpose of marching on City Hall over every issue." It was clear to southwest regional OEO officials that a merger between two groups with such strikingly different philosophies about how to solve the problems of poverty was going to be a difficult, if not impossible, process.[37]

Federal OEO inspectors who visited Houston during February 1967 agreed that a merged community action agency was the ideal solution, but all of them also noted in their reports that the competing philosophies and preferred tactics of the two groups would make a merger extremely unlikely. One inspector reflected on the "major philosophical differences" between the two organizations, while another pointed out that each organization was "operating separately and increasingly at cross-purposes" and argued that "initial steps to achieve greater coordination between the two agencies have in one sense only served to reinforce existing antagonisms." Another OEO inspector wrote in her report that directors of H-HCEOO and HAY were "mutually suspicious of each other," but she optimistically noted that "the strengths of each organization offset the weaknesses of the other." All of the federal inspectors agreed, however, that despite the major philosophical differences between the two organizations, the city of Houston desperately needed a single community action agency to carry out the War on Poverty and implement the full effect of the concept of community action. As one inspector concluded, "Could they forget their rivalry and, through a consolidation, work together, concentrating on the determination of objectives, program priorities and organizational goals and on the mobilization and coordination of resources in the community, Houston would have a strong and viable community action program." Another inspector ended her inspection report by stating that "even at this time we can conclude from our observations in Houston that both the provision of social services and community organizing tend to become ends in themselves, to the detriment of the ultimate goal, unless programs contain elements of both community organization and social services." With a merger, the inspector argued, Houston's community action program could become a model to illustrate the need for both approaches and an understanding of the totality of the concept of community action.[38]

Southwest regional OEO officials acted on these reports and began pushing more forcefully for a merger between H-HCEOO and HAY during the first few months of 1967. William Finister, an analyst for the southwest region, suggested that the regional office use each organization's funding request as leverage to encourage them to agree to a merger plan. Finister noted that for the 1967 fiscal year, HAY had requested $2.2 million and H-HCEOO had requested $3 million, and he argued that "the easiest way to get them to merge would be to tell both CAA's that Houston will only receive X dollars this year with separate funding, but that if they merge Houston will get X + bonus dollars." Southwest OEO officials responded favorably to Finister's suggestion, and in late February they notified representatives from H-HCEOO and HAY that the two organizations must merge to create a single community action agency by April 30, 1967, and that no further grants would be made except to a single agency in Houston. Additionally, southwest OEO officials warned that if H-HCEOO and HAY were unable to settle their differences and work together, a completely new community action agency might be created for the city of Houston.[39]

During this controversy over the proposed merger, Congressman Bush and Mayor Welch both attempted to enter the fray in order to gain more control over the poverty program in Houston. In mid-March 1967 OEO officials in Washington met separately with Bush and Welch to address their concerns about the power struggle shaping up within Houston's community action program. Congressman Bush, who had already told OEO officials that he strongly opposed H-HCEOO's focus on community organizing and expressed his displeasure about the organization's voter registration drive in Houston, worried that HAY's service-delivery approach would be lost in a merger of the two community action agencies in the city. Mayor Welch made it clear that he wanted more control over the activities of the merged community action agency than he had had over H-HCEOO, and OEO officials quickly recognized that Welch would use the increasingly negative public image of H-HCEOO "as a lever against present H-HCEOO leadership in a power struggle now going on for control of the Houston CAP program." During the meetings with Bush and Welch it also became apparent that the two politicians would continue working together to rein in Earl Allen and the rest of H-HCEOO's community organization staff. They would be able to exert even more influence over the poverty program in Houston since President Johnson had named Welch to the National Advisory Council of OEO.[40]

After the meetings, OEO officials concluded that the mayor and his allies, including Bush, would continue to battle H-HCEOO leaders for control of the community action program in Houston and stated that the situation in the city would "remain warm for some time." They retained their faith in H-HCEOO chairman Ballew, however, and noted that as head of the largest community action agency in Houston, Ballew had shown himself to be "liberal, savvy, and in all respects well-connected." OEO officials continued, "Bush and others may disagree with him, but I doubt that they will be able to push him around easily. Ballew himself senses the situation as one of an impending power struggle for the CAP program, where there is some need for increased self-policing by H-HCEOO. He sees Mayor Welch as the principal antagonist, and he is very interested in learning who is responsible for the Mayor's appointment to the National Advisory Council of OEO." Although Welch and Bush had begun working together to control the War on Poverty in Houston, OEO officials remained confident that, under Ballew's leadership, H-HCEOO would remain the dominant organization and would continue the work they had begun the previous year.[41]

OEO officials underestimated the power of Welch and Bush, however, even if they correctly gauged the tenacity and determination of Ballew. The mayor had effectively used information from the Settegast protest and the TSU Riot to discredit H-HCEOO's community-organizing tactics not only among Houston residents uninvolved in the poverty program but also among some H-HCEOO board members and poor residents themselves. There is evidence that Welch instructed members of his staff to cultivate animosity against H-HCEOO's community organizers in the Settegast area by illustrating how Earl Allen and his organizers had bypassed respectable middle-class leadership in the neighborhoods and had turned young people against their elders. Welch had also used information collected from Houston police chief Herman Short to launch a public smear campaign against individual community organizers employed by H-HCEOO and had supplied this confidential information to a local radio station to be broadcast all over the city. By March 1967 Welch was able to secure the support of Congressman Bush, who was already opposed in principle to a massive antipoverty program funded by the federal government, especially if it meant poor people would be organized to challenge local power structures. With his appointment to the National Advisory Council of OEO, Welch enjoyed a rapidly increasing amount of influence over the poverty program in his city. Regardless of how dedicated Ballew was to the Alinsky model of community organization and empowerment of the poor, neither he nor his organization had the strength to challenge the city's public officials and expect to emerge victorious when those local officials were determined to undermine Ballew's entire antipoverty philosophy and were willing to use nearly all of the powerful weapons at their disposal. In the clash over the future of democracy in Houston, Welch and Bush simply had more power to enforce their limited interpretation.[42]

Mayor Welch's assault on the H-HCEOO staff had a profound effect on the board of directors and on Executive Director Charles Kelly. After the turmoil in Settegast, Kelly and the board decided to pull the community organizers out of the neighborhoods and reassign them to different parts of the city. Many board members who had once supported Ballew's vision for dedicating H-HCEOO to organizing poor people to challenge local elected officials were now beginning to back off from that commitment. In the wake of the controversy in Settegast and the attacks by Mayor Welch and Police Chief Short, the H-HCEOO board of directors convened a special meeting to develop a new community development plan without the input of Ballew or Allen. This new community development plan was a total repudiation of the Saul Alinsky method; it called for placing an experienced social service worker in each neighborhood to direct poor residents to the proper service agency rather than attempting to organize them. Earl Allen's community organization staff knew this shift would eventually mean an end to their methods of organizing the poor to challenge the city's public officials, and this realization was partly responsible for the staff revolt that took place in April 1967. Ironically, however, the demonstrations led by Allen at H-HCEOO headquarters served to push the H-HCEOO board into an even more defensive position as Allen lost additional support among board members. With southwest regional OEO officials putting constant pressure on the H-HCEOO board of directors to approve a merger plan to create a single community action agency for Houston, many board members were fearful that Allen's protests would harm their efforts to bring about a successful merger with HAY.[43]

From the very first suggestion that H-HCEOO and HAY should merge to form a single community action agency for the city of Houston, H-HCEOO chairman Ballew opposed the idea on the grounds that H-HCEOO's community organization efforts would be drowned out by HAY's emphasis on the delivery and coordination of social services and its members' aversion to using confrontational tactics to challenge the city's public officials. For much of the time Ballew also had the support of the majority of the board of directors, many of whom had been willing to allow Ballew and Allen to experiment with the Alinsky method even if they did not share the chairman's confrontational philosophy and his commitment to community organization. Southwest regional OEO officials began threatening to cut funding to both agencies in the spring of 1967 if no merger could be worked out. Reeling under a heavy barrage of attacks from Mayor Welch and Police Chief Short, however, many H-HCEOO board members became much more receptive to the idea of a merger with HAY. Not only did a majority of the H-HCEOO board support a negotiated merger between the two organizations by April 1967, but a significant number of them were also willing to back off from their previous commitment to community organizing, as evidenced by the new community development plan many of them developed at the end of March. While a majority of H-HCEOO board members began making overtures toward HAY officials for fear that failure to do so would mean extinction and possibly the end of community action in Houston, Ballew remained bitterly opposed to the idea of a merger.

It became clear in early April 1967 that no successful merger between H-HCEOO and HAY could occur with Ballew as chairman of H-HCEOO, and several board members decided that Ballew would have to be removed as an obstacle to a successful merger. Sensing this development and recognizing that the H-HCEOO board was beginning to move the poverty program in a much more cautious direction, Ballew announced that he would not seek reelection as chairman. During a meeting on April 10, 1967, the H-HCEOO board of directors continued their shift to a more limited program by electing Francis Williams, a prominent African American attorney in Houston and former head of the city's NAACP chapter, as the new chairman. Upon accepting the position, Williams separated himself from the previous leadership by pointing out that he was certainly no militant. "My views are well-known," Williams told reporters. "I'm NAACP, not SNCC, not CORE, not Stokely Carmichael. I'm for negotiation, time-honored, tried and true methods." The new chairman vowed that his first priority would be to solve the twin problems of a merger with HAY and the staff revolt that was taking place, and he argued that both issues would be handled quickly and efficiently. Williams envisioned after the merger a single community action agency for Houston that would find out from poor residents themselves what types of social services they needed and help locate and coordinate these services for the poor in Houston. At no point during his talk with reporters did Williams touch on the subject of community organizing or confrontational tactics, despite the fact that this issue had caused a major rift within the organization that was still unresolved. Outgoing chairman Ballew stated that Williams was inheriting "a can of worms," and even Williams called the job he accepted "a hot potato." Williams continued, "But I didn't feel I could shirk it. Somebody has to bell the cat. Somebody has to try, because the program is of great importance to this city."[44]

Williams immediately began working toward a successful merger between H-HCEOO and HAY. Even before Williams officially began in his new position as H-HCEOO chairman, southwest regional OEO officials began contacting him in an attempt to speed up the merger process. At the urging of Fred Baldwin, a southwest OEO representative assigned to Houston, Williams called a meeting in late April 1967 between the boards of H-HCEOO and HAY in order to come up with a plan to merge the two organizations and create a single community action agency. During this meeting held on April 20, 1967, representatives from H-HCEOO and HAY finally agreed to a merger plan that would combine aspects of each organization to create the Harris County Community Action Association (HCCAA). The plan called for every member from each agency's board and executive committee to be included on the new board of directors. A fifteen-member steering committee, elected by the new board, would oversee the merger process. In an effort to satisfy Mayor Welch, the plan also called for the mayor to appoint an additional twenty-five members to the board of directors of the new organization and one person to the steering committee.[45]

The most important negotiation associated with the merger, and the issue that had prevented any successful attempt at bringing the two organizations together in the past, was the role each staff would play in the newly merged community action agency. Unlike Ballew, Francis Williams and a majority of the H-HCEOO board members were now willing to compromise on this issue, and the concessions they made on this point had significant implications for the future role of community organizers in the newly created HCCAA. The merger plan stated that the former HAY staff members would continue to focus on delivery and coordination of social services for poor residents in Houston. The plan stated that they would "serve primarily as a community forum for planning, recommending policies and programs and conducting public hearings." Former H-HCEOO staff, according to the merger plan, would continue to focus on community organization, but with a strikingly different definition of community organization from the one Ballew and Allen had developed in the fall of 1966. Within HCCAA, community organization would be "defined as assisting groups to seek solutions, through orderly petitioning and public voice, to serious problems in poverty stricken neighborhoods that affect the rights of their residents as citizens, the conditions under which they live and work, and their needs for additional public and private support." Community organizers would still have a role to play in the new community action agency for Houston, but their stated goals and duties had been considerably revised so their activities would not be so challenging to the city's public officials. Although this compromise seemed to offer a way to pacify Welch and ensure the continuation of the War on Poverty in Houston, in reality it merely exacerbated the rift among the staff and heightened the tensions among poverty workers who held different beliefs about how to solve the problems of poverty. These tensions would continue to plague the new organization and hamper its ability to confront poverty in Houston in an effective and meaningful way, and after May 1967 Williams would thoroughly mishandle these two competing factions within the organization.[46]

By mid-May 1967 both H-HCEOO and HAY had approved the merger plan. On May 16, the Harris County Community Action Association came into existence as Houston's single community action agency with Francis Williams as chairman of the board of directors. Only a few months prior to the creation of HCCAA, the merger of H-HCEOO and HAY seemed a remote possibility. The sharp philosophical differences between members of each organization reflected a significant disagreement about the meaning of community action and the role of community organizers in the fight against poverty in Houston. As chairman of H-HCEOO, William Ballew had committed his agency to the Saul Alinsky model of community organization and empowerment of the poor and had adopted confrontational tactics to challenge the city's public officials and attempt to reform its institutions. HAY officials, on the other hand, were firmly committed to the nonconfrontational aspects of community action, which included the delivery and coordination of social welfare services. The only way these two organizations could come together to produce a single community action agency was for one of them to back off from a firm commitment to its preferred solution for solving the problems of poverty. This is precisely what occurred. In response to sustained attacks from the city's public officials, H-HCEOO officials gradually abandoned Ballew's commitment to the Alinsky philosophy, and in the process they tamed their own community organization staff. The limited view of democracy had won and the city's Community Action Program would no longer be committed to expanding the meaning of democracy in Houston.[47]

Four events during the spring of 1967—the Settegast revolt, the TSU Riot, the staff uprising, and the forced merger of H-HCEOO and HAY—worked to put H-HCEOO leaders on the defensive and opened up a space for several local officials to reassert their authority over the poverty program in Houston. By redefining the concept and goals of community organizing, H-HCEOO officials made their organization more acceptable to the HAY board of directors and to the city's public officials. Francis Williams and other H-HCEOO board members who helped this process along probably ensured that the community action program would continue in Houston without additional attacks from Mayor Welch, Congressman Bush, or Police Chief Short, but in abandoning community-organizing efforts, they also undercut the successes Earl Allen and his staff had achieved in the city and ensured they would not be repeated in the future. As Ballew watched the organization he led for more than a year slip away, he noted that the new HCCAA board could become simply "a debating society, and the executive committee can become a tool of local government." By this time, however, the majority of former H-HCEOO board members had turned their backs on Ballew and committed themselves to a more cautious vision for the Community Action Program in Houston.[48]

FIVE

A Triumph for the Limited Vision of Democracy

New Leadership and the Expulsion of the Organizers, 1967–1969

In August 1967 Fred Baldwin, administrator of the Community Action Program for the OEO's southwest regional office, sent a lengthy memo to the office's director, Walter Richter, updating him on the status of several community action agencies throughout the region. Baldwin provided matter-of-fact details about community action agencies in Albuquerque, Dallas, and a few other locations, but he saved for last his report on the "Houston situation"—a term many OEO officials began using by the summer of 1967 to refer to recent events in the city. The Harris County Community Action Association (HCCAA), an organization born of the merger between the aggressive and confrontational Houston–Harris County Economic Opportunity Organization (H-HCEOO) and the more cautious Houston Action for Youth (HAY), had been through a troubling summer filled with ideological disputes, internal divisions, and negative publicity. Baldwin did not even feel the need to recount the recent events in Houston or to provide an analysis of the situation. Rather, he used a quotation from Leo Tolstoy's *War and Peace* to stress to Richter that the War on Poverty was larger than the "Houston situation" and to urge him to keep everything in its proper perspective. Baldwin quoted from Book VIII of *War and Peace*, in which Tolstoy described the Battle of Borodino:

> Napoleon, standing on the knoll, looked through a field glass, and in its small circlet saw smoke and men, sometimes his own and sometimes Russians, but when he looked again with the naked eye, he could not tell where what he had seen was.
>
> He descended the knoll and began walking up and down before it. Occasionally he stopped, listened to the firing, and gazed intently at the battlefield. But not only was it impossible to make out what was happening from where he was standing down below, or from the knoll above on which some of his generals had taken their stand,

but even from the fleches themselves. .... From the battlefield adjutants he had sent out, and orderlies from his marshals, kept galloping up to Napoleon with reports of the progress of the action, but all these reports were false, both because it was impossible in the heat of battle to say what was happening at any given moment and because many of the adjutants did not go to the actual place of conflict but reported what they had heard from others; and also because while an adjutant was riding more than a mile to Napoleon circumstances changed and the news he brought was already becoming false.[1]

The imagery of a fierce and chaotic battle that Baldwin conjured in his quotation was certainly fitting to what had transpired in Houston since the merger. In order to facilitate a successful merger with HAY, members of the H-HCEOO board of directors had moved in a more cautious and less confrontational direction by abandoning the Saul Alinsky method and ousting William Ballew, a dedicated Alinsky disciple, from the organization. While this strategy was adequate for making H-HCEOO more acceptable to Houston's public officials and led to a successful merger, a surprising number of aggressive community organizers remained on the HCCAA staff, including Earl Allen. Nevertheless, this process of moving HCCAA in a direction that was more cautious, more amenable to the city's public officials, less confrontational, and less committed to community organizing and empowerment of the poor continued under the direction of Francis Williams, who led the antipoverty effort over the next two years as HCCAA chairman and later as HCCAA executive director.

Between May 1967 and the end of 1969, Williams and his allies on the HCCAA board and staff were victorious in defeating the confrontational organizers who remained in the community action agency after the merger. In doing so, they rendered the organization more cautious and also established a close working relationship with the city's public officials, particularly Mayor Louie Welch. These efforts ensured that the War on Poverty would no longer challenge the boundaries of democracy in Houston. Yet Williams's efforts produced several unintended consequences, the most important of which was that his attempts to rein in HCCAA's more aggressive and confrontational activities alienated the two constituencies that had made the organization thrive: the poor, who supplied local support for the poverty program; and grassroots antipoverty activists, who provided the bulk of the foot soldiers for the War on Poverty in the city. In the process, although Williams undoubtedly guaranteed the short-term survival of HCCAA, many of Houston's poor residents and grassroots antipoverty activists became disillusioned with the entire War on Poverty. As a result, during these two years there were no major victories for Houston's poor that came as a result of HCCAA's activities. By 1969 HCCAA was a large bureaucratic machine that dispensed an array of social services but lacked the support and confidence of the very people who had enabled the Houston antipoverty program to achieve a modest level of success in the past.

The first step Williams and his allies took to change their new organization was calling for the creation of an entirely new board of directors and executive committee. The new 150-member board would consist of 50 poor residents from the target neighborhoods, 50 individuals appointed by Houston's civic organizations, 25 appointed by the mayor, and 25 appointed by the county judge. The new 24-member executive committee would be made up of 8 individuals chosen by the poor, 8 chosen by civic organizations, 4 chosen by the mayor, and 4 chosen by the county judge. Houston's public officials thus enjoyed control of one-third of HCCAA's board and executive committee. As the *Houston Chronicle* reported, having the mayor and county judge play important roles in the community action agency's planning and implementation of programs would ensure that HCCAA's activities would be "unlikely to raise hackles this year as it did last. . . . HCCAA looks like an organization built on the mistakes of its predecessors, neither as strict and structured as HAY, nor as apt to run amok as [H-HCEOO]."[2]

Williams and his allies also decided that Charles Kelly remained entirely too committed to Ballew's vision to be allowed to continue serving as executive director of HCCAA, a position he had held with H-HCEOO since 1966. Instead, Williams and other board members wanted the job to go to Franklin Harbach, the chairman of the Neighborhood Centers Association (NCA), who was nearing retirement. Williams hoped that Harbach would be able to lead the newly created organization through its first year or two and set it on a course resembling the liberal settlement-house style of the NCA. A federal OEO inspector overseeing the merger described Harbach as a "1930s liberal who has been active in the settlement house movement," and a *Houston Chronicle* reporter referred to him as a moderate liberal who preferred "negotiation to head-on assault." Though Harbach declined the offer, citing his imminent retirement and his unwillingness to get involved in HCCAA's internal divisions, Williams's overtures toward someone like Harbach to head up the city's community action agency was illustrative of the more cautious direction he sought for the organization.[3]

According to a federal OEO inspector assigned to Houston to oversee the merger, Mayor Louie Welch and County Judge Bill Elliott were eager to be brought back into the poverty program after being shut out by Ballew. Even before the conclusion of the successful merger between the two antipoverty organizations, several H-HCEOO board members began forging a closer link between Houston's public officials and their agency. By the time the merger was complete, a federal OEO inspector could claim with confidence that there were significantly "closer working arrangements of H-HCEOO with Houston authorities." To make sure that his office would be consistently kept informed of the new community action's activities, Mayor Welch arranged for several former HAY employees to act as inside informants who would report to the mayor's aides on the actions of the new HCCAA staff. In a special inspection report filed in August 1967, an OEO inspector stated that "HAY strategy was to infiltrate the militants with informers and pass on all intelligence to the Mayor—through [mayoral aide Blair] Justice—to help the mayor put down any direct, concerted activity," such as poverty workers involving themselves in protests. With several former HAY staff members working as inside informants on the HCCAA staff, Welch believed he would never be unaware of the activities of poverty workers in Houston again.[4]

Federal OEO inspectors were extremely skeptical about the renewed relationship between Houston's community action agency and the city's public officials. Several inspectors warned that Welch's eagerness to be involved in the War on Poverty in the city most certainly stemmed from his desire to control HCCAA's activities. As one OEO inspector stated, Welch's past behavior relative to the community action program in Houston showed that he was "capable of putting his name to biased and unsubstantiated allegations about OEO-related persons," and despite the closer working relationship, "we expect that output of this nature from the Mayor's Office may continue indefinitely." Welch had changed tactics, but it was clear that his ideas about the proper role of Houston's community action agency remained the same as what they had been when he launched a concerted attack on Ballew and the Alinsky-style organizers.[5]

In June 1967 HCCAA received an OEO grant for $5 million to carry out its agenda for the next year. Through its programs and projects, HCCAA's leaders showed just how much more moderate and nonconfrontational the agency had become since the days when Ballew implemented his vision for the community action program. In several areas of operation—the oversight of the Legal Services program, the administration of the Head Start program, the continuation of the Settegast Clinic, the implementation of various programs and services in poor neighborhoods, and the management of the community organization department—Williams and his allies on the HCCAA board of directors not only showed that their methods for attacking poverty in Houston had become more cautious but also that there would be no effort made to continue expanding the meaning of democracy. To make matters even worse, poor Houston residents began losing their confidence in the War on Poverty because under the direction of Williams and his allies the impotent tactics and strategies of HCCAA meant that the poor would no longer be empowered to claim power over their own lives.[6]

One of the clearest examples of HCCAA's shift to a more limited program and its impact on the fight against poverty in Houston was the organization's handling of the Legal Services program. By the summer of 1967 the Houston Legal Foundation had failed to produce an impressive record of providing legal aid to the poor and, of more importance, had not lived up to expectations set by Ballew and other OEO officials who hoped Houston's program could produce transformative change in the lives of poor people and possibly reform the legal system that played an important role in keeping people in poverty. When he pushed for the creation of a large and robust Legal Services program in 1966, Ballew firmly believed that legal aid would be an excellent vehicle to empower the poor to challenge the city's structural forces that kept them subjugated and mired in poverty. At its inception in Houston in 1966, an OEO official commented that the Houston Legal Foundation's proposed program represented the country's most far-reaching and potentially socially transformative Legal Services program; this official frequently used the words "social revolution" and "agents of change" when referring to the program and its attorneys. When OEO officials stressed to HLF leaders the necessity of accepting civil rights cases in October 1966, Ballew most certainly was hopeful that the Legal Services program in Houston would attempt to challenge significant pillars of local power and reform institutions that affected the lives of poor people.[7]

By July 1967, however, the Houston Legal Foundation had only three remaining fully operational neighborhood law offices. Even these remaining offices were plagued with staff shortages and a general lack of awareness among poor residents about their existence. The types of cases that attorneys handled in these law offices did not possess the socially transformative potential for which Ballew had hoped when he advocated the program. Rather, more than 50 percent of the cases involved divorce, annulment, separation, child custody, paternity, and adoption. A handful of the remaining cases contained elements that may have had the potential for social reform, but the majority of them involved wage claims, bankruptcy, workmen's compensation issues, and other personal matters. There was also growing criticism from residents of Houston's African American and Mexican American neighborhoods that the foundation was not adequately aggressive about pursuing civil rights cases. While the HLF provided much-needed legal services to poor individuals in a limited area of Houston, the overall program was a far cry from what Ballew had envisioned at the launch of the Legal Services program in the city.[8]

A more urgent problem facing the Houston Legal Foundation was a very unstable financial situation caused by the HCCAA board's neglect of the organization and its financial well-being. In September 1967 Judge Sam Johnson resigned from his position as the foundation's executive director to become a judge on the fourteenth Court of Civil Appeals, which left the HLF without a permanent executive director for the rest of the year. During the last few months of 1967 the foundation fell into financial trouble caused mostly by improper spending. The southwest regional OEO office performed an audit of the organization that showed the HLF had spent $14,284 for items not permitted under OEO guidelines, including employee salaries that exceeded federal limits and expensive office equipment. Southwest regional OEO officials strongly urged HLF administrators to address their financial troubles or risk having their federal funding completely cut off. Without an active executive director and with little encouragement or direction from HCCAA, however, the HLF sank further into financial turmoil by the end of the year.[9]

The Houston Legal Foundation hired a new executive director in January 1968 and finally ironed out its financial troubles the following month, but the organization's difficulties did not end there. A new set of problems erupted when OEO inspectors discovered that the HLF did not have enough representatives of the poor on its board of directors to meet federal guidelines for "maximum feasible participation" of the poor. A federal OEO inspection during the summer of 1968 revealed that the HLF had no poor residents or even representatives of the poor on its board of directors; the twenty-one-member board was instead made up of state and federal judges, local school officials, and lawyers. HLF administrators defended their exclusion of the poor by arguing that poor people were not qualified to determine policy for a legal aid organization. Federal OEO officials responded with another threat to cut off funding unless the organization's board of directors devised a plan to include poor residents in the decision-making processes of the group.[10]

With this latest threat of withholding funds, several HLF board members decided to use the Houston press to fight this battle with OEO officials. After a board meeting in which a majority of the members voted down a plan to add poor residents to the board, several members openly expressed their opposition to appointing poor people to the board to a *Houston Post* reporter, who was writing a three-part series on the conflict. While one member compared placing poor residents on the HLF board to a medical surgeon including heart patients on his surgical team, Harry Patterson, chairman of the board, stated, "We feel this is a professional organization that should be operated on the highest ethical concepts—and that non-attorney control would dilute this concept." Patterson also argued that the foundation was already in compliance because poor residents were currently represented by four members of the board, three of whom were African American and one of whom was Mexican American. Patterson did not mention, however, that three of these men were attorneys, one was the dean of the Texas Southern University law school, and none were poor or elected by the poor.[11]

Harold Scarlett, the *Houston Post* reporter following this story, provided great insight into what was at the root of this conflict. In the second part of his series, Scarlett argued that "a much deeper issue underlies this surface struggle" than the supposed problem of including the poor on the organization's board of directors. The real issue, according to at least one board member that Scarlett quoted, was "whether the Houston Legal Foundation is going to engage in law reform and social reform." It was clear to many observers that there was a growing reluctance to use the organization to expand democracy in Houston. The HLF had pledged itself to solving legal problems for poor individuals, but it shied away from attempting to reform the legal system to work more fairly for poor residents or filing suits that would have far-reaching implications, such as those involving civil rights or school desegregation. Some poor residents had even begun to complain that the foundation was created by powerful members of Houston's elaborate power structure to serve as "a pacifier [and] a remover of hangnails rather than a surgeon cutting out the deeply imbedded causes of poverty." Several board members retorted that the organization had an advisory board that poor residents could join if they wanted to have a voice in the operations of the foundation. Poor residents, however, complained that the advisory board was often ignored because the board's policy was "just to keep the lid on" any potentially volatile situation that might arise.[12] HLF board members, as Scarlett pointed out, "do not feel social crusading is their proper function."[13] These board members believed that including laymen on the board would "reduce the effectiveness of the board and distort the primary function of HLF, which is to provide legal services instead of participating in social reforms." HLF board chairman Patterson so strongly opposed the idea of placing poor residents on the board that he threatened cancellation of the Legal Services program in Houston altogether rather than conform to the federal policy of "maximum feasible participation" of the poor.[14]

By the summer of 1968 HCCAA leaders had been almost totally uninvolved in the administration of Houston's Legal Services program for more than a year. Near the end of the summer, however, at the urging of the southwest regional OEO office, HCCAA officials finally offered to end their silence and help negotiate a reconciliation between the two parties. The plan that HCCAA officials drew up, and the one eventually adopted by the HLF board, was indicative of how far the boards of both organizations had gotten from Ballew's vision for a robust and socially transformative Legal Services program for Houston. Under the new arrangement, four representatives of the poor would be seated on the HLF board of directors with full voting power. These representatives would not be elected by the poor, but instead they would be appointed by the HLF advisory board, which in theory was composed of poor residents. The most surprising part of the plan, however, was the edict that the advisory board would no longer have any authority to make recommendations to HLF board members on matters of policy or procedure or to initiate grievance procedures against the board. This action by the HLF board was a clear attempt to limit the role that poor residents would play in the organization, especially considering the four poor residents on the board would be outnumbered by the twenty-one other members and would have no one to appeal to for support within the organization. Russell L. Hayes, vice chairman of the HLF advisory board, interpreted this action by the board as spite. "All I have to say," Hayes told the *Houston Post*, "is the action by the board . . . completely negates the power of the [advisory] board and cuts off the line of communication with the people."[15]

By the time the HLF board of directors got around to outlining procedures for the placement of four poor residents on its board in September 1968, OEO officials had backed off from their commitment to the maximum feasible participation of the poor. On September 13 the regional OEO Legal Services administrator sent a letter to the new executive director of HLF informing him that his organization had fulfilled its agreement for including poor residents on the board, even though not a single poor person or representative of the poor had yet been appointed to the board. At no point during this ordeal did HCCAA officials try to intervene in a way that would have guaranteed poor residents a place on the policymaking board of the Houston Legal Foundation. This failure of both organizations to respond to the demands of the poor further alienated them from Houston's poor residents. By the end of 1968 poor residents were once again complaining that they were being left out of the administration of the Legal Services program. When Hayes appeared at an HCCAA meeting in October 1968 to voice the concerns of poor residents, the HCCAA board chairman declared his comments out of order and quickly ended the meeting. The poor were rapidly losing their voice in the poverty program in Houston, and the first major setback was suffered within the Houston Legal Foundation. William Ballew had hoped that the HLF would implement a widespread Legal Services program in Houston that would challenge the status quo and even expand the meaning of democracy. Without constant pressure exerted by HCCAA leadership on the HLF board of directors, however, the Legal Services program in the city was allowed to evolve into a simple deliverer of services. It most certainly had failed to become the socially transformative foundation Ballew had envisioned.[16]

In a development similar to the ordeal with the Houston Legal Foundation, it became apparent after the merger that HCCAA leaders were not willing to pursue reforms using the Head Start program. In particular, the HCCAA board was reluctant to push for change in the one area where the Head Start program actually had the greatest potential for reform, which was the desegregation of Houston's public schools. Racial segregation in public schools was the most logical issue targeted by reformers using the Head Start preschool program, because they could demand compliance with federal desegregation orders before making funding available. In 1965 and 1966 the Houston Independent School District (HISD) had administered an almost completely segregated Head Start program in the city, but with each passing year OEO officials and local reformers pushed more forcefully for desegregation. By the spring of 1967, OEO officials decided to deliver on their promise to cut off all Head Start funding to organizations that refused to desegregate their programs. Because HISD board members refused to desegregate their facilities in preparation for the 1967 summer program, OEO officials warned HCCAA board members that unless HISD complied with federal desegregation orders, a different organization would receive the $1.5 million grant to administer Head Start during the summer of 1967.[17]

HCCAA board members, mired in internal controversy caused by the merger negotiations and under continued assault from the city's public officials, were in no position to push for the desegregation of Houston's schools to comply with Head Start requirements. Rather than using their position as the governing body for the poverty program to demand that HISD take steps to meet federal desegregation requirements so as to avoid losing the Head Start program, HCCAA board members simply agreed to fund a different agency to administer the program. In May, board members chose Aid to Culturally Deprived Children (ACDC), a Catholic organization run by a local priest and a handful of educators, to sponsor Head Start for the summer of 1967. Not possessing adequate resources to administer a citywide preschool program, ACDC's Head Start suffered from low enrollment, an inactive parent program, and segregated facilities based on residential patterns in Houston and inadequate transportation. ACDC director Father Emile Farge blamed HCCAA for the low enrollment and lack of parent participation by pointing out that HCCAA board members had failed to initiate a widespread recruitment effort as they had done in the past for HISD. "Recruiting for Head Start was supposed to start in March with 50 paid workers," proclaimed a reporter for the *Houston Chronicle* in agreement with Farge. "But the staff of what is now the Community Action Assn. was more concerned with merging their two anti-poverty agencies than with recruiting children."[18]

HCCAA board members appeared equally indifferent about the problems of segregation that extended beyond the boundaries of the city into other parts of Harris County. During a routine inspection of Head Start centers in midsummer 1967, federal OEO officials found that the summer Head Start programs in Aldine, Cypress-Fairbanks, and Alief, as well as one administered by the Northeast Houston Independent School District, all operated in segregated facilities. Southwest regional OEO officials worked closely with Head Start sponsors in these areas to solve the problems and push for desegregation, but they received no assistance from HCCAA board members or staff in their efforts. The more cautious administrators who took control of HCCAA made it clear in the summer of 1967 that they were not interested in using the Head Start program to advance educational reform in Houston.[19]

In the fall of 1967 HCCAA board members—giving up any hope of educational reform in Houston—abandoned the Head Start program completely. They opted instead to administer a year-round preschool program through their own day care centers located in the target neighborhoods. The new preschool program was significantly smaller than Head Start, serving only about one-fourth of the number of preschoolers previously enrolled in Head Start. While Head Start was a program that had the potential to further an educational reform agenda because it required the use of desegregated facilities, HCCAA's new preschool program was simply a service that could be delivered to poor residents in a limited area. As one HCCAA official explained it, the most important part of this new program was that it would allow parents to receive childcare while they worked. Though day care for children of working parents was an important service, especially because it often allowed single-parent families to have an income, the Head Start program was designed with much grander expectations and was often used by activists to push for significant changes in the country's educational system. By the fall of 1967, however, it was clear that HCCAA board members were no longer interested in social change or educational reform, and their abandonment of the Head Start program was further evidence of this shift.[20]

During the summer of 1968, federal OEO officials once again convinced HISD to administer a summer Head Start program because they feared not having a program in Houston at all and still hoped to bring about school desegregation in Houston. HCCAA board members remained aloof from the entire process other than providing the standard paperwork needed for HISD to receive federal funding. Before OEO approved funding, Alfredo Garcia, civil rights coordinator for the southwest regional OEO office, warned that Houston was an area where the Head Start program might once again run into segregation problems. OEO officials tried to impress upon HISD representatives that their program must strictly adhere to federal guidelines regarding desegregation of facilities, and HISD representatives made vague statements to the effect that guidelines would be followed. OEO agreed to fund HISD's summer Head Start program in 1968; but soon after the program began, it was clear that very little attempt had been made to ensure the program was administered in a desegregated environment. In June Garcia charged that HISD officials tried to conceal the segregated nature of their program from federal inspectors by not reporting the ethnic breakdown of the students and staff. Garcia ordered a thorough investigation of the HISD Head Start program that not only revealed racially segregated facilities but also showed HISD had intentionally excluded hiring Mexican American staff members even though Mexican American students made up 20 percent of the enrollees.[21]

There is no evidence that OEO officials took any significant action to force HISD to comply with desegregation requirements, and presumably this was partly due to the fact that HCCAA board members refused to provide any support in pushing for educational reform in Houston. In the fall of 1968 the HCCAA board of directors simply took control of all of Houston's summer Head Start programs and placed them in their day care centers rather than attempt to reform HISD segregation practices. Similar to the ordeal with the Houston Legal Foundation, Houston's Head Start program evolved into yet another service delivered to poor residents. Important as that service may have been, it did not produce any opportunities for educational reform as Ballew had envisioned. Without HCCAA administrators putting pressure on their delegate agencies to comply with federal guidelines, there was little hope that Houston's Head Start would attack educational inequality or affect its impact on the city's poor.

In addition to abandoning the goals of social, legal, and educational reform, the new HCCAA board of directors also allowed the Settegast Clinic—one of William Ballew and Earl Allen's greatest accomplishments—to fall into financial trouble due to the new board's neglect. In the fall of 1966 Allen had organized Settegast residents and launched a protest campaign aimed at the Harris County Hospital District, demanding the creation and maintenance of a permanent health clinic in the neighborhood. When the hospital district agreed to these demands, Ballew and Allen believed they had proven the worth of confrontational community-organizing tactics as an effective component of the fight against poverty. While the hospital district agreed to create a permanent branch of the charity hospital in Settegast, however, there was a misunderstanding about which organization would fund the clinic once it was established. Ballew and Allen believed the responsibility fell squarely on the shoulders of the hospital district board members, and Ballew undoubtedly would have used the community action agency to continue putting pressure on the hospital district to deliver on its promises of accessible healthcare to the residents of Settegast. Because of HCCAA's changed priorities after the merger, however, board members took very little action to ensure the hospital district would continue to fund the clinic after the initial ninety-day contract expired in the summer of 1967.[22]

In June 1967, as the Settegast Clinic was rapidly running out of cash and with no prospects for additional funding on the horizon, the HCCAA board of directors passed a resolution asking the Harris County Hospital District to fund the clinic on a permanent basis. A resolution, of course, did not have the same sense of urgency as a public demonstration, and the hospital district responded by agreeing to fund the clinic for an additional ninety days until another agency could be located to provide permanent funding. A group of African American doctors began meeting during this time and decided to appeal directly to OEO to fund the clinic, but this solution could only be temporary because it was not OEO policy to fund these types of programs directly. Several HCCAA board members interpreted this appeal to OEO as a circumvention of their authority over poverty funds for the entire city and threatened to cut off funding to the clinic altogether. Although OEO agreed to fund the Settegast Clinic on a temporary basis, and the Harris County Hospital District eventually accepted responsibility for the clinic on a permanent basis as part of its neighborhood clinic program, the HCCAA board showed little interest in preserving this impressive accomplishment achieved under Ballew's tenure.[23]

The HCCAA board of directors initiated a handful of new projects and programs in 1967 that are also illustrative of the more cautious turn they took after the merger and the clear move away from confrontation. In June 1967 the new HCCAA board, in cooperation with the National Council on Aging, launched Project FIND, which was designed to use volunteers to seek out the aging poor and help them locate social services available to them. In September HCCAA chairman Francis Williams announced the initiation of a parent and child program created "to strengthen parental skills in taking care of youngsters and also to help families on the poverty level overcome some of the social and economic problems they face." As part of this program, HCCAA established several Parent and Child Centers in target neighborhoods to work closely with parents to equip them with parenting skills. The HCCAA board also helped create the Foster Grandparents program in cooperation with Protestant Charities of Houston that "recruits, trains, and employs persons over age 60, with low incomes, to serve neglected and deprived children who lack close personal relationships with adults." The program's directors placed approximately sixty older persons in local Houston hospitals to provide care for children whose parents were either absent or unable to be at the hospital for lengthy periods of time. Francis Williams and his allies on the board also placed a heavy emphasis on establishing social service programs that resembled the work HAY had been doing before the merger, including Foster Care and Counseling for Troubled Youth, Family Life Improvement and Home Management, and a Generic Counseling Service.[24]

Though many of these programs were heartwarming and undoubtedly made some poor people's lives more bearable, they were all clearly products of the more cautious philosophy that had overtaken the HCCAA board of directors in 1967. In designing these service delivery programs, board members never attempted to attack poverty by redistributing power or expanding democracy; they just tried to address the symptoms of poverty by alleviating some of its ill effects. Project FIND was simply a program for locating traditional social welfare services for the elderly poor, and programs such as the Parent and Child Centers and the other counseling service projects harked back to the tactic of attempting to change the behavior of poor people rather than addressing the structural forces that kept them locked in a cycle of poverty. These programs initiated by the HCCAA board of directors in 1967, which consumed the majority of the organization's resources, showed just how far the implementers of the War on Poverty in Houston had gotten away from the Saul Alinsky method.

By far the largest and most costly service program that the new HCCAA board launched in 1967 was the Concentrated Employment Program (CEP), which was designed in conjunction with the Texas Employment Commission to help locate jobs for unemployed and underemployed persons in Houston. Like HCCAA's other social service delivery programs, however, the CEP program had very little potential for reform. To make matters worse, CEP administrators, armed with a $5 million grant from OEO, squandered their resources, alienated the poor people that the program was designed to help, and failed to provide any tangible results for Houston's unemployed population. The main thrust of the program was job training, but HCCAA chairman Francis Williams misled Houston's poor residents into believing that CEP would be able to accomplish more than simply training residents for jobs. Williams implied that CEP would attack employment discrimination and might even create new jobs, and in the process raised expectations for the program beyond what it was capable of delivering. After announcing the CEP program, Williams criticized the city of Houston's meager efforts to provide equal employment opportunities and insinuated that CEP would be able to address some of these problems. He stated, "What has been done has been so negligible that the man in the street doesn't know that they are doing anything." Williams failed to mention, however, that a job-training program such as CEP was not designed to push for reform in hiring practices that would result in more jobs being available for the city's poor.[25]

Due to bureaucratic wrangling over various contracts, the CEP program was slow to get started in Houston. In order to provide comprehensive job training for Houston's poor, HCCAA needed to enter into contracts with several delegate agencies, such as the Houston Independent School District and the Texas Employment Commission, in order to administer various components of CEP. The most problematic impediment to the initiation of the program was whether or not the HCCAA board could enter into contracts with delegate agencies that did not require their own boards to include a significant number of poor residents or representatives of the poor. Under Ballew's direction, in 1966 the HCCAA board notified all delegate agencies that HCCAA expected poor residents to compose one-third of each of their boards by July 1968. The new members of the board, however, dispensed of this requirement despite the opposition of a few remaining progressives on the board. To add insult to injury, HCCAA board members also passed a resolution to eliminate the Manpower Advisory Committee, a group of poor residents elected from the target neighborhoods to advise the board on how the manpower programs affected poor Houston residents. The new board members made it clear that they alone would administer the CEP program without interference from the poor, and several members spoke in favor of creating an advisory committee composed of representatives from Houston's business leaders rather than the city's poor communities.[26]

CEP administrators continued Francis Williams's tactic of falsely raising the hopes of Houston's poor by implying that there was an abundance of jobs in the city. This tactic inevitably caused CEP enrollees to become disillusioned once they graduated from the program and still could not secure employment. By the summer of 1968, it was clear to most observers that the most the CEP program could accomplish was to equip enrollees with skills for jobs that did not exist. CEP administrators simply had no power to create jobs in Houston or to force the city's employers to cease their discriminatory hiring practices. The CEP program came under a tremendous amount of criticism in late 1968, and the HCCAA board never delivered on the promises made about what the job-training program could realistically accomplish.[27]

The new HCCAA board's shift to a more limited program was clearly illustrated in the programs and projects in which its members engaged after the merger. Nowhere was it more evident that the new community action agency had abandoned the Saul Alinsky method than in the new board's management of the community organization department and the remaining Alinsky-style organizers on the staff. After Francis Williams and his allies successfully took control of the HCCAA board and oversaw the merger, their most pressing problem was the fact that many confrontational community organizers, including Earl Allen, were still on the organization's employment rolls and remained committed to using the War on Poverty to expand democracy in Houston. Challenging mainstream definitions of democracy, however, was no longer the goal of HCCAA. Both during and after the merger, the new board was completely averse to confrontation or controversy of any kind. In order to render the organization more amenable to the city's public officials, Williams and other board members knew they would have to put controls on Allen and eventually defeat the Alinsky disciples who remained in the organization.[28]

As the first step in this process of controlling and eventually purging the confrontational organizers from HCCAA, Francis Williams assigned Hartsell Gray to supervise Earl Allen and his community organization staff. Gray had been an Episcopal minister in a congregation that U.S. congressman George H. W. Bush attended in Houston, and he played an important role in Bush's successful campaign for election to Congress in 1966. With Bush's help, Gray was appointed to the H-HCEOO board of directors in 1965. The two remained close friends after Bush moved to Washington in 1966, with Gray providing the freshman congressman with information about the poverty program in Houston. Gray had been a member of the H-HCEOO board of directors and had served on the personnel committee when William Ballew and Executive Director Charles Kelly recommended hiring Earl Allen as director of community organization in the fall of 1966. Gray vehemently opposed hiring Allen because he disagreed with Allen's confrontational tactics, but the overwhelming majority of the H-HCEOO board at the time was supportive of Ballew's vision and approved of Allen's hiring. Gray remained a foe of Allen and his community organization staff, however, and he was among the most outspoken board members who attacked Allen's methods in Settegast in the spring of 1967. During the merger negotiations in May 1967, Gray was a strong supporter of taming H-HCEOO in order to merge with the more cautious HAY.[29]

As part of the effort to rein in some of the activities of Allen's community organization staff and make the merger a success, Gray had been a significant contributor to the drawing up of a new Community Development Work Plan designed to professionalize members of Allen's staff and refocus them toward less confrontational activities. The new plan, which was carried over into the merged community action agency, called for the community organization staff to undergo retraining. Their duties were changed to include locating services for poor residents rather than organizing them to confront local elected officials or make demands on the city's institutions. Gray and several others on the HCCAA board were so confident that the new Community Development Work Plan would empower the board to control the community organization staff that they reinstated Pluria Marshall, who had been involved in protests and demonstrations on the campus of Texas Southern University in May 1967.[30]

As soon as the merger was complete, the new HCCAA executive committee met in June 1967 to decide how to reorganize the two staffs from H-HCEOO and HAY and to determine which staff members to retain in the new community action agency. In a surprising change of course, Gray strongly urged the committee to allow Earl Allen to continue in his current position, now called "director of community development," because he was the only staff member who had personal contact with militant African American leaders in Houston. There was, however, one important stipulation; Gray insisted that the new executive committee appoint him as the deputy director of resource development and, of most importance, that they designate Gray as Allen's immediate supervisor. Gray was determined to control Allen and the other organizers on the staff, and he assured the committee that Allen's confrontational tactics would diminish once Allen was put under Gray's close supervision. A majority of the HCCAA executive committee agreed, and in June 1967 Hartsell Gray—a man who had opposed hiring Allen, attacked his methods incessantly, helped rewrite the plan for organizing poor neighborhoods to make the tactics less confrontational, and was bent on controlling the confrontational organizers on the staff—became Allen's supervisor and was responsible for overseeing the implementation of the new community development plan.[31]

Federal OEO inspectors who evaluated Houston's new merged community action agency in the summer of 1967 were skeptical about the new arrangement. In a report sent to OEO officials in Washington, these inspectors expressed concern that the authors of HCCAA's new Community Development Work Plan had failed to define clearly the long-range goals of Allen's staff and that board members were unaware of the mission of the community development department. Most alarming to the federal inspectors, however, were their interactions with Hartsell Gray. One OEO inspector noted that Gray "is more sensitive to the voices of the locally elected officials than to any other community element," and because of this he "has attempted to cloak the efforts of the CAA under the mantle of 'moderate, liberal' leadership of Harris County . . . [and] has seen his task as a staff member to keep the dissident staff members quiet thereby neutralizing Earl Allen or forcing his resignation."[32]

Inspectors were uncertain about Gray's motivations for wanting to shape the future direction for the community action agency in Houston. Gray proclaimed himself to be a believer in the "democratic process," but few could determine what he meant by that term. Gray publicly supported increased participation by poor residents in the poverty program through elections but at the same time stated that ultimate control of the War on Poverty in Houston rested with local public officials. It was also evident to the federal OEO inspectors that Gray was willing to use sinister methods to "neutralize" Allen and his staff; one OEO official described Gray as "the most Byzantine character in a Byzantine city." For example, federal inspectors discovered that in addition to Houston police chief Herman Short, Gray had also been providing much of the negative information regarding the activities of HCCAA employees to Bush and Welch, particularly with regard to the TSU Riot and the turmoil in Settegast. The inspectors agreed that the poverty program in Houston would be better off without Gray, but none of them believed it would be possible for the HCCAA board to terminate his employment without Gray creating a major controversy for the organization through his connections to Bush and Welch.[33]

Members of the federal OEO inspection team noted that in addition to impediments created by Gray, Earl Allen and his staff were also being attacked by other forces in the city. Inspectors concluded that Earl Allen and his staff were "capable, militant, and close to the mood of the 'folk,'" but their worthwhile efforts were being thwarted by pillars of the Houston establishment, including the "liberal political organization" and the "traditional business" interests in the city. "A fear of controversy," continued the inspector, "seems as evident among 'liberal' [HCCAA] board members as among the conservatives. The legitimacy of CAP personnel being a part of community efforts to petition the power structure for redress of real grievances is in doubt. The word 'demonstration' has taken on an awesome, fear-inspiring meaning within OEO organizations, in spite of the vital part demonstrations have played in the social development of our country and their central meaning to our democratic tradition." The federal OEO inspector continued, "[Earl] Allen believes that no meaningful community action can occur in a city like Houston without some confrontation between the impoverished citizens of the slums and the power structure. . . . As Allen . . . told me, 'In Houston there is no such thing as a peaceful demonstration.' All demonstrations are, a priori, non-peaceful and unlawful." The inspector concluded that Mayor Welch had taken full advantage of the HCCAA board's defensiveness and the widespread fear of rioting by "planting stories that the CAP staff is 'Black Power infiltrated' and other such pot-shots."[34]

These developments that occurred in the first few months after the merger deepened the divisions within HCCAA, particularly between the board and Allen's staff, as Gray took it upon himself to purge the Alinsky-style organizers from the organization. Despite changes on the board and modifications to the community development plan, Earl Allen and much of his staff remained firmly committed to the Saul Alinsky method and to the necessity for open conflict and confrontation with Houston's public officials. HCCAA leadership, however, had been growing more cautious since the merger, and most approved of Gray's attempts to control Allen and his staff. As soon as Gray took over as deputy director of resource development in June 1967, he immediately began circumventing Allen's authority over his community development staff, redirecting community organizers toward less controversial activities. He also purged from the HCCAA staff the remaining Alinsky disciples who refused to be controlled by Gray and the new board of directors.[35]

Serious difficulties began immediately after Gray assumed his new position as Allen's supervisor. As Allen was busy reorganizing his staff after a somewhat chaotic melding of staff members from H-HCEOO and HAY, Gray made his first move to undercut Allen's authority over his own staff. Stating that he did not trust Allen to administer any portion of the new community development plan, Gray arbitrarily reassigned forty-six of Allen's community organizers away from the neighborhoods where Allen had placed them and ordered them to work in several HCCAA neighborhood centers under the supervision of James Williams, a former HAY staff member. A few days later Gray removed twenty-three of Allen's community development specialists from the field and ordered them to undergo training in the central HCCAA office for several weeks. Gray readily admitted to a federal inspector that he intentionally diverted Allen's staff in order to get them out of the target neighborhoods, where many board members believed they were stirring up too much trouble and threatening the reputation of the poverty program.[36]

Following the reassignment of the community development staff without consulting Allen, Gray began reprioritizing the duties of Allen's staff to focus on various "crash programs," such as recruiting for summer Head Start and the Neighborhood Youth Corps, advertising for the Job Fair planned in conjunction with Mayor Welch's office, and gathering resources for a summer youth recreation program. Several of these "crash programs" were very poorly planned, and when this lack of planning drew criticism from the HCCAA board and from poor Houston residents, Gray used the negative publicity to attack Allen and his community development staff even more viciously. Gray had developed a habit of simultaneously demeaning Allen in board meetings and implying that Allen had lost his own authority over the staff while also giving the impression that Allen was deliberately attempting to radicalize staff members and carry out a Black Power agenda. Gray made statements to the board such as, "I tell Allen what I want, and he does it," while at the same time accusing Allen of allowing Black Power advocates and "SNCC types" to infiltrate the community development staff. According to a federal inspector, Mayor Welch and Congressman Bush, who by this time were on edge about the prospect of continued demonstrations, undoubtedly prompted Gray to attack Allen in this way. Welch was so concerned about Allen's activities in Houston's poor neighborhoods that he ordered undercover police surveillance of Allen and certain members of his staff. By mid-summer 1967 Gray had decided that the only way to satisfy Welch and Bush and to rid the HCCAA community development staff of SNCC operatives was to force Earl Allen to resign as community development director and to professionalize the staff by purging the more aggressive community organizers from the organization.[37]

The TSU 5 indictments handed down in the summer of 1967 provided Gray and his allies with the ammunition they needed to begin ridding HCCAA of the more confrontational organizers on Allen's staff. In early June a Houston grand jury issued indictments against five Texas Southern University students, charging them with murdering Houston police officer Louis R. Kuba and attempting to murder two other officers who were injured during the TSU Riot in the previous month. It is unclear whether the grand jury had access to police information showing that Kuba was killed by a ricocheting bullet fired by another police officer, but that revelation would have mattered very little since the grand jury charged the students not with firing the actual shots but with "setting in motion the violence that took the rookie officer's life and wounded the other two." As District Attorney Carol Vance explained, "One engaged in any riot whereby an illegal act is committed, shall be deemed guilty of the offense of riot according to the character and degree of such offense, whether the said illegal act was perpetrated by him or by those with whom he is participating. All persons are principals who are guilty of acting together in the commission of an offense." In an even more shocking affront to reality, grand jury foreman W. A. Ruhmann stated that the jury also found "that our law enforcement officials acted with due restraint. . . . With numerous rumors of police brutality, we find that the law enforcement officers acted in the best interests of the community. We find that this trouble was caused or encouraged by a few agitators and troublemakers." After the grand jury issued the indictments, District Judge Fred Hooey denied bond to the group of students now referred to as the "TSU 5." It took two weeks for attorneys provided by the NAACP to convince a judge to set bond for the five defendants, but in mid-June the TSU 5 were allowed to post bail and leave the Houston city jail. The trial was set to begin in July, but then a protest of the scheduled trial in the Third Ward near the TSU campus turned violent as several demonstrators broke store windows and set small fires. In response to the violence, a district judge granted a continuance and postponed the trial of the TSU 5 until the fall of 1967.[38]

HCCAA and the TSU 5 first crossed paths in early July 1967 when the HCCAA board of directors launched Project Go, a temporary summer recreation program designed to "cool down the long hot summer" in Houston. With a $600,000 grant from OEO, HCCAA officials hired more than four hundred young people to staff Project Go and employed them as recreation workers and neighborhood developers. An HCCAA board member described the summer program as an attempt to provide constructive activities for Houston's youth and keep them from causing any trouble in the city. He stated, "We know from experience that summer trouble often starts because there are young people on the street with nothing to do. We propose to hire the troublemakers as the neighborhood developers, and keep them busy collecting data, helping the poor find jobs and pointing out services to people who need them. This will help cool down the long hot summer." In early July, as HCCAA employees moved from the planning stages to the implementation of Project Go, program administrators decided to hire two rather prominent "troublemakers" in Houston who were then part of the TSU 5. That month they hired Trazawell Franklin and Floyd Nichols, both under indictment for the murder of Officer Kuba, to work in the summer recreation program.[39]

The hiring of Franklin and Nichols did not cause any immediate problems for HCCAA as Project Go got off to a smooth start in mid-July. A small army of newly hired HCCAA staff members fanned out over the Houston area and provided recreational activities for children between the ages of one and twelve at parks and recreation centers located in the children's own neighborhoods. Mayor Welch's office even helped organize a citywide job fair to work in conjunction with Project Go to provide employment for teenagers who were too old for the summer recreation program. Several HCCAA board members publicly applauded their own efforts to hire potential rioters and other troublemakers and turn them into productive citizens.[40]

The problem started during the first week in August, however, when Hartsell

Gray discovered that Franklin and Nichols had been hired as part of Project Go without his knowledge. Though the stated purpose of the program was to hire militant agitators and allow them to participate in the constructive work of the poverty program, Gray interpreted the employment of Franklin and Nichols as simply another step in Allen's plan to fill his staff with Black Power advocates and troublemakers. Gray immediately notified Congressman Bush that HCCAA had hired these two men, and Bush in turn told Mayor Welch and Police Chief Short. By the time OEO officials were made aware of the situation in late July, Gray had already made the news public in an effort to discredit Allen and his staff even further.[41]

Southwest regional OEO director Walter Richter rushed to Houston the next day to meet with Mayor Welch and to try to prevent the situation from inflicting an additional blemish on the poverty program. At Welch's insistence, Richter strongly encouraged HCCAA chairman Francis Williams to terminate Franklin's and Nichols's employment with the community action agency and to relieve them of their duties immediately. Since Williams was determined to give the poverty program a better image in Houston and was under increasing pressure from Gray and his allies to get rid of the militants in the organization, he complied with Richter's request: on August 4, he fired Franklin and Nichols. In an effort to blunt the inevitable reaction from the militant black community in Houston, however, Williams also arranged for a local labor union to employ Franklin and Nichols for the rest of the summer. According to Williams, Franklin and Nichols accepted the decision without opposition; they said they understood the reason for their termination and that they would happily assume their new positions with the labor union the following week.[42]

A few days after Williams fired Franklin and Nichols, Mayor Welch publicly applauded the decision in an interview with the *Houston Post*. Welch stated that he was shocked to learn that the HCCAA board would hire two men facing murder charges, but he was confident that Williams would "not tolerate this sort of thing" because his philosophy was "apparently different from those first promoted within" the community action agency. "Williams appears dedicated to making the organization what it is intended to be," continued Welch, "[which is] one that fights poverty and not a civil rights organization."[43]

Many members of Houston's black community, however, were already fuming about the TSU 5 indictments. They believed the charges were illegitimate and most likely the products of a racist mayor and police chief. They greeted the news of Franklin's and Nichols's termination with outrage and bitterness. The firings even prompted an angry letter from Roy Wilkins, executive director of the NAACP, in which he chastised Sargent Shriver for allowing this miscarriage of justice to occur within the poverty program. Wilkins pointed out that OEO guidelines prevented local community action agencies from hiring any person convicted of being involved in a riot, but those guidelines said nothing about a person charged and not convicted. He stated, "The dismissal of these . . . students, based upon charges which have been preferred but not yet determined, is an excellent example of prejudgment. Moreover, the abuse of discretion evidenced by their discharge is precisely the type of behavior which the Negro community has come to expect, to resent and to protest by methods which are becoming increasingly more violent. . . . The termination of these students' employment with the OEO program, based upon charges which have not been submitted to trial contradicts the principle, embodied in our Constitution, that all persons shall be presumed innocent until proven guilty." Despite these pleadings, Shriver and southwest regional OEO officials never wavered in their support of the decision to terminate the employment of Franklin and Nichols.[44]

Hartsell Gray used the momentum created by the firings to begin advocating for the complete elimination of the Community Development Program and the dismissal of Earl Allen and his entire staff. Gray was convinced that SNCC members had control of Project Go and that Franklin and Nichols were simply the first of many needed terminations on the HCCAA staff. He told a federal inspector that the only way to wrest control of the poverty program from SNCC militants was to rid the organization of Earl Allen and his Community Development staff. Gray stated, "All of the problems in this community have been caused by HCCAA staff members." In a highly suspect accusation, Gray claimed that Allen told his staff members that "the Negro must be taught to hate the Whites before some action can take place." However improbable Gray's statements may have been, the fact remained that because of the Project Go incident, by August 1967 he had enough support on the HCCAA board of directors and executive committee to deliver on his threat to expel Allen and his staff from the organization.[45]

By this time Earl Allen could read the handwriting on the wall. HCCAA would never again be a vehicle for expanding democracy in Houston, and therefore his services would no longer be needed in the organization. Near the end of the first week in August he tendered his resignation to the HCCAA board of directors. Citing the firing of Franklin and Nichols, Allen stated that he could no longer administer the Community Development program for HCCAA because Hartsell Gray was bent on eliminating his entire operation in Houston. During a lengthy interview with Saralee Tiede of the *Houston Chronicle*, Allen said that his resignation from HCCAA should be interpreted as "the admission of a militant Negro professional that he cannot work in the politically charged atmosphere of the antipoverty program," and he reiterated his commitment to the use of confrontational tactics to empower Houston's poor. He continued, "Numbers are usually the only strength poor people have. It's a very honorable technique in the whole scheme of things for creating a bargaining atmosphere and it should not be denied the folk who have no alternative." The HCCAA board of directors and Allen's superiors in the organization had become so afraid of open conflict, he argued, that he could no longer carry out his plan for community development. "My powers to hire and fire staff were curtailed," Allen exclaimed, "while criticism often resulted in staff being transferred over my objection. The result of criticism was always an order to cool it. As a result the staff was frustrated and demoralized. We were always getting ready, never really getting in to do something." Allen argued that the problems he faced in the poverty program were systemic problems with the entire antipoverty effort. He stated, "There is a basic contradiction in the war on poverty. The agencies charged with affecting [sic] change are themselves threatened by change." Allen's solution, therefore, was to create a privately funded independent antipoverty organization capable of changing the status quo and free of ties to the existing order in Houston. He promised that his new organization would be dedicated to empowering poor people and minorities in the city, and he said its motto would be "Don't burn, baby, let's build, because we have the tools."[46]

Before launching their own antipoverty organization, Allen and his supporters wanted to create a forum where HCCAA staff members could register their displeasure with the agency and the way it conducted the War on Poverty in the city. On August 8, 1967, Allen and approximately a hundred community development staff members staged a protest at HCCAA headquarters demanding Allen's reinstatement, with increased authority over the community development program; and the rehiring of Project Go employees Trazawell Franklin, Floyd Nichols, and Kelton Sams. Sams had worked as a liaison between the Project Go staff and Allen's community development department and had been one of Allen's closest and most trusted allies in the organization. After Sams appeared on a radio panel discussion the previous day and spoke about the poverty program in Houston without permission from the HCCAA board, Hartsell Gray persuaded Francis Williams to fire Sams rather than give him a simple warning. After walking a picket line for several hours, many of the protesters began blocking the entrances to the HCCAA building and refusing to allow anyone to enter or exit. When Francis Williams returned from lunch that afternoon, he had to force his way through the picketers in order to reach the door. Once inside, Williams called the Houston police and asked them to remove the protesters. Police officers arrived within minutes to disperse the crowd. The protesters agreed to leave peacefully, but Allen and Sams vowed they would return the next day until changes were made to the poverty program.[47]

Williams and Gray were furious about HCCAA employees being involved in protests against the organization. The next day they fired twenty-three employees they had witnessed picketing with Allen and Sams. Williams stated that the reason for the firings was that these employees failed to report to their assigned posts on the day of the protest, but it was clear that Williams and Gray wanted to send a message to any other HCCAA employee who was considering challenging their authority over the poverty program. The firings also represented the latest development in Gray's attempt to purge the organization of those individuals loyal to Earl Allen. By the end of the summer, Gray's crusade to clean up the HCCAA staff was well on its way to completion.[48]

One of the fears consuming Williams, Gray, and other members of the HCCAA board was that a riot could break out in Houston and poverty workers could possibly be implicated in it. Other than the police riot on the campus of Texas Southern University in May 1967, Houston had been mostly spared the racial violence that plagued other major cities in the mid-1960s. At the same time, no one in Houston interpreted the absence of an outbreak of violence for an absence of racial tension. After riots caused widespread destruction in Watts, Newark, Detroit, and many other American cities, Houstonians understandably were on edge about the possibility of a major riot in their city. This fear that gripped much of Houston undoubtedly had a profound effect on the administration of the War on Poverty in the city and created an atmosphere conducive to the purging of the more aggressive community organizers from the organization.

In August 1967, the fear of an urban riot occurring in Houston played a role in an episode involving HCCAA that bordered on farce. This drama involved an HCCAA supplies officer and an order for several surplus rifle scopes from the U.S. Air Force. This incident pushed HCCAA leaders into an even more defensive position and prompted Williams and others to dissociate themselves from the alleged troublemakers even further. The saga began in July when George T. Miller, a sixty-four-year-old white Houstonian and HCCAA property control manager, placed an order for seven surplus telescopic rifle scopes from Kelly Air Force Base in San Antonio, Texas, without getting approval from any of his superiors in the organization. Although Miller would later claim that he wanted to purchase the scopes in order to build microscopes from the lenses to use in an HCCAA job-training program, there is some evidence that this explanation was fabricated after the story broke in August. Regardless of Miller's motive, on August 3 agents with the Houston office of the Federal Bureau of Investigation (FBI) decided to investigate the matter quietly before the local press discovered the story. The FBI did, however, notify the OEO Office of Inspection that they were conducting an investigation, and OEO officials called the Houston Police Department's Intelligence Division to make them aware of what was going on. Two days later FBI officials determined that neither Miller nor HCCAA had violated any federal law and ended the investigation.[49]

The FBI's decision not to pursue the investigation any further infuriated members of the Houston Police Department, especially Police Chief Herman Short, who decided to take matters into his own hands. During a routine news conference on August 11, Short insinuated to reporters that Miller had attempted to order the telescopic rifle scopes and poverty workers wanted to use them for violent purposes. Stating that he was filled with "such a feeling of disgust and outrage," Short showed members of the press the order form submitted by HCCAA and pointed out that the wording "specifically asked for scopes equipped with standard range settings that could be attached to high-powered rifles." When reporters approached George Miller about the order, Miller claimed he could not remember submitting any order for rifle scopes and stated that the order may have been submitted without his signature. A day later, however, Miller held his own news conference and stated that he indeed ordered the surplus rifle scopes and that they were to be converted into micro-scopes for a job-training program. The *Houston Chronicle* quoted a master gunsmith, however, who argued that "there is no conceivable way a telescopic sight can be converted into a microscope." Predictably, a controversy soon arose over exactly what use an antipoverty agency would have with military-grade rifle sights.[50]

Upon receiving the details of this developing story from his home district, Congressman Bush demanded a full congressional investigation into the rifle scope order. On August 14 Bush addressed the House of Representatives and stated that the entire rifle scope incident "indicates a gross stupidity on the part of OEO" and that poverty workers in Houston were "totally lacking in judgment." Bush continued, "In this critical summer period of civil unrest, a citizen of Houston might well believe that the scopes were ordered for use in a disturbance. After reading of the sniping incidents in Detroit, Newark, and other cities, it is understandable that a Houston citizen might view an order for scopes as a threat to the peace of his community." It was understandable for Houston citizens to make this assumption, according to Bush, but even he implied that it was unlikely that HCCAA would order rifle sights to use in a riot. As he stated to Congress, there were several possible explanations for the or-der. Although the mystery of the rifle scope episode was never solved to many observers' satisfaction, the most probable explanation for the rifle scope order boiled down to political graft. Bush suggested to Congress that Miller or one of his employees wanted to obtain the scopes to give to their friends to use on their deer-hunting rifles.[51]

Despite the fact that Bush recognized the improbability that HCCAA employ-ees wanted to use the rifle sights in case a riot broke out in Houston, he nonethe-less went a step further in order to link the poverty program and the potential for riots even more closely. For example, Bush reminded the representatives that very recently HCCAA had come under fire for hiring potential rioters. "The ordering of the scopes," Bush continued, "was revealed only a week after the facts were released that the Houston OEO had hired two young men under indictment for murder in connection with the death of a police officer in the recent disturbances at Texas Southern University." Because of these two incidents, Bush demanded a full congressional investigation of the poverty program in Houston and urged investigators to ascertain why HCCAA employees would have required rifle scopes to fight poverty in the city.[52]

After Bush's call for an investigation, federal investigators from the U.S. Air Force, the OEO Office of Inspection, and the FBI rushed to Houston to conduct a complete inventory of all HCCAA's possessions. More important, Bush succeeded in persuading the House Education and Labor Committee to initiate a full investigation of all of HCCAA's activities in Houston, a development that brought national attention to these local controversies. This investigation would prove to be short lived and its report inconclusive, but in the fall of 1967 the Senate Committee on Government Operations, under the direction of Arkansas senator John L. McClellan, pursued a more comprehensive inquiry into the connection between Houston's community action agency and the potential for urban riots in the city. Bush wanted to make a connection in people's minds between the poverty program and urban riots, and by using the rifle scope fiasco in Houston he was able to accomplish that goal. Although federal investigators eventually accepted Miller's explanation that the lenses from the scopes were to be used to build microscopes for a job-training program and approved the delivery of the lenses without the scopes, the entire event added yet another blemish to an organization already under attack for its alleged ties to Black Power militants and potential rioters. After the rifle scope incident, HCCAA leaders, particularly Francis Williams and Hartsell Gray, became even more cautious in their outlook, distancing their organization even further from supposed militants. At the same time, Welch and Short once again ramped up their attack on the poverty program in Houston.[53]

The increasingly cautious approach of HCCAA's administrators and their purging of the more aggressive community organizers led to even deeper divisions within the community action agency and caused a rapid decline in support from Houston's poor neighborhoods. A striking indication that HCCAA had lost the support of many of Houston's poor residents was the incredibly low voter turnout during elections to place poor residents on the HCCAA board of directors. In the midst of Earl Allen's protests against the organization in mid-August 1967, HCCAA board members, under pressure from OEO officials in Washington, tried to meet federal guidelines for including the poor on their board by holding elections in several poor neighborhoods in the city. HCCAA employees set up thirty-eight polling places located in nine target areas and kept them open all day in order to ensure a high voter turnout. Their hopes were dashed, however, when less than 1 percent of eligible voters in the poor neighborhoods showed up at the polls. In one district, not a single person voted, and the result was that no representative was sent to the board from that area.[54]

Even more damaging to the reputation of HCCAA than low voter turnout, however, was a rapidly increasing number of poor residents who began speaking out against the organization and expressing their disappointment with the poverty program. During a meeting in July 1967, as Hartsell Gray was attempting to rein in the activities of Allen and his community organization staff, several residents from one of the neighborhoods where Gray had removed HCCAA community organizers arrived to lodge their complaints with the board. One resident expressed outrage that, since Allen's staff members had been removed, neighborhood centers were being closed down and a complete communication breakdown was threatening to occur between poverty workers and poor residents. Another resident complained that the few HCCAA employees who remained in her neighborhood refused to speak with poor residents and instead simply made notes about the activities of community organizers in the area. A third resident informed the board that the director of the neighborhood center in her area frequently refused to allow residents to use the HCCAA facility for meetings and other events. All of the residents who attended the meeting agreed that their neighborhoods desperately needed community organizers to return and continue the work they began under Allen's direction.[55]

These complaints went largely unaddressed, and poor residents began complaining to reporters from the local newspapers in order to make their voices heard. A team of *Houston Chronicle* reporters visited four of HCCAA's ten target areas around the city in early September 1967 to ascertain how much the War on Poverty had helped Houston's poor. Their final report described their mission as "uncomfortable and soul-depressing" as they witnessed firsthand the seemingly incurable "want, deprivation and misery of body and spirit." Many of the poor residents made very critical comments about the federal War on Poverty and how the local community action agency administered it. "For all but a few," the report stated, "the federal War on Poverty is no more than a slogan. It is as distant in effect as the Civil War is in time." One resident they interviewed proclaimed, "Some poor people are being helped by the poverty program. But the very poor are not." By 1968 several poor Houstonians had resorted to writing letters to President Johnson to inform him that the people of Houston were quickly losing faith in the War on Poverty because of the way in which the HCCAA board administered the program.[56]

By far the loudest complaints about how HCCAA employees and the board administered the poverty program in Houston came from Mexican Americans in Area 9, a poor area near the ship channel on the east side of the city. In February 1968 Hector del Castillo, president of a Mexican American community group in the area, sent a letter to southwest regional OEO director Walter

Richter expressing his shock and outrage that the HCCAA board of directors had recently diverted more than $300,000 from Area 9 and used it for programs in a section of the city with no Mexican American residents. Later in the month A. D. Asios, the chairman of the Area 9 Committee on the HCCAA board of directors, expressed his alarm to Richter that for six months the HCCAA board had completely neglected Area 9. Asios proclaimed that he was very angry that the area was then being offered "a token program which is totally inadequate, unequal in its application and completely discriminatory." Richter responded to both men by trying to shift the blame from HCCAA to the delegate agencies that were responsible for implementing the programs in Area 9. Richter admitted that there had been problems extending programs into the area but promised that Francis Williams would adequately address their concerns.[57]

Apparently the response from Richter and the action taken by Williams did not satisfy Mexican Americans in Area 9. In August 1968 they approached Texas state representative Lauro Cruz from Houston with their grievances about the poverty program. Cruz was able to convince officials at the southwest regional OEO office that an inspection should be performed to investigate the allegations being made about HCCAA's neglect of the Mexican American community in Houston. The inspection team found that the HCCAA board was indeed guilty of neglecting Houston's Mexican American community in programming, using discriminatory hiring practices and denying Mexican Americans a voice in the planning and implementation of the poverty program in the city. Although OEO officials outlined several steps that the HCCAA board could take to remedy these problems, by the end of 1968 very little had been accomplished; Mexican American residents of Area 9 continued to complain about the poverty program.[58]

While HCCAA administrators became more cautious in their implementation of the War on Poverty in Houston, the Reverend Wallace B. Poteat, Ecumenical Fellowship Latin American Channel (EF-LAC) project activists, and VISTA volunteers attempted to continue with their more aggressive and confrontational approach to community action designed to expand the meaning of democracy in the city. In the Third Ward, VISTA volunteers organized residents to go to Houston city council meetings to put pressure on the councilmen to build a public library in their neighborhood. A VISTA volunteer in the Fifth Ward organized a neighborhood council to pressure the city council to build more parks and other outdoor recreational areas in their neighborhood. Another volunteer in the Fifth Ward organized the tenants who lived in homes owned by the same landlord and pressured the owner to repaint all of their houses. After achieving this victory, this newly formed tenant union successfully persuaded city officials to pave the roads and install streetlights in their neighborhood. In an impoverished neighborhood near the ship channel, a VISTA volunteer began holding meetings to educate residents about how to set up their own credit union, and in another area on the east side VISTA organized parents into a committee to monitor school board decisions that affected schools in their neighborhood and to arrange extracurricular activities for their children. In another neighborhood a VISTA volunteer organized a Golden Age Club for senior citizens to provide activities and lobby the city council in the interests of retired persons.[59]

After living in Houston's poor neighborhoods and witnessing firsthand the daily lives of those living in poverty, nearly all of the VISTA volunteers recognized the need for welfare reform. This was true all over the country. As poverty workers came into close contact with families that depended on welfare payments, primarily through Aid to Families with Dependent Children (AFDC), it quickly became apparent that changes in the welfare system were needed. Many poverty workers across the country discovered that a number of loosely knit grassroots organizations had already been formed, mainly by mothers, to advocate for higher welfare payments and better treatment from caseworkers. With assistance provided by community organizers, many of whom were VISTA volunteers, the National Welfare Rights Organization was born in 1967 out of these local pressure groups. As historian Premilla Nadasen has argued, "The welfare rights movement was perhaps one of the most important political and social struggles of the 1960s."[60]

VISTA volunteers in Houston quickly recognized the need for welfare reform, but few could locate existing welfare rights organizations in the city like those found in other parts of the country. In July 1967, VISTA volunteer Frank Barrett argued that, based on his experiences in many of Houston's poor neighborhoods, "one of the great problems of this wealthy city is the plight of the welfare recipient in Houston and the distinct aura of the 1930s which surrounds the administration of public assistance." Barrett proposed that VISTA volunteers begin organizing the poor into cohesive groups that would be able to pressure the Harris County Welfare Department and the Commissioners Court to increase the amount of welfare payments and demand fair treatment for all Houston citizens receiving welfare support. Barrett described the impossibility of poor and relatively powerless individuals to effectively deal with the welfare establishment in Houston and argued that only through organization could welfare recipients be empowered to make demands on the city's welfare bureaucracy. Going a step further, Barrett advocated using lawyers from the Houston Legal Foundation to demand real reform of the welfare system by filing lawsuits against pillars of the welfare establishment whose administrators abused the system or treated recipients unfairly. The VISTA volunteer, argued Barrett, would thus serve as a catalyst for reform and could assist attorneys by using the local media to expose flaws and inequalities in the city's welfare system. Most important, Barrett argued, an effort to push for welfare rights in Houston would empower poor residents to demand justice from a system that had thus far denied it to them. Barrett's report had a profound effect on EF-LAC project directors and other VISTA volunteers working in Houston, and by the end of the year VISTA volunteers in all areas of Houston had begun organizing welfare rights organizations.[61]

Several inevitable clashes between VISTA volunteers working to empower poor Houston residents and the city's public officials and other defenders of the status quo began to occur more regularly in 1967. As VISTA volunteers continued to focus on community organizing, many of them came into direct conflict with reactionary forces in Houston. Arsonists started fires in the VISTA-run East End Teen Center near the ship channel twice between November 1966 and January 1967, the second of which almost burned the center to the ground. Rev. Poteat commented in the wake of the second fire that the neighborhood "is a breeding ground for crime and antagonistic racial feelings." During an EF-LAC trustees meeting held after an investigation concluded that both fires were the result of arson, Rev. Poteat proclaimed that the arsonists must have really believed the Ku Klux Klan when they charged EF-LAC organizers with "orgies" in the teen center. L. S. Sedita, a landlord in the Third Ward who owned the building in which the VISTA volunteers had established a teen recreation center, evicted the VISTA tenants after receiving multiple complaints from his other tenants about profanity, drinking, and fighting at the center. Rev. Poteat and the VISTA volunteers were able to get five hundred neighborhood residents to sign a petition demanding they be allowed to stay in the building, but Sedita refused to budge. Ironically, the teens who frequented the center had just voted to name the building the "Sedita Recreation Center." After the VISTA volunteers got some publicity surrounding these issues, landlords began arbitrarily raising the rents on their apartments and community centers. Critics of the VISTA volunteers in Houston also accused the EF-LAC project of being a haven for draft dodgers, a charge Rev. Poteat vehemently denied by pointing to the fact that many of Houston's VISTA volunteers were veterans of the U.S. Armed Forces and also the fact that VISTA service did not exempt a volunteer from military service.[62]

In addition to property destruction and public accusations, one VISTA volunteer, in a report on the conditions in Houston, recounted a number of hostile actions against their programs: "The day of the last fire some of the local segregationists tried to break a chair over my head in a restaurant. The Chairman of the Board of the project was shot at by a local Klaner. The Ku Klux Klan used to call the director of the project at home at 3 a.m." The Houston Police Department, which Rev. Poteat always argued was infiltrated by members of the Ku Klux Klan and the John Birch Society, was openly antagonistic to VISTA volunteers in poor neighborhoods. In January 1967, the same month that arsonists set fire to the East End Teen Center for the second time, officers from the Houston Police Department's Criminal Intelligence Division began a confidential investigation of a VISTA volunteer in Houston because they believed he had "Civil Rights political affiliations."[63] While the East End Teen Center was burning to the ground in the middle of the night on January 2, 1967, police officers arrested VISTA volunteer Marc Jacobs and charged him with loitering simply because he was standing on the front lawn of his rented home across the street from the fire and at one time attempted to help extinguish the fire. As the officers were taking him to the police station, they accused him of being an atheist and a beatnik and made numerous "offensive statements about VISTA." Houston Legal Foundation attorneys eventually convinced the courts that police officers misinterpreted Jacobs's attempts to help contain the fire as obstructing their work, but police harassment continued. When Frank Barrett, a VISTA volunteer in the ship channel area, provided emergency transportation to the hospital for neighborhood residents, he received six separate citations by the Houston Police Department within a twenty-four-hour period for having a local residence but an out-of-state driver's license. The charges were clearly spurious and Barrett was never prosecuted in court, but this kind of harassment from Houston police officers severely hindered the work of the VISTA volunteers in the city. Police officers also repeatedly harassed two female VISTA volunteers in the Third Ward for being the only white women in the neighborhood. In the midst of increasing concern over rioting in urban ghettos that began in 1965, Rev. Poteat warned that "unless communication at the grass-roots level between the white community and the black community is opened up, understood, and supported by the white community, Houston may be in for serious trouble."[64]

An additional problem that the VISTA volunteers faced beginning in 1967 was an increasing number of conflicts with HCCAA, the city's official community action agency. Before May 1967, VISTA volunteers in Houston had received enormous support from H-HCEOO, particularly because William Ballew, Charles Kelly, and Earl Allen were sympathetic to the tactics employed by the VISTA volunteers. Beginning during the summer of 1967, as Francis Williams and Hartsell Gray attempted to shift the activities of the recently merged HCCAA in a more cautious direction, away from community organizing and empowerment of the poor, the work of many VISTA volunteers inevitably clashed with that effort. In fact, VISTA volunteers in Houston became some of the most vocal critics of HCCAA's shift to a more limited program of social service delivery. During an inspection of HCCAA in late August 1967, a federal OEO inspector noted that the VISTA volunteers in particular were the most critical of Williams. "The VISTAs like and sympathize with the major militant leaders," stated the inspector, "feel they are the natural leaders of the ghettos, and are alarmed at the cleanup that Williams is doing." An open feud between HCCAA and the EF-LAC project began early in 1968 when several Mexican American organizations in the ship channel area, together with VISTA volunteers, protested the way the community action association planned to spend a $300,000 grant from the federal government in the area. Mexican American civic leaders proclaimed that HCCAA would only agree to fund "a token program, inadequate in comparison to needs, unequal in application and totally discriminatory." EF-LAC organizers argued that the tactic of HCCAA was to develop antipoverty measures in their offices and implement them in neighborhoods regardless of whether residents wanted these programs or not. In an interview with the *Houston Chronicle*, Francis Williams, HCCAA executive director, exclaimed that if the residents of poor neighborhoods in the ship channel area did not want the federal funds spent on programs in their area, then HCCAA would be happy to spend the money elsewhere.[65]

Federal OEO inspectors placed the blame for this dwindling support among poor residents and grassroots antipoverty activists squarely on the shoulders of the conflicting factions within HCCAA that had existed since before H-HCEOO and HAY had merged to form a single community action agency for the city. According to the inspection team, the internal divisions within HCCAA were incredibly harmful to the entire antipoverty effort in the city because petty squabbles were filtering out into the staff in the target neighborhoods. As long as the staff remained divided, there was little hope that poor people would be-come confident in the work being done in their neighborhoods. One inspector believed that Hartsell Gray was mostly to blame for these internal divisions because of his arbitrary firings and reassignment of HCCAA personnel. The in-spector remarked that because of Gray's actions, "the poor are very suspicious of HCCAA." With no unity and very little sense of direction among themselves, HCCAA leaders could hardly expect to inspire confidence or trust among Hous-ton's poor residents.[66]

HCCAA administrators not only suffered from diminishing support from the very people they were supposed to be helping, they also faced declining support from OEO officials in Washington who were beginning to back off of their com-mitment to the concept of community action as well as from some members of Congress who started increasing their attacks on the entire poverty program. As historian Allen J. Matusow has shown, national OEO officials were in retreat by 1967, and it was inevitable that local community action agencies would follow. "In 1967," argued Matusow, "the question was not whether CAP would continue to promote change but whether it would even be permitted to exist." There were certainly enough anti–War on Poverty votes in Congress to abolish OEO, and, according to Matusow, it fell to an unlikely savior of the poverty program to ensure its continuance. Democratic Representative Edith Green of Oregon, who since the early days of the juvenile delinquency program had opposed the very concept of community action, submitted a last-minute change to the OEO re-authorization bill in October 1967 that ultimately persuaded enough of the bill's previous opponents to support it. This development saved the War on Poverty from being unceremoniously terminated just three years after its inception.[67]

Although the Community Action Program did not end in 1967, the shape and direction of the program changed dramatically after Congress passed the OEO reauthorization bill in October. The Green Amendment essentially allowed local governments to take control of local community action agencies, effectively giving mayors the power to dominate agencies that had become too meddlesome to the status quo. The irony of the situation lay in the fact that by the fall of 1967 most local community action agencies had backed off from any previous commitment to aggressive community action and had become little more than dispensers of social services. The Green Amendment simply codified what had already taken place in nearly every town and city in the country and ruled out the possibility of any community action agency successfully appealing to federal OEO guidelines in its quest to challenge local power structures. After the Green Amendment passed, federal regulations were on the side of local governments.[68]

The passage of the Green Amendment had long-term consequences for the War on Poverty in Houston, but its immediate effect was to encourage HCCAA administrators to make their organization even more amenable to city government officials. The HCCAA board of directors had scheduled a second round of elections to place more poor residents on the board for February 1968, but after the passage of the Green Amendment southwest regional OEO officials advised the board to postpone the elections until the effects of the amendment on local community action agencies became clearer. Once the elections had been postponed, it became apparent that in order for HCCAA to continue its role in implementing the War on Poverty and receive funding from OEO, Mayor Welch would have to give the organization official designation as Houston's community action agency. The Green Amendment thus gave Welch the power to require whatever changes he desired in HCCAA's structure and to withhold official sanction if HCCAA leaders refused to comply.[69]

The southwest regional OEO office dispatched OEO field analyst Hamah King to Houston in early April 1968 to assist HCCAA leaders in meeting the new guidelines and to help make any needed organizational changes to satisfy Welch. Since Francis Williams and Hartsell Gray had been successful in purging the Alinsky disciples from the HCCAA rolls, Welch's only major requirement was that the organization centralize control of the poverty program into a much smaller board of directors. Rather than a 150-member board of directors, Welch desired a 21-member board composed of 7 representatives of public officials, 5 from private organizations, and 9 representatives of the poor. Members of the HCCAA board quickly agreed to these terms, and on June 30, 1968, Welch officially designated the organization as the legitimate community action agency for the city of Houston.[70]

By the end of 1968 HCCAA, faced with diminished support from national OEO officials and having lost credibility in Houston's poor neighborhoods, had become nothing more than a deliverer of social services with a centralized and bureaucratic governing board. In July, Francis Williams moved into the position of executive director and the HCCAA board elected Joe Foy, a prominent Houston businessman and vice president of the Houston Natural Gas Corporation, as chairman. Foy promised that he would lead the organization "out of the wilderness" and into the business of delivering much-needed services to poor residents of Houston. A *Houston Chronicle* reporter noted optimistically that Foy and the board would now enjoy greater control over the organization than previous boards and that HCCAA had recently replaced much of their staff with trained professional social workers.[71]

HCCAA's new programs and activities during 1968 are illustrative of the organization's commitment to the delivery of social services and complemented the services the organization began offering the previous year. In April HCCAA administrators initiated a program called the "Special Community Action Program" (SCAP), which reassigned the majority of the community organizers who remained on the HCCAA staff and placed them in neighborhood centers where they were instructed to help poor residents locate needed social services. In July HCCAA employees launched a $750,000 youth summer camp for poor children and teenagers that provided activities such as swimming, recreation, and arts and crafts. That summer HCCAA also held a job fair in downtown Houston to bring employers and potential employees together, and it also instituted a neighborhood health services program to provide temporary federally funded medical services in poor neighborhoods. In September HCCAA got approval from OEO to administer Project MoneyWise, a consumer education program aimed at Houston's elderly population. As historian Allen J. Matusow argued, "Instincts for self-preservation having prevailed over formal commitments to change, once militant CAAs rapidly evolved into tame dispensers of services." Having rid the organization of activists who wanted to use the War on Poverty to expand democracy in Houston, HCCAA officials were determined to show that their organization now "served—not threatened—local authority."[72]

Williams's and Gray's success in purging the confrontational organizers and making their organization more palatable to the city's public officials undoubtedly helped ensure HCCAA's continued existence. But in a short time they also made HCCAA so cautious and racked with internal divisions that the organization lost the support of Houston's poor people. By 1969 HCCAA was large, bureaucratic, centralized, overly sensitive to the wishes of public officials, and alienated from the very people it was created to help. Little hope remained that such a cautious HCCAA could bring about social change capable of empowering the poor and expanding the meaning of democracy in Houston. As Tolstoy once described the Battle of Borodino, in a similar way the War on Poverty in Houston had been filled with starts and stops, illusory victories, discouraging defeats, and misinformation, and the experience frustrated any attempt to ascertain progress in the fight against the evils of poverty. The city's community action agency, once dominated by idealistic antipoverty activists determined to try a new approach to solving the problems of poverty through an aggressive interpretation of the community action concept, had become little more than a bureaucratic charity organization based on the same service delivery philosophy that had failed to lift people out of poverty for decades. As often occurs in history, the defenders of the status quo had won. The real losers in this battle were not the Alinsky-style community organizers who once controlled the poverty program in the city but the people living in poverty who had their hopes and expectations raised, only to have them dashed when it was no longer politically expedient to fight on their behalf.

By 1969 HCCAA had ceased to be a positive force for social change in Houston and no longer threatened to challenge the limited interpretation of democracy that had prevailed in the city. Yet the War on Poverty continued, albeit in modified form. The election of Richard Nixon signaled massive changes in the federal antipoverty program. Although local circumstances continued to shape its implementation in Houston, in the final years of the War on Poverty the diminished federal support for an active community action agency doomed the federal antipoverty program to failure and culminated in the end of the War on Poverty by the mid-1970s.

National Changes with Local Results

De-escalation of the War on Poverty, 1969–1976

The first four years of the War on Poverty saw a diverse group of grassroots activists struggling against the city's public officials, defenders of the status quo, and sometimes each other. This group included community organizers dedicated to the principles of Saul Alinsky; religious activists, who combined Old Testament prophetic social justice advocacy and Christian social gospel with confrontational politics in their sponsorship of VISTA volunteers; and more moderate advocates of social service delivery. They all shared in a quest to use the federal War on Poverty to expand the meaning of democracy in Houston.

As the experiences of these activists have shown, local implementers of the War on Poverty were indispensable for carrying out the poverty war on the ground, and in many ways they shaped the contours of the program. Yet they were not alone in engaging in these battles of the War on Poverty, nor did they create their own war on poverty in Houston without assistance. Rather, grassroots antipoverty activists in Houston used federal programs, resources, and governmental authority to wage their battle against poverty in the city. In many cases grassroots activists were also able to expand these federal programs into vehicles for social change in their crusade for racial and economic justice and the expansion of democracy. The federal government was equally important, however, in determining what the War on Poverty could accomplish. It was this fluid relationship between the federal government and grassroots activists that determined the fate of the War on Poverty in Houston.

In short, the federal government, in addition to grassroots activists, was key to implementing the War on Poverty in Houston. This work's focus on the grassroots activists who implemented the poverty programs in Houston has revealed several important points about how the War on Poverty operated on the ground. But at the same time we must not lose sight of the significance of the federal government in relating this story. Actions of War on Poverty administrators at the national, state, and regional levels affected the implementation of programs at the local level, even while grassroots antipoverty activists at times transformed these programs in their efforts to empower Houston's poor residents. Nowhere was the importance of the federal government illustrated more vividly, however, than in the 1969–1976 period when diminished federal support for the struggle against poverty doomed it to failure on the ground in Houston. The conviction and determination of grassroots activists were crucial factors in the implementation of the War on Poverty in the city, but it was virtually impossible for these activists to continue their efforts in the absence of federal support, funding, and authority. Grassroots activists in Houston had been propelled by the federal mandate to fight a War on Poverty. But the federal government's abrupt retreat from its commitment to fight poverty took the wind out of their sails. The result, of course, was disastrous for the War on Poverty. It meant that local activists would no longer be able to use the federal antipoverty program to challenge mainstream definitions of democracy in Houston.

Many historians of the War on Poverty have portrayed the Green Amendment, passed by Congress in the fall of 1967 as part of the OEO reauthorization bill, as the end of the story of community action and even of the entire War on Poverty.[1] It is easy to understand why this interpretation has persisted. The Green Amendment codified into law a phenomenon that had been occurring at least since 1966—namely, the practice of city mayors and other local public officials taking control of community action agencies (CAAs). Once public officials regained a firm grip on these agencies, there was little chance that these agencies would be able to carry out their original mission, which almost always required challenging the status quo to reform local institutions and the local establishment. The Green Amendment, therefore, guaranteed the legal right of mayors to take control of local community action agencies, even if it neither required them to do so nor stipulated the manner in which they could do it.

As with nearly every other aspect of the War on Poverty, local circumstances dictated how the Green Amendment would affect local community action agencies and the entire antipoverty program on the ground. In Houston, although it resulted in significant changes to the Harris County Community Action Association (HCCAA), the passage of the Green Amendment did not prompt Mayor Welch or any other public official to assume immediate control over the organization. Rather, the Green Amendment launched a process that continued into the early 1970s in which the mayor assisted in HCCAA's gradual but steady decline into irrelevance in the city. Meanwhile, VISTA volunteers in Houston, who were unaffected by the Green Amendment because their sponsoring agencies were autonomous and not bound to HCCAA, continued to organize poor residents and use confrontational tactics until 1972. In Houston, therefore, the Green Amendment represented not the end of the poverty program but rather the beginning of the final act of the War on Poverty in the city.[2]

To a much greater degree than the Green Amendment, national political developments beginning in 1969 weighed heavily on the course of the War on Poverty in Houston. Upon assuming the presidency that year, Richard Nixon, the candidate many Americans believed would crack down on 1960s-style political activism, lacked a clearly defined domestic agenda for his administration. During the campaign Nixon had occasionally blamed the Democrats for skyrocketing crime rates and runaway inflation and left voters assuming he would eliminate much of the Great Society, but he rarely spoke out on domestic issues with much conviction. Despite Nixon's apparent lack of interest in domestic affairs, however, the new president did have, in historian Irwin Unger's words, "a constellation of prejudices with policy implications." Above all, Nixon "considered the Great Society primarily a payoff to blacks and Hispanics and deplored the supposed kowtowing to black militants and white left-liberals of his predecessor. . . . Poverty was not a shame; it was a misfortune that could be overcome by people who applied themselves." Nixon himself had come from a poor family, and he believed in the American myth of the self-made man. His own personal background, combined with his beliefs about the causes of poverty and the effects of federal programs to eradicate it from society, determined how the new president would change the War on Poverty over the next several years.[3]

Despite his opposition to much of the philosophy surrounding the War on Poverty, in his first term Nixon did not begin eliminating poverty programs as many of his supporters had wished. Rather than bringing the War on Poverty to a halt, the new president put a major emphasis on decentralizing power in an effort to do away with government bureaucracy. Calling his loosely formed domestic agenda the "New Federalism," Nixon wanted to take the power that Lyndon Johnson and the liberals had amassed for the federal government and return it to state and local governments. Nixon and the Republicans sharply disagreed with Johnson and many liberal Democrats about where political power should be lodged. Johnson and many War on Poverty planners believed that state and local agencies were at best inept and at worst protectors of a social and racial caste system, particularly in the South. Their solution, as part of the War on Poverty, was to create a federal agency like the Office of Economic Opportunity that could carry out a strong domestic reform agenda and in the process bypass state and local power structures in an effort to empower society's disadvantaged. Nixon's New Federalism, on the other hand, offered the opposite argument by suggesting that the federal government had failed to solve society's problems and calling for the restoration of power to governors, mayors, and other pillars of the nation's local establishments. In a sense, Nixon's domestic policy assumptions created an atmosphere that allowed for an extension of the same spirit that had produced the Green Amendment in 1967.[4]

On August 8, 1969, Nixon delivered a speech to the nation outlining his vaguely defined domestic policy. The president said that for the previous eight years the liberals had turned the federal government into "a bureaucratic monstrosity, cumbersome, unresponsive, ineffective," and he committed his administration to the task of shrinking its power. As for the War on Poverty, Nixon promised to restructure the Job Corps and to reshape rather than abolish the Office of Economic Opportunity. OEO had "a vital place in our efforts to develop new programs and apply new knowledge," Nixon said, but it would be severely reduced in size and transformed into a "laboratory agency" to experiment with new ways of solving the problems of the poor. Once antipoverty methods proved successful, they would be transferred out of OEO and into appropriate agencies for implementation. Rather than being the administrative body responsible for directing the War on Poverty all over the nation, OEO would come to serve as a small experimental agency and be removed from the day-to-day operations of the federal poverty program.[5]

The application of Nixon's New Federalism to the War on Poverty was simple and direct. Nixon retained the antipoverty programs that had proven their effectiveness, but he turned the administration of them over to state and local governments and agencies. Soon after his speech on his domestic agenda in August 1969, Nixon closed fifty-nine Job Corps centers and sharply cut funding to those that remained. The president also appointed several of his allies to top OEO positions, most significantly Illinois Republican representative Donald Rumsfeld as the new head of OEO. Nixon made a significant change to the position, however, by placing the OEO director in the executive cabinet, thereby making it easier for the president to watch closely over OEO's activities. Rumsfeld, in turn, appointed several anti-OEO advocates to administer OEO's Office of Planning, Research, and Evaluation (OPRE). These appointees predictably concluded that many War on Poverty programs were ineffective, unpopular among public officials, and in need of either elimination or drastic change. Thus Nixon's strategy—to refrain from openly attacking popular OEO programs but simultaneously to fill top OEO positions with critics of the War on Poverty—had the effect of reducing the size of OEO without making the new president appear as an opponent of its programs.[6]

Nixon and Rumsfeld's actions to curb the activities of several programs had profound implications for the War on Poverty at the local level. In 1970 Nixon instructed Rumsfeld to strip the Legal Services program of its law reform potential and place local personnel under the direction of public officials. Rumsfeld even went so far as to threaten to replace the popular national director of the program if he failed to carry out the president's wishes. Predictably, Nixon and

Rumsfeld got their way. In 1971 and 1972 Nixon transferred the wildly popular Head Start program to the Department of Health, Education, and Welfare (HEW) and slowed its growth. In 1973 Nixon got Congress to pass the Comprehensive Employment and Training Act, which moved the Job Corps to the Department of Labor and other manpower programs to local government agencies. After Nixon's landslide reelection in 1972, the president moved to attack OEO and the entire War on Poverty more openly. He severely cut funding to the agency; for example, in 1969 funding for OEO was $1.9 billion, yet by 1973 Nixon had reduced that amount to $328 million. In January 1975, after Nixon's resignation, President Gerald Ford closed OEO completely but allowed a remnant of the Community Action Program to survive under the newly created Community Services Administration. By this point, however, CAP was a simple deliverer of services and totally uninterested in reform.[7]

These national developments within OEO greatly affected operations at the agency's southwest regional office in Austin, which was responsible for supervising the War on Poverty in Houston. By April 1969 Rumsfeld was busy charting a new course for OEO that reflected Nixon's desire to decentralize War on Poverty programs and reduce the size of government bureaucracy. In his speech at the press conference where Nixon announced his appointment, Rumsfeld promised to find out what worked and what did not and to eliminate ineffective programs. "The President has talked of the voices we have lost amid the shouting," Rumsfeld proclaimed, invoking Nixon's appeal to the Silent Majority during the campaign, "the voices of quiet anguish, the voices that speak without words, the voices of the heart." The new OEO director pledged to make the War on Poverty successful by rendering its programs more appealing to the group of American citizens who were responsible for Nixon's victory the previous year—the Great Silent Majority of mostly white and middle-class citizens who had grown weary of 1960s social activism, racial conflict, annual urban riots, protests, demonstrations, and aggressive community organizers who stirred up the poor. Rumsfeld's most significant change to OEO came when he began transforming it from the administrative body for the War on Poverty into an experimental agency. According to Rumsfeld, OEO would become a laboratory for testing various approaches to solving poverty, as Nixon had promised in his August speech. Once a program proved its effectiveness, it would be moved out of OEO and into the proper federal agency to administer it, such as HEW or the Department of Labor. Nixon had made it clear that he wanted "a good Nixon Republican" to direct the federal War on Poverty, and it seemed that in Rumsfeld he got exactly what he wished for.[8]

By the end of the summer in 1969, Rumsfeld had embarked on a plan for the complete reorganization of the OEO bureaucracy. He appointed a task force to travel to all regional OEO offices and report back to Washington about each office's activities. The report generated by these visits called for a major reorganization of OEO at all levels. According to the report, there was an urgent need for OEO officials to delegate certain programs to other federal or local agencies, overcome management deficiencies plaguing the agency, and, most important, "reorient the agency to the new thrust of this [presidential] administration." Above all, Nixon and Rumsfeld wanted to rid OEO of bureaucrats. The reorganization plan accordingly called for the merger or elimination of several OEO offices and positions, the integration of many of the office's activities, and the restructuring of regional offices to ensure closer financial control by the new director. In a memo sent to all OEO employees in August, Rumsfeld stressed the need to implement these organizational changes rapidly.[9]

Once Rumsfeld's efforts to reorganize the OEO bureaucracy were underway, the new director turned his attention to the fate of the Community Action Program (CAP). During a speech in October 1969, the new OEO director outlined a redefined mission for CAP that would reflect the Nixon administration's commitment to the Silent Majority. In a clear attempt to make CAP more palatable for the Republican Party's enlarged constituency of mostly white middle-class Americans, Rumsfeld stressed the need to broaden the appeal of community action. "We have operated too long on the assumption that the poor have natural enemies with whom it is useless to talk," Rumsfeld stated, and this "prophecy has been self-fulfilling. We have created enemies, many of whom might have been natural friends if we had sought them out." The poor, according to Rumsfeld, had been "treated as a separate nation at war with the rest, as if only they were the ones calling for improved services, as if only they were pointing to the decaying blight of our cities, as if only they felt institutions were unresponsive to their needs, as if only they wanted social change. . . . It is not just the poor who will benefit from change." Rumsfeld promised that under his direction, CAP would unite the poor and nonpoor to create an alliance to solve the problems of poverty.[10]

In his effort to broaden the base of support for community action, Rumsfeld told his staff that they would have to work together to clarify the goals and sharpen the objectives of CAP. The expectations placed on CAP in the past had been unreasonable and unrealistic, Rumsfeld told them, and in the future local community action agencies must rely on a whole system of public and private institutions to solve the problems of the poor. Community action agencies were ill equipped to complete the tasks of planning, coordinating, and providing solutions to the nation's poverty on their own, but an attack on poverty was still possible if most of the effort could be expended by state and local governments, city and county welfare agencies, and the private sector. In other words, poverty could still be defeated if fought in a more cautious way without upsetting the traditional balance of power and without challenging more limited conceptions of democracy.[11]

In order to promote this partnership between local community action agencies and established institutions, Rumsfeld made it clear that while community action agencies should be advocates for the poor, they should never alienate the nonpoor. Above all, this meant that local antipoverty activists associated with CAP would be forced to drop the use of confrontational tactics in the fight against poverty. "If CAA efforts are dominated by the kind of confrontation tactics which divide communities and further isolate the poor from other groups instead of bringing them into closer relations with the community," Rumsfeld warned, "Community Action will soon be without the broad support it must have. And the really good efforts of CAAs would go down the drain. The results would be tragic for this country—the poor and the nonpoor alike." Confrontational tactics on behalf of the poor, of course, would threaten this middle-class support and produce a backlash against the poverty program, which in reality had already begun before Nixon's election in 1968. In fact, there was very little need for the type of changes Rumsfeld called for in this speech because the majority of local community action agencies had been effectively tamed by years of attacks, and they were no longer engaged in confrontational tactics. Nevertheless, Rumsfeld's statements made it clear that the Community Action Program would cease to have official sanction to offend the middle class, and in the OEO reorganization plan he made sure staffers who agreed with his plan would have more direct control over the types of activities in which members of local CAAs engaged.[12]

All of these changes in the War on Poverty at the national and regional levels beginning in 1969 had a tremendous effect on the local antipoverty effort in Houston, particularly on the Harris County Community Action Association (HCCAA). Local elected officials had effectively neutralized any confrontational politics that had existed in the organization by the end of the previous year, but HCCAA nevertheless continued to play the most important role in the administration of the War on Poverty in the city. HCCAA already suffered from an overbearing local power structure, hostility from many of Houston's poor, and diminished support from OEO officials in Austin and Washington. But beginning in 1969, the city's community action agency began a steady decline into irrelevance. By the time Nixon took office, HCCAA was simply a benign deliverer of social services, but even those services were scaled back during the first few years of his administration. The organization was also beset with administrative difficulties, including a tumultuous board restructuring and a lengthy absence of an executive director that ultimately proved to be the final nail in the coffin of community action in Houston. The changes in Washington, coming at a time when HCCAA desperately needed guidance and a renewed sense of mission, virtually ensured that the agency would become a nonentity in Houston's War on Poverty.

The restructuring of the HCCAA board that began during the summer of 1969 illustrated how much the agency had grown alienated from the people it was designed to serve. Mayor Louie Welch had been successful during the previous year in forcing the HCCAA board of directors to centralize control over the War on Poverty in the city by reducing the size of the board and increasing the representation of public officials. HCCAA went without an executive director for several months during the fall of 1969 and spring of 1970, and Welch worked to gain even more control over the organization during this time of uncertainty. In July the board's representatives of Houston's public officials voted as a bloc to remove members of the city's NAACP chapter from HCCAA's board and prevent any organization representing the Mexican American population from being appointed. According to an OEO inspector sent from Austin, this particular meeting was an attempt by the city's public officials and HCCAA leadership to hold an unannounced election meeting to avoid votes by other members of the board or allow them to force their will on the board by determining its composition. Southwest regional OEO officials responded by declaring HCCAA's meeting null and void and ordered its board to schedule another meeting with a quorum present to elect representatives.[13]

Southwest regional OEO representatives noted that Welch was "extremely unhappy with our action" to require HCCAA to comply with federal OEO guidelines, but in the end Houston's community action agency was forced to hold another meeting to elect representatives in a democratic way or else face a loss of funding. The problems, however, did not end there, particularly with regard to HCCAA's relationship with the city's Mexican American population. As the 1960s led into the 1970s in Houston, the city's Mexican American population became increasingly organized around civil rights issues and more vocal in their displeasure with the city's public officials. In a special report on the impact of the War on Poverty on Mexican Americans in Texas, federal OEO inspectors noted that HCCAA failed to reach a large number of Mexican Americans in Houston because the agency created target neighborhoods where poor whites and African Americans were in the majority. Mexican American activists in Houston had begun demanding a strict apportionment of federal dollars spent on poor Mexican Americans in the city proportionate to their percentage in the population. But HCCAA board members refused to alter their budget, and they argued that the Mexican American population already benefited from War on Poverty programs to a greater degree than their numbers warranted. In May 1970, after the HCCAA board had consistently refused to address these problems, members of the Mexican American Youth Organization (MAYO), a militant

Chicano group, appeared at a meeting of HCCAA and threatened several board members because they had failed to name a Mexican American to one of the vacant top-level positions within the agency. Having already alienated a large segment of Houston's poor population the previous year, HCCAA board members continued to draw the ire of the city's poor residents who believed the agency was not serving their needs. Without pressure from Austin and Washington, HCCAA continued its decline into an agency that had little effect on Houston's poor and often provoked the anger of many of the city's poor residents.[14]

Mayor Welch and other city officials could read the handwriting on the wall. While OEO officials at the national level were rapidly changing the face of the War on Poverty and becoming increasingly condemnatory of activist community action agencies, HCCAA was embroiled in its own controversies and suffered from mismanagement and a lack of direction. Houston's public officials correctly surmised that HCCAA would no longer be of much consequence in the city. This was quite a change from the previous relationship between Welch and implementers of the local War on Poverty. At one time Houston's community action agency was an activist antipoverty organization that could use the threat of organized protest to win concessions from city officials. There is no doubt that Welch was extremely apprehensive about the prospect of mass demonstrations occurring in his city, and as a result he had been responsive to public demands to address the problems of poverty in Houston in the past. During the winter of 1966–1967, community organizers were able to win a series of small yet significant victories for the city's poor by confronting Welch and other public officials and coercing them into taking action on behalf of poor Houston residents. Even as late as February 1969, Welch and his staff sought to extend city services to four well-organized low-income areas in the northern part of the city; this decision was made before, as a confidential internal memo stated, the mayor was "forced or unpleasantly pressured" into taking the action. This is precisely the reason community organizing had been moderately effective in Houston and why grassroots activists had been able to achieve a few victories. Welch responded to large numbers of citizens exerting pressure from the community.[15]

By 1969, however, Welch had learned his lesson about approving federal funding to fight poverty in Houston without retaining control over how the money would be spent and, of more importance, what types of programs would be funded and who would administer them. The mayor and other public officials' actions to reduce HCCAA to a simple deliverer of services and to force the organization's leaders to abandon community organization over the previous two years had, by design, allowed Welch to pursue alternative avenues to fight poverty in Houston. These actions would show he cared about the plight of the poor in his city but at the same time not require him to give up any of his power or allow his constituents to be threatened. Beginning in 1969 Welch took advantage of President Nixon's efforts to decentralize power in the War on Poverty and began to advocate using federal block-grant programs to fight urban blight in Houston that could be administered by branches of the city government rather than by pesky poor people or rabble-rousing antipoverty activists. In the process, Welch stole any authority HCCAA still had as the administrative body for the War on Poverty in Houston. Taking cues from the new presidential administration, he secured his own power over how federal antipoverty funds would be spent in his city.

The most glaring example of how Welch accomplished this goal—of circumventing HCCAA's little remaining power and taking almost complete control of the War on Poverty in Houston—was his transformation into a vocal advocate for Houston's participation in the Model Cities program. Like many other moderate politicians in the emerging Sunbelt South, Welch had always been attracted to federal funding for improvements to the city of Houston as long as there were no strings attached. During the War on Poverty he welcomed federal funds that bypassed HCCAA and did not invite interference from the poor. The Model Cities program became a tool for some Sunbelt mayors to regain control of local wars on poverty that had become irritants to local public officials. Houston's experience with the federal program shows just how directly the changes at the national level determined the course of the War on Poverty for those at the grassroots.[16]

Lyndon Johnson and his advisers conceived of Model Cities (then called Demonstration Cities) in 1966, but the program was extremely slow to get off the ground. The idea for a massive federal program to attack blight in the nation's decaying urban centers initially came from United Auto Workers president Walter Reuther and Detroit mayor Jerome Cavanagh. The two men submitted a report to Johnson in May 1965 calling for a plan to rebuild the nation's inner cities and make up for the failings of Urban Renewal. Like much of the War on Poverty, the solution for the country's decaying urban centers would involve coordination of all the public and private resources available to help rebuild the cities, while at the same time allowing inner-city residents to have a voice in its implementation. In the original plan, Houston was to be chosen as one of six "Demonstration Cities" that would prove the effectiveness of this new approach to solving urban problems. Although Johnson and his staff were initially cold to the idea of a revamped Urban Renewal program, the Watts riot that occurred in Los Angeles that summer gave fresh urgency to the problems of the cities. It was in the wake of Watts that Johnson assembled a task force to study Reuther and Cavanagh's proposal. The president and his advisers responded favorably to the task force's report in December. But as he had done with the proposal for the Community Action Program a few months prior, the president expanded Model Cities from an experiment in rebuilding the nation's cities into a full-fledged government program that would fund sixty-six cities of all sizes selected from hundreds of applications. The White House spent the first half of 1966 drumming up grassroots support for Model Cities and defending it against attacks by congressmen claiming it would reward rioters. Finally in November Johnson signed the Demonstration Cities and Metropolitan Development Act of 1966 before officially changing the name of the program to "Model Cities" and placing it in the recently created Department of Housing and Urban Development (HUD). The federal program would not be as large in its first year as Johnson hoped, however, because the Senate designated 1967 as a planning year, and as a result it was not until 1968 that many local politicians from cities like Houston began paying attention to the new federal program for the nation's cities.[17]

Although Welch was not overly eager to obtain a Model Cities grant during the planning year, in mid-1967 he did permit a few members of his staff to draw up an application for Houston. In July HUD officials released a list of cities, including four in Texas, that had been approved for a Model Cities planning grant, but Houston was not among them. The city's rejected application revealed a problem peculiar to the city of Houston that would haunt Welch's later efforts to obtain a Model Cities grant. Houston, unlike any other major city in the United States, had no zoning laws. According to Houston historian David McComb, early efforts to promote city planning and to enact land-zoning ordinances began during the 1910s and 1920s, only to be defeated by real estate agents and the Houston Property Owners' League, whose spokesmen argued that "such planning was discriminatory, arbitrary, and damaging to small property owners and real estate interests."[18]

Another attempt to pass a zoning ordinance occurred during the 1930s and resulted in a series of land zoning hearings at City Hall. Antizoning advocates argued that "zoning would throttle city growth and would interfere with the constitutional right to hold property." As the debate dragged on into the late 1940s, several Houstonians opposed to zoning ordinances had even harsher words for the proposal. Zoning laws, according to opponents, would "create a dangerous club in the hands of any dictatorial administration." One prominent leader of the antizoning faction in Houston proclaimed that "a zoning ordinance is an exercise of the police power of government. . . . Houston was built by men of vision, not by slide-rule experts armed with an omniscient egotism and a pocket full of silly statistics." Another antizoning activist exclaimed that zoning "just goes back to the idea of Joe Stalin, that one man can figure out everything—the whole plan." Hugh Roy Cullen, a reactionary but nonetheless influential voice in city politics, stated that Houston was "doing too well to try this un-American, German plan." Houston residents predictably went to the polls and defeated this latest zoning plan by a two-to-one margin. Zoning came up as an issue once more in the early 1960s, but was again defeated, not to return as a major issue in Houston city politics until the Model Cities application once again made zoning laws a hot political topic in the late 1960s.[19]

According to McComb, one significant consequence of Houston's lack of zoning ordinances has been the inability of the city to benefit from any federal urban renewal projects. The federal government has insisted on some degree of city planning in order to determine eligibility for federal funding to attack urban blight, but this type of planning was exactly what Houstonians deliberately and consistently avoided. When HUD began awarding Model Cities planning grants during the summer of 1967, federal officials inevitably left Houston off their list because an absence of zoning ordinances meant little or no control over how the money would be spent in the city. HUD officials were explicit in their reason for rejecting Houston's application; without control over land use, city officials could not guarantee Model Cities funds would be used to carry out the mission of the program. HUD secretary Robert Weaver made it clear to Welch that HUD officials sincerely wanted Houston to be a part of the Model Cities program despite the city's reluctance to pass zoning laws. If a zoning ordinance was out of the question, Weaver suggested that the mayor advocate an alternative measure that would grant the city government some power over land use in the city. Welch had not yet been persuaded to become an advocate for the new federal program, however, and Weaver's overtures had little effect. By the end of 1967, federal officials had approved the Model Cities applications of sixty-three cities, with Houston being the only major American city that could not qualify for even a planning grant.[20]

Beginning in January 1968, Mayor Welch began to warm up to the idea of making a bigger push to get Model Cities funding. The timing of his shift from indifference to open advocacy was quite telling of his intentions. During the last few months of 1967, Welch, along with other city officials and local politicians, had successfully tamed HCCAA and watched approvingly as the once-confrontational community action agency became embroiled in internal battles over the purging of the group's aggressive community organizers. With HCCAA effectively neutralized, Welch began searching for ways to bring federal anti-poverty funds to Houston without having to go through the city's community action agency. In the Model Cities program, Welch discovered that he could secure a block grant from the federal government without having to abide by the wishes of HCCAA. A direct grant program like Model Cities would allow Welch to enjoy much more control over how the money would be spent in the city than he had over community action funds in Houston.

As the city's rejected application stated the previous year, the first step in persuading HUD officials to approve Houston's Model Cities application was to convince city council members to pass an ordinance that would allow for land control in the city. Upon returning to Houston from Washington, where he had met with HUD secretary Robert Weaver to ascertain the exact requirements, Welch told the city council that the city only needed to pass a moderate housing code rather than a full-fledged zoning ordinance in order to qualify for Model Cities funding. A few months prior, a group called the "Citizens' Advisory Committee on Low Rent Housing" had submitted a proposal to the council for a city housing code in their effort to make Houston eligible to receive federal assistance for building low-rent housing projects in the city. Under the proposed housing code, the mayor would appoint a "building official" who would "inspect substandard houses in a systematic manner and also answer tenants' complaints." This building official could also order improvements in substandard housing to bring it up to a series of minimum standards, which included requirements that each house be equipped with running water and connected to an approved sewer system; have a bathroom inside the house; be water-, rodent-, and insect-proof; be able to be heated to seventy degrees; and have a safe garbage container. During the first few months of 1968, Welch urged members of the city council to pass this housing code—not necessarily to gain federal funds to construct low-rent housing but to prepare Houston to receive Model Cities funding.[21]

City Council members were skeptical about the proposed housing code and made several complaints about the implications of its passage. Several of the charges that some council members leveled against the proposed housing code were strikingly reminiscent of the arguments against passing zoning laws in Houston in the past. A *Houston Post* reporter wrote in January 1968, "Some claim the code is too tough and concentrates dangerous powers in the hands of a 'building official' who would work directly for the mayor under the Board of Appeals, which also would be chosen by the mayor." Shockingly, several councilmen were concerned about the requirement that every house have an indoor bathroom and running water because it would be too strict for many homeowners. According to an engineer employed by the city, the indoor bathroom requirement "will affect several thousand of the 12,000 dwellings that have either septic tanks or outdoor privies." One city councilman expressed sympathy for landlords and homeowners who lacked the means to make improvements to their homes. "No one has answered me satisfactorily," he charged, "on what happens when [the building official] orders a fellow who can't afford it to make $5,000 in improvements on his house." Despite these reservations, Welch remained confident that the city council would eventually pass the proposed housing code, and he called for a series of informal meetings between councilmen and representatives of the Citizens' Committee on Low Rent Housing in order to iron out a compromise.[22]

While the city council debated the housing code, Welch and other public officials continued moving forward in their preparation of a Model Cities application that could be approved. In the process, Welch made it clear that HCCAA was not welcome in the discussions. In an effort to push the community action agency even further to the sidelines of the antipoverty fight in Houston, Welch and other city officials drew up a new Model Cities grant application in March 1968 that designated the Community Welfare Planning Association (CWPA), rather than HCCAA, as the required social planning board for the implementation of the federal program in Houston. The CWPA was the central coordinating board for the traditional welfare agencies in Houston and had been integral to the creation in 1965 of the city's first community action agency, which was extremely limited in scope and almost totally controlled by public officials. The CWPA had been mostly shut out of the poverty program in Houston since William Ballew took over the city's community action agency in 1966 and adopted confrontational tactics, but the Model Cities program offered the CWPA a way back in. Several CWPA staff members made sure they were involved in writing up the Model Cities application for the city and assured Welch they would provide the necessary support to get it approved. Welch accepted the offer and held up his end of the bargain when it came time to designate a social planning board for the implementation of the Model Cities program in Houston.[23]

In selecting a demonstration area of the city where the first-year Model Cities planning grant would be used, Welch also sought to keep HCCAA from being involved in the program. He and other city officials chose a small area in the old inner city that had been served by Houston Action for Youth (HAY) before the merger between HAY and H-HCEOO to create HCCAA in May 1967. The new HCCAA had retained the more cautious ex-HAY officials who already administered programs in that particular area, and there were very few community organizers who worked in this particular part of the city. In focusing on this area for the Model Cities demonstration, Welch sent another clear message that HCCAA, especially its community organizers, would be left out of this federal program.[24]

Unfortunately for Welch, by the fall of 1968 the Houston City Council had not yet approved the proposed housing code required for the Model Cities application. As one HUD official told President Johnson, without some way of ensuring proper land use, Houston's Model Cities application was "clearly in no shape to be approved." Welch was determined to find a way for his city to take advantage of this massive federal program, so in October 1968 he sent Blair Justice, one of his staffers, to Washington to meet with HUD officials and White House personnel in order to convince Model Cities administrators that the program would be effective in Houston. During this visit, Welch and Justice decided to change tactics. Rather than trying to coax the city council into passing the housing code, the mayor and his staff would convince HUD officials that Houston's existing deed-restriction system provided sufficient control over land use in the city to make its Model Cities application approvable.[25]

In reality, this argument was quite a stretch. Deed restrictions in Houston usually applied to the city's affluent neighborhoods, whose residents wanted to keep the atmosphere residential so as to ward off undesirable business developments like gas stations and in some cases to bar home sales to nonwhites. For example, according to Houston historian David McComb, the deed restrictions in the affluent River Oaks neighborhood "restricted the land to allow only one resident or family per lot, no hospitals, no duplexes, no apartments, only Caucasian ownership, no livestock, no dumping, and no signs." The HUD requirement of a city land-control ordinance, however, was designed to ensure that a city governmental body existed and possessed the authority to carry out the Model Cities program in an effective way. As the Demonstration Cities and Metropolitan Development Act of 1966 stated, HUD must verify that "local administrative procedures are available for carrying out the program on a consolidated and coordinated basis . . . [and] the program is consistent with comprehensive planning in the entire urban or metropolitan area." Zoning ordinances were tailor-made for guaranteeing that these requirements would be met, but Houston's refusal to legislate zoning laws illustrated the city's deliberate avoidance of the type of comprehensive citywide planning that the Model Cities program required. Deed restrictions were clearly not intended to aid in planning an entire urban area; if anything, deed restrictions were another way to shun the very planning that Model Cities tried to encourage by offering affluent Houston residents a way of controlling their own neighborhoods without forcing them to approve of citywide zoning ordinances. Nevertheless, at Welch's request Justice met with HUD officials in Washington and tried to persuade them that Houston's deed restrictions were an adequate means of land control in the city. Justice also contacted Larry Temple, special counsel to President Johnson, who promised to look into the matter.[26]

Blair Justice's visit to Washington helped bring the Houston situation to the attention of key Washington officials, but problems with its Model Cities application remained. Larry Temple kept his promise to look into Houston's application, but what he discovered was not what Welch and Justice had hoped for. After contacting HUD officials to inquire about Houston's application status, Temple received a response from Robert Wood, undersecretary of HUD. Wood informed Temple that the problems with Houston's application were insurmountable without a zoning ordinance for the city. Without some form of land control, Wood stated, "there is a grave doubt that Houston could make the required impact on its environmental and housing problems." The city's deed restriction system, according to Wood, was a totally inadequate method of land control because its requirements were enforced not by the city government but by individual residents. Wood also alluded to the fact that the city had been unable to benefit from Urban Renewal funding in the past for precisely the same reasons. "In short," Wood concluded, "the inability of Houston to use one of the major government-funded tools (urban renewal) provided for sharing the problems that face it, makes it a high risk for model cities funding.... To make an exception for Houston from the requirements of ... Model Cities would undermine the future effectiveness" of the program.[27]

Welch's efforts to persuade Washington officials to approve Houston's Model Cities application, however, did not end with the conclusions drawn by HUD administrators. On December 4, 1968, Welch had a telephone conversation with President Johnson on the subject of his city's application. Although the specific content of this conversation is unknown, it is clear that Welch was able to convince the outgoing president to instruct HUD to approve Houston's application for a Model Cities planning grant. Just ten days prior to Welch and Johnson's conversation, HUD officials had reiterated their judgment that Houston's application was unacceptable. After Welch's appeal to the president, despite the fact that nothing on the application had changed, HUD officials suddenly reversed their ruling and awarded Houston a Model Cities planning grant of nearly $270,000. After more than a year of telling Houston officials that without an effective means of controlling land use in the city the application could not be approved, HUD officials suddenly agreed with Welch and Justice that the deed restriction system was sufficient. Although this was no guarantee that the city would receive a full Model Cities grant in the years to come, it was nevertheless an impressive political accomplishment for Welch and the city of Houston.[28]

Welch was happy to bask in his victory among Houstonians, and he used the occasion to drive HCCAA even further out of the fight against poverty and urban blight in the city. After HUD officials announced the approval of Houston's Model Cities planning grant, Welch, in a blatant disregard for everything the Community Action Program had tried to achieve in Houston, proclaimed that *"for the first time,* the way is clear for a coordinated attack on all of the problems of the poor." According to Welch and Justice, the planning grant would bring improvements "in all areas of urban living—health, employment, education, crime and delinquency, housing and welfare and the total physical environment including such things as streets, parks, drainage and utilities." Blair Justice also told Houstonians that they could reasonably expect more than $20 million in federal Model Cities funding over the next several years. Welch and Justice had become champions of using federal funding to fight poverty in Houston, even though they and other city officials had provided very minimal support for the city's community action agency and had even attacked its community organizers, who for several years had been attempting to accomplish what Welch now supported.[29]

The mayor's disingenuousness about why he was an advocate for the Model Cities program, however, did not end with his newfound appreciation for attacking the root causes of poverty. Welch also pretended to have become a strong supporter of the ideal of maximum feasible participation of the poor in the poverty program. The mayor proclaimed that Urban Renewal had been a failure all over the country because the program did not include poor people in its planning and implementation. Model Cities, according to Welch, was different because it took into account the wishes of the poor. Yet Welch had deliberately excluded HCCAA from participation in Houston's Model Cities grant, despite the fact that HCCAA had a potential avenue for including the poor in the program through its neighborhood councils. While appearing to care about the plight of the poor, in reality Welch had successfully taken control of antipoverty funding in the city and removed HCCAA from the center of the poverty program in Houston.[30]

When Richard Nixon assumed the presidency in January 1969, he disliked the Model Cities program because of the large federal bureaucracy it created, particularly within HUD. At the same time, however, the new president believed that a program like Model Cities fit in quite well with his overall agenda of decentralization and his effort to give local governments control of the War on Poverty. Though he was somewhat conflicted, Nixon allowed the Model Cities program to continue. In Houston, Welch was moving swiftly to implement the planning grant and prepare for a full Model Cities grant application the next year. In January 1969 Welch created a Model Cities department within the city government and appointed George McGonigle, former executive at the Humble Oil Company, as Model Cities director. The mayor also continued to court the involvement of the Community Welfare Planning Association (CWPA), rather than HCCAA, as the organization that would assess the community impact of Model Cities decisions and improvements and ensure citizen participation in the program. By April 1969 Welch had created a sizable city government bureaucracy to administer the Model Cities program.[31]

As this process of creating a city agency to direct the Model Cities program moved forward, Welch assumed a steadily increasing amount of power over the poverty program in Houston as he centralized the administration of a large part of it in the city government. With HCCAA beset with administrative difficulties, internal conflicts, and a clear lack of direction due to the lengthy absence of an executive director, Welch was able to consolidate his own authority over the War on Poverty. As other Sunbelt politicians welcomed federal funding so long as they could control how it would be spent, Welch had become an open advocate of the Model Cities program precisely because, unlike with the Community Action Program, he could control every aspect of it through his own Model Cities department within the city government. In the process, he was also able to marginalize HCCAA even further. No longer would most of the federal anti-poverty funds flow into an organization outside of the city bureaucracy. From then on, according to the plan, Welch would enjoy determining how a large portion of the federal money coming into his city would be spent.

By 1973, Nixon was ready to end the Model Cities program. In its place, the president implemented his revenue-sharing plan, which was never able to address the problems of the nation's cities adequately. More important, however, despite the closing down of Model Cities, the mayor was able to use the program to push HCCAA to the sidelines in the fight against poverty in Houston. The entire process was emblematic of how changes in the War on Poverty in Washington greatly affected the poverty program at the local level. Welch and other city officials, as well as many HCCAA administrators, responded to Nixon's efforts to decentralize power and return authority back to local governments. While HCCAA scrambled to regroup, Welch assumed control of the poverty program in Houston. By becoming an advocate of the Model Cities program, Welch was able to take control of federal antipoverty initiatives and marginalize HCCAA while also appearing to fight on behalf of the poor.[32]

While Welch pursued Model Cities funding for the city and HCCAA increasingly became irrelevant in the War on Poverty, the Volunteers in Service to America (VISTA) program in Houston attempted to sustain its somewhat clandestine strategy of expanding democracy by continuing to employ the tactics of community organization and empowerment of the poor. For the previous three years the Reverend Wallace B. Poteat, EF-LAC project activists, and VISTA volunteers had largely flown under the radar of local officials in their quest to effect social change in Houston by organizing the poor. Beginning in 1969, however, VISTA volunteers in Houston experienced a marked increase in harassment from the city's police department, particularly its criminal intelligence division. Although VISTA volunteers were able to carry out their direct attack on poverty in the city for a longer period of time than the Community Action Program did, they nevertheless eventually suffered significant defeats at the hands of the city's public officials who wanted to stop the volunteers' aggressive community-organizing and confrontational tactics. By 1972 the VISTA program in Houston was a shell of its former self, and late that year the sponsoring organizations bid farewell to their last volunteer.

The final demise of the VISTA program in Houston did not, however, come solely as a result of attacks by local officials. In addition to police harassment, the city's VISTA volunteers suffered from a changing focus in Washington. As Nixon had reorganized OEO, consolidated power in the White House, and placed loyal allies in charge of key programs, the new president likewise sought to centralize control over VISTA and reorient the volunteer program away from confrontational tactics. Although an ideological attack on the VISTA program was not to come until Nixon's second term in office, which was after the VISTA program had ended in Houston, the new president did successfully lay the groundwork for the assault on VISTA between 1969 and 1972 by reorganizing the federal bureaucracy overseeing the volunteer program. As historian T. Zane Reeves has shown, Nixon assigned the task of evaluating the VISTA program's alleged accomplishments to the newly created Office of Management and Budgeting (OMB), whose staff members were interested in quantitative measurements of the War on Poverty's effectiveness. VISTA, however, was not a program with accomplishments that were easily quantifiable, and predictably the OMB was not satisfied with anecdotal stories of success.[33]

Nixon also instructed staff members of OEO's Office of Planning, Research, and Evaluation (OPRE) to investigate and submit detailed reports on all War on Poverty activities. OPRE's report on VISTA justified the eventual attack on the program. Even before the investigation began, according to Reeves, OPRE investigators were "convinced that VISTA projects were proposing political organization for the poor rather than self-help programs for them." OPRE's final report on VISTA, argued Reeves, "revealed an activist culture at VISTA that confirmed conservatives' worst fears." Authors of the report concluded that, for the majority of the volunteers, their experience as VISTA volunteers politicized and radicalized them, exposed them to leftist political ideologies, and made them suspicious of the government and of the intent of federal social programs.[34]

Nixon knew he could not simply eliminate the VISTA program outright for fear that a political showdown with a mostly sympathetic Congress and several popular VISTA support groups would threaten his chances of reelection. Rather than simply cutting the VISTA program from the War on Poverty, the president, as he had done with the Job Corps and Head Start, removed the VISTA program from OEO's jurisdiction and placed it in a new agency called "ACTION" that would oversee the activities of national voluntary service, including VISTA and the Peace Corps. According to Reeves, the conservative ideologues who staffed ACTION believed if VISTA remained in OEO, its activist culture and radicalizing tendencies would be retained. They believed that "drastic action must be taken that would change the organizational cultures in antipoverty programs. Only if agency volunteers and staff carried an achievement ethic to the poor would there be any hope of liberating the poor from poverty. In their assessment, VISTA had done more harm than good for the poor." By 1971 Nixon had begun directing his appointees within ACTION to instill an explicitly conservative ideology into the VISTA program that would eliminate all community-organizing activities and establish conservative alternatives to VISTA for college-aged volunteers. According to Reeves, this new conservative ideology driving VISTA would eliminate efforts to expand democracy in cities like Houston, allow administrators to have greater control over the volunteer program, and rid it of "an embarrassing legacy of activist idealism."[35]

During the first two years of Nixon's efforts to reorient the VISTA program to be more in line with conservative principles, most VISTA volunteers in Houston remained committed to community organization and empowerment of the poor. The Reverend Wallace Poteat and other members of the Ecumenical Fellowship's Latin American Channel (EF-LAC) project, the major VISTA sponsoring organization in Houston, remained steadfast in their pledge to eradicate the evil of poverty in the city using prophetic religion and Saul Alinsky–style community organization. One way Rev. Poteat tried to continue the fight against poverty in Houston using VISTA volunteers was to team up with the Reverend Earl Allen's organization, known as Human Organizational, Political, and Economic Development, Incorporated (HOPE). Following the turmoil within Houston's community action agency when the HCCAA board forced him to resign in August 1967, Allen created his own antipoverty organization to continue using tactics of aggressive community organizing and protest demonstrations to force confrontations with the city's public officials. In 1968 both Rev. Poteat and Rev. Allen worked to strengthen the ties between HOPE members and VISTA volunteers and devised several antipoverty projects on which the two groups could work together. During an EF-LAC board meeting in February, Allen made it clear that HOPE community organizers were attempting to teach the poor the power of collective action and confrontation and that the VISTA volunteers must agree with this approach if they wanted to work with HOPE organizers. Rev. Poteat assured Allen that the VISTA volunteers were indeed committed to the same confrontational tactics and that he had personally notified VISTA administrators that the EF-LAC project was interested in receiving only militant volunteers in the future rather than "nice middle-class kids." Over the next two years the relationship between EF-LAC and HOPE would grow stronger, until by 1970 new VISTA volunteers arriving in Houston to work with the EF-LAC project were immediately assigned to a training program led by Earl Allen and other HOPE leaders to teach the new volunteers how to organize the poor and confront local public officials in their effort to combat poverty in Houston.[36]

Houston's VISTA program also went through a leadership change in 1968 and 1969 that showed how committed the volunteers and members of the sponsoring agencies remained to community organization and confrontational tactics. In early 1968 Rev. Poteat announced that he would resign at the end of the year to assume a position in Tulsa, Oklahoma, directing a War on Poverty program similar to the EF-LAC project. In August 1968 EF-LAC project members held a meeting to select Rev. Poteat's replacement. The EF-LAC board had narrowed their pool of candidates to two finalists, Barry Kraut and Paul Allen. Kraut worked at a local Presbyterian church in the city and had served for several years on the EF-LAC board, while Allen currently directed an antipoverty program in Washington, D.C. During the meeting, the board allowed both Kraut and Allen to explain their antipoverty philosophy and describe how they would lead the EF-LAC project and the VISTA volunteers in the city. It became clear early in the meeting that Kraut held a very limited view of what the proper role of a VISTA volunteer was in a community, while Allen demonstrated that he would be a better fit with the organization created by Rev. Poteat to organize the poor and confront the evil of poverty. While Kraut stated that he viewed the VISTA volunteer program as a model for the poor to teach them how to join the middle class, Allen proclaimed that the role of the volunteers was to force the establishment to change when needed. The focus, according to Allen, should be on organizing the poor in order to empower them to challenge local public officials and institutions and bring about needed structural changes in Houston. At the end of the meeting, EF-LAC board members and VISTA volunteers voted overwhelmingly to name Paul Allen the new director of the project.[37]

Houston's VISTA volunteers continued to develop new and innovative programs to combat poverty in the city through 1971. In 1969 the VISTA volunteers established projects that included an urban arts program to help develop any latent talent among poor residents, a welfare rights organization, the strengthening of neighborhood centers, community organizing to put pressure on the Legal Services program to fight for the rights of the poor, and a free educational system called the "University of Thought" that attracted more than a thousand students during the summer of 1969. Later in the year, after Houston's Legal Services personnel proved to be impervious to pressure from the city's poor residents and their VISTA allies, volunteers developed a VISTA legal program to "educate the poor in, and enable the poor to act upon, their rights under the law." The VISTA legal program would go further, however, in its effort to attack poverty and expand democracy in the city. The VISTA lawyer would be encouraged to "go beyond the individual services approach of legal aid by developing a working knowledge of a specific area of law that has direct impact upon the poor." These areas of expertise might include consumer advocacy, school desegregation and discrimination, economic development, discrimination in health services, human rights in employment and law enforcement, housing issues, discrimination in public services and utilities, and welfare rights. All the while VISTA volunteers continued to pressure the Legal Services program in Houston to fulfill its mission as a catalyst for law reform.[38]

A community-organizing effort in which the VISTA volunteers put a large amount of effort, and one that aroused the indignation of public officials like

Mayor Welch, was an attempt to include poor residents in the decision-making processes of the proposed Model Cities program. Welch had become attracted to Model Cities precisely because he could bypass the community action agency and ignore poor residents in his attempt to secure federal funds to make improvements to the city, even though he had openly advocated the involvement of the poor in the program. Unfortunately for Houston's poor people, HCCAA's board and staff members were in no position to demand the inclusion of poor Houston residents in the program's planning stages. The mayor had not considered, however, that the city's VISTA volunteers might begin organizing poor residents to claim their rightful place in the Model Cities program. As early as May 1968, VISTA volunteers and members of the EF-LAC project expressed concern that Welch was attempting to keep total control over Model Cities and to prevent residents from having a voice in how federal funds might be used in Houston. By the end of the year, EF-LAC project members and VISTA volunteers had familiarized themselves with the Model Cities legislation and were determined to make sure that Welch followed the federal requirement that residents of a city must consent to the mayor's plan for Model Cities funding.[39]

During the summer of 1969, after the city council approved the application for a Model Cities grant and Welch had created a government department to oversee the program in Houston, VISTA volunteers initiated an organizing drive in the city's poor neighborhoods to create a Model Cities Citizens' Council, as stipulated by the program's requirements. As a VISTA newsletter stated in July, Houston's volunteers were "devoting much of their effort in the time before the August 3rd election in letting the neighborhoods know that they should have a voice and they have a mandate to become a part of Model Cities if this program is going to become what it can be." Despite the mayor's public pronouncements, citizen involvement in the Model Cities program in Houston was simply too much democratic participation for Welch and his appointed officials in charge of implementing the program in the city. In October 1969 Houston's Model Cities director George McGonigle contacted Benton Russell, one of the city's VISTA sponsoring officials, and strongly suggested that he regain control of the activities of the VISTA volunteers, particularly with regard to organizing poor residents to make demands on the city's Model Cities department. Russell replied to McGonigle first by explaining the relationship between the VISTA sponsoring agency and volunteers. "The projects in which [the volunteers] work are 'their' projects," Russell stated, "and although we are interested and concerned about them, we could never dictate policy to them in autocratic or bureaucratic methods. Our direction is through advice and counsel. We do not 'instruct.' We are their sponsors, if you will, not their bosses." With regard to citizen participation in the Model Cities program, Russell scolded McGonigle: "I think we should perhaps examine our programs which we in our middle-class, middle-aged way undertake. I am sure we do not see the problems exactly as the younger generation, but let us not condemn their actions when they do what seems best. . . . If the [Model Cities] program is worthwhile, it can stand on its merits. Let's make sure, however, that our program is 'of' the poor and not 'for' the poor. Let's be sure that our program is listening to and abiding by the will of the area people, for this is what model cities is all about. If we have put together such a program, then I don't think we have much to fear from well-meaning VISTAS." In other words, Russell granted full sanction to the VISTA volunteers' efforts to organize the poor to make sure they would be allowed to participate in the decision-making processes of the Model Cities program.[40]

It was probably no coincidence that in 1969, as the VISTA volunteers ramped up their efforts to develop innovative programs to empower the poor and placed a major emphasis on including the poor in the Model Cities program, the Houston Police Department launched a series of harassment campaigns against the volunteers. In January HPD Intelligence Division officers began conducting surveillance of a support group for former presidential contender Eugene McCarthy, and in a report they noted that several VISTA volunteers attended an organizational meeting for the group. HPD officers also began focusing on the volunteers' alleged misuse of government vehicles. In May an officer on patrol near the construction site for Houston's new airport came upon a government-issued vehicle that contained Dorothy Brown, a white VISTA volunteer, in "an apparent embrace" with Terence Smith, an African American male. "This does not seem to be official business," the officer stated in his report, "so please report this to the proper authorities." HPD officials turned their report over to the General Services Administration (GSA), the federal agency responsible for overseeing use of government property, and GSA representatives subsequently performed an investigation of the charges and concluded there was no wrongdoing on the part of Dorothy Brown or the Houston VISTA program. Brown maintained that she had stopped the vehicle to discuss with Smith a particular problem he was having adjusting to life in Houston after recently moving from Alaska, and while they were having this conversation the police officer approached. EF-LAC project leaders did, however, give her a warning for not taking into consideration how the situation might have appeared to enemies of the War on Poverty and of the VISTA program in Houston.[41]

The rising amount of interest in, and resulting criticism of, the VISTA volunteers' activities in Houston, however, stemmed not only from the city's public officials but also from the community action agency. By the fall of 1969, as VISTA volunteers were launching organizational drives to create citizens committees to participate in Model Cities planning, HCCAA officials began showing a surprising amount of concern about the activities of the VISTA volunteers. In November the HCCAA board of directors, which included representatives of the mayor's office, appointed a special committee to study the role of Houston's VISTA volunteers in the War on Poverty in the city, allegedly at the request of the Texas OEO office. After making a few telephone calls, however, Houston VISTA supervisor Roger Armstrong discovered that the Texas OEO office had never ordered HCCAA to investigate the activities of VISTA volunteers in Houston. In an angry letter to HCCAA executive director Francis Williams, Armstrong exclaimed, "If HCCAA—its administration or its board—desires to know more about Houston's VISTA Project, we would be happy to supply you with information on its activities. . . . However, in the absence of any concrete reason why a special HCCAA Board committee should study the role of Houston's VISTA Project, you should be aware that we would consider the establishment of such a committee precipitous. It would be unwarranted and [cause] an undue negative reflection on Houston's VISTA Project and its existing sponsorship."[42]

When this threat of an investigation failed to bring the VISTA program under the control of the HCCAA board, several board members moved to consolidate all of Houston's VISTA volunteers under the direction of the HCCAA board. These board members were able to convince a state OEO official that HCCAA should run the VISTA program in the city, and this official submitted a formal request late that fall to consolidate all the VISTA volunteers in Houston under the direction of the HCCAA board. This strategy also failed; VISTA regional administrator Edward Dela Rosa rejected the request, stating that the "present sponsors have demonstrated the ability to carry out an effective VISTA program in Harris County." Dela Rosa also expressed hope that HCCAA officials and members of the city's VISTA sponsoring agencies would be able to resolve their disputes with each other and continue to carry out the War on Poverty in Houston in an effective way. As long as each group had such strikingly different and competing ideas about how to attack poverty and what role the poor should play, however, it seemed unlikely the friction between HCCAA and the VISTA program would resolve itself.[43]

Between 1969 and 1972, a series of changes at the national level damaged the VISTA program in Houston and ultimately brought it to an end. During an EF-LAC board meeting in February 1969, project director Paul Allen reported on a recent trip to Washington during which he noted several changes in the VISTA program. The national VISTA training centers were no longer recruiting young college-aged volunteers but rather individuals with bachelor's and master's degrees who were specialists in some particular field. The VISTA program was being professionalized, according to Allen, and national VISTA officials were calling for more direct supervision on the part of local sponsoring agencies. This national development ran counter to everything Houston's VISTA program stood for; its sponsoring agencies prided themselves on using young and idealistic volunteers who were free to attack poverty in the city with a remarkable amount of freedom to determine their own tactics. The national OEO office, under the direction of Donald Rumsfeld, was also trying to take more direct control over the VISTA program nationally and to use local community action agencies to control VISTA activities in local communities. This effort by the new OEO leadership prompted OEO official Paul Duncan to outline the place of VISTA in OEO in a position paper, which he sent to all regional OEO administrators in June 1969. In the position paper Duncan stated that VISTA must remain autonomous within the OEO structure because VISTA was "more a movement than a program" and "must be concerned with equity and idealism in order to produce results." VISTA must retain its independence from the establishment and from local community action agencies, according to Duncan, in order for the program to stay relevant to young people and to preserve the victories achieved by volunteers all over the country. "VISTA is working well," Duncan concluded, "[so] why make a change? Why risk a good thing?"[44]

Despite Duncan's pleadings, national OEO administrators continued their efforts over the next several years to strip the VISTA program of its autonomy and force volunteers to drop their confrontational tactics. By 1970, these national changes had produced visible effects on Houston's VISTA program, not the least of which was decreased morale among the volunteers and a nagging uncertainty about the future of the entire volunteer program. In a letter to Congressman George H. W. Bush in April 1970, Houston's VISTA supervisor Roger Armstrong expressed great concern that national developments in the VISTA program were negatively affecting the volunteer effort in Houston. "I think VISTAs are making clear," Armstrong stated, "that they feel that a number of recent actions by OEO both nationally and regionally indicate that there is a lack of support of VISTA by the Office of Economic Opportunity administration. They feel that these new developments will result in either making VISTA less effective in working with the poor or possibly could result in VISTA being cancelled altogether. . . . I feel that this would be tragic if true." Armstrong requested an urgent meeting with Bush in order to make sure that Bush supported the continuation of the VISTA program in Houston. The next month, after Bush had failed to respond favorably to Armstrong's overtures, Armstrong fired off another letter exclaiming that the VISTA volunteers in Houston "are deadly serious in their concern that someone listen to their cries of alarm. They do feel recent administrative decisions within the Office of Economic Opportunity have not been in the interests of the poor or of the VISTAs who are working on behalf of the poor." Armstrong again requested a personal meeting with Bush, but this also went unheeded.[45]

After failing to receive an adequate response from Congressman Bush, Armstrong sent an equally urgent letter to OEO director Donald Rumsfeld expressing alarm over the diminishing amount of support for community organizing and institutional change from national OEO and VISTA officials. After detailing a few of the VISTA-initiated programs in Houston, Armstrong stated that many VISTA volunteers in the city were "seeking social and institutional change. This . . . is needed if the causes as well as the symptoms of poverty are to be addressed. However, as you know there are certain special interest groups in society who are threatened by such change and react against it. It would be sad indeed if national and regional support of these VISTA efforts were to wither under the pressure of these reactionary forces." Armstrong pleaded with Rumsfeld to reply with words of encouragement that would show the VISTA volunteers in Houston that OEO continued to support their grassroots efforts, but Rumsfeld never responded to the letter.[46]

Most likely Rumsfeld did not reply to Armstrong's letter because he would not have been able to provide those reassuring words. Nationally, the VISTA program was being consolidated under the ACTION umbrella. Nixon was beginning to appoint conservative ideologues to top positions within that agency, a development that would ultimately change the nature of the federal volunteer program all over the country. VISTA volunteers and members of their sponsoring agencies in Houston felt these changes acutely by 1970. In an annual report on Houston's VISTA activities that year, VISTA supervisors lamented the fact that national developments had irreparably harmed the VISTA program in Houston. In addition to a lack of support for community organizing and empowerment of the poor, authors of the report presented a list of several additional decisions made by new OEO officials that had a negative effect on the VISTA program in Houston, including a withdrawal of the one-year draft deferment for volunteers, the perpetual vacancies in top-level VISTA positions in Washington, and a changed VISTA recruiting policy that steered many college-aged volunteers away from the program. "Many volunteers began to feel that the VISTA in the field was no longer being supported in his work," the report stated, and the result was "a drop in re-enrollment from 60% last year to 10% this year, and a decrease in expected new National Pool Volunteers by 50%." In just two years, the changes in the VISTA program at the national level had had a profoundly negative effect on the local volunteer program in Houston.[47]

In 1972 national VISTA and OEO officials made a decision that finally brought an end to the VISTA program in Houston. Once Nixon had moved the VISTA program into ACTION, the new agency changed the funding requirement for volunteer-sponsoring organizations. Whereas the VISTA sponsoring agency had been responsible for only 10 percent of the funding before 1972, ACTION's new requirement stipulated that the sponsoring agency must pay half of the cost of the volunteers' expenses. For Houston's VISTA program, the total sum would have been more than $12,000, an amount no VISTA sponsoring agency in the city could afford to pay. The current VISTA volunteers were allowed to continue their work until the end of the year, but many volunteers believed this was simply the first step in a process to eliminate the VISTA program completely from the War on Poverty. As a local newspaper reporter covering the VISTA story stated, the VISTA program in Houston thus "came to an end on a note of sorrow and bitterness." As a final blow to community organizing and confrontational tactics, the EF-LAC project, whose members had defined their mission based on using VISTA volunteers, finally disbanded in 1972 and ceased to be a force for social change in the city of Houston.[48]

With the VISTA program gone from Houston, HCCAA remained the only agency in the city charged with carrying out the War on Poverty in the early 1970s. By that time, however, HCCAA had become a simple deliverer of social services, but even those services were severely scaled back and the participation of the poor was virtually nonexistent. In 1976, after President Gerald Ford dismantled OEO and reorganized the community action agencies under the newly created Community Services Administration, HCCAA likewise reorganized and renamed itself the "Gulf Coast Community Services Association" (GCCSA), which still exists today. In order to accomplish this reorganization, however, GCCSA administrators made one final assault on the participation of the poor in the poverty program. In January 1976, just months before the organization became GCCSA, HCCAA board members voted to remove any administrative powers that remained within the ten delegate agencies, which were responsible for implementing the various community action initiatives in the target neighborhoods and for making sure the poor were involved in the planning and implementation of these programs. While the ten delegate agencies would still serve as a "voice for the poor," in reality they would have no power to enforce anything. Despite opposition from several parties, including the city NAACP chapter's president, who argued that the withdrawal of the administrative duties of the ten delegate agencies was "a gross disappointment to the idea of getting the program to the grassroots," the HCCAA board approved the plan. As evidenced by GCCSA documents detailing the organization's activities, by 1976 the War on Poverty in Houston consisted of a disorganized assortment of a few social services delivered by an agency totally uninterested in the expansion of democracy through the participation of the poor or the empowerment of those Houston residents who had been systematically denied power over their own lives.[49]

Between 1969 and 1976, the War on Poverty gradually came to a close in Houston. While the Green Amendment initiated this process in 1967 and 1968, the decline of the poverty program in the city took several years to play out as Mayor Welch and other public officials pushed the city's community action agency to the sidelines of the War on Poverty. More important, changes within OEO at the national and regional levels had profound effects on the War on

Poverty in Houston. Without a doubt, grassroots antipoverty activists who were responsible for implementing the poverty program on the ground in Houston were vital for the success of the War on Poverty, but equally important for its fate was the influence of the federal government and national OEO officials. The dynamic relationship between the federal government and local antipoverty activists had determined the course of the War on Poverty in Houston, and between 1969 and 1976 this relationship brought the poverty program to a close in the city. Whereas grassroots activists in the mid-1960s had enjoyed a remarkable amount of support from federal OEO officials to carry out an aggressive and confrontational Community Action Program capable of expanding democracy in Houston, beginning in 1969 they saw that support gradually disappear because of Nixon's reorientation of the poverty war. The Green Amendment, therefore, was the beginning of the end of the War on Poverty drama in the city of Houston because it launched a process that took several years to complete. The Nixon administration's efforts to reorient OEO away from confrontational tactics and to shrink the size of the poverty program's bureaucracy were thus the final blows to the War on Poverty in Houston. By 1976 there was virtually nothing left of what was once a vibrant, proactive, and confrontational program to address the problems of the poor in the city and make democracy meaningful in the lives of more Americans.

The War on Democracy

"Is democracy in crisis?" So began a 1975 report titled "The Crisis of Democracy" issued by the Trilateral Commission, a nongovernmental think tank made up of elite business and political figures and funded by David Rockefeller. According to Harvard political scientist Samuel P. Huntington, one of the report's authors, the decade of the 1960s had witnessed an explosion of grassroots activism that had resulted in an excess of democracy in the United States. Echoing John Adams's warning that there "never was a democracy that did not commit suicide," Huntington warned that democracy in the United States was in danger not because of any external threat or internal subversion, but because of an "overindulgence" in democracy. "A value which is normally good in itself," concluded Huntington, "is not necessarily optimized when it is maximized. . . . There are . . . potentially desirable limits to the indefinite extension of political democracy. Democracy will have a longer life if it has a more balanced existence." Where had all this excess democracy come from? Huntington traced this alarming development to the African American civil rights movement and the subsequent efforts by other minority groups to bring about racial equality. He also considered the outpouring of citizen participation during the 1960s, the "marches, demonstrations, protest movements, and 'cause' organizations" spawned by "blacks, Indians, Chicanos, white ethnic groups, students, and women." These efforts, according to Huntington, had put too much strain on American democracy by the 1970s and threatened to undermine the entire democratic experiment in the United States.[1]

The War on Poverty tells a different story about democracy in the 1960s. As its implementation in Houston reveals, there were opportunities to expand the meaning of democracy during the 1960s. The federal antipoverty program opened up a space to challenge mainstream definitions of democracy. Together with civil rights legislation, for a few years the federal government placed its power and authority behind the idea of broadening democracy, and a significant number of grassroots activists capitalized on these opportunities to change the status quo. Yet once activists and poor Houston residents began achieving a few victories, opponents organized to preserve a more limited interpretation of the meaning of democracy. In the end, it was this limited vision that prevailed over the more participatory form of democracy that activists had pushed for in their implementation of the War on Poverty. Specifically, the type of democracy that survived would have a place for racial minorities, women, and the poor to take part in the system of representative democracy through voting and office holding, but these groups would not be permitted to participate directly in the decision-making processes that affected their daily lives. This significant limitation applied especially to those living in poverty, as gains made in enlarging the number of Americans who could take part in the system of representative democracy primarily benefitted the middle class.

The efforts to broaden the definition of democracy in Houston using the War on Poverty reveal several important lessons about the nature of democracy in the United States. First, the conflict over democracy in Houston during these years shows that democracy is inherently unstable; it is constantly being renegotiated and redefined. Second, this episode reveals that democracy does not inevitably expand and there is no progressive march toward perfect democracy. Rather, any expansion of democracy requires conflict and struggle. Finally, democracy and power are inextricably intertwined and must be understood together. There can be no broadening of the meaning of democracy without an exercise and display of power.

The experiences of local activists in Houston as they struggled to use the War on Poverty to expand the meaning of democracy illustrate these three points about democracy. Grassroots activists in Houston, armed with a mandate from the federal government, challenged mainstream definitions of democracy and, at least for a short period of time, broadened the scope of local democracy in the city and empowered poor residents to take an active role in civic life. By demanding a voice in the decisions that affected their lives, local activists and poor Houston residents demanded a voice in local politics. At least for a brief moment, poor Houstonians and their activist allies achieved some important victories and managed to expand the meaning of democracy. The fluid interaction between federal policies and grassroots activists made it possible to use the War on Poverty to bring about social change in Houston and to make the concept of democracy meaningful in the lives of poor residents.

These efforts did indeed leave behind an important legacy in Houston. As historian Annelise Orleck has argued, "Antipoverty programs initiated under LBJ and built on, adapted by, and extended by several of his successors make up some of the most enduring and unassailable strands of the national social safety net." Although there was a shift in emphasis after 1969, President Nixon actually increased federal spending on social programs during his time in the White House. According to Orleck, in 2010 the 1,100 surviving community action agencies around the country received more than $9 billion in public and private funds. Several national programs, including the Job Corps, Volunteers in Service to America, Legal Services, Foster Grandparents, and Upward Bound, also continue to operate to this day.[2]

Similar to other locations, there were a handful of lasting achievements of the War on Poverty in Houston. The extension of water and sanitation services to remote low-income neighborhoods like Settegast began a process of equalizing municipal amenities across the entire city. The opening of the Settegast Clinic was only the first establishment of a public healthcare facility in one of Houston's poor neighborhoods. Today the Harris County Hospital District operates three hospitals, fifteen community health clinics, nine school-based facilities, a dialysis center, and several mobile health clinics. The Gulf Coast Community Services Association continues to operate several service programs in Houston's low-income neighborhoods, including housing assistance, a food pantry, a clothes closet, employment skills training, and the very popular Head Start preschool program. In conjunction with the civil rights movements in the city, the voter registration drives initiated by War on Poverty activists changed the face of electoral politics in Houston.[3]

While it is clear that a previous generation of historians overlooked many of these lasting consequences of President Johnson's antipoverty efforts, the question of whether the War on Poverty actually expanded democracy and empowered the poor is a more complicated matter and much more difficult to answer definitively. Although there were a significant number of grassroots activists and poor residents who attempted to use the War on Poverty to expand democracy in Houston, it seems that a more significant long-term consequence of these endeavors to expand democracy can be seen in the efforts to maintain a more limited interpretation of democracy. In Houston, the successes activists were able to achieve using the War on Poverty provoked a strong backlash from pillars of local power, and this counterattack was ultimately fatal for the building of a strong social movement in the city capable of continuing the march toward a fuller interpretation of democracy. This backlash, therefore, proved to be a more significant long-term consequence than any of the victories activists achieved in their use of the War on Poverty.

The face of democracy in America, as the Trilateral Commission report suggested, certainly looked different after the upheavals of the 1960s. Federal legislation passed in response to the civil rights movement has resulted in a more inclusive political arena where there is now a remarkable amount of voting and office holding among women and racial minorities. Yet while the realm of politics has become more accessible since the 1960s, the broader definition of democracy—including what democracy actually means in the lives of most Americans—remains for the most part unchanged. More American citizens have been brought into the mainstream political process, but the process itself emerged from the 1960s relatively unaltered. As the backlash against the War on Poverty shows, the idea of participatory democracy—where all citizens, however poor, would participate directly in the decision-making processes that affect their lives—went down in defeat. It is the limited interpretation of democracy—the one favored by most elites in Houston and across the nation— that ultimately prevailed and persists to the current day.

The efforts to preserve a narrow interpretation of democracy have persisted since the 1960s and continue in the twenty-first century. Examples are numerous. As of December 2011, fifteen state legislatures have approved photograph-identification requirements for voting, and several more are considering similar legislation. These measures are ostensibly directed at alleged voter fraud, but several studies have shown that photograph-identification requirements disproportionately disfranchise low-income and minority voters. The limitations of the U.S. Census often result in the exclusion of citizens and a corresponding loss of public resources and the advantages of proportional representation, which most often affects communities of color, immigrants, and the poor. Opponents of widespread political participation, even the mere act of voting, periodically support congressional redistricting plans to silence the voices of those same groups. In an even clearer example of an attempt to limit democratic participation, Congress in 2009 defunded the Association of Community Organizations for Reform Now (ACORN) amid a scandal where a few employees had given an undercover activist advice on running a brothel and hiding income. ACORN certainly had faults and was in need of more oversight, but to shut down an entire organization based on the actions of a handful of low-level employees was clearly excessive. It seems likely that the real outrage over ACORN had more to do with the organization's efforts to organize and empower the poor rather than a fleeting scandal. Finally, in January 2010, the U.S. Supreme Court handed down its decision in *Citizens United v. Federal Election Commission*, which invalidated any limits on donations to political campaigns by corporations. Rather than an excess of democracy, all of these examples show that the last forty years have witnessed a number of significant efforts to limit the definition of democracy and preserve a system that works best for social and political elites and the very wealthy.[4]

Is democracy in crisis? The implementation of the War on Poverty in Houston—especially what those experiences reveal about the relationship between democracy and power—suggests that the answer to this question is always yes. Democracy itself is inherently unstable, open to interpretation, and inextricably tied to power. As a result, it is constantly being redefined, renegotiated, and reimagined. Any expansion of democracy requires struggle, conflict, and even crisis. Yet this crisis is not something to lament; instead, it should compel us to attempt to understand the concept of democracy and its application more deeply.

NOTES

Introduction. The War on Poverty and the Expansion of Democracy

1. The chapter's opening epigraph is from Donald Rumsfeld, "Remarks at NACD Conference, Silver Spring Maryland," October 11, 1969, Box 2, Folder CAP (General), Office of Economic Opportunity, Southwest Region, VISTA, Central Files, Budget-Mexican American Affairs, Record Group 381, National Archives and Records Administration, Southwest Region, Fort Worth, Texas (hereafter cited as NARASW) (quotation). For the Johnson speech, see *Public Papers of the Presidents of the United States, 1963–1964*, vol. 1: Lyndon B. Johnson, "Remarks at the University of Michigan," May 22, 1964, 704–7 (first quotation); and Lyndon B. Johnson, "Annual Message to the Congress on the State of the Union," January 8, 1964, 112–18 (second quotation).

2. *Economic Opportunity Act of 1964*, S 2642, 88th Cong., 2nd sess., *United States Serial Set* 12616–3 (August 1964).

3. Matusow, *Unraveling of America*, 220, 270 (first and second quotations); Murray, *Losing Ground*, 9 (third quotation). Other examples with arguments similar to Murray's are Mead, *Beyond Entitlement*; and Magnet, *Dream and the Nightmare*. For other national histories of the War on Poverty, see Andrew, *Lyndon Johnson and the Great Society*; Davies, *From Opportunity to Entitlement*; Kaplan and Cuciti, *Great Society and Its Legacy*; Unger, *Best of Intentions*; Jackson, "The State, the Movement, and the Urban Poor"; Russell, *Economics, Bureaucracy, and Race*. For a recent Marxist interpretation of the War on Poverty that continues the tradition of asking the same questions about the eradication of poverty, see Stricker, *Why America Lost the War on Poverty*. Two important works that came before historians began studying the War on Poverty were Piven and Cloward, *Regulating the Poor*; and Ginzberg and Solow, *Great Society*.

4. Blair Justice to Louie Welch, memorandum, September 6, 1966, Box 33, Louie Welch Papers, Houston Metropolitan Research Center, Houston Public Library, Houston, Texas (hereafter cited as Welch Papers); Saralee Tiede, "Outlook Called Hopeful in War on Poverty Here," *Houston Chronicle*, January 1, 1967; "Settegast Area to Use Fire Hydrant Water," *Houston Chronicle*, September 6, 1966; "Urgent Steps OKd in Settegast Water Crisis," *Houston Post*, September 7, 1966; "Settegast Water Job Begun," *Houston Post*, September 8, 1966; Harold Scarlett, "Poverty's Captives: Planners Finally Get Some Action," *Houston Post*, November 10, 1966 (quotation).

5. "Beating Pregnant Woman Arouses Resentment," *Houston Informer*, January 14, 1967 (quotation); Ed Terrones to Edgar May, memorandum, March 15, 1967, Box 73, Folder CAP, Houston, Harris County, Texas, January–March 1967, OEO Inspection Divi-

sion, Inspection Reports, 1964–67, Record Group 381, National Archives and Records Administration, College Park, Maryland (hereafter cited as NARA); Saralee Tiede, "Settegast—A Powderkeg or a Community on the Move?," *Houston Chronicle*, January 22, 1967.

6. Ed Terrones to Edgar May, memorandum, March 15, 1967, Box 73, Folder CAP, Houston, Harris County, Texas, January–March 1967, OEO Inspection Division, Inspection Reports, 1964–1967, Record Group 381, NARA; Charles Kelly to Ed Terrones, March 17, 1967, Box 73, Folder CAP, Houston, Harris County, Texas, January–March 1967, OEO Inspection Division, Inspection Reports, 1964–1967, Record Group 381, NARA; Tiede, "Settegast—A Powderkeg or a Community on the Move?," (quotation).

7. Matusow, *Unraveling of America*, 254–55.

8. A sampling of these recent studies, but certainly not a comprehensive list, includes Orleck and Hazirjian, *War on Poverty*; Germany, *New Orleans after the Promises*; Ashmore, *Carry It On*; Kiffmeyer, *Reformers to Radicals*; Bauman, *Race and the War on Poverty*; Clayson, *Freedom Is Not Enough*; McKee, *Problem of Jobs*; Jordan, "Citizenship, Welfare Rights and the Politics of Respectability in Rural and Urban Mississippi, 1900–1980," PhD diss., University of Michigan, 2003; Orleck, *Storming Caesar's Palace*; Hazirjian, "Negotiating Poverty"; Quadagno, *Color of Welfare*; Braun, *Social Change and Empowerment of the Poor*. A fascinating study that does not focus the analysis on the grassroots but rather widens the lens to view the War on Poverty within the broad context of the international Cold War and the search for ways to enhance national security in the United States is Jardini, "Out of the Blue Yonder."

9. Ashmore, *Carry It On*; Germany, *New Orleans*, 5–11 (quotation); Bauman, *Race and the War on Poverty*, 5–9, 137–38.

10. Clayson, *Freedom Is Not Enough*.

11. Matusow, *Unraveling of America*, xx.

12. Castells, *City and the Grassroots*, 318–20.

13. Mattson, *Intellectuals in Action*, 5, 13 (quotation); Students for a Democratic Society, "Port Huron Statement," http://www.h-net.org/~hst306/documents/huron.html (accessed December 8, 2011); Kaufman, "Human Nature and Participatory Democracy." See also Cunningham, "Participatory Democracy"; Pateman, *Participation and Democratic Theory*; Dahl, *Democracy and Its Critics*, 225–31.

14. Andrew, *Lyndon Johnson*, 68; Matusow, *Unraveling of America*, 244–45. My use of the term "space" is informed primarily by Sara Evans and Harry Boyte's work on "free spaces" and their role in bringing about democratic change. See Evans and Boyte, *Free Spaces*.

15. Matusow, *Unraveling of America*, 245. See Office of Economic Opportunity, Community Action Program, *Community Action Program Guide* (Washington, D.C., February 1965); and Office of Economic Opportunity, Community Action Program, *Community Action Program Workbook* (Washington, D.C., March 1965).

16. Clayson, *Freedom Is Not Enough*, 66 (first quotation); McKee, "'This Government Is With Us': Lyndon Johnson and the Grassroots War on Poverty," in Orleck and Hazirjian, *War on Poverty*, 36 (second quotation).

17. Heale, " Sixties as History."

18. Kloppenberg, "From Hartz to Tocqueville."

19. Lemisch, "The American Revolution Seen from the Bottom Up," 3–45 (first quotation); Zinn, *People's History of the United States*, 11 (second quotation). The intellectual

godfather of this shift in emphasis to ordinary people was the British historian E. P. Thompson, particularly his *Making of the English Working Class*.

Chapter 1. Declaring a War on Poverty in the Midst of "Pervasive Conservatism"

1. McComb, *Houston*, 145.
2. Macdonald, "Our Invisible Poor."
3. Matusow, *Unraveling of America*, 246.
4. Cole, *No Color Is My Kind*; *Strange Demise of Jim Crow*; Schulman, *From Cotton Belt to Sunbelt*.
5. Cole, *No Color Is My Kind*, 42–43.
6. Chandler Davidson, "Negro Politics," 61. For additional information on the civil rights movement in Houston, see also Davidson, *Biracial Politics*. Once elected, Welch delivered on his promise and promptly fired Chief Shuptrine, replacing him with the more humane and racially tolerant H. Buddy McGill. Within a year, however, Welch had fired McGill, allegedly because he was too soft on the city's gambling industry, and replaced him with Herman Short. Short's reputation would eventually top that of Shuptrine as a notorious racist. See Davidson, "Negro Politics," 65.
7. Mel Young, "City Can Get $5 Million Yearly in Poverty Funds," *Houston Chronicle*, August 19, 1964; Office of Economic Opportunity, "Allotment among States of Funds Authorized by the Economic Opportunity Act of 1964," September 25, 1964, Box 1, Folder 4, Records of the General Counsel, President's Task Force in the War against Poverty, Record Group 381, National Archives and Records Administration, College Park, Maryland (hereafter cited as NARA).
8. Sam Kinch, "Dems May Make Poverty Act Major Issue in Election Drive," *Houston Chronicle*, August 22, 1964 (first quotation); "Democratic Party Platform of 1964," August 24, 1964, in John Woolley and Gerhard Peters, *The American Presidency Project*, http://www.presidency.ucsb.edu/platforms.php (accessed December 8, 2011) (second quotation).
9. Virginia F. Eastham to Mayor Louie Welch, October 16, 1964, Box 14, Louie Welch Papers, Houston Metropolitan Research Center, Houston Public Library, Houston, Texas (hereafter cited as Welch Papers) (first quotation); Mrs. John T. Carter to Mayor Louie Welch, November 2, 1964, Box 14, Welch Papers (second quotation). For an interesting account of the history of anticommunism and right-wing politics in Houston, see Carleton, *Red Scare!*.
10. "Elliott Raps Anti-Poverty Drive in City," *Houston Chronicle*, August 24, 1964 (first quotation); Oscar Griffin, "Republican Party Is Mounting Well-Oiled Campaign in Texas," *Houston Chronicle*, September 6, 1964; Bill Connolly, "Bush Says Liberals Stand Poor in Line," *Houston Chronicle*, October 17, 1964 (second quotation).
11. Mildred to President Lyndon Johnson, memorandum, November 4, 1964, Box 69, Folder 8, White House Central Files, Lyndon Baines Johnson Library, Austin, Texas (hereafter cited at LBJL); Oscar Griffin, "Harris County Vote Is Solid for Democrats," *Houston Chronicle*, November 4, 1964.
12. "Poverty Funds Bid by City Is Rejected," *Houston Chronicle*, September 26, 1965.
13. Minutes of Houston–Harris County Community Council Board of Directors, October 7, 1964, Box 2, Records of the Community Welfare Planning Association of Greater

Houston, Houston Metropolitan Research Center, Houston Public Library, Houston, Texas (hereafter cited as CWPA Collection).

14. Minutes of Houston–Harris County Community Council, August 24, 1964, Box 2, CWPA Collection (quotation); Minutes of Houston–Harris County Community Council Board of Directors, October 7, 1964, Box 2, CWPA Collection.

15. Minutes of Houston–Harris County Community Council Board of Directors, September 22, 1964, CWPA Collection; Minutes of Houston–Harris County Community Council Executive Committee, September 30, 1964, CWPA Collection; Minutes of Houston–Harris County Community Council Board of Directors, October 27, 1964, CWPA Collection; "Community Council Presses for Ammunition in Poverty War," *Houston Chronicle*, October 8, 1964; "Poverty Funds Bid by City Is Rejected," *Houston Chronicle*, September 26, 1965.

16. Mel Young, "$8 Million Poverty War in Harris!," *Houston Chronicle*, October 13, 1964; Howard Spergel, "Youth Unwanted," *Houston Post*, December 13, 1964; Minutes of Houston–Harris County Community Council Membership Committee, November 19, 1964, Box 2, CWPA Collection; Minutes of Houston–Harris County Community Council Committee on Appraisal of Needs, December 10, 1964, Box 2, CWPA Collection; Minutes of Houston–Harris County Community Council Board of Directors, October 7, 1964, Box 2, CWPA Collection.

17. Melvin Steakley, "HAY Program Called Inept," *Houston Chronicle*, November 13, 1964.

18. "New Plan Offered to Fight School Dropout Problem," newspaper clipping, Box 21, Folder 1, Records from Federal Government Agencies, Records from the Office of Economic Opportunity, 1964–1968, LBJL; Hugh Powers, "Klein Gets 1st Slice of Anti-Poverty Pie," *Houston Chronicle*, December 29, 1964; "Harris Agencies Ask U.S. for Youth-Training Funds," *Houston Chronicle*, January 7, 1965; Gale McNutt, "Anti-Poverty 'Big Business,'" *Houston Post*, April 8, 1965; Elmer Bertelsen, "Operation Headstart: A Program for Deprived Children," *Houston Chronicle*, April 14, 1965; "Headstart 'Goes for Broke,'" *Houston Chronicle*, April 15, 1965; Elmer Bertelsen, "'Head Start' to Open Children's Minds," *Houston Chronicle*, May 23, 1965.

19. Howard Spergel, "Youth Unwanted," *Houston Post*, December 13, 1964; Elmer Bertelsen, "Operation Headstart: A Program for Deprived Children," *Houston Chronicle*, April 14, 1965; "Headstart 'Goes for Broke,'" *Houston Chronicle*, April 15, 1965; Elmer Bertelsen, "'Head Start' to Open Children's Minds," *Houston Chronicle*, May 23, 1965.

20. Minutes of Houston–Harris County Community Council Board of Directors, January 26, 1965, Box 1, CWPA Collection; Minutes of Houston–Harris County Community Council Board of Directors, February 23, 1965, Box 1, CWPA Collection; "Poverty Funds Bid by City Is Rejected," *Houston Chronicle*, September 26, 1965; Sargent Shriver to Louie Welch, January 26, 1965, Welch Papers.

21. Minutes of Houston–Harris County Community Council Board of Directors, January 26, 1965, Box 1, CWPA Collection; Minutes of Houston–Harris County Community Council Board of Directors, February 23, 1965, Box 1, CWPA Collection; "Poverty Funds Bid by City Is Rejected," *Houston Chronicle*, September 26, 1965; Sargent Shriver to Louie Welch, January 26, 1965, Welch Papers (quotation); "Welch Will Attend Humphrey Meeting," *Houston Post*, March 6, 1965; Charles Culhane, "Welch Joins Study of Urban Problems," *Houston Post*, March 9, 1965; Theodore H. Berry, memorandum, March 26, 1965, Box 9, Folder Houston, Texas, 1965, Office of Economic Opportunity, Community Action Program, Records of the Director, State Files, 1965–1968, Record Group 381,

NARA; Fred Baldwin to Theodore H. Berry, Fred Hayes, and William Bozman, memorandum, March 29, 1965, Box 9, Folder Houston, Texas, 1965, Office of Economic Opportunity, Community Action Program, Records of the Director, State Files, 1965–1968, Record Group 381, NARA; "U.S. Aides, Welch Talk about Poverty Program," *Houston Post*, March 23, 1965.

22. Fred Baldwin to Theodore H. Berry, Fred Hayes, and William Bozman, memorandum, March 29, 1965, Box 9, Folder Houston, Texas, 1965, Office of Economic Opportunity, Community Action Program, Records of the Director, State Files, 1965–1968, Record Group 381, NARA (quotation); "U.S. Aides, Welch Talk about Poverty Program," *Houston Post*, March 23, 1965; "Welch Hints Poverty War Plans Vague," *Houston Chronicle*, March 23, 1965.

23. Fred Baldwin to Theodore H. Berry, Fred Hayes, and William Bozman, memorandum, March 29, 1965, Box 9, Folder Houston, Texas, 1965, Office of Economic Opportunity, Community Action Program, Records of the Director, State Files, 1965–1968, Record Group 381, NARA; "U.S. Aides, Welch Talk about Poverty Program," *Houston Post*, March 23, 1965; "Welch Hints Poverty War Plans Vague," *Houston Chronicle*, March 23, 1965.

24. Fred Baldwin to Theodore H. Berry, Fred Hayes, and William Bozman, memorandum, March 29, 1965, Box 9, Folder Houston, Texas, 1965, Office of Economic Opportunity, Community Action Program, Records of the Director, State Files, 1965–1968, Record Group 381, NARA. Philadelphia was the first city to experiment with the "maximum feasible participation" edict by holding elections in poor neighborhoods for seats on the city's community action agency board. Beneath the façade of grassroots democracy, however, Philadelphia's poverty program was being administered by one very wealthy, powerful man named Samuel L. Evans, who had ties to the city's mayor, James Tate. This revelation exposed corruption within both the community action agency and the mayor's office. See Matusow, *Unraveling of America*, 256–57.

25. "Rally Scheduled to Explain Johnson's War on Poverty," *Houston Chronicle*, March 28, 1965; Hank Ezell, "Latin Americans Must Unify for Poverty Aid, Cleric Says," *Houston Post*, March 29, 1965 (quotation).

26. "Welch Says Poverty Plan Near," *Houston Post*, April 8, 1965; "City Asked to Join LBJ Poverty Program," *Houston Chronicle*, April 8, 1965.

27. Houston–Harris County Community Council, "Tentative Proposal for a Community Action Program for Metropolitan Houston," March 30, 1965, Box 1, CWPA Collection.

28. Houston–Harris County Community Council, "Tentative Proposal for a Community Action Program for Metropolitan Houston," March 30, 1965, Box 1, CWPA Collection.

29. "Poverty Funds Bid by City Is Rejected," *Houston Chronicle*, September 26, 1965; Fred Baldwin to Theodore Berry, Fred Hayes, and Bill Bozman, Memorandum, May 10, 1965, Box 9, Folder Houston, Texas, 1965, Office of Economic Opportunity, Community Action Program, Records of the Director, State Files, 1965–1968, Record Group 381, NARA; Vince Ximenes to Bill Haddad, Memorandum, May 11, 1965, Box 77, Folder Texas OEO Program (Compilation) 1965 April thru July, Office of Economic Opportunity, Inspection Division, Inspection Reports, 1964–1967, Record Group 381, NARA.

30. Vince Ximenes to Bill Haddad, memorandum, May 11, 1965, Box 77, Folder Texas OEO Program (Compilation) 1965 April thru July, Office of Economic Opportunity, Inspection Division, Inspection Reports, 1964–1967, Record Group 381, NARA; Houston–Harris County Economic Opportunity Organization, "Articles of Incorporation," May 1965, Box 265, Folder Houston–Harris County Economic Opportunity Organization—

General, Leon Jaworski Papers, Texas Collection, Baylor University Library, Waco, Texas (hereafter cited as Jaworski Papers); Houston–Harris County Economic Opportunity Organization, "By-Laws," May 1965, Box 265, Folder Houston–Harris County Economic Opportunity Organization—General, Jaworski Papers.

31. Houston–Harris County Community Council, "Tentative Proposal for a Community Action Program for Metropolitan Houston," March 30, 1965, Box 1, CWPA Collection.

32. Vince Ximenes to Bill Haddad, Memorandum, May 11, 1965, Box 77, Folder Texas OEO Program (Compilation) 1965 April thru July, Office of Economic Opportunity, Inspection Division, Inspection Reports, 1964–1967, Record Group 381, NARA. County Judge Elliott later declined to run for the new congressional seat, opening the way for Republican George H. W. Bush to win his first election to the House of Representatives from Houston in 1966.

33. Vince Ximenes to Bill Haddad, Memorandum, May 11, 1965, Box 77, Folder Texas OEO Program (Compilation) 1965 April thru July, Office of Economic Opportunity, Inspection Division, Inspection Reports, 1964–1967, Record Group 381, NARA; Fred Baldwin to Theodore Berry, Fred Hayes, and Bill Bozman, Memorandum, May 10, 1965, Box 9, Folder Houston, Texas, 1965, Office of Economic Opportunity, Community Action Program, Records of the Director, State Files, 1965–1968, Record Group 381, NARA.

34. Houston–Harris County Economic Opportunity Organization, "Announcement," May 6, 1965, Box 266, Folder H-HCEOO Executive Committee Minutes, Jaworski Papers (first quotation); Vince Ximenes to Bill Haddad, Memorandum, May 11, 1965, Box 77, Folder Texas OEO Program (Compilation) 1965 April thru July, Office of Economic Opportunity, Inspection Division, Inspection Reports, 1964–1967, Record Group 381, NARA; Fred Baldwin to Theodore Berry, Fred Hayes, and Bill Bozman, Memorandum, May 10, 1965, Box 9, Folder Houston, Texas, 1965, Office of Economic Opportunity, Community Action Program, Records of the Director, State Files, 1965–1968, Record Group 381, NARA; Vince Ximenes to Bill Haddad, Memorandum, May 13, 1965, Box 77, Folder Texas OEO Program (Compilation) 1965 April thru July, Office of Economic Opportunity, Inspection Division, Inspection Reports, 1964–1967, Record Group 381, NARA (second quotation).

35. Vince Ximenes to Bill Haddad, Memorandum, May 13, 1965, Box 77, Folder Texas OEO Program (Compilation) 1965 April thru July, Office of Economic Opportunity, Inspection Division, Inspection Reports, 1964–1967, Record Group 381, NARA.

36. Vince Ximenes to Bill Haddad, Memorandum, May 13, 1965, Box 77, Folder Texas OEO Program (Compilation) 1965 April thru July, Office of Economic Opportunity, Inspection Division, Inspection Reports, 1964–1967, Record Group 381, NARA (quotations); Vince Ximenes to Bill Haddad, Memorandum, May 11, 1965, Box 77, Folder Texas OEO Program (Compilation) 1965 April thru July, Office of Economic Opportunity, Inspection Division, Inspection Reports, 1964–1967, Record Group 381, NARA.

37. Vince Ximenes to Bill Haddad, Memorandum, May 13, 1965, Box 77, Folder Texas OEO Program (Compilation) 1965 April thru July, Office of Economic Opportunity, Inspection Division, Inspection Reports, 1964–1967, Record Group 381, NARA (first quotation); Bill Haddad to Sargent Shriver, Memorandum, May 14, 1965, Box 77, Folder Texas OEO Program (Compilation) 1965 April thru July, Office of Economic Opportunity, Inspection Division, Inspection Reports, 1964–1967, Record Group 381, NARA; Sargent Shriver to Theodore Berry, Memorandum, May 15, 1965, Box 9, Folder Houston, Texas, 1965, Office of Economic Opportunity, Community Action Program, Records of the Director, State Files, 1965–1968, Record Group 381, NARA (second quotation); Fred Baldwin

to Theodore Berry, Fred Hayes, and Bill Bozman, Memorandum, May 21, 1965, Box 9, Folder Houston, Texas, 1965, Office of Economic Opportunity, Community Action Program, Records of the Director, State Files, 1965–1968, Record Group 381, NARA (third quotation); Theodore H. Berry, Memorandum, May 20, 1965, Box 9, Folder Houston, Texas, 1965, Office of Economic Opportunity, Community Action Program, Records of the Director, State Files, 1965–1968, Record Group 381, NARA.

38. Houston Action for Youth, "Application for Community Action Program," May 27, 1965, Box 266, Folder Houston Action for Youth Application for a Community Action Program, Jaworski Papers.

39. Fred Baldwin to Theodore Berry, Fred Hayes, and Bill Bozman, memorandum, May 21, 1965, Box 9, Folder Houston, Texas, 1965, Office of Economic Opportunity, Community Action Program, Records of the Director, State Files, 1965–1968, Record Group 381, NARA (quotation); Office of Economic Opportunity, "Houston, Texas (Conduct and Administration)," Press Release, July 2, 1965, Microfilm Reel 30, Records from Federal Government Agencies, Records from the Office of Economic Opportunity, 1964–1968, LBJL; "Governor OK's 38 More Head Start Projects," *Waco Tribune-Herald*, June 5, 1965, Newspaper Clipping, Box 22, Folder Miscellaneous, Records from Federal Government Agencies, Records from the Office of Economic Opportunity, 1964–1968, LBJL; Howard Spergel, "School Board OK's Anti-Poverty Plans," *Houston Post*, March 24, 1965; *Houston Chronicle*, August 3, 1965; *Houston Chronicle*, March 17, 1965.

40. Houston–Harris County Economic Opportunity Organization, "Application for Community Action Program (Initial Program Development Project)," June 10, 1965, Box 265, Folder Houston–Harris County Economic Opportunity Organization Application for Community Action Program (Initial Program Development Project), Jaworski Papers; Houston–Harris County Economic Opportunity Organization, "Summary of Proposal," June 1965, Box 2, Folder Economic Opportunity Workpapers February–June 1965, William V. Ballew Jr. Papers, 1965–1968, MS 254, Woodson Research Center, Fondren Library, Rice University (hereafter cited as Ballew Papers).

41. "Poverty Funds Bid by City Is Rejected," *Houston Chronicle*, September 26, 1965.

42. George Bush to Leon Jaworski, July 19, 1965, Box 265, Folder Houston–Harris County Economic Opportunity Organization Correspondence, Jaworski Papers (quotations).

43. "Poverty Funds Bid by City Is Rejected," *Houston Chronicle*, September 26, 1965; Houston–Harris County Economic Opportunity Organization, "Application for Community Action Program," August 20, 1965, Box 265, Folder Houston–Harris County Economic Opportunity Organization Application for Community Action Program, Jaworski Papers (quotation).

44. "Poverty Funds Bid by City Is Rejected," *Houston Chronicle*, September 26, 1965; Houston–Harris County Economic Opportunity Organization, "Application for Community Action Program," August 20, 1965, Box 265, Folder Houston–Harris County Economic Opportunity Organization Application for Community Action Program, Jaworski Papers.

45. "Poverty Funds Bid by City Is Rejected," *Houston Chronicle*, September 26, 1965.

46. "OEO Critic of Houston Panel Scored," *Houston Chronicle*, September 27, 1965 (quotations); Ellen Middlebrook, "Poverty Fund Denial Illogical, Jaworski Says," *Houston Post*, September 28, 1965.

47. "More Poor Members on Panel 'Illogical,'" *Houston Chronicle*, September 28, 1965 (emphasis added).

48. Paul D. White, "15 Leaders of Poor to Serve on Board," *Houston Post*, September 30, 1965; Jerry Zuber, "Poor Will Get Anti-Poverty Panel Seats," *Houston Chronicle*, September 30, 1965 (quotation); "Poverty War Misapprehensions Ended," *Houston Chronicle*, October 1, 1965.

49. Leon Jaworski to Community Action Program Office, Office of Economic Opportunity Southwest Region, October 20, 1965, Box 76, Folder Texas OEO Program (Compilation) 1965 October thru November, Office of Economic Opportunity, Inspection Division, Inspection Reports, 1964–1967, Record Group 381, NARA; Minutes of Houston–Harris County Economic Opportunity Organization Board of Directors, October 26, 1965, Box 1, CWPA Collection; Bill Crook to Marvin Watson, Memorandum, September 30, 1965, Box 16, Folder HE-HOVZ, White House Central Files, LBJL (first quotation); Bill Crook to Sargent Shriver, Memorandum, October 1, 1965, Box 16, Folder HE-HOVZ, White House Central Files, LBJL (second quotation); Donn Mitchell to Edgar May, Memorandum, November 7, 1965, Box 76, Folder Texas OEO Program (Compilation) 1965 October thru November, Record Group 381, NARA; Theodore Berry to Charles Kelly, November 15, 1965, Box 265, Folder Houston–Harris County Economic Opportunity Organization Correspondence, Jaworski Papers; "Grant Made for Poverty Project," *Houston Chronicle*, November 5, 1965; "$128,137 for Anti-Poverty Granted to Harris County," *Houston Post*, November 5, 1965.

50. Charles Culhane, "$3 Million in Poverty War Here," *Houston Post*, November 28, 1965; Charles Culhane, "Houston Probed by Anti-Poverty Team," *Houston Post*, December 11, 1965 (quotations).

51. Ivan Scott to Edgar May, Memorandum, November 2, 1965, Box 76, Folder Texas OEO Program (Compilation) 1965 October thru November, Record Group 381, NARA.

Chapter 2. Creating an Alternative Antipoverty Philosophy for Houston

1. Cate Ewing and Joy Hodge, "Winifred Pollack: Census Tract 18, Houston, Texas," Box 1, Houston Council on Human Relations VISTA Collection, Houston Metropolitan Research Center, Houston Public Library, Houston, Texas (hereafter cited as HCHR VISTA Collection).

2. Cate Ewing and Joy Hodge, "Winifred Pollack: Census Tract 18, Houston, Texas," Box 1, HCHR VISTA Collection (quotations); "VISTA," Houston Council on Human Relations Newsletter, Box 2, Folder 3, Houston Council on Human Relations Collection, Houston Metropolitan Research Center, Houston Public Library, Houston, Texas (hereafter cited as HCHR Collection).

3. "Splinter Group Has Its Own Church Now," *Houston Chronicle*, March 9, 1965; Ecumenical Fellowship United Church of Christ, "Contract with Wallace B. Poteat," September 23, 1964, Box 1, Folder Ecumenical Fellowship, Volunteers in Service to America Collection, Houston Metropolitan Research Center, Houston Public Library, Houston, Texas (hereafter cited as VISTA Collection); Vince Maggio to Council Members, September 25, 1964, Box 1, Folder Ecumenical Fellowship, VISTA Collection; Garden Villas United Church of Christ Board of Trustees to Garden Villas Members, October 28, 1964, Box 1, Folder Ecumenical Fellowship, VISTA Collection; Garden Villas United Church of Christ, "The Community Courier," October 31, 1964, Box 1, Folder Ecumenical Fellowship, VISTA Collection; Garden Villas United Church of Christ, "Annual Report," November 1964, Box 1, Folder Ecumenical Fellowship, VISTA Collection.

4. Ecumenical Fellowship, "Questions Asked of the Ecumenical Fellowship by Wil-

liam Luthe and Henry Damm," January 15, 1965, Box 1, Scrapbook, VISTA Collection (quotations); Charles Cross to Ed Weltge, November 2, 1964, Box 1, Folder Ecumenical Fellowship, VISTA Collection. The United Church of Christ had a long tradition of trying to become a truly multiracial and multicultural church and experienced varying degrees of success with that endeavor. See Walker, *Evolution of a UCC Style*, esp. chap. 2.

5. Ecumenical Fellowship, "Questions Asked of the Ecumenical Fellowship by William Luthe and Henry Damm," January 15, 1965, Box 1, Scrapbook, VISTA Collection.

6. For an interesting view of ecumenism and Rev. Poteat's church activism as a bridge between the nonviolent civil rights movement and the Black Power and Brown Power movements, see Behnken, *Fighting Their Own Battles*, 130–37.

7. Ecumenical Fellowship, "Questions Asked of the Ecumenical Fellowship by William Luthe and Henry Damm," January 15, 1965, Box 1, Scrapbook, VISTA Collection; Niebuhr, *Moral Man and Immoral Society*, xxvi–xxvii (quotations).

8. Chappell, *Stone of Hope*. See also Branch, *Parting the Waters*, 81, 84–87. Chappell disagrees with the effort to paint Niebuhr as a neo-orthodox theologian, arguing instead that Niebuhr had a foot in both the neo-orthodox and liberal theological camps. Chappell states, "Niebuhr insisted that he was not 'neo-orthodox'; he rejected Karl Barth's pessimism, Barth's Augustinian rejection of this world. Niebuhr sought to engage in political conflict, to fight oppression, and 'to mitigate the brutalities' of modern life, even while he held that complete success in such efforts was impossible. His biographers and other students of his work now emphasize that Niebuhr greatly exaggerated his own rejection of liberal theology. He was really criticizing liberalism from within, seeking to curb its excesses, not rejecting its engagement with this world and efforts to reform it. Fundamentalists routinely lumped Niebuhr with liberal theologians; to suggest that he was neo-orthodox, as historians persist in doing, is an equal and opposite error." Chappell, *Stone of Hope*, 27. Regardless of whether Niebuhr was truly a neo-orthodox theologian, what is significant for the present discussion is that Niebuhr had an incisive critique of liberalism and its relation to the possibility for social change and struggles for justice, and this criticism rang loud and clear for Rev. Poteat and his supporters.

9. Ecumenical Fellowship, "Questions Asked of the Ecumenical Fellowship by William Luthe and Henry Damm," January 15, 1965, Box 1, Scrapbook, VISTA Collection.

10. Wallace B. Poteat, "Minister's Report," January 1966, Box 1, Folder 3, VISTA Collection; Cox, *Secular City:*. Quotations from page 17, 105–8. Rev. Poteat was also greatly influenced by theologians Gibson Winter, Stephen C. Rose, Hans-Reudi Weber, and John A. T. Robinson, all of whom were writing on the same general topic as Harvey Cox in the 1960s. See Winter, *New Creation as Metropolis*; Rose, *Day the Country Mouse Expired*; Weber, *Salty Christians*; and Robinson, *Honest to God.*

11. Wallace B. Poteat, "Theology and Structure, Ecumenical Fellowship-LAC Project," March 1, 1966, Box 1, Scrapbook, VISTA Collection.

12. Ecumenical Fellowship, "Out of Adversity," n.d., Box 1, Folder 3, VISTA Collection.

13. National Council of Churches, "To the People of the Nation."

14. Wallace B. Poteat, "Theology and Structure, Ecumenical Fellowship-LAC Project," March 1, 1966, Box 1, Scrapbook, VISTA Collection.

15. For the life of Saul Alinsky, see Horwitt, *Let Them Call Me Rebel.*

16. Alinsky, *Reveille for Radicals*, 23–29.

17. Ibid., 29–30, 70.

18. Ibid., 82–83 (emphasis in original).

19. Ibid., 154.

20. Ibid., 208, 213, 215 (emphasis in original).

21. Ecumenical Fellowship, "Voice," February 28, 1965, Box 1, Folder Ecumenical Fellowship, VISTA Collection (quotation); Ecumenical Fellowship, "Voice," May 29, 1965, Box 1, Folder Ecumenical Fellowship, VISTA Collection; "Strategies for Community Change," *Social Action* (February 1965); "Justice and Beyond Justice," *Christian Century* 24 (February 1965): 227–28.

22. Jan Morgan, "Churchmen to Work in Harrisburg Area," *Houston Chronicle*, September 11, 1965 (first quotation); Melvin Steakley, "Ship Channel Area to Get Outside Aid in Self-Help," *Houston Chronicle*, April 24, 1965; Don Britton to Charles Cross, November 3, 1964, Box 1, Folder Ecumenical Fellowship, VISTA Collection; EF-UCC, "Voice," February 14, 1965, Box 1, Folder Ecumenical Fellowship, VISTA Collection; EF-UCC, "Voice," February 28, 1965, Box 1, Folder Ecumenical Fellowship, VISTA Collection; EF-UCC, "Voice," March 28, 1965, Box 1, Folder Ecumenical Fellowship, VISTA Collection; EF-UCC LAC Project, "Projected Program for LAC Project, Houston, Texas, 1965–1966," April 1965, Box 2, Folder The Lack Project, VISTA Collection; Wallace B. Poteat, "The Objectives of the LAC Project," August 1965, Box 1, Scrapbook, VISTA Collection (second quotation).

23. Students for a Democratic Society, "Port Huron Statement," The Sixties Project, University of Virginia, http://www2.iath.virginia.edu/sixties/HTML_docs/Sixties .html (accessed December 8, 2011) (first quotation); Houston SDS Newsletter, November 12, 1965, Box 1, VISTA Scrapbook, VISTA Collection (second quotation); Ecumenical Fellowship–Latin American Channel Project, "Why Does the Ecumenical Fellowship UCC-LAC Project Ask You to Support Our Cause?" n.d., Box 1, VISTA Scrapbook, VISTA Collection; Bud Poteat to EF-UCC Church Council Members, August 1, 1965, Box 1, Folder Ecumenical Fellowship, VISTA Collection.

24. EF-LAC Project, "The LAC (LACK) Project," May 16, 1966, Box 1, VISTA Scrapbook, VISTA Collection (quotation); EF-UCC LAC Project, "Projected Program for LAC Project, Houston, Texas, 1965–1966," April 1965, Box 2, Folder The Lack Project, VISTA Collection.

25. Wallace B. Poteat to Lawrence H. Noonan, September 30, 1966, Box 1, Folder 4, VISTA Collection (first quotation); Jan Morgan, "Churchmen to Work in Harrisburg Area," *Houston Chronicle*, September 11, 1965 (second quotation); Wallace B. Poteat, "The LAC (LACK) Project," May 16, 1966, Box 1, Scrapbook, VISTA Collection; EF-LAC, "Why Does the Ecumenical Fellowship UCC-LAC Project Ask You to Support Our Cause?" n.d., Box 1, Scrapbook, VISTA Collection (third quotation).

26. Many historians downplay or altogether ignore the contributions of VISTA volunteers to the overall War on Poverty. Several histories of the War on Poverty do not include a discussion of the VISTA program at all. These include Matusow, *Unraveling of America*; Davies, *From Opportunity to Entitlement*; and Andrew, *Lyndon Johnson and the Great Society*. Historian Irwin Unger briefly mentioned the VISTA program only to dismiss its importance by pointing out that VISTA "never became the same burr and irritant as community action and the Job Corps, perhaps as much for its lilliputian scale as for any other reason." See Unger, *Best of Intentions*, 185. Similarly, Susan Youngblood Ashmore has argued that the VISTA program was largely inconsequential across the South. See Ashmore, *Carry It On*, 59. Important exceptions to the general neglect of the VISTA program are Germany, *New Orleans after the Promises*, particularly chapter 4; and Kiffmeyer, "From Self-Help to Sedition."

27. Gillette, *Launching the War on Poverty*, 237–41. See also Crook and Thomas, *War-*

riors for the Poor; Reeves, *Politics of the Peace Corps and VISTA*; Schwartz, *In Service to America*; Balzano, "Political and Social Ramifications"; and Pass, "Politics of VISTA."

28. Gillette, *Launching the War on Poverty*, 237–41. In the section of his book devoted to the War on Poverty, historian Allen J. Matusow referred to early architects of community action like Boone and Hackett as "closet radicals." See Matusow, *Unraveling of America*, 243.

29. Edgar May quoted in Gillette, *Launching the War on Poverty*, 249–50.

30. Minutes of HCHR Executive Committee, February 17, 1966, Box 2, Folder 4, HCHR Collection; Waring Fincke, "The VISTA Volunteer," HCHR Newsletter, February 1966, Box 2, Folder 3, HCHR Collection; Minutes of HCHR Board of Directors, March 31, 1966, Box 2, Folder 4, HCHR Collection.

31. Rebekah McBride and James Byron Smith, "A Report on the Action of VISTA Volunteers in Census Tract 18," Box 1, Houston Council on Human Relations VISTA Collection, Houston Metropolitan Research Center, Houston Public Library (hereafter cited as HCHR VISTA Collection); "VISTA," HCHR Newsletter, April 1966, Box 2, Folder 3, HCHR Collection.

32. McBride and Smith, "A Report," HCHR VISTA Collection.

33. Ibid.

34. Ibid.

35. Cate Ewing and Joy Hodge, "Winifred Pollack: Census Tract 18, Houston, Texas," Box 1, HCHR VISTA Collection; "VISTA," HCHR Newsletter, Box 2, Folder 3, HCHR Collection.

36. Ewing and Hodge, "Winifred Pollack," HCHR VISTA Collection.

37. Ibid.

38. Ibid.

39. "VISTA," HCHR Newsletter, Box 2, Folder 3, HCHR Collection; David Gipson, "Report on VISTA Project in Census Tract #12," Box 1, HCHR VISTA Collection.

40. Gipson, "Report," HCHR VISTA Collection.

41. Ibid.

42. *The LAC Project VOICE*, January 22, 1967, Box 2, Folder 2, VISTA Collection.

Chapter 3. An Aggressive Vision for the Community Action Program

1. Leon Jaworski to Louie Welch and Bill Elliott, January 10, 1966, Box 265, Folder Houston–Harris County Economic Opportunity Organization—Correspondence, Leon Jaworski Papers, Texas Collection, Baylor University Library, Waco, Texas (hereafter cited as Jaworski Papers); Leon Jaworski to Houston–Harris County Economic Opportunity Organization Board of Directors, January 10, 1966, Box 265, Folder Houston–Harris County Economic Opportunity Organization—Correspondence, Jaworski Papers; Noe Perez, "Jaworski Quits Local Antipoverty Group," *Houston Chronicle*, January 11, 1966; Bo Byers, "Jaworski to Head Group to Study Texas Education," *Houston Chronicle*, January 6, 1966.

2. Minutes of Houston–Harris County Economic Opportunity Organization Board of Directors, January 10, 1966, Box 266, Folder H-HCEOO Board of Directors Minutes, Jaworski Papers; George Bush to Bill Ballew, January 15, 1966, Box 265, Folder Houston–Harris County Economic Opportunity Organization—Correspondence, Jaworski Papers; Leon Abramson, "Summary Report on the Investigative Task Force of the Ad Hoc Subcommittee on the War on Poverty Program," Box 6, Folder Report/Investigative Task

Force, March 1966, Ad-Hoc Subcommittee of War on Poverty, Records of the General Counsel, President's Task Force in the War Against Poverty, Record Group 381, National Archives and Records Administration, College Park, Maryland (hereafter cited as NARA) (quotation); Noe Perez, "Jaworski Quits Local Antipoverty Group," *Houston Chronicle*, January 11, 1966; "Bush Is 7th District Congress Candidate," *Houston Chronicle*, January 16, 1966.

3. W. V. Ballew Jr., "The Way We Were," Address Delivered at the Twentieth Anniversary Symposium of the Gulf Coast Community Services Association, November 19, 1986, Box 1, W. A. V. Ballew Collection, Houston Metropolitan Research Center, Houston Public Library, Houston, Texas (hereafter cited as Ballew Collection); Minutes of Houston–Harris County Economic Opportunity Organization Board of Directors, January 10, 1966, Box 266, Folder H-HCEOO Board of Directors Minutes, Jaworski Papers.

4. Ballew, " Way We Were. For the life of Saul Alinsky, see Horwitt, *Let Them Call Me Rebel*.

5. Austin Scott, "Saul Alinsky, Professional Radical, Aids 'Have-Nots,'" *Houston Chronicle*, February 20, 1966; Noe Perez, "Slum-Dweller Organizer Hits Poverty War," *Houston Chronicle*, February 25, 1966 (quotations).

6. W. V. Ballew Jr., "The Anti-Poverty Program in Houston," Address Delivered to the Young Presidents' Club of Houston, Texas, August 17, 1966, in author's possession.

7. William V. Ballew, "Anti-Poverty Program," October 3, 1966, Box 1, Folder 3, William V. Ballew Jr. Papers, 1965–1968, MS 254, Woodson Research Center, Fondren Library, Rice University, Houston, Texas (hereafter cited as Ballew Papers).

8. William V. Ballew to Charles Kelly, memorandum, November 2, 1966, Box 1, Folder 3, Ballew Papers.

9. Minutes of Houston–Harris County Economic Opportunity Organization Board of Directors, June 7, 1966, Box 265, Folder H-HCEOO Information, Jaworski Papers.

10. John Moore, "Houston Lawyers' Plan to Defend Poor Watched," *Houston Post*, May 1, 1966; Dick Raycraft, "Legal Aid Available for Needy," *Houston Chronicle*, February 13, 1966. This series of Supreme Court decisions included *Gideon v. Wainwright* (1963), *Massiah v. United States* (1964), and *Miranda v. Arizona* (1966).

11. Donnie Moore, "Legal Aid Fund for Poor OK'd," *Houston Post*, April 26, 1966.

12. E. Clinton Bamberger, Address to the Southwest Regional Office of Economic Opportunity, March 24, 1966, Box 12, Records from Federal Government Agencies, Records of the Office of Economic Opportunity, 1964–1968, Lyndon Baines Johnson Library, Austin, Texas (quotations); Office of Economic Opportunity, "Grant Profile for Houston Legal Foundation through H-HCEOO," April 1966, Box 12, Records from Federal Government Agencies, Records of the Office of Economic Opportunity, 1964–1968, LBJL.

13. Office of Economic Opportunity, "Justice: Legal Services: First Annual Report of the Program of the Office of Economic Opportunity to the American Bar Association at the Annual Convention," August 1966, Box 12, Records from Federal Government Agencies, Records of the Office of Economic Opportunity, 1964–1968, LBJL; Minutes of Houston–Harris County Community Council, Committee on Economic Opportunity and Related Programs, May 6, 1966, Box 1, Records of the Community Welfare Planning Association of Greater Houston, Houston Metropolitan Research Center, Houston Public Library, Houston, Texas (hereafter cited as CWPA collection); Sargent Shriver to Lyndon Johnson, memorandum, May 17, 1966, Box 16, White House Central Files, LBJ Library (hereafter cited as WHCF); John Johnson to Charles Kelly, August 15, 1966, Box 10, Folder Audit, Office of Economic Opportunity, Southwest Region, Community

Action Programs, District Supervisors, Records Relating to City Economic Opportunity Boards, 1965–1968, Record Group 381, National Archives and Records Administration, Southwest Region, Fort Worth, Texas (hereafter cited as NARASW); Donnie Moore, "Legal Aid Fund for Poor OK'd," *Houston Post*, April 26, 1966; "Legal Aid for Poor Gets Funds," *Houston Post*, May 18, 1966; Harold Scarlett, "Poverty's Hostages: Money for Charts—or Bread?" *Houston Post*, November 11, 1966; "Legal Foundation Opens 2 New Branch Offices," *Houston Post*, November 10, 1966.

14. Robert D. Ford to Robert Eckels, September 7, 1966, Box 1, Folder Legal Services Program, William V. Ballew Papers, 1965–1968, MS 254, Woodson Research Center, Fondren Library, Rice University, Houston, Texas (hereafter cited as Ballew Papers); Robert D. Ford to Mrs. Melvyn Davis, September 15, 1966, Box 1, Folder Legal Services Program, Ballew Papers; Fred P. Graham, "Houston to Avoid Rights Legal Aid," *New York Times*, September 26, 1966, newspaper clipping, Box 2, Folder Anti-Poverty Material and Speeches 1965–1966, Ballew Papers; William H. Crook to William V. Ballew, September 1966, Box 59, Folder Houston Texas CAA 1968, OEO CAP Records of the Director, Subject Files, 1965–1969, Record Group 381, NARA; Theodore M. Berry to Earl Johnson, memorandum, September 21, 1966, Box 59, Folder Houston Texas CAA 1968, OEO CAP Records of the Director, Subject Files, 1965–1969, Record Group 381, NARA; Earl Johnson to Theodore M. Berry, September 22, 1966, Box 59, Folder Houston Texas CAA 1968, OEO CAP Records of the Director, Subject Files, 1965–1969, Record Group 381, NARA; Pat Reed, "Schools May Face Race Suit," *Houston Post*, September 9, 1966.

15. Robert D. Ford to Robert Eckels, September 7, 1966, Box 1, Folder Legal Services Program, Ballew Papers; Robert D. Ford to Mrs. Melvyn Davis, September 15, 1966, Box 1, Folder Legal Services Program, Ballew Papers; Fred P. Graham, "Houston to Avoid Rights Legal Aid," *New York Times*, September 26, 1966, newspaper clipping, Box 2, Folder Anti-Poverty Material and Speeches 1965–1966, Ballew Papers; William H. Crook to William V. Ballew, September 1966, Box 59, Folder Houston Texas CAA 1968, OEO CAP Records of the Director, Subject Files, 1965–1969, Record Group 381, NARA; Theodore M. Berry to Earl Johnson, memorandum, September 21, 1966, Box 59, Folder Houston Texas CAA 1968, OEO CAP Records of the Director, Subject Files, 1965–1969, Record Group 381, NARA; Earl Johnson to Theodore M. Berry, September 22, 1966, Box 59, Folder Houston Texas CAA 1968, OEO CAP Records of the Director, Subject Files, 1965–1969, Record Group 381, NARA; Pat Reed, "Schools May Face Race Suit," *Houston Post*, September 9, 1966; Anthony Partridge to Earl Johnson, memorandum, October 12, 1966, Box 59, Folder Houston Texas CAA 1968, OEO CAP Records of the Director, Subject Files, 1965–1969, Record Group 381, NARA; Earl Johnson to Sargent Shriver, memorandum, November 2, 1966, Box 59, Folder Houston Texas CAA 1968, OEO CAP Records of the Director, Subject Files, 1965–1969, Record Group 381, NARA; Felton West, "Legal Group Given OEO Order," *Houston Post*, November 18, 1966, newspaper clipping, Box 1, Folder Legal Services Program, Ballew Papers; Saralee Tiede, "City's Legal Foundation," *Houston Chronicle*, November 23, 1966, Box 2, Folder Anti-Poverty Material and Speeches 1965–1966, Ballew Papers (quotation).

16. Houston Legal Foundation, "Report to the Board of Directors of H-HCEOO on the Opening of Law Offices and the Hiring of Lawyers," 1966, Box 1, Folder Legal Services Program, Ballew Papers.

17. Elmer Bertelsen, "How Head Start Fared This Year," *Houston Chronicle*, February 13, 1966.

18. William H. Crook to Theodore Berry, memorandum, May 26, 1966, Box 14, OEO

CAP Records of the Director, State Files, 1965–1968, Record Group 381, NARA; William H. Crook to Sargent Shriver, memorandum, June 3, 1966, Box 14, OEO CAP Records of the Director, State Files, 1965–1968, Record Group 381, NARA; Astor Kirk to Theodore Berry, telegram, June 7, 1966, Box 14, OEO CAP Records of the Director, State Files, 1965–1968, Record Group 381, NARA; Office of Economic Opportunity, "Houston, Texas (Summer Head Start)," press release, June 15, 1966, Microfilm Reel 35, Records from Federal Government Agencies, Records from the Office of Economic Opportunity, 1964–1968, LBJ Library; "$834,551 Sought for 'Head Start,'" *Houston Chronicle*, February 25, 1966; Elmer Bertelsen, "Schools to Expand on Head Start," *Houston Chronicle*, March 1, 1966; "$2.2 Million Sought for Head Start Plan," *Houston Chronicle*, March 31, 1966; "'Segregated' Head Start Projects Hit," *Houston Chronicle*, May 22, 1966.

19. Office of Economic Opportunity, "Houston, Texas (Conduct and Administration)," press release, March 10, 1966, Microfilm Reel 30, Records from Federal Government Agencies, Records from the Office of Economic Opportunity, 1964–1968, LBJL; William Finister to William H. Crook, memorandum, June 1, 1966, Box 75, OEO Inspection Division, Inspection Reports, 1964–67, Record Group 381, NARA; Office of Economic Opportunity, "Houston, Texas (Conduct and Administration)," press release, June 17, 1966, Microfilm Reel 30, Records from Federal Government Agencies, Records from the Office of Economic Opportunity, 1964–1968, LBJL (quotation); Office of Economic Opportunity, "Houston, Texas (Conduct and Administration)," press release, August 26, 1966, Microfilm Reel 30, Records from Federal Government Agencies, Records from the Office of Economic Opportunity, 1964–1968, LBJL; Houston–Harris County Economic Opportunity Organization, newsletter, July 21, 1966, Box 265, Folder H-HCEOO Information, Jaworski Papers; "Aid Granted for Parent Education," *Houston Chronicle*, March 2, 1966. For the history of the Alley Theatre in Houston, see Matthew C. Ross, "Nina Vance, 1914–1980: Visionary, Founder, Innovator." http://www.alleytheatre.org /Alley/Nina_Vance_EN.asp?SnID=1847439053 (accessed February 13, 2009).

20. Houston–Harris County Economic Opportunity Organization, newsletter, July 21, 1966, Box 265, Folder H-HCEOO Information, Jaworski Papers; Office of Economic Opportunity, "Houston, Texas (Conduct and Administration)," press release, June 15, 1966, Microfilm Reel 30, Records from Federal Government Agencies, Records from the Office of Economic Opportunity, 1964–1968, LBJL (quotation); Bess Attwell to H-HCEOO Board of Directors, memorandum, March 11, 1966, Box 1, Folder Correspondence January–June 1966, Ballew Papers.

21. Charles Kelly to Don Hess, July 26, 1966, Box 13, Folder Administrative, Texas, 1966, OEO CAP Records of the Director, State Files, 1965–1968, Record Group 381, NARA; "Resume of Proposals," March 23, 1966, Box 1, Folder Minutes 1966, Ballew Papers; William Ballew to Lucile Johnson, 8 April 1966, Box 1, Folder Correspondence January–June 1966, Ballew Papers; Minutes of H-HCEOO Board of Directors, April 10, 1966, Box 1, Folder Minutes 1966, Ballew Papers.

22. Charles Kelly to Don Hess, July 26, 1966, Box 13, Folder Administrative, Texas, 1966, OEO CAP Records of the Director, State Files, 1965–1968, Record Group 381, NARA; "E. E. Allen Named to EOO Post," *Houston Post*, November 20, 1966; H-HCEOO, "Resume of Proposals," March 23, 1966, Box 1, Folder Minutes 1966, Ballew Papers; William Ballew to Lucile Johnson, April 8, 1966, Box 1, Folder Correspondence January–June 1966, Ballew Papers; Minutes of H-HCEOO Board of Directors, April 10, 1966, Box 1, Folder Minutes 1966, Ballew Papers; Earl Allen, interview by Wesley G. Phelps, December 11, 2008, Houston, Texas (quotation).

23. Earl E. Allen to All Community Organization Staff, memorandum, December 9, 1966, Box 59, Folder Houston Texas CAA 1968, OEO CAP Records of the Director, Subject Files, 1965–1969, Record Group 381, NARA; Office of Economic Opportunity, Office of Inspection, "Houston–Harris County Economic Opportunity Organization," February 1967, Box 10, Folder Contracts, Office of Economic Opportunity, Southwest Region, Community Action Programs, District Supervisors, Records Relating to City Economic Opportunity Boards, 1965–1968, Record Group 381, NARASW; E. R. Brown to Marlene Futterman, memorandum, February 13, 1967, Box 73, Folder CAP, Houston, Harris County, Texas, Jan.–Mar. 1967, OEO Inspection Division, Inspection Reports, 1964–1967, Record Group 381, NARA; Harold Scarlett, "Poverty's Hostages: After a Year, Crucial Corner Turned?" *Houston Post*, November 12, 1966 (quotation).

24. Earl E. Allen to All Community Organization Staff," memorandum, December 9, 1966, Box 59, Folder Houston Texas CAA 1968, OEO CAP Records of the Director, Subject Files, 1965–1969, Record Group 381, NARA (quotation); Office of Economic Opportunity, Office of Inspection, "Houston–Harris County Economic Opportunity Organization," February 1967, Box 10, Folder Contracts, Office of Economic Opportunity, Southwest Region, Community Action Programs, District Supervisors, Records Relating to City Economic Opportunity Boards, 1965–1968, Record Group 381, NARASW; E. R. Brown to Marlene Futterman, memorandum, February 13, 1967, Box 73, Folder CAP, Houston, Harris County, Texas, January–March 1967, OEO Inspection Division, Inspection Reports, 1964–1967, Record Group 381, NARA; Earl Allen, interview.

25. Earl E. Allen to All H-HCEOO Personnel, memorandum, December 21, 1966, Box 59, Folder Houston Texas CAA 1968, OEO CAP Records of the Director, Subject Files, 1965–1969, Record Group 381, NARA; Marlene Futterman, "Inspection Report for H-HCEOO and HAY," February 1967, Box 73, Folder CAP, Houston, Harris County, Texas, January–March 1967, OEO Inspection Division, Inspection Reports, 1964–1967, Record Group 381, NARA.

26. Earl E. Allen to All H-HCEOO Personnel, memorandum, December 21, 1966, Box 59, Folder Houston Texas CAA 1968, OEO CAP Records of the Director, Subject Files, 1965–1969, Record Group 381, NARA (quotations); Saralee Tiede, "Outlook Called Hopeful in War on Poverty Here," *Houston Chronicle*, January 1, 1967.

27. Earl Allen, interview; Saralee Tiede, "Settegast—a Powderkeg or a Community on the Move?," *Houston Chronicle*, January 22, 1967.

28. Houston–Harris County Economic Opportunity Organization, "The Settegast Report: A Program for Community Development," August 31, 1966, Box 59, Folder Houston Texas CAA 1968, OEO CAP Records of the Director, Subject Files, 1965–1969, Record Group 381, NARA.

29. Ibid.

30. Ibid.

31. Ibid. In addition to Ben Taub Hospital, a public health facility that was closer to Settegast was Jefferson Davis Hospital, but it had such a high mortality and infection rate that it seems no one in Houston who was interested in living would walk through the doors. The disgusting conditions and the ineptitude of Jefferson Davis's staff were revealed in de Hartog, *The Hospital*.

32. Ibid.

33. Ibid.

34. Tiede, "Settegast. "

35. Blair Justice to Louie Welch, memorandum, September 6, 1966, Box 33, Louie

Welch Papers, Houston Metropolitan Research Center, Houston Public Library, Houston, Texas (hereafter cited as Welch Papers); Sarelee Tiede, "Outlook Called Hopeful in War on Poverty Here," *Houston Chronicle*, January 1, 1967 (first quotation); Harold Scarlett, "Poverty's Captives: Planners Finally Get Some Action," *Houston Post*, November 10, 1966 (second quotation); "Water Emergency," *Houston Post*, September 9, 1966 (third quotation).

36. Blair Justice to Louie Welch, memorandum, September 6, 1966, Box 33, Welch Papers; Blair Justice to Louie Welch, memorandum, September 19, 1966, Box 33, Welch Papers; Darrell Williams to Gene Gatling, September 21, 1966, Box 33, Welch Papers; Louie Welch to Darrell Williams, September 28, 1966, Box 33, Welch Papers; Louie Welch to D. H. Germany, September 28, 1966, Box 33, Welch Papers; Blair Justice to Louie Welch, memorandum, September 30, 1966, Box 33, Welch Papers; Joe Smith, "Schools without Water: Children Are Sent Home," *Houston Post*, n.d., newspaper clipping, Box 33, Welch Papers; Sarelee Tiede, "Outlook Called Hopeful in War on Poverty Here," *Houston Chronicle*, January 1, 1967; Harold Scarlett, "Poverty's Captives: Planners Finally Get Some Action," *Houston Post*, November 10, 1966 (quotation).

37. Minutes of Houston–Harris County Economic Opportunity Organization Executive Committee, December 19, 1966, Box 73, Folder CAP, Houston, Harris County, Texas, July–September 1967, OEO Inspection Division, Inspection Reports, 1964–1967, Record Group 381, NARA; Saralee Tiede, "EOO to Ask Hospital District to Set Up Settegast Clinic," *Houston Chronicle*, December 15, 1966 (quotation); H-HCEOO, "Narrative Statements on Needs and Functions, Decentralized Medical Facility, Settegast Community," December 1966, Box 1, Folder Minutes 1966, Ballew Papers.

38. Office of Economic Opportunity, Office of Inspection, "Houston CAP," February 1967, Box 10, Folder Contracts, Office of Economic Opportunity, Southwest Region, Community Action Programs, District Supervisors, Records Relating to City Economic Opportunity Boards, 1965–1968, Record Group 381, NARASW; Minutes of Houston–Harris County Economic Opportunity Organization Executive Committee, February 23, 1967, Box 73, Folder CAP, Houston, Harris County, Texas, July–September 1967, OEO Inspection Division, Inspection Reports, 1964–67, Record Group 381, NARA; Minutes of Houston–Harris County Economic Opportunity Organization Executive Committee, January 23, 1967, Box 1, Folder Minutes 1967, Ballew Papers; H-HCEOO, "Announcement of Grand Opening of Settegast Clinic," January 28, 1967, Box 1, Folder Correspondence January–February 1967, Ballew Papers; William Ballew to Ralph Yarborough, February 2, 1967, Box 1, Folder Correspondence January–February 1967, Ballew Papers (quotation).

39. Saralee Tiede, "Outlook Called Hopeful in War on Poverty Here," *Houston Chronicle*, January 1, 1967; Harold Scarlett, "Poverty's Captives: Planners Finally Get Some Action," *Houston Post*, November 10, 1966; "Residents March in Protest: Sunnyside Fights 'Instant Slums,'" *Houston Post*, November 8, 1966 (quotations).

40. Harold Scarlett, "Poverty's Captives: Planners Finally Get Some Action," *Houston Post*, November 10, 1966 (first quotation); E. R. Brown to Marlene Futterman, memorandum, February 13, 1967, Box 73, Folder CAP, Houston, Harris County, Texas, January–March 1967, OEO Inspection Division, Inspection Reports, 1964–1967, Record Group 381, NARA (second quotation); Marlene Futterman, "Inspection Report for H-HCEOO and HAY," February 1967, Box 73, Folder CAP, Houston, Harris County, Texas, January–March 1967, OEO Inspection Division, Inspection Reports, 1964–67, Record Group 381, NARA (third quotation).

41. "New Head Start Project Opened for 90 Children," *Houston Chronicle*, January 30,

1966; "Anti-Poverty Workers to Seek Out Unemployed," *Houston Chronicle*, April 3, 1966 (first quotation); James Harper, "On the Texas Battlefront: Poverty War Lacks Unity," *Houston Post*, March 19, 1967 (second quotation).

42. Ed Torrenes to Edgar May, memorandum, February 10, 1966, Box 76, OEO Inspection Division, Inspection Reports, 1964–1967, Record Group 381, NARA; Office of Economic Opportunity, "Houston, Texas (Conduct and Administration)," press release, June 29, 1966, Microfilm Reel 30, Records from Federal Government Agencies, Records from the Office of Economic Opportunity, 1964–1968, LBJL; Office of Economic Opportunity, "Texas Receives Three Operation Medicare Alert Grants," press release, February 14, 1966, Microfilm Reel 30, Records from Federal Government Agencies, Records from the Office of Economic Opportunity, 1964–1968, LBJL; "Only Few Aged Have Applied for Medicare," *Houston Chronicle*, January 9, 1966; "If You Are Over 65 . . . Medicare Deadline Near," *Houston Chronicle*, January 16, 1966; "Houston Gets Grant for Medicare Work," *Houston Chronicle*, February 3, 1966; "Medicare Deadline March 31; 2397 Apply at Houston Office," *Houston Chronicle*, March 20, 1966; "Harris County May Top Medicare Sign-Up Average," *Houston Chronicle*, April 1, 1966.

43. Office of Economic Opportunity, Office of Inspection, "Houston–Harris County Economic Opportunity Organization and Houston Action for Youth, Inc.," February 1967, Box 10, Folder Contracts, Office of Economic Opportunity, Southwest Region, Community Action Programs, District Supervisors, Records Relating to City Economic Opportunity Boards, 1965–1968, Record Group 381, NARASW (first quotation); Office of Economic Opportunity, Office of Inspection, "Houston CAP," February 1967, Box 10, Folder Contracts, Office of Economic Opportunity, Southwest Region, Community Action Programs, District Supervisors, Records Relating to City Economic Opportunity Boards, 1965–1968, Record Group 381, NARASW (second quotation); E. R. Brown to Marlene Futterman, memorandum, February 13, 1967, Box 73, Folder CAP, Houston, Harris County, Texas, January–March 1967, OEO Inspection Division, Inspection Reports, 1964–1967, Record Group 381, NARA.

44. Office of Economic Opportunity, Office of Inspection, "Houston CAP," February 1967, Box 10, Folder Contracts, Office of Economic Opportunity, Southwest Region, Community Action Programs, District Supervisors, Records Relating to City Economic Opportunity Boards, 1965–1968, Record Group 381, NARASW (first quotation); Office of Economic Opportunity, Office of Inspection, "Houston–Harris County Economic Opportunity Organization and Houston Action for Youth, Inc.," February 1967, Box 10, Folder Contracts, Office of Economic Opportunity, Southwest Region, Community Action Programs, District Supervisors, Records Relating to City Economic Opportunity Boards, 1965–1968, Record Group 381, NARASW (second quotation and "rock the boat"); E. R. Brown to Marlene Futterman, memorandum, February 13, 1967, Box 73, Folder CAP, Houston, Harris County, Texas, January–March 1967, OEO Inspection Division, Inspection Reports, 1964–1967, Record Group 381, NARA (third quotation).

Chapter 4. A Closing Window of Opportunity for Expanding Democracy

1. James M. Simons to Edgar May, memorandum, January 26, 1967, Box 73, Folder CAP, Houston, Harris County, Texas, January–March 1967, OEO Inspection Division, Inspection Reports, 1964–1967, Record Group 381, National Archives and Records Administration, College Park, Maryland (hereafter cited as NARA); Peter Spruance to Edgar May, memorandum, March 20, 1967, Box 59, Folder Houston Texas CAA 1968, OEO CAP Rec-

ords of the Director, Subject Files, 1965–1969, Record Group 381, NARA; George Bush to Frank Harmon, January 25, 1967, Box 1, Folder Correspondence January–February 1967, William V. Ballew Jr. Papers, 1965–1968, MS 254, Woodson Research Center, Fondren Library, Rice University, Houston, Texas (hereafter cited as Ballew Papers) (quotation).

2. James M. Simons to Edgar May, memorandum, January 26, 1967, Box 73, Folder CAP, Houston, Harris County, Texas, January–March 1967, OEO Inspection Division, Inspection Reports, 1964–1967, Record Group 381, NARA; "Prober Says EOO Fire Arson," *Houston Post*, January 18, 1967.

3. "Beating Pregnant Woman Arouses Resentment," *Houston Informer*, January 14, 1967 (quotation); Ed Terrones to Edgar May, memorandum, March 15, 1967, Box 73, Folder CAP, Houston, Harris County, Texas, January–March 1967, OEO Inspection Division, Inspection Reports, 1964–1967, Record Group 381, NARA; Saralee Tiede, "Settegast—a Powderkeg or a Community on the Move?," *Houston Chronicle*, January 22, 1967.

4. Ed Terrones to Edgar May, memorandum, March 15, 1967, Box 73, Folder CAP, Houston, Harris County, Texas, January–March 1967, OEO Inspection Division, Inspection Reports, 1964–1967, Record Group 381, NARA; Charles Kelly to Ed Terrones, March 17, 1967, Box 73, Folder CAP, Houston, Harris County, Texas, January–March 1967, OEO Inspection Division, Inspection Reports, 1964–1967, Record Group 381, NARA; Minutes of Houston–Harris County Economic Opportunity Organization Board of Directors, January 11, 1967, Box 1, Folder Minutes January–April 1967, Ballew Papers; Saralee Tiede, "Settegast—a Powderkeg or a Community on the Move?," *Houston Chronicle*, January 22, 1967 (quotation).

5. Ed Terrones to Edgar May, memorandum, March 15, 1967, Box 73, Folder CAP, Houston, Harris County, Texas, January–March 1967, OEO Inspection Division, Inspection Reports, 1964–1967, Record Group 381, NARA; Charles Kelly to Ed Terrones, March 17, 1967, Box 73, Folder CAP, Houston, Harris County, Texas, January–March 1967, OEO Inspection Division, Inspection Reports, 1964–1967, Record Group 381, NARA; Settegast Residents, "Settegast Day," January 16, 1967, Box 2, Folder Anti-Poverty News Clippings 1967–1968, Ballew Papers; Saralee Tiede, "Settegast—a Powderkeg or a Community on the Move?," *Houston Chronicle*, January 22, 1967 (quotation).

6. James M. Simons to Edgar May, memorandum, February 23, 1967, Box 73, Folder CAP, Houston, Harris County, Texas, January–March 1967, OEO Inspection Division, Inspection Reports, 1964–1967, Record Group 381, NARA; Ed Terrones to Edgar May, memorandum, March 15, 1967, Box 73, Folder CAP, Houston, Harris County, Texas, January–March 1967, OEO Inspection Division, Inspection Reports, 1964–1967, Record Group 381, NARA; Charles Kelly to Ed Terrones, March 17, 1967, Box 73, Folder CAP, Houston, Harris County, Texas, January–March 1967, OEO Inspection Division, Inspection Reports, 1964–1967, Record Group 381, NARA; "Welch Favors Ending Some Poverty Projects," *Houston Post*, March 14, 1967; Charles Kelly to Ed Terrones, March 17, 1967, Box 1, Folder Correspondence March–July 1967, Ballew Papers.

7. Office of Economic Opportunity, Office of Inspection, "Houston CAP," February 1967, Box 10B, Folder Inspection and Evaluation Reports, OEO, Southwest Region, Community Action Programs, District Supervisors, Records Relating to City Economic Opportunity Boards, 1965–1968, Houston, Record Group 381, National Archives and Records Administration, Southwest Region, Fort Worth, Texas (hereafter cited as NARASW); Minutes of Houston–Harris County Economic Opportunity Organization Executive Committee, February 23, 1967, Box 73, Folder CAP, Houston, Harris County, Texas, July–September, 1967, NARA (quotation).

8. Saralee Tiede, "Settegast—a Powderkeg or a Community on the Move?," *Houston Chronicle*, January 22, 1967 (quotations). There is some evidence that Mayor Louie Welch and his aide Blair Justice encouraged and exploited this animosity between Settegast residents and H-HCEOO community organizers; see Blair Justice to Louie Welch, memorandum, February 21. 1967, Box 33, Louie Welch Papers, Houston Metropolitan Research Center, Houston Public Library, Houston, Texas (hereafter cited as Welch Papers); and Blair Justice to Louie Welch, memorandum, September 23, 1966, Box 33, Welch Papers.

9. Saralee Tiede, "Settegast—a Powderkeg or a Community on the Move?," *Houston Chronicle*, January 22, 1967 (first and second quotation); "Protest Poverty Program," *Houston Chronicle*, March 2, 1967 (third quotation).

10. "EOO Staff Ordered Relocated," *Houston Post*, April 20, 1967 (quotation); Reid Beveridge, "Settegast Youth Stage Sit-In over Transfer of EOO Staffers," *Houston Chronicle*, April 22, 1967.

11. *Handbook of Texas Online*, s.v. "Texas Southern University," by Cary D. Wintz, http://www.tshaonline.org/handbook/online/articles/TT/kct27.html (accessed November 10, 2008); Watson, *Race and the Houston Police Department*, 78 (quotations). For an interesting report of the TSU Riot, see Bill Helmer, "Nightmare in Houston," *Texas Observer*, June 9–23, 1967.

12. Watson, *Race and the Houston Police Department*, 78–81; "Negroes Stage Noisy Rally Downtown," *Houston Post*, March 12, 1967 (quotations).

13. Watson, *Race and the Houston Police Department*, 81; Blair Justice to Louie Welch, memorandum, April 12, 1967, Box 33, Welch Papers; Blair Justice to Louie Welch, memorandum, April 19, 1967, Box 33, Welch Papers; Ken Fairchild to Louie Welch, memorandum, April 27 1967, Box 33, Welch Papers; Joyce Jane Weedman and Ted D'Andriole, "Boycott at TSU Fizzles and Classes about Normal," *Houston Chronicle*, March 29, 1967; "Carmichael's UH Speech Will Go On," *Houston Post*, April 12, 1967; Donnie Smith, "'Organize Black People': Carmichael Outlines Plans for Houston," *Houston Post*, April 14, 1967 (quotation); "UH Hall Crowded for Carmichael Talk," *Houston Informer*, April 15, 1967; "Fear for Violence, Loss of Credits Return Calm to TSU," *Houston Informer*, April 1, 1967. For more on Welch's fear of urban riots in Houston, see Clayson, "The War on Poverty and the Fear of Urban Violence in Houston, 1965–1968," *Gulf South Historical Review* 18 (2003): 38–59.

14. The Reverend F. D. Kirkpatrick, Millard Lowe, Lee Otis Johnson, Rhone Lewis, and William Richards, "Student Power Speaks Out," April 1967, Box 73, Folder CAP, Houston, Harris County, Texas, April–June 1967, OEO Inspection Division, Inspection Reports, 1964–67, Record Group 381, NARA; Watson, *Race and the Houston Police Department*, 81–82.

15. Gus Taylor to Pluria Marshall, December 2, 1966, Box 73, Folder CAP, Houston, Harris County, Texas, April–June 1967, OEO Inspection Division, Inspection Reports, 1964–1967, Record Group 381, NARA; Spencer Bayles to William P. Hobby Jr., December 9, 1966, Box 73, Folder CAP, Houston, Harris County, Texas, April–June 1967, OEO Inspection Division, Inspection Reports, 1964–67, Record Group 381, NARA; Pluria Marshall to Gus Taylor, December 30, 1966, Box 73, Folder CAP, Houston, Harris County, Texas, April–June 1967, OEO Inspection Division, Inspection Reports, 1964–1967, Record Group 381, NARA; Pluria Marshall to Gus Taylor, memorandum, March 3, 1967, Box 73, Folder CAP, Houston, Harris County, Texas, April–June 1967, OEO Inspection Division, Inspection Reports, 1964–1967, Record Group 381, NARA; Peter Spruance to Edgar May, memorandum, April 7, 1967, Box 73, Folder CAP, Houston, Harris County, Texas, April–

June 1967, OEO Inspection Division, Inspection Reports, 1964–1967, Record Group 381, NARA; Hal Wimberly, "Fund Misuse?: OEO Probes TSU Protest," *Houston Post*, April 9, 1967; Saralee Tiede, "EOO to Ask Hospital District to Set Up Settegast Clinic," *Houston Chronicle*, December 15, 1966.

16. Edwin Becnel to Earl E. Allen, memorandum, April 1967, Box 73, Folder CAP, Houston, Harris County, Texas, April–June 1967, OEO Inspection Division, Inspection Reports, 1964–1967, Record Group 381, NARA; Earl Allen to Gus Taylor, memorandum, April 1967, Box 73, Folder CAP, Houston, Harris County, Texas, April–June 1967, OEO Inspection Division, Inspection Reports, 1964–1967, Record Group 381, NARA; Pluria Marshall to Edwin Becnel, memorandum, April 7, 1967, Box 73, Folder CAP, Houston, Harris County, Texas, April–June 1967, OEO Inspection Division, Inspection Reports, 1964–1967, Record Group 381, NARA (quotation); Edwin Becnel to Earl E. Allen, memorandum, April 7, 1967, Box 73, Folder CAP, Houston, Harris County, Texas, April–June 1967, OEO Inspection Division, Inspection Reports, 1964–67, Record Group 381, NARA.

17. Ray Reusche to Edgar May, memorandum, May 26, 1967, Box 73, Folder CAP, Houston, Harris County, Texas, April–June 1967, OEO Inspection Division, Inspection Reports, 1964–67, Record Group 381, NARA; KTRH Radio, "Allegations Made Pertaining to EOO Workers," April 7, 1967, Box 73, Folder CAP, Houston, Harris County, Texas, April–June 1967, OEO Inspection Division, Inspection Reports, 1964–67, Record Group 381, NARA; Peter Spruance to Edgar May, memorandum, April 10, 1967, Box 73, Folder CAP, Houston, Harris County, Texas, April–June 1967, OEO Inspection Division, Inspection Reports, 1964–67, Record Group 381, NARA; Minutes of Houston-Harris County Economic Opportunity Organization Executive Committee, April 17, 1967, Box 73, Folder CAP, Houston, Harris County, Texas, July–September 1967, OEO Inspection Division, Inspection Reports, 1964–67, Record Group 381, NARA.

18. KTRH Radio, "Allegations Made Pertaining to EOO Workers," April 7, 1967, Box 73, Folder CAP, Houston, Harris County, Texas, April–June 1967, OEO Inspection Division, Inspection Reports, 1964–67, Record Group 381, NARA; James M. Simons to Edgar May, memorandum, April 10, 1967, Box 73, Folder CAP, Houston, Harris County, Texas, April–June 1967, OEO Inspection Division, Inspection Reports, 1964–67, Record Group 381, NARA.

19. James M. Simons to Edgar May, memorandum, April 10, 1967, Box 73, Folder CAP, Houston, Harris County, Texas, April–June 1967, OEO Inspection Division, Inspection Reports, 1964–67, Record Group 381, NARA (first quotation); Peter Spruance to Edgar May, memorandum, April 19, 1967, Box 73, Folder CAP, Houston, Harris County, Texas, April–June 1967, OEO Inspection Division, Inspection Reports, 1964–67, Record Group 381, NARA (second quotation).

20. Watson, *Race and the Houston Police Department*, 83–84; Peter Spruance to Edgar May, memorandum, May 17, 1967, Box 73, Folder CAP, Houston, Harris County, Texas, April–June 1967, OEO Inspection Division, Inspection Reports, 1964–67, Record Group 381, NARA; Fred Baldwin to Walter Richter, memorandum, May 17, 1967, Box 73, Folder CAP, Houston, Harris County, Texas, April–June 1967, OEO Inspection Division, Inspection Reports, 1964–67, Record Group 381, NARA.

21. Peter Spruance to Edgar May, memorandum, May 17, 1967, Box 73, Folder CAP, Houston, Harris County, Texas, April–June 1967, OEO Inspection Division, Inspection Reports, 1964–67, Record Group 381, NARA.

22. Watson, *Race and the Houston Police Department*, 84–85 (quotation); Fred Baldwin to Walter Richter, memorandum, May 17, 1967, Box 73, Folder CAP, Houston, Harris

County, Texas, April–June 1967, OEO Inspection Division, Inspection Reports, 1964–67, Record Group 381, NARA; Peter Spruance to Edgar May, memorandum, May 25, 1967, Box 73, Folder CAP, Houston, Harris County, Texas, April–June 1967, OEO Inspection Division, Inspection Reports, 1964–67, Record Group 381, NARA; Ray Reusche to Edgar May, memorandum, May 26, 1967, Box 73, Folder CAP, Houston, Harris County, Texas, April–June 1967, OEO Inspection Division, Inspection Reports, 1964–67, Record Group 381, NARA; David Beckwith and Fred Harper, "NAACP Offers TSU Peace Plan," *Houston Chronicle*, May 19, 1967; "FBI to Probe TSU Civil Rights Charge," *Houston Post*, May 19, 1967. Disagreement remains over who was responsible for firing the first shot of the "TSU Riot." The Reverend Bill Lawson stated, "The police started shooting before we went in. . . . The police ran over our backs charging the dormitory." See Watson, *Race and the Houston Police Department*, 84.

23. Ray Reusche to Edgar May, memorandum, May 26, 1967, Box 73, Folder CAP, Houston, Harris County, Texas, April–June 1967, OEO Inspection Division, Inspection Reports, 1964–67, Record Group 381, NARA (first and second quotations); Herman Short to Louie Welch, memorandum, May 1967, Box 33, Welch Papers (third and fourth quotations).

24. Minutes of Houston–Harris County Economic Opportunity Organization Executive Committee, April 17, 1967, Box 73, Folder CAP, Houston, Harris County, Texas, July–September 1967, OEO Inspection Division, Inspection Reports, 1964–67, Record Group 381, NARA; Ray Reusche to Edgar May, memorandum, May 26, 1967, Box 73, Folder CAP, Houston, Harris County, Texas, April–June 1967, OEO Inspection Division, Inspection Reports, 1964–67, Record Group 381, NARA (quotation).

25. James M. Simons to Edgar May, memorandum, April 12, 1967, Box 73, Folder CAP, Houston, Harris County, Texas, April–June 1967, OEO Inspection Division, Inspection Reports, 1964–67, Record Group 381, NARA.

26. James M. Simons to Edgar May, memorandum, April 10, 1967, Box 73, Folder CAP, Houston, Harris County, Texas, April–June 1967, OEO Inspection Division, Inspection Reports, 1964–67, Record Group 381, NARA; Peter Spruance to Edgar May, memorandum, April 10, 1967, Box 73, Folder CAP, Houston, Harris County, Texas, April–June 1967, OEO Inspection Division, Inspection Reports, 1964–67, Record Group 381, NARA; Peter Spruance to Edgar May, memorandum, April 11, 1967, Box 73, Folder CAP, Houston, Harris County, Texas, April–June 1967, OEO Inspection Division, Inspection Reports, 1964–67, Record Group 381, NARA; Peter Spruance to Edgar May, memorandum, April 12, 1967, Box 73, Folder CAP, Houston, Harris County, Texas, April–June 1967, OEO Inspection Division, Inspection Reports, 1964–67, Record Group 381, NARA; James M. Simons to Edgar May, memorandum, April 12, 1967, Box 73, Folder CAP, Houston, Harris County, Texas, April–June 1967, OEO Inspection Division, Inspection Reports, 1964–67, Record Group 381, NARA; Minutes of Houston–Harris County Economic Opportunity Organization Executive Committee, April 17, 1967, Box 73, Folder CAP, Houston, Harris County, Texas, July–September 1967, OEO Inspection Division, Inspection Reports, 1964–67, Record Group 381, NARA; "'Railroad' Shouted: EOO Elects and Adjourns," *Houston Post*, April 11, 1967; "Three Area EOO Officials Suspended," *Houston Chronicle*, April 16, 1967.

27. Earl E. Allen, "Statement of Concerns, Grievances, and Recommendations, Presented to the Executive Committee," April 17, 1967, Box 73, Folder CAP, Houston, Harris County, Texas, January–March 1967, OEO Inspection Division, Inspection Reports, 1964–67, Record Group 381, NARA.

28. Earl E. Allen, "Statement of Concerns, Grievances, and Recommendations, Presented to the Executive Committee," April 17, 1967, Box 73, Folder CAP, Houston, Har-

ris County, Texas, January–March 1967, OEO Inspection Division, Inspection Reports, 1964–67, Record Group 381, NARA.

29. Earl E. Allen, "Statement of Concerns, Grievances, and Recommendations, Presented to the Executive Committee," April 17, 1967, Box 73, Folder CAP, Houston, Harris County, Texas, January–March 1967, OEO Inspection Division, Inspection Reports, 1964–67, Record Group 381, NARA.

30. Ray Reusche to Edgar May, memorandum, May 26, 1967, Box 73, Folder CAP, Houston, Harris County, Texas, April–June 1967, OEO Inspection Division, Inspection Reports, 1964–67, Record Group 381, NARA.

31. "Welch Returns from Anti Poverty Meeting," *Houston Post*, March 17, 1967; "Welch Favors Ending Some Poverty Projects," *Houston Post*, March 14, 1967 (quotation).

32. Louie Welch to OEO, Washington, D.C., n.d., Box 4, Folder Reports on the Success of OEO Programs, OEO Southwest Region, Records of the Director, Central Files, 1967–69, Record Group 381, NARASW (quotations); Edgar May to Bertrand Harding, memorandum, May 26, 1967, Box 73, Folder CAP, Houston, Harris County, Texas, April–June 1967, OEO Inspection Division, Inspection Reports, 1964–67, Record Group 381, NARA; Edgar May to Walter Richter, memorandum, May 26, 1967, Box 73, Folder CAP, Houston, Harris County, Texas, April–June 1967, OEO Inspection Division, Inspection Reports, 1964–67, Record Group 381, NARA; Peter Spruance to Edgar May, memorandum, May 29, 1967, Box 73, Folder CAP, Houston, Harris County, Texas, October–December 1967, OEO Inspection Division, Inspection Reports, 1964–67, Record Group 381, NARA; Edgar May to Bertrand Harding, memorandum, June 20, 1967, Box 73, Folder CAP, Houston, Harris County, Texas, April–June 1967, OEO Inspection Division, Inspection Reports, 1964–67, Record Group 381, NARA.

33. On February 21, 1967, mayoral aide Blair Justice sent a memorandum to Mayor Welch stating, "In regard to the E.O.O., I would recommend that you wait until the letter is received, as promised, from Isiah Moore, President of the Settegast Heights Civic Club. This would be concrete evidence of the position taken by the people in the area regarding E.O.O. activities. Meanwhile, if you want, copies of the intelligence reports can be sent to George Bush." See Blair Justice to Louie Welch, memorandum, February 21, 1967, Box 33, Welch Papers.

34. Blair Justice to Louie Welch, memorandum, February 21, 1967, Box 33, Welch Papers; James M. Simons to Edgar May, memorandum, February 23, 1967, Box 73, Folder CAP, Houston, Harris County, Texas, January–March 1967, OEO Inspection Division, Inspection Reports, 1964–67, Record Group 381, NARA; Peter Spruance to Edgar May, memorandum, March 20, 1967, Box 59, Folder Houston Texas CAA 1968, OEO CAP Records of the Director, Subject Files, 1965–1969, Record Group 381, NARA; E. R. Brown to Joseph Fagan, memorandum, March 21, 1967, Box 73, Folder CAP, Houston, Harris County, Texas, January–March 1967, OEO Inspection Division, Inspection Reports, 1964–67, Record Group 381, NARA.

35. Office of Economic Opportunity, Office of Inspection, "Houston CAP," February 1967, Box 10B, Folder Inspection and Evaluation Reports, OEO, Southwest Region, Community Action Programs, District Supervisors, Records Relating to City Economic Opportunity Boards, 1965–1968, Houston, Record Group 381, NARASW; Office of Economic Opportunity, Office of Inspection, "Houston–Harris County Economic Opportunity Organization and Houston Action for Youth, Inc.," February 1967, Box 10B, Folder Inspection and Evaluation Reports, OEO, Southwest Region, Community Action Programs, District Supervisors, Records Relating to City Economic Opportunity Boards, 1965–

1968, Houston, Record Group 381, NARASW; Marlene Futterman, "Inspection Report for HHCEOO and HAY," February 1967, Box 73, Folder CAP, Houston, Harris County, Texas, January–March 1967, OEO Inspection Division, Inspection Reports, 1964–67, Record Group 381, NARA; Judith Segal to Robert A. Levine, memorandum, February 13, 1967, Box 10B, Folder Inspection and Evaluation Reports, OEO, Southwest Region, Community Action Programs, District Supervisors, Records Relating to City Economic Opportunity Boards, 1965–1968, Houston, Record Group 381, NARASW; E. R. Brown to Marlene Futterman, memorandum, February 13, 1967, Box 73, Folder CAP, Houston, Harris County, Texas, January–March 1967, OEO Inspection Division, Inspection Reports, 1964–67, Record Group 381, NARA.

36. Marlene Futterman, "Inspection Report for HHCEOO and HAY," February 1967, Box 73, Folder CAP, Houston, Harris County, Texas, January–March 1967, OEO Inspection Division, Inspection Reports, 1964–67, Record Group 381, NARA (quotation); Office of Economic Opportunity, Office of Inspection, "Houston CAP," February 1967, Box 10B, Folder Inspection and Evaluation Reports, OEO, Southwest Region, Community Action Programs, District Supervisors, Records Relating to City Economic Opportunity Boards, 1965–1968, Houston, Record Group 381, NARASW; Office of Economic Opportunity, Office of Inspection, "Houston–Harris County Economic Opportunity Organization and Houston Action for Youth, Inc.," February 1967, Box 10B, Folder Inspection and Evaluation Reports, OEO, Southwest Region, Community Action Programs, District Supervisors, Records Relating to City Economic Opportunity Boards, 1965–1968, Houston, Record Group 381, NARASW.

37. Saralee Tiede, "War on Poverty Groups Must Merge," *Houston Chronicle*, November 20, 1966; Fred Baldwin to William Ballew, October 17, 1966, Box 1, Folder Correspondence October–December 1966, Ballew Papers; Sarelee Tiede, "HAY-EOO Merger Idea Meeting with Opposition," *Houston Chronicle*, January 15, 1967 (quotations).

38. Office of Economic Opportunity, Office of Inspection, "Houston CAP," February 1967, Box 10B, Folder Inspection and Evaluation Reports, OEO, Southwest Region, Community Action Programs, District Supervisors, Records Relating to City Economic Opportunity Boards, 1965–1968, Houston, Record Group 381, NARASW (first quotation); Office of Economic Opportunity, Office of Inspection, "Houston–Harris County Economic Opportunity Organization and Houston Action for Youth, Inc.," February 1967, Box 10B, Folder Inspection and Evaluation Reports, OEO, Southwest Region, Community Action Programs, District Supervisors, Records Relating to City Economic Opportunity Boards, 1965–1968, Houston, Record Group 381, NARASW (second quotation); Marlene Futterman, "Inspection Report for HHCEOO and HAY," February 1967, Box 73, Folder CAP, Houston, Harris County, Texas, January–March 1967, OEO Inspection Division, Inspection Reports, 1964–67, Record Group 381, NARA (third and fourth quotations); Judith Segal to Robert A. Levine, memorandum, February 13, 1967, Box 10B, Folder Inspection and Evaluation Reports, OEO, Southwest Region, Community Action Programs, District Supervisors, Records Relating to City Economic Opportunity Boards, 1965–1968, Houston, Record Group 381, NARASW (fifth quotation); Jerome Sohme to Theodore Berry, memorandum, February 9, 1967, Box 17, Folder Administrative Texas 1967, OEO CAP Records of the Director, State Files, 1965–1968, Record Group 381, NARA; E. R. Brown to Marlene Futterman, memorandum, February 13, 1967, Box 73, Folder CAP, Houston, Harris County, Texas, January–March 1967, OEO Inspection Division, Inspection Reports, 1964–67, Record Group 381, NARA.

39. William Finister, "Interim Report on Houston," February 1967, Box 17, Folder Ad-

ministrative Texas 1967, OEO CAP Records of the Director, State Files, 1965–1968, Record Group 381, NARA (quotation); James M. Simons to Edgar May, memorandum, February 23, 1967, Box 73, Folder CAP, Houston, Harris County, Texas, January–March 1967, OEO Inspection Division, Inspection Reports, 1964–67, Record Group 381, NARA; Peter Spruance to C. B. Patrick, memorandum, March 27, 1967, Box 59, Folder Houston Texas CAA 1968, OEO CAP Records of the Director, Subject Files, 1965–1969, Record Group 381, NARA.

40. Peter Spruance to Edgar May, memorandum, March 20, 1967, Box 59, Folder Houston Texas CAA 1968, OEO CAP Records of the Director, Subject Files, 1965–1969, Record Group 381, NARA (quotation); E. R. Brown to Joseph Fagan, memorandum, March 21, 1967, Box 73, Folder CAP, Houston, Harris County, Texas, January–March 1967, OEO Inspection Division, Inspection Reports, 1964–67, Record Group 381, NARA.

41. Peter Spruance to Edgar May, memorandum, March 20, 1967, Box 59, Folder Houston Texas CAA 1968, OEO CAP Records of the Director, Subject Files, 1965–1969, Record Group 381, NARA.

42. Blair Justice to Louie Welch, memorandum, February 21, 1967, Box 33, Welch Papers.

43. Saralee Tiede, "U.S. Pushes Faster Poverty Unit Merger," *Houston Chronicle*, March 30, 1967; Peter Spruance to Edgar May, memorandum, April 10, 1967, Box 73, Folder CAP, Houston, Harris County, Texas, April–June 1967, OEO Inspection Division, Inspection Reports, 1964–67, Record Group 381, NARA; James M. Simons to Edgar May, memorandum, April 12, 1967, Box 73, Folder CAP, Houston, Harris County, Texas, April–June 1967, OEO Inspection Division, Inspection Reports, 1964–67, Record Group 381, NARA; Fred Baldwin to Francis Williams, April 14, 1967, Box 73, Folder CAP, Houston, Harris County, Texas, April–June 1967, OEO Inspection Division, Inspection Reports, 1964–67, Record Group 381, NARA.

44. Saralee Tiede, "New EOO Head Has Red-Hot Job, but Cool Judgment to Work It," *Houston Chronicle*, April 16, 1967 (quotations); "Atty. Williams New H-HCEOO Head; Staff Griefs Head," *Houston Informer*, April 15, 1967; Minutes of Houston–Harris County Economic Opportunity Organization Executive Committee, March 27, 1967, Box 1, Folder Minutes 1967, Ballew Papers.

45. Fred Baldwin to Francis Williams, April 14, 1967, Box 73, Folder CAP, Houston, Harris County, Texas, April–June 1967, OEO Inspection Division, Inspection Reports, 1964–67, Record Group 381, NARA; Peter Spruance to Edgar May, memorandum, May 1, 1967, Box 73, Folder CAP, Houston, Harris County, Texas, April–June 1967, OEO Inspection Division, Inspection Reports, 1964–67, Record Group 381, NARA; Ray Reusche to Edgar May, memorandum, May 4, 1967, Box 73, Folder CAP, Houston, Harris County, Texas, April–June 1967, OEO Inspection Division, Inspection Reports, 1964–67, Record Group 381, NARA; "2 Poverty Agencies to Discuss Merger," *Houston Chronicle*, April 18, 1967; "Two Poverty Panels Seek Merger Here," *Houston Chronicle*, April 21, 1967; "Anti-Poverty Committee Plans EOO, HAY Merger," *Houston Post*, April 23, 1967.

46. "Two Poverty Panels Seek Merger Here," *Houston Chronicle*, April 21, 1967 (quotations); "Anti-Poverty Committee Plans EOO, HAY Merger," *Houston Post*, April 23, 1967.

47. Peter Spruance to Edgar May, memorandum, May 17, 1967, Box 73, Folder CAP, Houston, Harris County, Texas, April–June 1967, OEO Inspection Division, Inspection Reports, 1964–67, Record Group 381, NARA; Peter Spruance to Edgar May, memorandum, May 29, 1967, Box 74, Folder Texas OEO Program (Compilation) 1967 May–July, OEO Inspection Division, Inspection Reports, 1964–67, Record Group 381, NARA; Fred

Harper, "EOO Approves Plan to Merge with HAY," *Houston Chronicle*, April 27, 1967; Saralee Tiede, "Williams Heads Merged Antipoverty Group Here," *Houston Chronicle*, May 19, 1967; "HCCAA Formed Following Merger of HHCEOO-HAY," *Houston Informer*, May 20, 1967; Saralee Tiede, "City's Anti-Poverty Organizations Merge," *Houston Chronicle*, May 16, 1967.

48. Saralee Tiede, "City's Anti-Poverty Organizations Merge," *Houston Chronicle*, May 16, 1967.

Chapter 5. A Triumph for the Limited Vision of Democracy

1. Fred Baldwin to Walter Richter, memorandum, August 25, 1967, Box 1, Folder CAP Administrator Memoranda (2), Office of Economic Opportunity, Southwest Region, Community Action Program Correspondence, Memos, CAP Administrator-Family Planning, Record Group 381, National Archives and Records Administration, Southwest Region, Fort Worth, Texas (hereafter cited as NARASW).

2. Peter Spruance to Edgar May, memorandum, May 1, 1967, Box 73, Folder CAP, Houston, Harris County, Texas, April–June 1967, Office of Economic Opportunity, Inspection Division, Inspection Reports, 1964–67, Record Group 381, National Archives and Records Administration, College Park, Maryland (hereafter cited as NARA); Saralee Tiede, "City's Anti-Poverty Organizations Merge," *Houston Chronicle*, May 16, 1967; Saralee Tiede, "New Poverty Agency Appears More Effective Than Two Predecessors," *Houston Chronicle*, June 11, 1967 (quotation).

3. Peter Spruance to Edgar May, memorandum, May 1, 1967, Box 73, Folder CAP, Houston, Harris County, Texas, April–June 1967, Office of Economic Opportunity, Inspection Division, Inspection Reports, 1964–67, Record Group 381, NARA (first quotation); Ray Reusche to Edgar May, memorandum, May 4, 1967, Box 73, Folder CAP, Houston, Harris County, Texas, April–June 1967, Office of Economic Opportunity, Inspection Division, Inspection Reports, 1964–67, Record Group 381, NARA; Saralee Tiede, "New Poverty Agency Appears More Effective Than Two Predecessors," *Houston Chronicle*, June 11, 1967 (second quotation).

4. Ray Reusche to Edgar May, memorandum, May 26, 1967, Box 73, Folder CAP, Houston, Harris County, Texas, April–June 1967, Office of Economic Opportunity, Inspection Division, Inspection Reports, 1964–67, Record Group 381, NARA (first quotation); James M. Simons to Edgar May, memorandum, August 17, 1967, Box 73, Folder CAP, Houston, Harris County, Texas, July–September 1967, Office of Economic Opportunity, Inspection Division, Inspection Reports, 1964–67, Record Group 381, NARA (second quotation); Edgar May to Walter Richter, memorandum, May 17, 1967, Box 73, Folder CAP, Houston, Harris County, Texas, April–June 1967, Office of Economic Opportunity, Inspection Division, Inspection Reports, 1964–67, Record Group 381, NARA; Peter Spruance to Edgar May, memorandum, May 17, 1967, Box 73, Folder CAP, Houston, Harris County, Texas, April–June 1967, Office of Economic Opportunity, Inspection Division, Inspection Reports, 1964–67, Record Group 381, NARA.

5. Peter Spruance to Edgar May, memorandum, May 29, 1967, Box 74, Folder Texas OEO Program (Compilation) 1967 May–July, Office of Economic Opportunity, Inspection Division, Inspection Reports, 1964–67, Record Group 381, NARA.

6. Office of Economic Opportunity, "Grant Profile for HCCAA, Program Administration, Neighborhood Centers, and Community Development," June 16, 1967, Microfilm Reel #35 (Head Start, South Dakota to Vermont, State Summaries), Records from Federal

Government Agencies, Records of the Office of Economic Opportunity, 1964–1968, Lyndon Baines Johnson Library, Austin, Texas (hereafter cited as LBJL).

7. See chapter 3 for a description of Ballew's vision for the Houston Legal Foundation.

8. Office of Economic Opportunity, Community Action Program, "CAP Narrative Progress Report on Houston Legal Foundation," July 1967, Box 10, Folder Audit, Office of Economic Opportunity, Southwest Region, Community Action Programs, District Supervisors, Records Relating to City Economic Opportunity Boards, 1965–1968, Houston, Record Group 381, NARASW; "Community Action in Houston and Harris County as of November 1, 1967," November 1, 1967, Box 73, Folder CAP, Houston, Harris County, Texas, October–December 1967, Office of Economic Opportunity, Inspection Division, Inspection Reports, 1964–67, Record Group 381, NARA; "Legal Foundation Will Meet with OEO Official," *Houston Post*, July 16, 1968.

9. Gordon Gooch to Daniel E. Trevino, February 6, 1968, Box 10, Folder General Correspondence, January–July 1968, Office of Economic Opportunity, Southwest Region, Community Action Programs, District Supervisors, Records Relating to City Economic Opportunity Boards, 1965–1968, Houston, Record Group 381, NARASW; Texas Office of Economic Opportunity, "Weekly News Memo #57," February 14, 1968, Box 20, Folder Texas OEO Weekly News Memo, Records from Federal Government Agencies, Records of the Office of Economic Opportunity, 1964–1968, LBJL; Saralee Tiede, "Houston Legal Foundation May Lose Funds," *Houston Chronicle*, December 19, 1967.

10. Walter Richter to Harry W. Patterson, June 26, 1968, Box 1, Folder Correspondence, June–October 1968, Office of Economic Opportunity, Southwest Region, Records of the Director, Correspondence, 1967–69, Record Group 381, NARASW; "Talks Planned to Avoid Loss of Law Funds," *Houston Chronicle*, July 12, 1968; "Legal Foundation Will Meet with OEO Official," *Houston Post*, July 16, 1968.

11. Harold Scarlett, "Legal Foundation In Crisis," *Houston Post*, July 21, 1968.

12. Harry W. Patterson to Walter Richter, June 21, 1968, Box 1, Folder Correspondence, June–October 1968, Office of Economic Opportunity, Southwest Region, Records of the Director, Correspondence, 1967–69, Record Group 381, NARASW; Harold Scarlett, "Lawyers Draw the Line," *Houston Post*, July 22, 1968 (quotations).

13. Harold Scarlett, "Legal Board Decision Due," *Houston Post*, July 23, 1968.

14. Carlos Conde, "Poor People Win 4 Seats as HLF Board Members," *Houston Chronicle*, July 24, 1968.

15. William Shireman to Carver Daffin, August 20, 1968, Box 10, Folder General Correspondence, August–December 1968, Office of Economic Opportunity, Southwest Region, Community Action Programs, District Supervisors, Records Relating to City Economic Opportunity Boards, 1965–1968, Houston, Record Group 381, NARASW; Francis J. Duggan to William Shireman, August 23, 1968, Box 10, Folder General Correspondence, August–December 1968, Office of Economic Opportunity, Southwest Region, Community Action Programs, District Supervisors, Records Relating to City Economic Opportunity Boards, 1965–1968, Houston, Record Group 381, NARASW; Joe H. Foy to Walter Richter, August 29, 1968, Box 1, Folder Correspondence, June-October 1968, Office of Economic Opportunity, Southwest Region, Records of the Director, Correspondence, 1967–69, Record Group 381, NARASW; Carlos Conde, "Poor People Win 4 Seats as HLF Board Members," *Houston Chronicle*, July 24, 1968; Tommy West, "Legal Board to Add 4 Representatives of Poor," *Houston Post*, August 21, 1968 (quotation).

16. Minutes of Harris County Community Action Association Board of Directors, October 7, 1968, Box 10, Folder Board Minutes, Office of Economic Opportunity, South-

west Region, Community Action Programs, District Supervisors, Records Relating to City Economic Opportunity Boards, 1965–1968, Houston, Record Group 381, NARASW; "Foundation to Get U.S. Funds Without Poor," *Houston Post*, September 26, 1968.

17. Office of Economic Opportunity, "Grant Profile for HCCAA Summer Head Start," May 23, 1967, Microfilm Reel #35 (Head Start, South Dakota to Vermont, State Summaries), Records from Federal Government Agencies, Records of the Office of Economic Opportunity, 1964–1968, LBJL; Saralee Tiede, "A World of Wonder Is Opening Up for Deprived Children: But Operation Head Start Has Fallen Short of Its Objectives," *Houston Chronicle*, July 16, 1967.

18. Saralee Tiede, "A World of Wonder Is Opening Up for Deprived Children: But Operation Head Start Has Fallen Short of Its Objectives," *Houston Chronicle*, July 16, 1967.

19. Office of Economic Opportunity, Office of Inspection, "Inspector's Field Report for Inspection of Head Start in Aldine ISD, Delegate of H-HCEOO," June 29, 1967, Box 10B, Folder Inspection and Evaluation Reports, Office of Economic Opportunity, Southwest Region, Community Action Programs, District Supervisors, Records Relating to City Economic Opportunity Boards, 1965–1968, Houston, Record Group 381, NARASW; Office of Economic Opportunity, Office of Inspection, "Inspector's Field Report for Inspection of Head Start in Cypress–Fairbanks ISD, Delegate of H-HCEOO," June 29, 1967, Box 10B, Folder Inspection and Evaluation Reports, Office of Economic Opportunity, Southwest Region, Community Action Programs, District Supervisors, Records Relating to City Economic Opportunity Boards, 1965–1968, Houston, Record Group 381, NARASW; Office of Economic Opportunity, Office of Inspection, "Inspector's Field Report for Inspection of Head Start in Alief ISD, Delegate of H-HCEOO," July 3, 1967, Box 10B, Folder Inspection and Evaluation Reports, Office of Economic Opportunity, Southwest Region, Community Action Programs, District Supervisors, Records Relating to City Economic Opportunity Boards, 1965–1968, Houston, Record Group 381, NARASW; Office of Economic Opportunity, Office of Inspection, "Inspector's Field Report for Inspection of Head Start in Northeast Houston ISD, Delegate Agency of H-HCEOO," July 12, 1967, Box 10B, Folder Inspection and Evaluation Reports, Office of Economic Opportunity, Southwest Region, Community Action Programs, District Supervisors, Records Relating to City Economic Opportunity Boards, 1965–1968, Houston, Record Group 381, NARASW; Shirley P. Powell to Richard E. Orton, telegram, July 20, 1967, Box 10B, Folder Inspection and Evaluation Reports, Office of Economic Opportunity, Southwest Region, Community Action Programs, District Supervisors, Records Relating to City Economic Opportunity Boards, 1965–1968, Houston, Record Group 381, NARASW; Morgan Groves to Betsy Gelb, August 1, 1967, Box 10B, Folder Inspection and Evaluation Reports, Office of Economic Opportunity, Southwest Region, Community Action Programs, District Supervisors, Records Relating to City Economic Opportunity Boards, 1965–1968, Houston, Record Group 381, NARASW.

20. Saralee Tiede, "Harris to Abandon Head Start; Year-Round Program Scheduled," *Houston Chronicle*, October 6, 1967; "A Year-Round Head Start Program," *Houston Chronicle*, October 8, 1967.

21. Alfredo Garcia to Fred Baldwin, memorandum, November 17, 1967, Box 1, Folder Director's Office, Memoranda, Office of Economic Opportunity, Community Action Program Correspondence, Memos, CAP Administrator–Family Planning, Record Group 381, NARASW; Betsy Gelb to Rex Carey, February 20, 1968, Box 10, Folder General Correspondence, January–July 1968, Office of Economic Opportunity, Southwest Region, Community Action Programs, District Supervisors, Records Relating to City Economic

Opportunity Boards, 1965–1968, Houston, Record Group 381, NARASW; Earl Rhine to Glen Fletcher, telegram, February 23, 1968, Box 10, Folder General Correspondence, January–July 1968, Office of Economic Opportunity, Southwest Region, Community Action Programs, District Supervisors, Records Relating to City Economic Opportunity Boards, 1965–1968, Houston, Record Group 381, NARASW; Alfredo Garcia to Walter Richter, memorandum, June 7, 1968, Box 10, Folder General Correspondence, January–July 1968, Office of Economic Opportunity, Southwest Region, Community Action Programs, District Supervisors, Records Relating to City Economic Opportunity Boards, 1965–1968, Houston, Record Group 381, NARASW; Alfredo Garcia to Walter Richter, memorandum, July 3, 1968, Box 10, Folder General Correspondence, January–July 1968, Office of Economic Opportunity, Southwest Region, Community Action Programs, District Supervisors, Records Relating to City Economic Opportunity Boards, 1965–1968, Houston, Record Group 381, NARASW.

22. Saralee Tiede, "Federal Funds Sought to Help 'Cool Down' Hot Summer Here," *Houston Chronicle*, June 2, 1967.

23. Saralee Tiede, "Federal Funds Sought to Help 'Cool Down' Hot Summer Here," *Houston Chronicle*, June 2, 1967; Mary Jane Schier, "Hospital Board OKs Settegast Clinic Tab," *Houston Post*, June 30, 1967; "Med Forum Asking $1 Million from OEO," *Houston Chronicle*, August 30, 1967; Moselle Boland, "Medical Forum Asks U.S. Aid without HCCAA OK," *Houston Chronicle*, October 7, 1967; "Salary Disputes Alter Plans of Clinic for Poor," *Houston Chronicle*, October 8, 1967; Minutes of Harris County Community Action Association Executive Committee, September 18, 1967, Box 73, Folder Community Action Program, Houston, Harris County, Texas, July–September 1967, Office of Economic Opportunity, Inspection Division, Inspection Reports, 1964–67, Record Group 381, NARA; Bob Golter to Phil Hardberger, memorandum, October 15, 1967, Box 74, Folder Texas OEO Program (Compliation), 1967 August–October, Office of Economic Opportunity, Inspection Division, Inspection Reports, 1964–67, Record Group 381, NARA.

24. "'Project FIND' Urged as Aid to Aged Poor," *Houston Chronicle*, June 9, 1967; "Community Action Unit Gets Grant," *Houston Chronicle*, September 15, 1967 (first quotation); "Poverty Plan to Assist Those under 3, Parents," *Houston Post*, September 30, 1967; Office of Economic Opportunity, "Houston and Harris County Parent and Child Center," press release, September 14, 1967, Box 73, Folder CAP, Houston, Harris County, Texas, July–September 1967, Office of Economic Opportunity, Office of Inspection, Inspection Reports, 1964–67, Record Group 381, NARA; Texas Office of Economic Opportunity, "Weekly News Memo #40," October 5, 1967, Box 20, Folder Texas OEO Weekly News Memos (3), Records from Federal Government Agencies, Records from the Office of Economic Opportunity, 1964–1968, LBJL; Ben Haney to Earl Rhine, memorandum, January 9, 1968, Box 10, Folder General Correspondence, January–July 1968, Office of Economic Opportunity, Southwest Region, Community Action Programs, District Supervisors, Records Relating to City Economic Opportunity Boards, 1965–1968, Houston, Record Group 381, NARASW; Earl Rhine to Francis Williams, March 8, 1968, Box 10, Folder General Correspondence, January–July 1968, Office of Economic Opportunity, Southwest Region, Community Action Programs, District Supervisors, Records Relating to City Economic Opportunity Boards, 1965–1968, Houston, Record Group 381, NARASW; Office of Economic Opportunity, "The Foster Grandparent Program," October 20, 1967, Box 1, Folder CAP Administrator, Memoranda, Office of Economic Opportunity, Southwest Region, CAP Correspondence, Memos, CAP Administrator–Family

Planning, Record Group 381, NARASW (second quotation); Protestant Charities of Houston, "First Quarterly Report for Foster Grandparent Program," January 1, 1968, Box 10A, Folder Quarterly Reports, Office of Economic Opportunity, Southwest Region, Community Action Programs, District Supervisors, Records Relating to City Economic Opportunity Boards, 1965–1968, Houston, Record Group 381, NARASW; Protestant Charities of Houston, "Second Quarterly Report for the Foster Grandparent Program," April 1, 1968, Box 10A, Folder Quarterly Reports, Office of Economic Opportunity, Southwest Region, Community Action Programs, District Supervisors, Records Relating to City Economic Opportunity Boards, 1965–1968, Houston, Record Group 381, NARASW; Protestant Charities of Houston, "Quarterly Report for Foster Grandparent Program, April–June 1968," June 1, 1968, Box 10A, Folder Quarterly Reports, Office of Economic Opportunity, Southwest Region, Community Action Programs, District Supervisors, Records Relating to City Economic Opportunity Boards, 1965–1968, Houston, Record Group 381, NARASW; Protestant Charities of Houston, "Quarterly Report for Foster Grandparent Program, July–September 1968," September 1, 1968, Box 10A, Folder Quarterly Reports, Office of Economic Opportunity, Southwest Region, Community Action Programs, District Supervisors, Records Relating to City Economic Opportunity Boards, 1965–1968, Houston, Record Group 381, NARASW; "Community Action in Houston and Harris County as of November 1, 1967," Box 73, Folder CAP, Houston, Harris County, Texas, October–December 1967, Office of Economic Opportunity, Inspection Division, Inspection Reports, 1964–67, Record Group 381, NARA.

25. "HCCAA Expects Funds for Manpower Project," *Houston Post*, June 30, 1967 (quotation); "Big Manpower Project to be Proposed to OEO," *Houston Post*, June 6, 1967; Texas Office of Economic Opportunity, "Weekly News Memo #27," July 5, 1967, Box 20, Folder Texas OEO Weekly News Memos (2), Records from Federal Government Agencies, Records from the Office of Economic Opportunity, 1964–1968, LBJL.

26. Minutes of Harris County Community Action Association Executive Committee, September 18, 1967, Box 73, Folder CAP, Houston, Harris County, Texas, July–September 1967, Office of Economic Opportunity, Inspection Division, Inspection Reports, 1964–67, Record Group 381, NARA.

27. Minutes of Harris County Community Action Association, Cooperative Area Manpower Planning System Committee, June 13, 1968, Box 10, Folder Board Minutes, Office of Economic Opportunity, Southwest Region, Community Action Programs, District Supervisors, Records Relating to City Economic Opportunity Boards, 1965–1968, Houston, Record Group 381, NARASW; Walter Richter to George Bush, August 27, 1968, Box 10, Folder General Correspondence, August–December 1968, Office of Economic Opportunity, Southwest Region, Community Action Programs, District Supervisors, Records Relating to City Economic Opportunity Boards, 1965–1968, Houston, Record Group 381, NARASW; Carlos Conde, "Harris Poverty Agency Fires Job Training Chief," *Houston Chronicle*, October 9, 1968; Ann James, "New CEP Director Has Eye on Jobs," *Houston Post*, December 19, 1968.

28. James M. Simons to Edgar May, memorandum, May 24, 1967, Box 73, Folder CAP, Houston, Harris County, Texas, April–June 1967, Office of Economic Opportunity, Inspection Division, Inspection Reports, 1964–67, Record Group 381, NARA.

29. Philip Hardberger to Sargent Shriver, memorandum, August 25, 1967, Box 74, Folder Texas OEO Program (Compilation) 1967 August–October, Office of Economic Opportunity, Inspection Division, Inspection Reports, 1964–67, Record Group 381, NARA; Ben Haney to Jack Tinkle, memorandum, August 17, 1967, Box 10B, Folder In-

spection and Evaluation Reports, Office of Economic Opportunity, Southwest Region, Community Action Programs, District Supervisors, Records Relating to City Economic Opportunity Boards, 1965–1968, Houston, Record Group 381, NARASW; Saralee Tiede, "City's Anti-Poverty Organizations Merge," *Houston Chronicle*, May 16, 1967.

30. Gus Taylor to Earl Allen, memorandum, April 18, 1967, Box 73, Folder CAP, Houston, Harris County, Texas, April–June 1967, Office of Economic Opportunity, Inspection Division, Inspection Reports, 1964–67, Record Group 381, NARA; Gus Taylor to Charles Kelly, memorandum, 25 April 1967, Box 73, Folder CAP, Houston, Harris County, Texas, April–June 1967, Office of Economic Opportunity, Inspection Division, Inspection Reports, 1964–67, Record Group 381, NARA; Ben Haney to Jack Tinkle, memorandum, August 17, 1967, Box 10B, Folder Inspection and Evaluation Reports, Office of Economic Opportunity, Southwest Region, Community Action Programs, District Supervisors, Records Relating to City Economic Opportunity Boards, 1965–1968, Houston, Record Group 381, NARASW; "Community Action in Houston and Harris County as of November 1, 1967," November 1, 1967, Box 73, Folder CAP, Houston, Harris County, Texas, October–December 1967, Office of Economic Opportunity, Inspection Division, Inspection Reports, 1964–67, Record Group 381, NARA; Ken Fairchild to Louie Welch, memorandum, June 30, 1967, Box 33, Welch Papers; Saralee Tiede, "New Poverty Agency Appears More Effective Than Two Predecessors," *Houston Chronicle*, June 11, 1967.

31. Ben Haney to Jack Tinkle, memorandum, August 17, 1967, Box 10B, Folder Inspection and Evaluation Reports, Office of Economic Opportunity, Southwest Region, Community Action Programs, District Supervisors, Records Relating to City Economic Opportunity Boards, 1965–1968, Houston, Record Group 381, NARASW; Saralee Tiede, "New Poverty Agency Appears More Effective Than Two Predecessors," *Houston Chronicle*, June 11, 1967.

32. Ben Haney to Jack Tinkle, memorandum, August 17, 1967, Box 10B, Folder Inspection and Evaluation Reports, Office of Economic Opportunity, Southwest Region, Community Action Programs, District Supervisors, Records Relating to City Economic Opportunity Boards, 1965–1968, Houston, Record Group 381, NARASW.

33. Philip Hardberger to Sargent Shriver, memorandum, August 25, 1967, Box 74, Folder Texas OEO Program (Compilation) 1967 August–October, Office of Economic Opportunity, Inspection Division, Inspection Reports, 1964–67, Record Group 381, NARA.

34. James M. Simons to Edgar May, memorandum, May 24, 1967, Box 73, Folder CAP, Houston, Harris County, Texas, April–June 1967, Office of Economic Opportunity, Inspection Division, Inspection Reports, 1964–67, Record Group 381, NARA.

35. James M. Simons to Edgar May, memorandum, May 24, 1967, Box 73, Folder CAP, Houston, Harris County, Texas, April–June 1967, Office of Economic Opportunity, Inspection Division, Inspection Reports, 1964–67, Record Group 381, NARA; Ray Reusche to Edgar May, memorandum, May 26, 1967, Box 73, Folder CAP, Houston, Harris County, Texas, April–June 1967, Office of Economic Opportunity, Inspection Division, Inspection Reports, 1964–67, Record Group 381, NARA; Ben Haney to Jack Tinkle, memorandum, August 17, 1967, Box 10B, Folder Inspection and Evaluation Reports, Office of Economic Opportunity, Southwest Region, Community Action Programs, District Supervisors, Records Relating to City Economic Opportunity Boards, 1965–1968, Houston, Record Group 381, NARASW.

36. Ben Haney to Jack Tinkle, memorandum, August 17, 1967, Box 10B, Folder Inspection and Evaluation Reports, Office of Economic Opportunity, Southwest Region,

Community Action Programs, District Supervisors, Records Relating to City Economic Opportunity Boards, 1965–1968, Houston, Record Group 381, NARASW.

37. Ben Haney to Jack Tinkle, memorandum, August 17, 1967, Box 10B, Folder Inspection and Evaluation Reports, Office of Economic Opportunity, Southwest Region, Community Action Programs, District Supervisors, Records Relating to City Economic Opportunity Boards, 1965–1968, Houston, Record Group 381, NARASW (quotations); Peter Spruance to Edgar May, memorandum, May 29, 1967, Box 74, Folder Texas OEO Program (Compilation) 1967 May–July, Office of Economic Opportunity, Inspection Division, Inspection Reports, 1964–67, Record Group 381, NARA; Blair Justice to Louie Welch, memorandum, June 5, 1967, Box 33, Welch Papers; Blair Justice to Louie Welch, memorandum, June 27, 1967, Box 33, Welch Papers.

38. Bob Tutt, "Murder Is Charged in Riot at TSU," *Houston Chronicle*, June 2, 1967 (quotations); "Hearing for TSU Students June 12," *Houston Post*, June 7, 1967; "Delay to be Granted in Case of 5 TSU Students," newspaper clipping, Box 59, Folder Houston Texas CAA 1968, Office of Economic Opportunity, CAP Records of the Director, Subject Files, 1965–1969, Record Group 381, NARA; Peter Spruance to Edgar May, memorandum, July 25, 1967, Box 73, Folder CAP, Houston, Harris County, Texas, July–September 1967, Office of Economic Opportunity, Inspection Division, Inspection Reports, 1964–67, Record Group 381, NARA.

39. Saralee Tiede, "Federal Funds Sought to Help 'Cool Down' Hot Summer Here," *Houston Chronicle*, June 2, 1967 (quotation); Edgar May to Walter Richter, memorandum, August 3, 1967, Box 59, Folder Houston Texas CAA 1968, Office of Economic Opportunity, CAP Records of the Director, Subject Files, 1965–1969, Record Group 381, NARA.

40. Saralee Tiede, "Federal Funds Sought to Help 'Cool Down' Hot Summer Here," *Houston Chronicle*, June 2, 1967; "Job Fair to Aid Low-Income Area Youths," *Houston Chronicle*, July 16, 1967; Fred Harper, "4000 More Jobs Being Sought for Area Youths," *Houston Chronicle*, July 23, 1967.

41. Edgar May to Walter Richter, memorandum, August 3, 1967, Box 59, Folder Houston Texas CAA 1968, Office of Economic Opportunity, CAP Records of the Director, Subject Files, 1965–1969, Record Group 381, NARA; Tom McRae to Edgar May, memorandum, August 3, 1967, Box 74, Folder Texas OEO Program (Compilation) 1967 August–October, Office of Economic Opportunity, Inspection Division, Inspection Reports, 1964–67, Record Group 381, NARA.

42. "Report on Houston, Texas," August 1967, Box 73, Folder CAP, Houston, Harris County, Texas, July–September 1967, Office of Economic Opportunity, Inspection Division, Inspection Reports, 1964–67, Record Group 381, NARA; Edgar May to Walter Richter, memorandum, August 3, 1967, Box 59, Folder Houston Texas CAA 1968, Office of Economic Opportunity, CAP Records of the Director, Subject Files, 1965–1969, Record Group 381, NARA; Tom McRae to Edgar May, memorandum, August 3, 1967, Box 74, Folder Texas OEO Program (Compilation) 1967 August–October, Office of Economic Opportunity, Inspection Division, Inspection Reports, 1964–67, Record Group 381, NARA; Tom McRae to Edgar May, memorandum, August 4, 1967, Box 73, Folder CAP, Houston, Harris County, Texas, July–September 1967, Office of Economic Opportunity, Inspection Division, Inspection Reports, 1964–67, Record Group 381, NARA; Astor Kirk to C. Anderson Davis, August 9, 1967, Box 1, Folder August 1967, Office of Economic Opportunity, Southwest Region, Records of the Deputy Director, Correspondence, 1967–70, Record Group 381, NARASW; Franklin G. Moffitt to Edgar May, memorandum, Oc-

tober 31, 1967, Box 73, Folder CAP, Houston, Harris County, Texas, January–March 1967, Office of Economic Opportunity, Inspection Division, Inspection Reports, 1964–67, Record Group 381, NARA; "Report on Houston, Texas," August 1967, Box 73, Folder CAP, Houston, Harris County, Texas, July–September 1967, Office of Economic Opportunity, Inspection Division, Inspection Reports, 1964–67, Record Group 381, NARA; "Firing of TSU Pair Applauded," *Houston Post*, August 8, 1967.

43. "Firing of TSU Pair Applauded," *Houston Post*, August 8, 1967 (quotations); "Report on Houston, Texas," August 1967, Box 73, Folder CAP, Houston, Harris County, Texas, July–September 1967, Office of Economic Opportunity, Inspection Division, Inspection Reports, 1964–67, Record Group 381, NARA.

44. "Report on Houston, Texas," August 1967, Box 73, Folder CAP, Houston, Harris County, Texas, July–September 1967, Office of Economic Opportunity, Inspection Division, Inspection Reports, 1964–67, Record Group 381, NARA; Roy Wilkins to Sargent Shriver, August 25, 1967, Box 17, Folder Administrative, Texas, 1967, Office of Economic Opportunity, CAP Records of the Director, State Files, 1965–1968, Record Group 381, NARA (quotations); Theodore H. Berry to J. S. Spencer, memorandum, August 10, 1967, Box 59, Folder Houston Texas CAA 1968, Office of Economic Opportunity, CAP Records of the Director, Subject Files, 1965–1969, Record Group 381, NARA; Sargent Shriver to Roy Wilkins, September 5, 1967, Box 17, Folder Administrative, Texas, 1967, Office of Economic Opportunity, CAP Records of the Director, State Files, 1965–1968, Record Group 381, NARA.

45. Ben Haney to Jack Tinkle, memorandum, August 17, 1967, Box 10B, Folder Inspection and Evaluation Reports, Office of Economic Opportunity, Southwest Region, Community Action Programs, District Supervisors, Records Relating to City Economic Opportunity Boards, 1965–1968, Houston, Record Group 381, NARASW.

46. Tom McRae to Edgar May, memorandum, August 4, 1967, Box 73, Folder CAP, Houston, Harris County, Texas, July–September 1967, Office of Economic Opportunity, Inspection Division, Inspection Reports, 1964–67, Record Group 381, NARA; Ben Haney to Jack Tinkle, memorandum, August 17, 1967, Box 10B, Folder Inspection and Evaluation Reports, Office of Economic Opportunity, Southwest Region, Community Action Programs, District Supervisors, Records Relating to City Economic Opportunity Boards, 1965–1968, Houston, Record Group 381, NARASW; Saralee Tiede, "Beliefs of the Civil Rights Leader Who Quit HCCAA," *Houston Chronicle*, August 13, 1967 (quotations).

47. "Police Halt Picketing at HCCAA," *Houston Post*, August 9, 1967; "Report on Houston, Texas," August 1967, Box 73, Folder CAP, Houston, Harris County, Texas, July–September 1967, Office of Economic Opportunity, Inspection Division, Inspection Reports, 1964–67, Record Group 381, NARA; Tom McRae to Edgar May, memorandum, August 11, 1967, Box 10B, Folder Inspection and Evaluation Reports, Office of Economic Opportunity, Southwest Region, Community Action Programs, District Supervisors, Records Relating to City Economic Opportunity Boards, 1965–1968, Houston, Record Group 381, NARASW.

48. Walter Richter to Sargent Shriver and Bertram Harding, memorandum, August 15, 1967, Box 59, Folder Houston Texas CAA 1968, Office of Economic Opportunity, CAP Records of the Director, Subject Files, 1965–1969, Record Group 381, NARA; "OEO, AF, FBI Probing Harris Poverty Agency Order for Rifle Scopes," *Houston Chronicle*, August 15, 1967.

49. "Chronology of Events Relating to HCCAA's Attempting to Procure Seven Telescopic Sights through GSA," August 1967, Box 73, Folder CAP, Houston, Harris County,

Texas, July–September 1967, Office of Economic Opportunity, Inspection Division, Inspection Reports, 1964–67, Record Group 381, NARA. See "OEO, AF, FBI Probing Harris Poverty Agency Order for Rifle Scopes," *Houston Chronicle*, August 15, 1967.

50. Associated Press, "Telescopic Sights," August 1967, newspaper clipping, Microfilm Reel #30 (Grant Profiles), Records from Federal Government Agencies, Records of the Office of Economic Opportunity, LBJL (first quotation); Ken Sheets, "Poverty Official Can't Recall Ordering Telescopic Gun Sights," *Houston Chronicle*, August 13, 1967 (second and third quotations); "Chronology of Events Relating to HCCAA's Attempting to Procure Seven Telescopic Sights through GSA," August 1967, Box 73, Folder CAP, Houston, Harris County, Texas, July–September 1967, Office of Economic Opportunity, Inspection Division, Inspection Reports, 1964–67, Record Group 381, NARA.

51. Congressman George Bush of Houston, "Investigation of OEO Requested—Accusation of Ordering Rifle Sights for Use in Riots," on August 14, 1967, to the U.S. House of Representatives, 90th Cong., clipping, Box 73, Folder CAP, Houston, Harris County, Texas, July–September 1967, Office of Economic Opportunity, Inspection Division, Inspection Reports, 1964–67, Record Group 381, NARA (quotations); "OEO, AF, FBI Probing Harris Poverty Agency Order for Rifle Scopes," *Houston Chronicle*, August 15, 1967; Charles Culhane, "Tower, Bush Seek Anti-Poverty Quiz," *Houston Post*, August 15, 1967.

52. Congressman George Bush of Houston, "Investigation of OEO Requested—Accusation of Ordering Rifle Sights for Use in Riots," on August 14, 1967, to the U.S. House of Representatives, 90th Cong., clipping, Box 73, Folder CAP, Houston, Harris County, Texas, July–September 1967, Office of Economic Opportunity, Inspection Division, Inspection Reports, 1964–67, Record Group 381, NARA.

53. "U.S. Checks HCCAA's Use of Surplus Goods," *Houston Post*, August 16, 1967; "Welch Taking Poverty Hassle to White House," *Houston Chronicle*, August 18, 1967; "Rifle Scopes Withdrawn from Surplus," *Houston Chronicle*, August 29, 1967; "Lenses from Scopes OK'd for HCCAA Use," *Houston Chronicle*, August 29, 1967; "Air Force Will Fill CAA Order for Rifle Sights," *Houston Post*, August 29, 1967; Judy Raab to Ed Torrones, memorandum, August 25, 1967, Box 73, Folder CAP, Houston, Harris County, Texas, July–September 1967, Office of Economic Opportunity, Inspection Division, Inspection Reports, 1964–67, Record Group 381, NARA; Francis Williams to Dan Perkins, September 13, 1967, Box 74, Folder Texas OEO Program (Compliation) 1967 August–October, Office of Economic Opportunity, Inspection Division, Inspection Reports, 1964–67, Record Group 381, NARA; Francis Williams to Max Perkins, September 15, 1967, Box 73, Folder CAP, Houston, Harris County, Texas, July–September 1967, Office of Economic Opportunity, Inspection Division, Inspection Reports, 1964–67, Record Group 381, NARA; Ed Torrones and Tom McRae to Edgar May, memorandum, September 15, 1967, Box 73, Folder CAP, Houston, Harris County, Texas, July–September 1967, Office of Economic Opportunity, Inspection Division, Inspection Reports, 1964–67, Record Group 381, NARA.

54. Francis Williams to Fred Baldwin, July 14, 1967, Box 1, Folder Director's Office Memoranda, Office of Economic Opportunity, Southwest Region, CAP Correspondence, Memos, CAP Administrator–Family Planning, Record Group 381, NARASW; Fred Holt to Earl Rhine, memorandum, August 1, 1967, Box 1, Folder Director's Office Memoranda, Office of Economic Opportunity, Southwest Region, CAP Correspondence, Memos, CAP Administrator–Family Planning, Record Group 381, NARASW; "Districts to Elect HCCAA Board," *Houston Chronicle*, August 13, 1967; "Turnout Slim in Election of Poverty Board," *Houston Chronicle*, August 15, 1967.

55. Minutes of Harris County Community Action Association Executive Committee, July 6, 1967, Box 73, Folder CAP, Houston, Harris County, Texas, July–September 1967, Office of Economic Opportunity, Inspection Division, Inspection Reports, 1964–67, Record Group 381, NARA.

56. Carlton Carl, Jane Manning, and Susan Caudill, "Houston's Poor: Their Plights and Their Hopes," *Houston Chronicle*, September 10, 1967 (quotations); Mildred Robinson to Lyndon Johnson, September 25, 1968, Box 10, Folder General Correspondence, August–December 1968, Office of Economic Opportunity, Southwest Region, Community Action Programs, District Supervisors, Records Relating to City Economic Opportunity Boards, 1965–1968, Houston, Record Group 381, NARASW; Freddye M. Thompson to Lyndon Johnson, September 25, 1968, Box 10, Folder General Correspondence, August–December 1968, Office of Economic Opportunity, Southwest Region, Community Action Programs, District Supervisors, Records Relating to City Economic Opportunity Boards, 1965–1968, Houston, Record Group 381, NARASW.

57. Hector del Castillo to Walter Richter, February 2, 1968, Box 10, Folder General Correspondence, January–July 1968, Office of Economic Opportunity, Southwest Region, Community Action Programs, District Supervisors, Records Relating to City Economic Opportunity Boards, 1965–1968, Houston, Record Group 381, NARASW; A. D. Asios to Walter Richter, February 23, 1968, Box 1, Folder Correspondence, February–April 1968, Office of Economic Opportunity, Southwest Region, Records of the Director, Correspondence, 1967–69, Record Group 381, NARASW (quotation); Walter Richter to Hector del Castillo, February 2, 1968, Box 10, Folder General Correspondence, January–July 1968, Office of Economic Opportunity, Southwest Region, Community Action Programs, District Supervisors, Records Relating to City Economic Opportunity Boards, 1965–1968, Houston, Record Group 381, NARASW; Walter Richter to A. D. Asios, February 5, 1968, Box 1, Folder Correspondence, February–April 1968, Office of Economic Opportunity, Southwest Region, Records of the Director, Correspondence, 1967–69, Record Group 381, NARASW.

58. Walter Richter to Lauro Cruz, August 20, 1968, Box 1, Folder Correspondence, June–October 1968, Office of Economic Opportunity, Southwest Region, Records of the Director, Correspondence, 1967–69, Record Group 381, NARASW; Lauro Cruz to Walter Richter, telegram, August 20, 1968, Box 4, Folder Telegrams, Office of Economic Opportunity, Southwest Region, Records of the Director, Central Files, 1967–69, Record Group 381, NARASW; Francis Williams to Morgan Groves, September 16, 1968, Box 10, Folder General Correspondence, August–December 1968, Office of Economic Opportunity, Southwest Region, Community Action Programs, District Supervisors, Records Relating to City Economic Opportunity Boards, 1965–1968, Houston, Record Group 381, NARASW; Fred D. Baldwin to Regional CAP Administrator, memorandum, September 18, 1968, Box 10, Folder General Correspondence, August–December 1968, Office of Economic Opportunity, Southwest Region, Community Action Programs, District Supervisors, Records Relating to City Economic Opportunity Boards, 1965–1968, Houston, Record Group 381, NARASW; Joe H. Foy to Abraham Ramirez, October 23, 1968, Box 10, Folder General Correspondence, August–December 1968, Office of Economic Opportunity, Southwest Region, Community Action Programs, District Supervisors, Records Relating to City Economic Opportunity Boards, 1965–1968, Houston, Record Group 381, NARASW; Hamah King to Joe H. Foy, November 1968, Box 10, Folder Audit, Office of Economic Opportunity, Southwest Region, Community Action Programs, Dis-

trict Supervisors, Records Relating to City Economic Opportunity Boards, 1965–1968, Houston, Record Group 381, NARASW; Walter Richter to Fred Baldwin, Hamah King, and Morgan Groves, memorandum, October 24, 1968, Box 10, Folder General Correspondence, August–December 1968, Office of Economic Opportunity, Southwest Region, Community Action Programs, District Supervisors, Records Relating to City Economic Opportunity Boards, 1965–1968, Houston, Record Group 381, NARASW; Morgan Groves to Hamah King, memorandum, November 14, 1968, Box 10, Folder Field Trip Reports, Office of Economic Opportunity, Southwest Region, Community Action Programs, District Supervisors, Records Relating to City Economic Opportunity Boards, 1965–1968, Houston, Record Group 381, NARASW.

59. HCHR, "Accomplishments of VISTA during 1967," Box 1, HCHR VISTA Collection; HCHR, "VISTA Report," Box 1, HCHR VISTA Collection; Bob Paddock, "Activities," July 21, 1967, Box 1, HCHR VISTA Collection; Frank and Linda Barrett, "Houston Council on Human Relations," July 21, 1967, Box 1, HCHR VISTA Collection; Eileen Hayes, Gail Whitaker, James Jensen, and John Edgar, "First Ward," Box 1, HCHR VISTA Collection; Keith Johnson, "Cottage Grove," July 31, 1967, Box 1, HCHR VISTA Collection; Toni Johns, "5th Ward Bottoms," n.d., Box 1, Folder Vista Repts 1966–1967, HCHR VISTA Collection.

60. Nadasen, *Welfare Warriors*, xiv. For additional histories of the welfare rights movement, see West, *National Welfare Rights Movement*; and Bailis, *Bread of Justice*.

61. Frank Barrett, "A Report-Proposal to the Board of Directors of the HCHR," July 25, 1967, Box 1, HCHR VISTA Collection (quotation); Bob Newman to Bill Hale, memorandum, "Programs This Volunteer Is Involved In," July 31, 1967, Box 1, HCHR VISTA Collection; Frank and Linda Barrett, "Houston Council on Human Relations," July 21, 1967, Box 1, HCHR VISTA Collection; HCHR, "Accomplishments of VISTA during 1967," Box 1, HCHR VISTA Collection.

62. "Fire Engine on Way to Arson Blaze Kills Man," news clipping, Box 1, VISTA Scrapbook, VISTA Collection (first quotation); Minutes of EF-LAC Trustees, January 5, 1967, Box 2, Folder 5, VISTA Collection; Minutes of EF-LAC Trustees, February 15, 1967, Box 2, Folder 5, VISTA Collection (second quotation); "500 Ask Reversal of VISTA Eviction Order," *Houston Post*, June 12, 1967; Minutes of EF-LAC Board of Directors, September 20, 1967, Box 2, Folder 5, VISTA Collection; Wallace B. Poteat to Mrs. Birdell Truitt, October 16, 1967, Box 1, Folder 4, VISTA Collection.

63. Lieutenant M. L. Singleton, memorandum, January 29, 1967, Box 73, Folder CAP, Houston, Harris County, Texas, January–March 1967, OEO, Inspection Division, Inspection Reports, 1964–67, Record Group 381, NARA. Members of the Houston Police Department's Criminal Intelligence Division had received their training and authority during the red scare that occurred in Houston beginning in 1954. That year the Texas state legislature passed the Suppression of the Communist Party Act, which created a new statewide police officer training program that taught "subversive ideologies, economics, propaganda, espionage, sabotage, and counterintelligence." "The ultimate result of [the training program]," argued historian Don Carleton, "would be the investigatory excesses and civil rights abuses by . . . local police in such cities as Houston in the 1960s and 1970s." See Carleton, *Red Scare*, 264–65.

64. "Greetings from Houston," Box 1, VISTA Scrapbook, VISTA Collection (first quotation); Minutes of EF-LAC Trustees, February 15, 1967, Box 2, Folder 5, VISTA Collection; *LACK Project VOICE*, April 1, 1967, Box 1, VISTA Scrapbook, VISTA Collection (second quotation); James M. Simons to Edgar May, memorandum, March 6, 1967, Box 73, Folder

CAP, Houston, Harris County, Texas, January–March 1967, OEO Inspection Division, Inspection Reports, 1964–67, Record Group 381, NARA; "Lack Project Voice," May 1, 1967, Box 2, Folder 2, VISTA Collection.

65. Saralee Tiede, "Two Houston Poverty Groups Asked to Merge by Government," *Houston Chronicle*, news clipping, n.d., Box 2, Folder 7, VISTA Collection; John P. Murray to Mr. Reid Martin, August 29, 1967, Box 2, Folder 8, HCHR Collection; Saralee Tiede, "Anti-Poverty Program Hit by City's Mexican-Americans," *Houston Chronicle*, n.d., news clipping, Box 1, VISTA Scrapbook, VISTA Collection (second quotation); Ted D'Andriole, "Poverty Spending Dispute Aired," *Houston Chronicle*, no date, news clipping, Box 1, VISTA Scrapbook, VISTA Collection; Philip Hardberger to Sargent Shriver, memorandum, August 25, 1967, Box 74, Folder Texas OEO Program (Compilation) 1967 August–October, OEO Inspection Division, Inspection Reports, 1964–67, Record Group 381, NARA (first quotation). See chapter 4 of this dissertation for background on H-HCEOO's shift to a more limited program in 1967.

66. Earl Rhine to Francis Williams, March 15, 1968, Box 10, Folder General Correspondence, January–July 1968, Office of Economic Opportunity, Southwest Region, Community Action Programs, District Supervisors, Records Relating to City Economic Opportunity Boards, 1965–1968, Houston, Record Group 381, NARASW (quotation); Hamah King to Fred Baldwin, memorandum, May 3, 1968, Box 10, Folder General Correspondence, January–July 1968, Office of Economic Opportunity, Southwest Region, Community Action Programs, District Supervisors, Records Relating to City Economic Opportunity Boards, 1965–1968, Houston, Record Group 381, NARASW; Morgan Groves to Hamah King, memorandum, August 13, 1968, Box 10, Folder General Correspondence, August–December 1968, Office of Economic Opportunity, Southwest Region, Community Action Programs, District Supervisors, Records Relating to City Economic Opportunity Boards, 1965–1968, Houston, Record Group 381, NARASW.

67. Matusow, *Unraveling of America*, 269.

68. Ibid.

69. Francis Williams to Walter Richter, January 3, 1968, Box 1, Folder Correspondence, November 1967–February 1968, Office of Economic Opportunity, Southwest Region, Records of the Director, Correspondence, 1967–69, Record Group 381, NARASW; Walter Richter to Francis Williams, January 5, 1968, Box 10, Folder General Correspondence, January–July 1968, Office of Economic Opportunity, Southwest Region, Community Action Programs, District Supervisors, Records Relating to City Economic Opportunity Boards, 1965–1968, Houston, Record Group 381, NARASW; Walter Richter to Francis Williams, January 5, 1968, Box 1, Folder Correspondence, November 1967–February 1968, Office of Economic Opportunity, Southwest Region, Records of the Director, Correspondence, 1967–69, Record Group 381, NARASW.

70. Walter Richter to Louie Welch, April 10, 1968, Box 1, Folder Correspondence, April–May 1968, Office of Economic Opportunity, Southwest Region, Records of the Director, Correspondence, 1967–69, Record Group 381, NARASW; Fred Baldwin to Bill Elliott, May 1, 1968, Box 10, Folder General Correspondence, January–July 1968, Office of Economic Opportunity, Southwest Region, Community Action Programs, District Supervisors, Records Relating to City Economic Opportunity Boards, 1965–1968, Houston, Record Group 381, NARASW; Hamah King to Fred Baldwin, memorandum, May 3, 1968, Box 10, Folder General Correspondence, January–July 1968, Office of Economic Opportunity, Southwest Region, Community Action Programs, District Supervisors, Records Relating to City Economic Opportunity Boards, 1965–1968, Houston, Record

Group 381, NARASW; Carl Walker to Walter Richter, June 30, 1968, Box 10, Folder General Correspondence, January–July 1968, Office of Economic Opportunity, Southwest Region, Community Action Programs, District Supervisors, Records Relating to City Economic Opportunity Boards, 1965–1968, Houston, Record Group 381, NARASW.

71. Carlos Conde, "His Job: To Lead HCCAA Out of the Wilderness," *Houston Chronicle*, July 14, 1968.

72. MIS Report, "Quarterly Narrative Report for HCCAA, for period ending 3/31/68," April 1, 1968, Box 10B, Folder MIS Report, Office of Economic Opportunity, Southwest Region, Community Action Programs, District Supervisors, Records Relating to City Economic Opportunity Boards, 1965–1968, Houston, Record Group 381, NARASW; Morris Kagan to Lula M. Jones, August 16, 1968, Box 10, Folder General Correspondence, August–December 1968, Office of Economic Opportunity, Southwest Region, Community Action Programs, District Supervisors, Records Relating to City Economic Opportunity Boards, 1965–1968, Houston, Record Group 381, NARASW; Minutes of Harris County Community Welfare Planning Association Executive Committee, February 28, 1968, Box 1, Community Welfare Planning Association Papers, HMRC; "Poverty Area Youths Going to Summer Camp," *Houston Chronicle*, July 14, 1968; Texas Office of Economic Opportunity, "Weekly News Memo #73," June 12, 1968, Box 20, Folder Texas OEO Weekly News Memo (3), Records from Federal Government Agencies, Records of the Office of Economic Opportunity, LBJL; Hamah King to Fred Baldwin, memorandum, August 22, 1968, Box 10, Folder General Correspondence, August–December 1968, Office of Economic Opportunity, Southwest Region, Community Action Programs, District Supervisors, Records Relating to City Economic Opportunity Boards, 1965–1968, Houston, Record Group 381, NARASW; Texas Office of Economic Opportunity, "Weekly News Memo #70," June 12, 1968, Box 20, Folder Texas OEO Weekly News Memo (3), Records from Federal Government Agencies, Records of the Office of Economic Opportunity, LBJL; Rex L. Carey to Francis Williams, May 27, 1968, Box 10, Folder General Correspondence, January–July 1968, Office of Economic Opportunity, Southwest Region, Community Action Programs, District Supervisors, Records Relating to City Economic Opportunity Boards, 1965–1968, Houston, Record Group 381, NARASW; Francis Williams to Carter Klopton, September 16, 1968, Box 10, Folder General Correspondence, August–December 1968, Office of Economic Opportunity, Southwest Region, Community Action Programs, District Supervisors, Records Relating to City Economic Opportunity Boards, 1965–1968, Houston, Record Group 381, NARASW; Matusow, *Unraveling of America*, 270 (quotation).

Chapter 6. National Changes with Local Results

1. See especially Matusow, *Unraveling of America*; Andrew, *Lyndon Johnson and the Great Society*; and Cazenave, *Impossible Democracy*.

2. See chapter 5 for the immediate effects of the Green Amendment on the War on Poverty in Houston in 1967 and 1968.

3. Unger, *Best of Intentions*, 301.

4. Ibid., 302–3.

5. Ibid., 316–18. A significant part of Nixon's plan to reduce the power of the federal government and reduce the welfare bureaucracy was a guaranteed annual income through the Family Assistance Plan (FAP). See Unger, *Best of Intentions*, 309–30; and Davies, *From Opportunity to Entitlement*, 211–33.

6. Unger, *Best of Intentions*, 303, 331; Matusow, *Unraveling of America*, 270; Reeves, *Politics of the Peace Corps & VISTA*, 47, 67; Bertrand M. Harding to All OEO Employees, memorandum, April 21, 1969, Box 3, Folder 8, Office of Economic Opportunity, Southwest Region, VISTA, Central Files, Mexican-American Affairs–Regional Services Branch, Record Group 381, National Archives and Records Administration, Southwest Region, Fort Worth, Texas (hereafter cited as NARASW); Godfrey Sperling Jr., "We Are All Poor When We Fail to Heed . . . ," *Christian Science Monitor*, April 25, 1969, newspaper clipping, Box 3, Folder 8, Office of Economic Opportunity, Southwest Region, VISTA, Central Files, Mexican-American Affairs–Regional Services Branch, Record Group 381, NARASW.

7. Unger, *Best of Intentions*, 331–32; Matusow, *Unraveling of America*, 270.

8. Bertrand M. Harding to All OEO Employees, memorandum, April 21, 1969, Box 3, Folder 8, Office of Economic Opportunity, Southwest Region, VISTA, Central Files, Mexican-American Affairs–Regional Services Branch, Record Group 381, NARASW (first quotation); Godfrey Sperling Jr., "We Are All Poor When We Fail to Heed . . . ," *Christian Science Monitor*, April 25, 1969, newspaper clipping, Box 3, Folder 8, Office of Economic Opportunity, Southwest Region, VISTA, Central Files, Mexican-American Affairs–Regional Services Branch, Record Group 381, NARASW; John Osborne, "The President and the Poor," *New Republic*, May 24, 1969, newspaper clipping, Box 3, Folder 8, Office of Economic Opportunity, Southwest Region, VISTA, Central Files, Mexican-American Affairs–Regional Services Branch, Record Group 381, NARASW (second quotation).

9. Bertrand M. Harding to Regional Directors, memorandum, May 9, 1969, Box 1, Folder 20, Office of Economic Opportunity, Southwest Region, VISTA, Correspondence, 1969—Copies of Letters Sent, 1969, Central Files (Address-Blank Form), Record Group 381, NARASW; Donald Rumsfeld to All OEO Personnel, memorandum, August 11, 1969, Box 3, Folder 8, Office of Economic Opportunity, Southwest Region, VISTA, Central Files, Mexican-American Affairs–Regional Services Branch, Record Group 381, NARASW (quotation); Office of Economic Opportunity, "Background on OEO Reorganization," August 12, 1969, Box 3, Folder 8, Office of Economic Opportunity, Southwest Region, VISTA, Central Files, Mexican-American Affairs–Regional Services Branch, Record Group 381, NARASW.

10. B Mac to Ed Dela Rosa, memorandum, October 22, 1969, Box 2, Folder 2, Office of Economic Opportunity, Southwest Region, VISTA, Central Files, Budget–Mexican-American Affairs, Record Group 381, NARASW.

11. B Mac to Ed Dela Rosa, memorandum, October 22, 1969, Box 2, Folder 2, Office of Economic Opportunity, Southwest Region, VISTA, Central Files, Budget–Mexican-American Affairs, Record Group 381, NARASW; Office of Economic Opportunity, "Background on OEO Reorganization," August 12, 1969, Box 3, Folder 8, Office of Economic Opportunity, Southwest Region, VISTA, Central Files, Mexican-American Affairs–Regional Services Branch, Record Group 381, NARASW.

12. B Mac to Ed Dela Rosa, memorandum, October 22, 1969, Box 2, Folder 2, Office of Economic Opportunity, Southwest Region, VISTA, Central Files, Budget–Mexican-American Affairs, Record Group 381, NARASW (quotation); Office of Economic Opportunity, "Background on OEO Reorganization," August 12, 1969, Box 3, Folder 8, Office of Economic Opportunity, Southwest Region, VISTA, Central Files, Mexican-American Affairs–Regional Services Branch, Record Group 381, NARASW.

13. Hamah R. King to Frank Partida, February 27, 1970, Box 6, Folder 1, Office of Economic Opportunity, Southwest Region, Records of the Deputy Director, Central Files,

1969–70, Record Group 381, NARASW; Hamah R. King to Harry Davis, July 14, 1969, Box 6, Folder 1, Office of Economic Opportunity, Southwest Region, Records of the Deputy Director, Central Files, 1969–70, Record Group 381, NARASW; Walter H. Richter to Harry Davis, August 1, 1969, Box 6, Folder 1, Office of Economic Opportunity, Southwest Region, Records of the Deputy Director, Central Files, 1969–70, Record Group 381, NARASW.

14. Walter H. Richter to Donald Rumsfeld, memorandum, August 12, 1969, Box 1, Folder 2, Office of Economic Opportunity, Southwest Region, Records of the Director, Central Files, 1967–69, Record Group 381, NARASW (quotation); Arthur D. Jones to Blair Justice, memorandum, March 3, 1970, Box 33, Louie Welch Papers, Houston Metropolitan Research Center, Houston Public Library, Houston, Texas (hereafter cited as Welch Papers); Cynthia Carrington to Joe P. Maldonado, memorandum, April 20, 1970, Box 1, Folder 7, Office of Economic Opportunity, Records of the Office of Operations, Records of the Field Coordination Division, Subject File, 1968–1972, Record Group 381, National Archives and Records Administration, College Park, Maryland (hereafter cited as NARA); Blair Justice to Louie Welch, memorandum, May 5, 1970, Box 33, Welch Papers.

15. "Mayor's Aide Says Report Misunderstood," *Houston Chronicle*, February 11, 1969, newspaper clipping, Box 33, Welch Papers. See chapter 3 for how Houston's community action agency forced confrontations with Welch and other public officials and won a few small but significant victories in the fight against poverty in the city.

16. For analyses of how Sunbelt politicians took advantage of federal funding, see Cobb, *Most Southern Place on Earth*, especially 253–s76; and Schulman, *From Cotton Belt to Sunbelt*, especially 188–98.

17. Unger, *Best of Intentions*, 199, 221–33. The six cities included in Reuther and Cavanagh's plan were Houston, Washington, D.C., Detroit, Chicago, Philadelphia, and Los Angeles. For the national narrative of the Model Cities program, see Andrew, *Lyndon Johnson and the Great Society*, 131–62; and Bernstein, *Guns or Butter*, 458–70.

18. Robert Wood to Barefoot Sanders, memorandum, July 27, 1967, Box 8, Folder 1, White House Central Files, Local Government (Ex LG), Lyndon Baines Johnson Library, Austin, Texas (hereafter cited at LBJL); Fred Bohen to Joe Califano, memorandum, September 9, 1967, Box 8, Folder 1, White House Central Files, Local Government (Ex LG), LBJL; McComb, *Houston: A History*, 139–44 (quotation).

19. McComb, *Houston: A History*, 217–20.

20. Ibid., 220; Beverly Massey to Fred Baldwin, Joe Carpenter, and Ben Haney, memorandum, July 26, 1967, Box 1, Folder 2, Office of Economic Opportunity, Southwest Region, CAP Correspondence, Memos, CAP Administrator–Family Planning, Record Group 381, NARASW; Robert Wood to Barefoot Sanders, memorandum, July 27, 1967, Box 8, Folder 1, White House Central Files, Local Government (Ex LG), LBJL; Fred Bohen to Joe Califano, memorandum, September 9, 1967, Box 8, Folder 1, White House Central Files, Local Government (Ex LG), LBJL; Fred D. Baldwin to All CAP Staff, memorandum, November 16, 1967, Box 1, Folder 1, Office of Economic Opportunity, Southwest Region, CAP Correspondence, Memos, CAP Administrator–Family Planning, Record Group 381, NARASW; Texas Office of Economic Opportunity, "Weekly News Memo #47," November 22, 1967, Box 20, Folder 4, Records from Federal Government Agencies, Records from the Office of Economic Opportunity, 1964–1968, LBJL.

21. Ellen Middlebrook, "Welch Sees Model-City Aid in House Code OK," *Houston Post*, January 28, 1968.

22. Ibid.

23. Minutes of Community Welfare Planning Association Executive Committee, March 27, 1968, Box 1, Records of the Community Welfare Planning Association of Greater Houston, Houston Metropolitan Research Center, Houston Public Library, Houston, Texas (hereafter cited as CWPA Collection).

24. Minutes of Community Welfare Planning Association Executive Committee, March 27, 1968, Box 1, CWPA Collection.

25. Unknown Author to Lyndon Johnson, memorandum, October 14, 1968, Box 8, Folder 1, White House Central Files, Local Government (Ex LG), LBJL (quotation); Larry Temple to Blair Justice, October 19, 1968, Box 16, Folder 1, White House Central Files, Local Government (GEN LG), LBJL.

26. Unknown Author to Lyndon Johnson, memorandum, October 14, 1968, Box 8, Folder 1, White House Central Files, Local Government (Ex LG), LBJL; Larry Temple to Blair Justice, October 19, 1968, Box 16, Folder 1, White House Central Files, Local Government (GEN LG), LBJL; McComb, *Houston: A History*, 221 (first quotation); *Demonstration Cities and Metropolitan Development Act of 1966*, Public Law 89–754, 89th Cong., 2d sess. (November 4, 1966) (second quotation).

27. Robert Wood to Larry Temple, memorandum, December 3, 1968, Box 8, Folder 1, White House Central Files, Local Government (Ex LG), LBJL.

28. Larry Temple to Lyndon Johnson, memorandum, December 3, 1968, Box 8, Folder 1, White House Central Files, Local Government (Ex LG), LBJL; Ellen Middlebrook, "$268,500 for Model Cities Planning Granted to Houston," *Houston Post*, December 13, 1968.

29. Ellen Middlebrook, "$268,500 for Model Cities Planning Granted to Houston," *Houston Post*, December 13, 1968 (emphasis added).

30. Ellen Middlebrook, "$268,500 for Model Cities Planning Granted to Houston," *Houston Post*, December 13, 1968.

31. Unger, *Best of Intentions*, 333–34; George McGonigle to George A. Parker, April 15, 1969, Box 5, Folder 6, Office of Economic Opportunity, Southwest Region, Records of the Model Cities Programs, Applications and Plans, Record Group 381, NARASW; City of Houston, "Model Cities Mid-planning Statement and First Year Action Plan," January 1970, Box 223, Folders 1–2, General Records of the Department of Housing and Urban Development, Model Cities Reports, 1966–73, Record Group 207, NARA; Marshall Kaplan, Sheldon P. Gans, and Howard M. Kahn, "The Planning Year of the Model Cities Program in Houston, Texas, A Case Study (1971): Report Prepared for the Department of Housing and Urban Development," January 29, 1973, Box 223, Folder Model Cities Program Second Round Planning Year, Houston, Texas, General Records of the Department of Housing and Urban Development, Model Cities Reports, 1966–73, Record Group 207, NARA; Edward McClure to Curtis Johnson, memorandum, May 19, 1969, Box 3, CWPA Collection; Theodore C. Carr to Edward McClure, May 20, 1969, Box 3, CWPA Collection; Minutes of the Houston–Harris County Community Council Board of Directors, June 9, 1969, Box 3, CWPA Collection; Minutes of the Community Welfare Planning Association of Greater Houston Executive Committee, June 30, 1969, Box 3, CWPA Collection; Blair Justice to Louie Welch, memorandum, April 20, 1970, Box 33, Welch Papers.

32. Unger, *Best of Intentions*, 335.

33. Reeves, *Politics of the Peace Corps and VISTA*, 44–47.

34. Ibid., 48–49. OPRE's study of VISTA also revealed that the politicization process began within the VISTA training centers scattered throughout the country. In Michael Balzano's policy analysis study of the VISTA training centers, however, the author con-

cludes that not all of the centers were radicalizing. See Balzano, "The Political and Social Ramifications of the VISTA Program: A Question of Ends and Means" (Ph.D. diss., Georgetown University, 1971). Reeves concluded that the majority of VISTA training centers did instill a radical political philosophy in the volunteers.

35. Reeves, *Politics of the Peace Corps and VISTA*, 49–51, 55–56. For a more detailed description of Nixon's reorganization of War on Poverty programs and his appointment of conservative ideologues to top positions, see Reeves, *Politics of the Peace Corps and VISTA*, chaps. 3–4.

36. Minutes of EF-LAC Board of Directors, February 21, 1968, Box 2, Folder 5, Volunteers in Service to America Collection, Houston Metropolitan Research Center, Houston Public Library, Houston, Texas (hereafter cited as VISTA Collection) (quotation); EF-LAC, "Resolutions Submitted to the Board of Trustees of the Lack Project," February 28, 1968, Box 2, Folder 2, VISTA Collection; Charles Hall to Earl Allen, April 9, 1970, Box 3, Folder 7, Houston Council on Human Relations Collection, Houston Metropolitan Research Center, Houston Public Library, Houston, Texas (hereafter cited as HCHR Collection).

37. "Houston Poverty Fighter Takes Battle to Tulsa," n.d., newspaper clipping, Box 2, Folder 7, VISTA Collection; EF-LAC, "Resolutions Submitted to the Board of Trustees of the Lack Project," February 28, 1968, Box 2, Folder 2, VISTA Collection; Minutes of EF-LAC Board of Directors, August 1968, Box 2, Folder 5, VISTA Collection.

38. Houston Council on Human Relations, newsletter, October 1969, Box 2, Folder 20, HCHR Collection; EF-LAC, "Lack Talk," July 1970, Box 2, Folder 2, VISTA Collection; "A Proposal for a VISTA Legal Program in the Houston Council on Human Relations-Lack VISTA Project," n.d., Box 1, Folder 5, VISTA Collection (quotations); "HCHR-Lack VISTA Project (Volunteers in Service to America): A Proposal," 1969, Box 1, Folder 5, VISTA Collection; Houston Council on Human Relations, newsletter, November 1969, Box 2, Folder 20, HCHR Collection; Benton S. Russell to Frank Partida, April 1, 1970, Box 3, Folder 10, HCHR Collection.

39. Minutes of EF-LAC Board of Directors, 28 May 1968, Box 2, Folder 5, VISTA Collection; Minutes of EF-LAC Board of Directors, October 23, 1968, Box 2, Folder 5, VISTA Collection.

40. Houston Council on Human Relations, newsletter, July 22, 1969, Box 2, Folder 20, HCHR Collection (first quotation); Benton S. Russell to G. L. McGonigle, October 15, 1969, Box 3, Folder 7, HCHR Collection (second and third quotations).

41. D. E. Williams to Bertrand Harding, May 13, 1969, Box 1, Folder 2, Office of Economic Opportunity, Southwest Region, VISTA, Correspondence, 1969—Copies of Letters Sent, 1969, Central Files (Address–Blank Form), Record Group 381, NARASW (quotations); Robert Perrin to D. E. Williams, June 5, 1969, Box 1, Folder 2, Office of Economic Opportunity, Southwest Region, VISTA, Correspondence, 1969—Copies of Letters Sent, 1969, Central Files (Address–Blank Form), Record Group 381, NARASW.

42. Roger D. Armstrong to Francis Williams, November 11, 1969, Box 3, Folder 7, HCHR Collection.

43. Edward Dela Rosa to B. C. Allen, November 20, 1969, Box 1, Folder 21, Office of Economic Opportunity, Southwest Region, VISTA, Correspondence, 1969—Copies of Letters Sent, 1969, Central Files (Address–Blank Form), Record Group 381, NARASW.

44. Minutes of EF-LAC Board of Directors, February 12, 1969, Box 2, Folder 5, VISTA Collection; Paul A. Duncan to Regional Administrators, memorandum, June 16, 1969, Box 1, Folder 4, Office of Economic Opportunity, Southwest Region, VISTA, Correspon-

dence, 1969—Copies of Letters Sent, 1969, Central Files (Address–Blank Form), Record Group 381, NARASW (quotations).

45. Roger D. Armstrong to George Bush, April 28, 1970, Box 3, Folder 7, HCHR Collection (first quotation); Roger D. Armstrong to George Bush, May 18, 1970, Box 3, Folder 7, HCHR Collection (second quotation).

46. Roger D. Armstrong to Donald Rumsfeld, May 27, 1970, Box 3, Folder 7, HCHR Collection (quotation); Roger D. Armstrong to George Bush, July 9, 1970, Box 3, Folder 7, HCHR Collection.

47. Houston Council on Human Relations, "1970 Annual Report," December 2, 1970, Box 3, Folder 10, HCHR Collection.

48. Jane Manning, "Fruits of VISTA Labor in Past Year Will Be Harvested for Long Time," *Houston Chronicle*, n.d., newspaper clipping, Box 2, Folder 7, VISTA Collection (quotation); Jim Ferguson, Joyce Shaw, W. M. McKenzie, and Ken Nicoll to Thomas L. McKenzie, June 30, 1972, Box 1, Folder 4, VISTA Collection. The VISTA program did not end nationally, as many volunteers in Houston feared, but the shape of the program changed dramatically in the early 1970s.

49. Tommy Miller, "Community Action Association Board Approves Reorganization," *Houston Chronicle*, January 14, 1976, newspaper clipping, Box 11, Folder 1, Community Services Administration, Region VI (Dallas, Texas), Records Relating to County Community Action Agencies, 1976–78, Record Group 381, NARASW (quotation). For the types of activities in which GCCSA members engaged in the late 1970s, see Fred Hofheinz to Ben Haney, with attached activity report, September 14, 1976, Box 11, Folder 1, Community Services Administration, Region VI (Dallas, Texas), Records Relating to County Community Action Agencies, 1976–78, Record Group 381, NARASW.

Conclusion. The War on Democracy

1. Crozier, Huntington, and Watanuki, *Crisis of Democracy*, 61, 114–15.

2. Annelise Orleck, "Conclusion: The War on Poverty and American Politics since the 1960s," in *The War on Poverty: A New Grassroots History, 1964–1980*, ed. Annelise Orleck and Lisa Gayle Hazirjian (Athens: University of Georgia Press, 2011), 439–44.

3. For Harris County Hospital District facilities, see Harris County Hospital District, "Facilities and Directions," http://www.hchdonline.com/about/facilities/directions.htm (accessed December 6, 2011). For the programs administered by the Gulf Coast Community Services Association, see Gulf Coast Community Services Association, "About GCCSA," http://www.gulfcoastcommunityservicesassociation.org/gccsaabout.html (accessed December 6, 2011).

4. For voter identification laws, see National Conference of State Legislatures, "Voter Identification Requirements," http://www.ncsl.org/default.aspx?tabid=16602 (accessed December 6, 2011); Brennan Center for Justice, New York University School of Law, "Voter ID," http://www.brennancenter.org/content/section/category/voter_id (accessed December 6, 2011); Timothy Vercellotti and David Anderson, "Protecting the Franchise, or Restricting It?: The Effects of Voter Identification Requirements on Turnout," http://www.eagleton.rutgers.edu/research/documents/VoterID_Turnout.pdf (accessed December 6, 2011); Judson Robinson III, "Voter ID Hits the Voiceless Hardest," *Houston Chronicle*, March 1, 2011. For limitations of the U.S. Census and redistricting efforts, see Ford Foundation, "Promoting Electoral Reform and Democratic Participation," http://www.fordfound.org/issues/democratic-and-accountable-government/promoting

-electoral-reform-and-democratic-participation (accessed December 6, 2011). For the controversy over ACORN, see Scott Shane, "A Political Gadfly Lampoons the Left via Youtube," *New York Times*, September 18, 2009; and Scott Shane, "Conservatives Draw Blood from ACORN," *New York Times*, September 15, 2009. For the *Citizens United* decision, see Adam Liptak, "Justices, 5–4, Reject Corporate Spending Limit," *New York Times*, January 21, 2010.

BIBLIOGRAPHY

Archival Sources

Houston Council on Human Relations Collection. Houston Metropolitan Research Center. Houston Public Library. Houston, Texas.

Houston Council on Human Relations VISTA Collection. Houston Metropolitan Research Center. Houston Public Library. Houston, Texas.

Leon Jaworski (1905–1982) Papers. Texas Collection. Baylor University Library. Waco, Texas.

Louie Welch (1918–2008) Papers. The Houston Metropolitan Research Center. Houston Public Library. Houston, Texas. White House Central Files. Lyndon Baines Johnson Library. Austin, Texas.

Records of the Community Services Administration [Office of Economic Opportunity]. Record Group 381. National Archives and Records Administration. College Park, Maryland.

Records of the Community Services Administration [Office of Economic Opportunity]. Records of the Southwest Regional Office, Austin, Texas, and Records of the Regional Operations Division, Region VI, Dallas, Texas. Record Group 381. National Archives and Records Administration, Southwest Region. Fort Worth, Texas.

Records of the Community Welfare Planning Association of Greater Houston. The Houston Metropolitan Research Center. Houston Public Library. Houston, Texas.

Records of the Department of Housing and Urban Development. Record Group 207. National Archives and Records Administration. College Park, Maryland.

Records of the Office of Economic Opportunity, 1964–1968. Lyndon Baines Johnson Library. Austin, Texas.

Volunteers in Service to America Collection. Houston Metropolitan Research Center. Houston Public Library. Houston, Texas.

William V. Ballew Papers. MS 254. Woodson Research Center. Fondren Library. Rice University. Houston, Texas.

Periodicals

Christian Century, 1965.
Houston Chronicle, 1964–1976.
Houston Forward Times, 1964–1976.
Houston Informer, 1964–1976.
Houston Post, 1964–1976.

New York Times, 1964–1976.
Social Action (Chicago, Illinois), 1965.
Texas Observer, 1967.
Waco Tribune-Herald, 1965.

Published Primary Sources

Alinsky, Saul D. *Reveille for Radicals*. Chicago: University of Chicago Press, 1946.

Cox, Harvey. *The Secular City: Secularization and Urbanization in Theological Perspective*. New York: Macmillan, 1965.

Crook, William H., and Ross Thomas. *Warriors for the Poor: The Story of VISTA, Volunteers in Service to America*. New York: William Morrow, 1969.

Crozier, Michael, Samuel P. Huntington, and Joji Watanuki. *The Crisis of Democracy*. New York: New York University Press, 1975.

Economic Opportunity Act of 1964, S 2642, 88th Cong., 2nd sess., United States Serial Set 12616-3 (August 1964).

de Hartog, Jan. *The Hospital*. New York: Atheneum, 1964.

Kaufman, Arnold. "Human Nature and Participatory Democracy." In *NOMOS III: Responsibility*, edited by Carl J. Friedrich. New York: Liberal Arts Press, 1960.

Macdonald, Dwight. "Our Invisible Poor." *New Yorker*, January 19, 1963, 82–134.

National Council of Churches. "To the People of the Nation." In *A Documentary History of Religion in America*, edited by Edwin S. Gaustad and Mark A. Noll, 509–12. Vol. 3. Grand Rapids, Mich.: W. B. Eerdmans, 2003.

Niebuhr, Reinhold. *Moral Man and Immoral Society: A Study in Ethics and Politics*. New York: Scribner, 1932.

Office of Economic Opportunity. Community Action Program. *Community Action Program Guide*. Washington, D.C., February 1965.

Office of Economic Opportunity. Community Action Program. *Community Action Program Workbook*. Washington, D.C., March 1965.

Public Papers of the Presidents of the United States, 1963–1964. Volume 1. Washington, D.C.: Federal Registrar Division, National Archives and Records Service, General Services Administration, 2002.

Robinson, John A. T. *Honest to God*. Philadelphia: Westminster Press, 1963.

Rose, Stephen. *The Day the Country Mouse Expired*. New York: National Student Christian Foundation, 1964.

Weber, Hans-Reudi. *Salty Christians*. New York: Seabury Press, 1963.

Winter, Gibson. *The New Creation as Metropolis*. New York: Macmillan, 1963.

Digital Sources

"Democratic Party Platform of 1964." American Presidency Project, University of California, Santa Barbara. http://www.presidency.ucsb.edu/platforms.php (accessed March 3, 2008).

Ross, Matthew C. "Nina Vance, 1914–1980: Visionary, Founder, Innovator." The Alley Theatre. http://www.alleytheatre.org/Alley/Nina_Vance_EN.asp?SnID=1947439053 (accessed September 9, 2008).

Students for a Democratic Society. "Port Huron Statement." The Sixties Project, University of Virginia. http://www2.iath.virginia.edu/sixties/HTML_docs/Sixties .html (accessed February 21, 2010).

Interviews

Allen, Earl. Interview by Wesley G. Phelps. Telephone, December 11, 2008. Houston, Texas.

Secondary Sources

Andrew, John A. *Lyndon Johnson and the Great Society*. Chicago: Ivan R. Dee, 1998.

Ashmore, Susan Youngblood. *Carry It On: The War on Poverty and the Civil Rights Movement in Alabama, 1964–1972*. Athens: University of Georgia Press, 2008.

Bailis, Lawrence Neil. *Bread of Justice: Grassroots Organizing in the Welfare Rights Movement*. Lexington, Mass.: Lexington Books, 1974.

Balzano, Michael Pasquale. "The Political and Social Ramifications of the VISTA Program: A Question of Ends and Means." Ph.D. diss., Georgetown University, 1971.

Bauman, Robert. *Race and the War on Poverty: From Watts to East L.A.* Norman: University of Oklahoma Press, 2008.

Behnken, Brian D. *Fighting Their Own Battles: Mexican Americans, African Americans, and the Struggle for Civil Rights in Texas*. Chapel Hill: University of North Carolina Press, 2011.

Bernstein, Irving. *Guns or Butter: The Presidency of Lyndon Johnson*. New York: Oxford University Press, 1996.

Branch, Taylor. *Parting the Waters: America in the King Years, 1954–63*. New York: Simon & Schuster, 1988.

Braun, Mark Edward. *Social Change and Empowerment of the Poor: Poverty Representation in Milwaukee's Community Action Programs, 1964–1972*. Lanham, MD: Lexington Books, 2001.

Carleton, Don E. *Red Scare!: Right-Wing Hysteria, Fifties Fanaticism, and Their Legacy in Texas*. Austin: Texas Monthly Press, 1985.

Castells, Manuel. *The City and the Grassroots: A Cross-Cultural Theory of Urban Social Movements*. Berkeley: University of California Press, 1983.

Cazenave, Noel A. *Impossible Democracy: The Unlikely Success of the War on Poverty Community Action Programs*. Albany: State University of New York Press, 2007.

Chappell, David L. *A Stone of Hope: Prophetic Religion and the Death of Jim Crow*. Chapel Hill: University of North Carolina Press, 2004.

Clayson, William S. "'The Barrios and the Ghettos Have Organized!': Community Action, Political Acrimony, and the War on Poverty in San Antonio." *Journal of Urban History* 28 (2002): 158–83.

———. "The War on Poverty and the Fear of Urban Violence in Houston, 1965–1968." *Gulf South Historical Review* 18 (2003): 38–59.

———. *Freedom Is Not Enough: The War on Poverty and the Civil Rights Movement in Texas*. Austin: University of Texas Press, 2010.

Cobb, James C. *The Most Southern Place on Earth: The Mississippi Delta and the Roots of Regional Identity*. New York: Oxford University Press, 1992.

Cole, Thomas R. *No Color Is My Kind: The Life of Eldrewey Stearns and the Integration of Houston*. Austin: University of Texas Press, 1997.

Cunningham, Frank. *Theories of Democracy: A Critical Introduction*. New York: Routledge, 2002.

Dahl, Robert A. *Democracy and Its Critics*. New Haven: Yale University Press, 1989.

Davidson, Chandler. "Negro Politics and the Rise of the Civil Rights Movement in Houston, Texas." Ph.D. diss., Princeton University, 1968.

———. *Biracial Politics: Conflict and Coalition in the Metropolitan South*. Baton Rouge: Louisiana State University Press, 1972.

Davidson, Robert H. "The War on Poverty: Experiment in Federalism." *Annals of the Academy of Political and Social Science* 385 (September 1969): 1–13.

Davies, Gareth. *From Opportunity to Entitlement: The Transformation and Decline of Great Society Liberalism*. Lawrence: University Press of Kansas, 1996.

Evans, Sara M. and Harry C. Boyte, *Free Spaces: The Sources of Democratic Change in America*. Chicago: University of Chicago Press, 1992.

Germany, Kent B. *New Orleans after the Promises: Poverty, Citizenship, and the Search for the Great Society*. Athens: University of Georgia Press, 2007.

Gillette, Michael L. *Launching the War on Poverty: An Oral History*. New York: Twayne, 1996.

Ginzberg, Eli, and Robert M. Solow, eds. *The Great Society: Lessons for the Future*. New York: Basic Books, 1974.

Hazirjian, Lisa Gayle. "Negotiating Poverty: Economic Insecurity and the Politics of Working-Class Life in Rocky Mount, North Carolina, 1929–1969." Ph.D. diss., Duke University, 2003.

Heale, M. J. "The Sixties as History: A Review of the Political Historiography." *Reviews in American History* 33 (March 2005): 133–52.

Horwitt, Sanford D. *Let Them Call Me Rebel: Saul Alinsky—His Life and Legacy*. New York: Knopf, 1989.

Jackson, Thomas F. "The State, the Movement, and the Urban Poor: The War on Poverty and Political Mobilization in the 1960s." In *The Underclass Debate: Views from History*, edited by Michael B. Katz, 403–39. Princeton: Princeton University Press, 1993.

Jacobs, Meg, William J. Novak, and Julian E. Zelizer, eds. *The Democratic Experiment: New Directions in American Political History*. Princeton: Princeton University Press, 2003.

Jardini, David Raymond. "Out of the Blue Yonder: The RAND Corporation's Diversification into Social Welfare Research, 1946–1968." Ph.D. diss., Carnegie Mellon University, 1996.

Jordan, Amy Kearney. "Citizenship, Welfare Rights and the Politics of Respectability in Rural and Urban Mississippi, 1900–1980." Ph.D. diss., University of Michigan, 2003.

Kaplan, Marshall, and Peggy L. Cuciti, eds. *The Great Society and Its Legacy: Twenty Years of U.S. Social Policy*. Durham, N.C.: Duke University Press, 1986.

Kiffmeyer, Thomas J. "From Self-Help to Sedition: The Appalachian Volunteers in Eastern Kentucky, 1964–1970." *Journal of Southern History* 64 (1998): 65–94.

Kiffmeyer, Thomas. *Reformers to Radicals: The Appalachian Volunteers and the War on Poverty*. Lexington: University Press of Kentucky, 2008.

Kloppenberg, James T. "From Hartz to Tocqueville: Shifting the Focus from Liberalism to Democracy in America." In *The Democratic Experiment: New Directions in American Political History*, edited by Meg Jacobs, William J. Novak, and Julian E. Zelizer, 350–80. Princeton: Princeton University Press, 2003.

Lemisch, Jesse. "The American Revolution Seen from the Bottom Up." In *Towards a New Past: Dissenting Essays in American History*, edited by Barton J. Bernstein, 3–45. New York: Pantheon, 1968.

Magnet, Myron. *The Dream and the Nightmare: The Sixties' Legacy to the Underclass*. New York: W. Morrow, 1993.

Mattson, Kevin. *Intellectuals in Action: The Origins of the New Left and Radical Liberalism, 1945–1970*. University Park: Pennsylvania State University Press, 2002.

Matusow, Allen J. *The Unraveling of America: A History of Liberalism in the 1960s*. New York: Harper & Row, 1984.

McComb, David G. *Houston: A History.* Austin: University of Texas Press, 1981.

McKee, Guian A. *The Problem of Jobs: Liberalism, Race, and Deindustrialization in Philadelphia.* Chicago: University of Chicago Press, 2008.

Mead, Lawrence. *Beyond Entitlement.* New York: Free Press, 1986.

Murray, Charles. *Losing Ground: American Social Policy, 1950–1980.* New York: Basic Books, 1984.

Nadasen, Premilla. *Welfare Warriors: The Welfare Rights Movement in the United States.* New York: Routledge, 2005.

Orleck, Annelise. *Storming Caesar's Palace: How Black Mothers Fought Their Own War on Poverty.* Boston: Beacon, 2005.

Orleck, Annelise, and Lisa Gayle Hazirjian, eds. *The War on Poverty: A New Grassroots History, 1964–1980.* Athens: University of Georgia Press, 2011.

Pass, David Jacob. "The Politics of VISTA in the War on Poverty: A Study of Ideological Conflict." Ph.D. diss., Columbia University, 1975.

Pateman, Carol. *Participation and Democratic Theory.* Cambridge: Cambridge University Press, 1976.

Piven, Frances Fox, and Richard A. Cloward. *Regulating the Poor: The Functions of Public Welfare.* New York: Pantheon Books, 1971.

Quadagno, Jill S. *The Color of Welfare: How Racism Undermined the War on Poverty.* New York: Oxford University Press, 1994.

Reeves, T. Zane. *The Politics of the Peace Corps and VISTA.* Tuscaloosa: University of Alabama Press, 1988.

Russell, Judith. *Economics, Bureaucracy, and Race: How Keynesians Misguided the War on Poverty.* New York: Columbia University Press, 2004.

Schulman, Bruce J. *From Cotton Belt to Sunbelt: Federal Policy, Economic Development, and the Transformation of the South, 1938–1980.* New York: Oxford University Press, 1991.

Schwartz, Marvin. *In Service to America: A History of VISTA in Arkansas, 1965–1985.* Fayetteville: University of Arkansas Press, 1988.

Self, Robert O., and Thomas J. Sugrue. "The Power of Place: Race, Political Economy, and Identity in the Postwar Metropolis." In *A Companion to Post-1945 America*, edited by Jean-Christophe Agnew and Roy Rosenzweig, 20–43. Malden, Mass.: Blackwell, 2002.

Sinha, Manisha, and Penny Von Eschen. *Contested Democracy: Freedom, Race, and Power in American History.* New York: Columbia University Press, 2007.

The Strange Demise of Jim Crow: How Houston Desegregated its Public Accommodations. Produced by Thomas R. Cole. Directed by David Berman. Distributed by University of Texas Press, 1997. 57 Minutes.

Stricker, Frank. *Why America Lost the War on Poverty—And How to Win It.* Chapel Hill: University of North Carolina Press, 2007.

Tarrow, Sidney. *Power in Movement: Social Movements and Contentious Politics.* Cambridge: Cambridge University Press, 1998.

Thompson, E. P. *The Making of the English Working Class.* New York: Pantheon, 1964.

Unger, Irwin. *The Best of Intentions: The Triumphs and Failures of the Great Society under Kennedy, Johnson, and Nixon.* New York: Doubleday, 1996.

Walker, Randi Jones. *The Evolution of a UCC Style: Essays in the History, Ecclesiology, and Culture of the United Church of Christ.* Cleveland: United Church Press, 2005.

Watson, Dwight. *Race and the Houston Police Department, 1930–1990: A Change Did Come.* College Station: Texas A&M University Press, 2005.

West, Guida. *The National Welfare Rights Movement: The Social Protest of Poor Women*. New York: Praeger, 1981.

Wintz, Cary D. "Texas Southern University." *Handbook of Texas Online*. http://tshaonline .org/handbook/online/articles/TT/kct27.html (accessed November 10, 2008).

Zinn, Howard. *A People's History of the United States*. New York: Harper Perennial, 2005.

INDEX